Hispanisms and Homosexualities

~

D1319130

Edited by Michèle Aina Barale,

Jonathan Goldberg, Michael Moon,

and Eve Kosofsky Sedgwick

Hispanisms

and Homosexualities

Sylvia Molloy and Robert McKee Irwin, Editors

Duke University Press   Durham and London   1998

© 1998 DUKE UNIVERSITY PRESS
All rights reserved
"The Politics of Posing" © 1998 Sylvia Molloy
Printed in the United States of America on acid-free paper
∞
Designed by Amy Ruth Buchanan
Typeset in Minion by Keystone Typesetting, Inc.
Library of Congress Cataloging-in-Publication Data
appear on the last printed page of this book.

Contents

~

Acknowledgments

~

This book grew out of a conference held in New York on 14 and 15 April 1994, which was sponsored jointly by the Schweitzer Program in the Humanities, the Department of Spanish and Portuguese, the Office of the Dean for the Humanities, and the Association of Lesbian and Gay Faculty, Administrators, and Staff at New York University. For their organizing efforts, we are grateful to Jessica Chalmers, research assistant to Sylvia Molloy, and José Reyes, administrative assistant in the Department of Spanish and Portuguese. We would also like to thank Inés Azar and Jorge Salessi, who participated in the conference but whose work is not included in this volume, and Carla Giaudrone, for her good-natured assistance with the final steps of the editing process. Finally, we are grateful to students and colleagues whose enthusiastic response to the conference and lively participation in it confirmed our belief in the importance and timeliness of our venture.

Introduction

~

Sylvia Molloy and

Robert McKee Irwin

Many of the contributors to this volume have at some point or another participated in, or even organized, panels on some aspect of queer scholarship related to Hispanic cultures. The mid- to late eighties were the heady days of the Lesbian and Gay Conferences at Yale, when we had panels with titles ranging from the academic dowdy ("Lesbian and Gay Literature in Latin America") to—as we got more brassy—the flamboyant: "Readers on the Verge of a Textual Breakdown." The question that lurked in the back of our minds was why we were having those panels in the first place, but in the thrill of what for many of us amounted to an academic coming out, the question more often than not went unanswered. Besides a random conjunction of more or less anecdotal facts—that many of us, panelists and audience, were queer, that the organizers and speakers were often Spanish, Latin Americans, or Latinos, that all of us taught Spanish or Latin American literatures and wrote about those literatures—was there anything, we asked ourselves, that justified the conjunction of nationality and homosexuality in specifically Hispanic terms? Were we really reflecting on an intersection that would further our intellectual practices, or were we creating a culture-specific space to which we could repair and into which we could fit queries that did not quite conform to hegemonic cultural formations and, within those formations, to constructions of sexualities that did not quite suit us? And who were "we," to begin with? That these questions went unanswered—that they may always go unanswered—does not preclude their being asked yet once again.

If the gesture that these Hispanic panels had in common was an academic coming out, what were we (are we) coming out to? What is the site of our visibility, of our performance? It may be useful to reflect, for a moment, on the particularly complex, even controversial, nature of Hispanism as an academic "field" before going any further. For what indeed does this term, grown so ample that it encompasses everything and nothing, *mean*? Handily, it describes the study of Spanish-speaking cultures, so that it includes Peninsularists and Latin Americanists, medievalists and modernists in its generous, deceptively innocent embrace. So accustomed are Hispanists to the term that one rarely pauses to think of its exceptional nature: one doesn't speak, after all, of Italianism, or Germanism, or Gallicism in the same sense. Hispanism, the Spanish dictionary tells us, besides being "an idiom peculiar to Spanish," is "Afición al estudio de las cosas de España," love for the study of things pertaining to Spain. That the term is closely related to *hispanidad,* which the same dictionary defines as the "conjunto y comunidad de los pueblos hispanos," the group and community formed by Hispanic peoples, shows the ideological nature of the construct, its indubitably expansionist bent. We tend to forget this as we go about our teaching, our writing, and use the term loosely, descriptively, as synonymous with Hispanic studies. We forget the fierce act of commitment that Hispanism, as an ideological construct, would exact of its practitioners, with its talk of love, group belonging, and communal loyalty, a loyalty to a mythical *patria* devoid of geographical boundaries that would bring together—unproblematically, of course—the cultures of a metropolis and those of its erstwhile colonies. Hispanism, this Hispanism, is more than a linguistic bond: it is a conviction, a passion, a temporal continuity, an imperial monument. If for some of us it may mean a (provisional) way of organizing the study of a set of cultures, we should remember that we are, most assuredly, in a minority; that what for us is functional, either as a way of organizing a subject of study or even as a means of postulating strategic identities, is for others an article of faith and a clear call to the heart.

It is useful to bring out these submerged meanings of Hispanism, not to resignify them, of course, but to reflect on their possible effect on the construction of Hispanic studies as a discipline and on the exclusion of dissident voices from that discipline. Indeed, strangely unfriendly to bricolage, Hispanism has traditionally conceived itself in monolithic terms, as an oddly defensive family whose members supposedly share basic cultural values and engage in common cultural practices. Hispanism—that particular construction of Hispanism—has not usually taken kindly to the practice of rereading and revising and has not in general appreciated diversion, reformulation, and, more generally, the unsettling impact of critical inquiry. Hispanism—that particular construction of Hispanism—was begging, one might say, to be queered. To visit sexual dissidence on it at this point is not an impertinent gesture but a destabilizing move, a propitious fracture—in sum, an invitation to reread texts whose productive mobility has been deadened by sheer canonicity. "The notion of a *definitive* text," Borges writes memorably, "belongs to religion or to fatigue" (106). It is against such notions of the definitive—be it a text, a field of knowledge, an academic discipline, or even a national identity—that the essays in this volume work. Ours was not, to be sure, the only destabilizing move possible: it was the one that we, as queer critics, chose to effect.

The Hispanism we have spoken of, that of the communal bonding in name of a Spanish (and by extension Latin American) essence that it behooves every Hispanist to represent and uphold, cherishes its classics, monumentalized in Spain's Golden Age. Several authors in this collection have chosen precisely to go back to those classics, reading them against the grain, pausing at the margins of texts and seeing texts as narratives of the marginal, the better to bring out the unheeded story, the invisible queer. Mary Gossy focuses on the construction of female subjectivity in sixteenth-century narrative, more precisely on female desire as trouble. In her rereading of María de Zayas's "Amar sólo por vencer," cross-dressing enables the unspeakable ("Whoever heard of a lady falling in love with another?" asks María de Zayas rhetorically) to be inscribed in discourse. Cross-dressing as a place to be—or rather, as a place to say that one is, as a place to inscribe one's being—is also explored by Israel Burshatin in his reading of the case of Elena/Eleno de Céspedes. Céspedes's very body, the site of diverse institutional interpretations resulting in diverging gender adjudications, is an unstable construct, indeed, a text in conflict: in each new reading of that regendered body, desire, citizenship, power, even race, are diversely allocated. Benigno Sifuentes-Jáuregui, in his essay on *Lazarillo de Tormes*, recontextualizes the picaresque as "case history," releasing it from the legal underpinnings of the *relación* so that it can, in turn, release its untold story. Analyzing the by now grudgingly accepted homographesis of the fourth chapter of the *Lazarillo,* Sifuentes seeks not to identify homosexual desire but to show "how the possibility or impossibility of homosexuality is written or marked in/on the text and, more importantly for us as hispanists, . . . how that homographetic marking in the *Lazarillo* has been *read* by our colleagues . . . as something that is morally wrong." Emilie Bergmann considers the reading and rewriting of another gender-troubled life, that of Sor Juana Inés de la Cruz, in colonial Mexico, as told by contemporary feminist filmmaker María Luisa Bemberg in her film *"Yo, la peor de todas"* [I, the worst of all]. Bergmann focuses on the ambiguity of the filmmaker's interpretive stance: Bemberg repeatedly points to (and even titillates her audience with) intimations of sexual dissidence while carefully avoiding any reference to Sor Juana's clearly homoerotic texts, thus creating an ambivalence that comes close to disavowal. Although purporting to be a strong recuperative feminist reading of this seventeenth-century figure, *"Yo, la peor de todas,"* as Bergmann shows, effectively disempowers Bemberg's subject.

Relations between nationalities and sexualities are uneasy at best; between nationalities and homosexualities, they are downright problematic, even personally dangerous, as many of us, growing up in Hispanic cultures, came to learn. If, as an academic discipline, Hispanism is suspicious of queer studies, in its larger sense—that "love of things Spanish" so suggestive of amorous bonds *pro patria*—it has always been downright unfriendly to queers. As one of the authors in this book succinctly puts it, "desire has therefore meant above all national desire." Nowhere is this better grasped than in concrete national situations, usually situations of change perceived as crises, in which nationalities are (re)defined and national identities are (re)constructed defensively. Several essays in this volume address the vexed intersection of the national and the homosexual in different Hispanic cultures, examining institutional systems of surveillance, patterns of manipulation and exclusion, as well as practices of resistance and dissimulation. Considering the aftermath of the Mexican Revolution, Daniel Balderston perceptively studies the paranoid rejection of *afeminamiento* and the anxiously strident construction of virility in Mexican official circles in the 1920s, where a witch-hunt was virtually declared on "hermafrodite[s] incapable of identifying with workers for social reforms."

Queers problematize national formations, be they conservative or progressive. When, in addition, specific ideological constructs are presented as exclusive formulations of the national (which is always more or less the case, of course; we refer here to the more blatant cases), the queer is deleted from political action or manipulated in culturally revealing ways. In his essay on Cuban homosexualities, Paul Julian Smith acutely analyzes the mixed reception of, and even acute resistance to, Néstor Almendros's *Improper Conduct* and Reinaldo Arenas's *Antes que anochezca* [Before night falls] on the part of progressive U.S. and European critics: perceived by these critics as uncomfortable narratives—because they spell out a repression at odds with critics' political beliefs or postulate identities that don't fit into critics' expectations—both Almendros's film and Arenas's memoir were promptly denounced on reductive ideological grounds.

In an acute analysis of Juan Goytisolo's *Paisajes después de la batalla* [Landscapes after the battle], Brad Epps scrutinizes the Spanish novelist's denunciation of ideology and his attempt, through parody, to equate communism and gay activism as repressive (and terrorist) political practices. In so doing, Epps shrewdly uncovers, under Goytisolo's defense of ambiguity and of *libertad, libertad, libertad,* highly problematic constructions of dissident sexual practices and, more specifically, of sexual—and national—subaltern others. A particularly perverse combination of the national and the homosexual is analyzed by Agnes Lugo-Ortiz in her essay on Puerto Rican culture. Lugo-Ortiz reads two transparently symbolic Puerto Rican stories in which impotence and abject self-mutilation are clearly used to signify colonial anxiety, and then relates those texts to "El asedio" [The siege] by Emilio Díaz Valcarcel, the only Puerto Rican narrative depicting a (foreseeably mannish) lesbian. Embodying a grotesque displacement of the "natural"—a "natural" that stands in here for the national, heterosexual, and "vital," that is, the nonintellectual—this lesbian clearly functions as an ideological vehicle, as one more monstrous emblem of Puerto Rican eviration. Finally, Rubén Ríos Avila further complicates the intersection of the national and the homosexual with a productive meditation on exile, a familiar component of many queer Latin American biographies. Considering Reinaldo Arenas and Manuel Ramos Otero, two Caribbean writers exiled in New York much like Martí before them, Ríos reflects on exile as a provocative critical condition, the site where the "unhomely" queer relocates his or her sexual/textual practice.

If, as some of these pieces illustrate, national genealogies and communal bonding have been often founded on the repression of the queer—queer as monstrous, queer as alien, queer as definitely "not us," not part of our national family—the queer can in turn affiliate him- or herself with alternative genealogies and construct dissident, queer family romances. Thus José Quiroga reflects on queer bloodlines, on precursors to whom one turns for recognition, on queer scenes of origins, such as the frivolous bickering between José Lezama Lima and Virgilio Piñera, the two tropical queens who are, arguably, two of the greatest Cuban writers of this century. Inviting readers to a communal recognition through that scene (one that Hispanism, traditional Hispanism, would never have dreamed of), Quiroga at the same time tempers that recognition with a careful reflection on the gains and losses of outing. In a related move, and going back to the turn of the century, Sylvia Molloy has attempted to reconstruct a scene of queer recognition around the act of *posing,* usually dismissed as frivolous and gender suspect (not to mention unpatriotic), and proposes that it be read as a significant political performance and a founding queer cultural practice.

Concentrating on performance, José Muñoz's essay focuses on the performance of Latino queerness within the public space and perceptively analyzes the way in which Pedro Zamora, the young Cuban American AIDS activist who was part of MTV's *The Real World,* through his rich performance as a Latino/queer/PWA successfully challenged prescribed representations of identity in the media and opened a space of resistance within the public sphere.

Searching for ways to facilitate queer readings of Latin American and Latino texts and, inspired by Henry Louis Gates's powerful yet gender-cautious rendering of Esu as an agent of hermeneutics, Oscar Montero takes that same Esu one step further, to her Cuban incarnation as Echu-Eleguá in Severo Sarduy's *De donde son los cantantes.* Destabilizing Gates's neat reading of this Echu-Eleguá as a tutelary figure in a search for origins, in fact revising the whole notion of a search for origins, Montero literally brings out the (tacky) queen—"Baldie, limping, Havana here I come!"—in Echu-Eleguá, reclaiming this "tropical chimera" as one possible emblem for a Latino and Latin American queer signifying practice.

Such an emblem is sought, of course, as a means to empowerment against a still relentlessly present pathologizing discourse. The troubled relation of psychoanalysis and homosexuality is made clear by Robert Irwin. Jorge Cuesta's paranoiac doctor employs the homophobic authority of psychoanalytic discourse in an attempt to contain the subversions of biology itself. The much earlier story of Eleno/a, as recounted by Burshatin, with its repeatedly pathologized gender nonconformity, is no less tragic. And Molloy, by looking at medical discourse itself, makes clear its frighteningly significant politically repressive aspect.

Out of this repressive, pathologizing atmosphere, various strategies of resistance have emerged. However, neither the identities of Hispanic writers who are generally thought of as "homosexual" nor identity politics in general are notions easily defined in the context of Hispanism. The complex, thoughtful, often disquieting reflections on identity politics offered in this book—explored by Montero, whose Latino identity politics depend on a Latin American author exiled to France; by Epps, who reveals fragmentary postmodern anti-identity politics to be as troubling as the gay rights politics and Marxism they are meant to replace; by Muñoz, whose essay shows how the identity politics of a gay Latino PWA might be too disquieting even for the liberal and funky MTV; by Ríos, who examines the unnerving complications that exiled homosexual writers inflict on notions of "national desire" back home—reflect not only the political sore points within the world (the many worlds) defined by the term *Hispanism* but also the ways in which the boundaries (not just sexual but national, racial, and political) of Hispanism begin to break down when confronted by Hispanism's own homosexualities. Furthermore, as seen in Gossy's rereading of a tale of cross-dressing as one of lesbian desire, in Burshatin's story of criminalized gender nonconformity, and in Irwin's case study of the anxiety of biological gender flux and its confusing confrontation with psychoanalytic discourse on sexuality, even in cultures where a male/female dichotomy is accentuated in national rhetoric (and, is, in fact, a basic element of grammar in the very language spoken), gender can hardly be reduced to the comforting sureness of a biologically defined binarism.

"Confrontations and paradigms must be dissolved, both the meanings and the sexes [must] be pluralized," writes Barthes in a burst of utopianism. "Meaning will tend toward its multiplication, its dispersion . . . and sex will be caught in no typology: there will be, for example, only *homosexualities*, whose plural will baffle any constituted, centered discourse" (69). Following this call to salutary dispersion, the essays in this book embrace the plural, not only of *homosexualities* but also of *hispanism*, decentered, noncapitalized *hispanisms*, hoping not only to stress diversity but, more pointedly, to question prescriptive normalcy, be it cultural or sexual. This collection would like to bring hispanisms into homosexualities and homosexualities into hispanisms, would like to propose queer readings of Spanish and Latin American literatures and cultures, but would also seek to queer univocal constructions of mainstream homosexualities with its own, oblique, not easily assimilated hispanisms. It aspires to bring out the "disappeared" queerness of each text, however strange or disquieting that queerness may seem—to the resistant readers of traditional hispanisms but also, more importantly, to us, queer hispanists.

These essays urge homosexualities and hispanisms to profitably contaminate each other; to heed Cristina Peri Rossi's playful and powerful admonition: "Be fruitful and divide / Multiply in vain" (76).

I

~

GENDER

AT

LOSS

Interrogating Hermaphroditism

in Sixteenth-Century Spain

⁓

Israel Burshatin

In 1546 Elena de Céspedes was born a female and a slave in Alhama de Granada. At age sixteen, however, her body was transformed into that of a hermaphrodite, as s/he would declare more than twenty years later while facing the tribunal of the Holy Office of the Inquisition in Toledo, where in July 1587 s/he was tried. Several serious charges brought her/him there—impersonating a man, sodomy, witchcraft, and scorn for [*sentir mal*] the sacrament of matrimony; the latter was the gravest of the accusations, provoked by her recent marriage to a woman, María del Caño. Married first to a man, Christóval Lombardo, a stonemason from Jaén, with whom she lived for only three months, Elena gave birth to their son. That was how her body was metamorphosed. According to the "Discourse of her/his life" [*Discurso de su vida*] that s/he presented orally to the Toledo tribunal, Elena's body extruded a penis during delivery of her first and only child, Christóval junior. The trial transcript, prepared by the tribunal secretary, gives the following account:

> Dixo que en realidad de verdad ésta es y fue hermafrodito, que tubo y tiene dos naturas, una de hombre y otra de muger. Y que lo que en esto pasa es que quando ésta parió como tiene dicho, con la fuerça que puso en el parto se le rompió un pellejo que benía sobre el caño de la orina y le salió una cabeza como medio dedo pulgar, que ansí lo señaló, que pareçía en su hechura cabeça de miembro de hombre, el qual, quando ésta tenía deseo y alteraçión natural le salía como dicho tiene, y quando

no estava con alteraçión se enmusteçía y recogía a la parte y seno donde
estava antes que se le rompiese el dicho pellejo.[1]

[She said that she really and truly is and was a hermaphrodite, that she
had and has two sexes, a man's and a woman's. That what happened was
that when she gave birth, as she has said, with the force that she applied
in labor she broke the loose skin that covered the urinary canal, and a
head came out [the length] of about half a big thumb, and she indicated
it so; in its shape it resembled the head of a male member, which when
she felt desire and natural excitement would come out as she has said,
and when she wasn't excited it would wilt and return to the place where
the skin had broken.]

Eleno's defense was that nature—and not her own cunning, as the inquisitors and the expert witnesses alleged—had wrought her sex change. The
evidence of gender dissidence adduced by his/her accusers was, s/he argued, traceable to the genital mutation that occurred during labor. It was
only after the birth of her penis that she altered her dress and social
persona. She privileged masculinity and took up the "male habit" [*tomó
hábito de hombre*]—the masculine clothing, personal style, and identity
that corresponded to *his* new physique. She also rewrote the female name
that she had been given as a slave. Discarding the feminine ending of
Elen*a*, he replaced it with the *o* ending of masculine nouns and crafted the
name Elen*o*, thereby signifying a gender reclassification suitable to a hermaphrodite. Thus transgendered and renamed, Eleno's social position im-
proved. In her previous life as a female, she had received limited training
in the garment trade and had held several low-paying positions traditionally associated with women. Postmanumission Elena had been employed as hose maker [*calcetera*] and weaver [*texedora*]. But postmeta-
morphosis Eleno rose to the more lucrative positions of tailor [*sastre*] and,
eventually, licensed surgeon, after spending three years in military service.

   Though hardly unknown, Eleno's life story has been largely relegated to
the periphery of historical investigation—never more than a curious foot-
note to the history of the Spanish Inquisition.[2] By reclaiming Eleno and
taking her/his account of self with the seriousness and sympathy it so
richly deserves, I am aware that I am also challenging the monocultural
assumptions of "hegemonic Hispanism," the institutionalization of which

has asserted the primacy of things Castilian, dragging with it the heavy cultural baggage of an array of myths of "purity"—of blood, nation, race, gender, genre, and ethos. These are founded on ideologies of cultural, racial, and gender difference, whereby Castilian national Catholicism and its pantheon of exalted—and typically male—writers and heroes triumph over enemies of the faith and the "race." In contrast with the cultural fluidity that still prevailed in early modern Spain, hegemonic Hispanism has encouraged a reductive and monocultural formation, what Juan Goytisolo astutely dubs the "super-Spanish bind" [*españolísimo vínculo*]. It is this repressive chain across the centuries, guarded by austere patriots and "zealous watchmen of truth" [*guardianes celosos de la verdad*], that has exerted undue influence on the practice of Hispanism (*Reivindicación* 139).[3]

Although in the twentieth century several of the field's most eminent practitioners have eloquently resisted aspects of the "super-Spanish bind," the ruling regimes of dimorphic gender and compulsory heterosexuality that inform it have only recently come under critical scrutiny. Although not immune to heterosexist biases himself, Goytisolo has exposed the strategies of exclusion and demonization of the "other," which in the peninsular context refers primarily to Islamic and Jewish communities, as well as the Christian converts descended from these. In Eleno's world, these ethnic groups and their cultural legacies had been deemed extraneous or toxic to the Christian polity, even though their contributions were constitutive elements of Spanish culture. Regional and linguistic differences notwithstanding, the sixteenth century witnessed the construction of the hegemonic "Spaniard" as an instrument of absolutist control. It is this idealized subject-position that a powerful strain of modern Hispanism has revered and redeployed. In Goytisolo's writing, the myth of Spanish identity holds that "indelible ethnic characteristics have held constant across centuries" [*perduración secular de ciertos caracteres étnicos imborrables*] (*Reivindicación* 139). By definition, this "super-Spanish bind" has barred women, racial "others" (Moors, Jews, Africans, Indians, etc.), and forms of sexual and gender dissidence that would belie the monocultural formations precariously poised on those exclusions. No matter how repressed their accomplishments or misrepresented their resistance might have been, these marginalized "others" were also at the heart of what Spanishness was about. Our engagement with diverse Hispanisms allows us to interrogate the Inquisition's record of Eleno's hermaphroditism and thereby reclaim Eleno's voice—one of exemplary *mestizaje* in its articulations of the African, the transgendered, and the subaltern—for the widening conversation of "Hispanisms and homosexualities."

Eleno's story is compelling in ways similar to the rich tradition of women's writing—especially in its autobiographical form—that feminist scholarship has recovered in recent years.[4] Although feminism has already transformed the field, received notions of what properly constitutes the canon of the "Golden Age" and the subjectivities allowed to emerge under those formations have largely excluded same-sex desire. Only certain marginalized forms have been included for purposes of disapprobation— "Oriental" aberrations happily eradicated from their (all too) fertile soil by the expulsions of Jews and Moriscos, or contained in criminalized depictions issuing from secular or inquisitional courts.[5] Rather than the repressive and falsely transcendental "super-Spanish bind," it is to the *articulations* among categories of difference that this study of Eleno's transgendering attends.[6] The inquisitional dossier—a marginalized and repressed site of the official culture—enables us to interrogate the record of "Golden Age" subjectivities and to begin to write a queer history of gender and sexual dissidence in Spain. Although Eleno's voice is also one ventriloquized by the official discourse that represented it, a reading sensitive to the subaltern will uncover Eleno's fashioning and positioning of self precisely at points of interdependence, where multiple discourses allow diverse articulations of sexuality, gender, and race. As we shall see, Eleno was able to assume difference while also avowing the requisite orthodoxy expected of the subject in Habsburg Spain.

Eleno, as well as her accusers, former medical colleagues, and the inquisitors who judged her, subscribed to a basic tenet of medieval and Renaissance corporeal knowledge: that physique and mores, sex and gender roles, are bound together by nature. As Joan Cadden writes, "Physiognomy, like the theory of temperaments, [was thought to yield] evidence about the relation of physical characteristics to expected roles and behavior patterns" (186). Religious and lay prohibitions against homosexual acts between women and between men

> were commonly put in terms of role reversals, bearing the implication that there is something inherently feminine about taking what was

construed as a passive role in intercourse and something inherently masculine about having sex with a woman. Early penitentials had used language that reflected those assumptions, and it turned up with some regularity later, both within and beyond ecclesiastical documents. . . . Like the prohibition of transvestism, which is associated, among other things, with preventing women from celebrating the mass, the ecclesiastical position against sexual acts between persons of the same sex carries the message of role differentiation, and like the tone of the medical and physiognomic texts which derogate masculine traits in women and feminine traits in men by calling them deceptions and hypocrisies, it communicates firm moral disapprobation. (Cadden 220)

What happens, then, with the "neuter" position; how does it affect the binary opposition between male and female, masculine and feminine, and the medical/social distinctions between the hot and dry complexion of man and the cold and wet temperament of woman? Is there really a one-sex body in medieval and Renaissance thought, as Thomas Laqueur has argued? Is there a viable middle position, a true intersex with corresponding social status?[7] Alan of Lille, writing in the second half of the twelfth century, maintained his carefully constructed model of nature as a system homologous with the rules of Latin grammar by banishing from his system the third term that would disrupt his "ethical grammar" of genders (Ziolkowski 95–103). Although Alan entertained the notion of placing eunuchs and sodomite males in a third category modeled after the neuter grammatical gender, he chose instead, as Cadden puts it, "to dismantle the rules of grammar by declaring that nature and grammar have just two genders and that neuter is a different type of form, a negative and confused category. Although 'neuter' presented an opportunity to construct a grammatical category corresponding to 'homosexuals,' Alan declined to make use of it and thus accorded individuals engaged in stigmatized acts no natural category, no ontological status" (225).

We find in Eleno's life story attempts to construct precisely a third, or neuter, position grounded in scientific and historical discourses and capable of furnishing a valid juridical basis for his transgendering. Eleno cited in his own defense examples from Pliny, Augustine, and Aristotle in order to insert his own story into the recognized sequences of natural history with the aim of securing a legal justification for what he argued was his *natural* turn from sex with a man (her husband was her only male partner) to sex with women. Eleno had many female sexual partners, and he married one of them, María del Caño, an event that the civil authorities in Ocaña and the inquisitors in Toledo would subsequently regard with contempt as same-sex marriage and evidence of Eleno's animus against the laws of the realm and the holy sacrament of matrimony.

Eleno's legal troubles began when an officer and fellow veteran of the War of the Alpujarras (1568–1570) recognized Eleno, who was at the time newly married to María del Caño and living with her as man and wife. The officer, el licenciado Ortega Velázquez, recalling Eleno's dubious army reputation as someone who had two sexes, was quite perturbed that Eleno and María were living in connubial bliss, "haciendo vida maridable." On trial in the provincial court in Ocaña, Eleno identified himself as a hermaphrodite, a "neuter," and a man:

> Preguntado en qué rreputación le tenían sus padres, deudos y vecinos deste confesante, si le tenían por onbre o muger, dixo que le tenyan por neutro y por onbre, que no era lo uno ny lo otro.

> [Asked about his reputation among his parents, relatives, and neighbors, whether they considered him to be a man or a woman, this person confessing said that they considered him to be neuter and a man, that he was neither the one nor the other.]

Eleno's location of self betwixt and between male and nonmale is characteristic of the hermaphrodite, who is ontologically caught amidst competing discourses—the legal and the scientific. As Julia Epstein defines this predicament:

> Hermaphrodites pose a particularly unsettling problem for medical jurisprudence. The law assumes a precise contrariety between two sexes, whereas medical science has for several centuries understood sex determination to involve a complex and indefinite mechanism that results in a spectrum of human sexual types rather than in a set of mutually exclusive categories. (101)

Daston and Park, in their examination of hermaphrodites in sixteenth-century France, conclude that homophobia played a decisive role in maintaining the "precise contrariety between two sexes" that Epstein describes (Daston and Park 7–8).

What exactly did Eleno understand by the term *neutro?* Covarrubias's lexicon, published in 1611, helps, but not much: "Neutro. *Apud grammaticos,* es el nombre que ni es masculino ni es femenino" [Neuter: In the writings of grammarians, is the name that is neither masculine nor feminine] (Covarrubias, s.v. "Neutro," 827). Covarrubias gives strictly a grammatical definition, one more suited to Latin than to the vernacular. Yet the clue that interests us in this entry is the linguistic structure that makes possible and validates gender indeterminacy. Eleno altered her name by substituting a masculine for a feminine ending and thereby rendered visible and socially meaningful his body's own new sense of an ending. But because Eleno was not regarded as a suitable name for a man—as the Ocaña tribunal would carefully point out—the result of both the name and Eleno's physical appearance (*lampiño,* without a beard) was to convey a curious mix of genders, which brought into play notions of altered gender and gender itself, rather than projecting the male persona that Eleno undoubtedly privileged.[8] For Eleno certainly knew that neuter was not a felicitous subject-position. However, as with Alan of Lille, the analogy with linguistic gender was ephemeral.

Eleno was a mulatto and a freed slave in a society obsessed with exalted origins and the so-called purity of bloodlines. After her emancipation and the death of her mother, who was a slave of African origins, Eleno relocated to the city of Granada, where s/he continued to apprentice in ever more skilled manufacturing jobs. It would have been a kind of social suicide for Eleno to acknowledge and claim for him/herself publicly the status of hermaphrodite, which at best would have set back his social aspirations. Nevertheless we learn from various testimonies presented at the Toledo trial that his popular reputation was that he had two sexes. It was this "local knowledge" of being a hermaphrodite that Eleno sought to revise when he submitted to several physical examinations as part of his application for a license to marry María. Satisfied that all the witnesses who looked at and touched Eleno's genitals declared that he was a fully endowed male, the vicar of Madrid granted his approval, thus enabling Eleno to marry María and to proclaim the unambiguous gender status that he had so assiduously pursued. If neuter was not a suitable subject-position, then neuter would only furnish an occasional locus, a sexuality to be transformed, and, all too briefly, a source of sensual pleasure.

We shall have to revise the notion that surgically assisted transgenderings occur only in modern times as we delve into Eleno's understanding of the neuter category. For Eleno, *neutro* initially signified a physical impediment to be overcome by a surgical procedure that would refashion the body and furnish the member necessary to play the masculine sexual role. Indeed, that Eleno had relations with women, and even married a woman after his surgery, was an opportunity not to be missed by the Toledo Inquisition, which dismissed Eleno's account of her transformation and, instead, staged on the body of the brown-skinned female who had formerly been a slave a cruel spectacle of phallocratic disapprobation and rank homophobia. If slavery was a condition that the law allowed to be superseded by manumission, femaleness, however, was not at all a condition that could be cast aside, even after proper medical intervention.

Asked during his civil trial in Ocaña how she could have married a woman if she was, as claimed, a neuter or hermaphrodite, Eleno replied that a surgeon had made it all possible:

Y que la causa de aberse casado siendo neutro fue que en Sanlúcar de Varrameda un licenciado Tapia, siendo este confesante de hedad de diez e ocho años, le curó y cortó un pellejo e pedazo de carne que tenía pegado al cuerpo en la parte de su natura y le dexó natura de onbre formada e asy comenzó usar de onbre y se casó y sentó con muger.

[The reason why she was married having been neuter was that in Sanlúcar de Barrameda a certain licentiate Tapia, when this person confessing was eighteen years old, cured him and cut off a piece of loose skin that was stuck to his body over his sex, which left him with male genitals fully formed. And that was how he began to act as a man, and he was married and settled down with his wife.]

The masculine gender role, understood as comprising corporeal, sexual, and social elements, necessitates possession of the phallus. According to this portion of Eleno's trial in Ocaña, having had the surgical procedure that left him with a fully working male member, Eleno's femaleness became a moot point. But in later testimony in front of the tribunal of the Inquisition in Toledo, we learn that the surgical procedure did nothing to diminish her femaleness and, in fact, fully rendered him *neutro* for the first and only time, bringing with it a great deal of carnal pleasure. In the narrative of Eleno's life, which he formally presented to the Toledo inquisitors, this unique, openly *neutro* affair emerged as a privileged moment in his erotic awakening.

Both the Ocaña and Toledo tribunals ordered physical exams to determine Eleno's true sex, and all the experts—physicians, surgeons, and midwives—declared unanimously that Eleno was female and bore no signs of ever having been what she said. Eleno related how she had lost her male genitalia—member and testicles—all the while insisting that scars and signs were still visible where the member had once hung. The expert witnesses who had previously assured the court of the archbishop of Toledo that Eleno was a man and not a hermaphrodite, and could therefore marry without impediment María del Caño, now accused Eleno of deception and traffic with the devil. Eleno held her ground, admitting only that she had concealed her female sex when, to marry María, she had to assuage the suspicions of the vicar of Madrid that Eleno was a "capon" [*capón*], as vicar Juan Baptista Neroni called Eleno when he noticed his lack of facial hair. Regardless of the specifics implied in the vicar's colorful interpellation of *capón*—castrated or sexually incapacitated male, hermaphrodite, or just perfectly "queer"—these conditions were incompatible with marriage. Moreover, Eleno's gender ambiguity, coupled with his brown skin and the brand of slavery burned into his face in early childhood, produced a "signature" of unremitting marginality. According to the dominant code of sexed bodies woven into in the rising discourse of hegemonic "Spanishness," Eleno as *capón* upset the exclusive contrariety of masculine and feminine that sustained the ruling ideology of the household.

Eleno's short-lived pleasures as a *neutro* occurred when he had his first sexual encounter with a woman. In this touching account, we perceive not the vicar's abject *capón* but a Tiresias figure who seduces his boss's pretty wife with his own narrative of transfiguration. Eleno's complex roles in the love triangle—"other" man, "other" woman—enrich his gender crossings and render his hermaphroditic body a potent source of attraction. In fact, the surgical procedures that he underwent in Sanlúcar de Barrameda did not negate Eleno's femaleness, as one might infer from her testimony in Ocaña; rather, the procedure enhanced a maleness that existed side by side with her female organs. But this was a dangerous, intergendered line to tread, and as he explained to the Toledo inquisitors, he would never again reveal himself fully to anyone else, not even his own wife. María was under considerable pressure to incriminate her husband. No doubt to shield herself from accusations of complicity, she insisted that she had been duped. Despite certain suspicions stemming from Eleno's reluctance to be touched and some bloody shirts, María was never really certain that Eleno could be other than a man.

Coming out as *neutro* occurred in Sanlúcar de Barrameda, where he worked as tailor and hose maker [*sastre* and *calcetero*]—or was it female *sastra* and *calcetera?* The trial transcript is ambiguous as to what sort of attire and style [*hábito*]—male, female, or "other"—Eleno had assumed at the time, but enough clues point to a mix-and-match approach to gender performance. Employed at the house of a linen merchant, Eleno was aroused by the beautiful and young Ana, the merchant's wife. In a moment of intimacy, while the husband was away on business, Eleno came out to Ana and revealed that she possessed a male member. Exposing her vulva and her penis, Eleno wooed Ana and promised to copulate with her as a man. She said she also spoke to Ana "half-disguised":

> Y quando ésta estubo en Sanlúcar de Barrameda, como tiene dicho, haçiendo una vez una obra de ofiçio de sastre como en tantas husaba, en casa de un mercader de lienzos que se llama Hernando de Toledo, quedando a solas con su muger, que se llamava Ana de Albánchez, que hera moça y hermosa, a ésta le vino gana de vesarla, y sin deçille cosa alguna la vesó. Y espantándose de esto ella, ésta la dixo que podría tener con ella giunta como hombre, lo qual la dijo medio disfraçado por la vergüenza que ésta tenía de deçilla que tenía dos sexos.

> [And when she was in Sanlúcar de Barrameda, as she has said, one day while working as he often had as a tailor at the home of the linen merchant, Hernando de Toledo, she came to be alone with the merchant's wife, who was called Ana de Albánchez; she was young and

pretty, and she felt like kissing her, and without saying anything, she kissed her. The merchant's wife was shocked by this, but she told her that she could couple with her as a man, which she told her half-disguised because she felt ashamed to tell her that she had two sexes.]

Eleno's *neutro* persona and physique so inflamed Ana's passion that it was she who took the initiative and an unusually shy Eleno to bed:

> Y la dicha Ana de Albánchez llevó a ésta a la cama. Y aunque estava alterada y tenía aquella caveza salida como tiene dicho y se echó ençima de ella, no la pudo haçer nada más de aquella demostraçión, y con esto ésta se lo mostró a la dicha Ana de Albánchez.

> [Ana de Albánchez took her to bed. And even though she was excited and the head had come out, as she has said, and lay down on top of her, she couldn't do any more to her than that demonstration and then she showed it to said Ana de Albánchez.]

In order to remove the physical impediment that thwarted their passion, Eleno went to see surgeon Tapia, who cut off the unwanted layer of skin, thereby enabling Eleno and Ana to consummate their love. The lovers carried on their affair for several months, undeterred by Ana's cuckolded husband.

> Y ésta quedó con abtitud de poder tener quenta con muger y bolvió a la dicha Ana de Albánchez, y con ella tubo muchas veçes quenta y actos como hombre, y estubo en su casa sin que su marido entendiese nada como quatro o çinco meses.

> [And she remained with the wherewithal to have relations with women, and she returned to Ana de Albánchez and had sex with her many times as a man, and she was with her in her house for about four or five months without her husband noticing anything.]

Their liaison came to an end only when a more powerful man, the town magistrate [*corregidor*], who was also in love with Ana, interfered with the cozy arrangement and ran Eleno out of town. It is remarkable, I believe, to find this unabashed expression of sexual desire between women—or, rather, between woman and "phallicized woman"⁹—in sixteenth-century Spain. In Eleno's eyes, Ana de Albánchez was young and pretty. And, therefore, Eleno was aroused, "and she felt like kissing her, and without saying anything, she kissed her."

Eleno's life story illustrates the complex articulations of sexuality, mores, and the body that remained a powerful model of sexuality well into the early modern period. Eleno's body is indeed the most important piece of evidence brought before the three tribunals that had something to say about his relations with women: the court of the archbishop of Toledo in Madrid, the provincial court [*audiencia*] in Ocaña, and the tribunal of the Holy Office of the Inquisition in Toledo. The medical experts agreed with Eleno that it was possible—in theory, at least—for a female to be transformed into a hermaphrodite, and accounts of these metamorphoses were well-known, even though increasingly relegated to the realm of the preternatural, as in Pliny's *Natural History*, Book 7, an often-cited source and one with a poignant connection to Eleno's own story.¹⁰ But the challenge to the ideology of the household posed by Eleno's marriage to a woman could not go unpunished—even if in Castile the Inquisition had no jurisdiction over "the unspeakable crime of sodomy" [*el delito nefando de sodomía*], which the Inquisition of Aragon did make it very much its business to prosecute. The inquisitors found Eleno guilty of bigamy, an elegant legal way out of the conundrum posed by Eleno's articulations of sex, gender, and race. But even though sodomy stayed in the closet of their medico-legal elucubrations, the inquisitors staged an elaborate and exemplary punishment on Eleno, "the bigamist." They released a text to be read publicly [*pregón*] to accompany the two hundred lashes Eleno received, one hundred in Toledo, where the trial occurred, and another hundred in Ciempozuelos, where Eleno and María were betrothed. The public text of the sentence was clearly meant to admonish women against the lure of other female tricksters [*burladoras*] who, like Eleno, might flout the gender norms of church and state and entice women into same-sex liaisons:

Esta es la justicia que manda hazer el Santo Officio de la Inquisición de Toledo a esta muger, porque siendo casanda engañó a otra muger y se casó con ella. So pena de su culpa la mandan açotar por ello y se recluya en un hospital por diez años para que sirva en él. Quien tal haze que así lo pague.

[This is the justice ordered by the Holy Office of the Inquisition of Toledo on this woman, because, being married, she fooled another woman and married her. For her guilt she is sentenced to be whipped and confined in a hospital for ten years so that she may serve there. As you sow so shall you reap.]

A more literal translation of the proverbial expression would read, "as you do, so shall you pay." But was the punishment truly equivalent to Eleno's crime? And what was, really, her crime? As we have seen, Eleno was found guilty only of bigamy, whereas the charges brought against her were much more broadly conceived and touched on all the major aspects of what Judith Butler has called "punishable phallicism" (*Bodies* 102): cross-dressing, dildo-assisted sex, and same-sex marriage.

The *pregón* plunges (re)feminized Elena in ritualized abjection. The text's rhetorical force derives from its enunciation during exemplary and violent events: auto-da-fé in Toledo's Zocodover (central market square), public reading of the sentence in front of the assembled parishioners in the church of Ciempozuelos, where the same-sex betrothal took place, and public lashings in the streets of both cities in the month of December 1588. A close reading of the *pregón* reveals that the equation so dramatically presented to edify the masses reiterates the abjecting strategy in prescribing—and policing—femininity: "[T]his woman, because, being married, she fooled another woman and married her." Having rejected Eleno's reading of his own anatomy as a phallicized body, the *pregón* interpellates woman: "*This* woman." The act of naming asserts femininity against the grain of prior readings of Eleno as "somebody who had two sexes" (his reputation in the army) or as *capón* (according to the vicar of Madrid).

The theatricals of abjuration and punishment reterritorialize Eleno's body.[11] "This woman" is the locus of punishment; "this woman" is, indeed, a woman. And here we can reformulate Montesquieu's famous question about—and challenge to—the troping of otherness: "How can one be Persian?"[12] We modify the question and ask, how can "one" be woman? Or rather, how might a phallicized woman (Eleno) be further transformed so that she can be a woman? Is a "return" possible? Does the flesh admit erasure? The Inquisition's formulaic "reconciliation" conjures up past misdeeds and exacts penance from Eleno, who performs the ritual abjuration of one convicted of "minor" [*de levi*] heretical offenses that are now indelibly entered into the public transcript—hence the bloody spectacle, the public shaming of the offending body whose masculine fiction will be violently corrected by yet another fiction. "This woman, because being married," no matter that the husband left her after three months and died soon afterward. This is a woman. This is a married woman—that is, married to a man. Femininity "is the forcible citation of a norm," writes Butler (*Bodies* 232). A married woman is the phallus, and the husband has the phallus. Eleno is, therefore, a married woman. But Eleno disavowed being the phallus and insisted that she had it—the loss of her penis and testicles notwithstanding, or, indeed, because of that castration. "She fooled another woman and married her." A woman can be fooled by another woman—a man, conversely, cannot be fooled.

This is the most obtuse aspect of the inquisitors' phantasmic restoration of hegemonic phallicism, because the dossier amply documents Eleno's rhetorical and morphological authoritativeness over many powerful male officials, including the vicar of Madrid, the parish priest of Ciempozuelos, and the physicians and surgeons who made the wedding possible by certifying that Eleno was a man and *not* a hermaphrodite. The restoration of phallic authority requires the iteration of the norm—gender (the sexed position) is assumed through the abjection of homosexuality (Butler, *Bodies* 111). A woman—Eleno's wife, María—was duped by another and married her. Feminine abjection finds a value equal to itself in the exemplary punishment. Eleno will be shown back to her true gender as the executioner rips her flesh apart two hundred times on the streets of Toledo and Ciempozuelos, to the amusement—and perhaps the horror— of the spectators, themselves vulnerable (or so the inquisitors say) to such female doubleness. But the system can be contested. The law produces the occasion for such challenges. So women can and do have sex with other women, and marry each other, and can live successfully as men and become soldiers and surgeons? Exemplary punishment maps out the limits of the law of dimorphic sex and gender, as well as the way to challenge those norms (Butler, *Bodies* 109).

In February 1589, less than two months into Eleno's ten-year sentence of confinement—and return to servitude—in King's Hospital [*Hospital del Rey*] in Toledo, caring for the sick and injured, Eleno again found her/ himself the center of controversy. The hospital administrator wrote to the inquisitors, begging them to relocate Eleno to another institution; s/he was too much to handle.

Que es grande el estorbo y enbaraço que a causado la entrada de la dicha Elena de Céspedes por la mucha gente que acude a verla y a curarse con ella.

[The presence of Elena de Céspedes has caused great annoyance and embarrassment from the beginning, since many people come to see and be healed by her.]

The return of the phallicized woman. The sick and injured of Toledo preferred to be cured by Eleno—to the consternation of the male physicians. The lines of Eleno's protean selves converged in this latest embodiment, a surgeon by inquisitional decree, but popularly, still, transgendered, her/his powers have been glorified by auto-da-fé, *pregón*, scourges, manumission, and, presumably, the gender-bending sight of a surgeon "properly" attired in skirts.

Notes

1   Eleno's life story is contained in the hitherto unpublished dossier of her/his trial, beginning in July 1587, at the Toledo court of the Inquisition, which also gathered the documents from two other legal venues: his initial prosecution by the provincial court in Ocaña some months earlier and the documents filed in 1584 to 1586 at the court of the archbishop of Toledo in Madrid, where Eleno successfully challenged the impediments raised in regard to his application for a license to marry a woman, María del Caño, on account of his intergendered appearance. The dossier contains summaries of the court sessions, depositions by expert and lay witnesses regarding Eleno's genital conformation, and testimonies by his wife, casual sexual partners, friends, neighbors, associates in his practice of surgery, and all those who had anything relevant to say about Eleno's mode of dress, sexual habits, anatomy, medical practice, and suspected demonic affiliations. The hitherto unpublished dossier gathered by the Inquisition is of considerable heft, more than 150 folios,

and remains the principal source of information about Eleno and his life. This and all subsequent citations from the trial summaries of Elena de Céspedes are from my transcription and translation of the dossier at the Archivo Histórico Nacional (Céspedes). The documents are written in various sixteenth-century hands. I give no page numbers because the originals lack consistent page or folio numbers. My transcriptions show some slight modifications to facilitate reading. I resolve all abbreviations (e.g., *dho* = *dicho*, *Mᵃ* = *María*), furnish accent marks and punctuation, and regularize the use of *u* and *v*.

2 Eleno's case has been mentioned or studied by the following: Lea, who misnames her "Elvira" (187–88); Barbazza; Escamilla; Folch Jou and Muñoz; and most recently Bullough and Bullough, who apparently cite (94–96) from an unpublished paper by Richard A. Kagan, which I have been unable to obtain.

3 English translation is mine, with my colleague Roberto Castillo-Sandoval's assistance gratefully acknowledged.

4 I cite only a few of many important contributions: Arenal and Schlau, Franco, Lagos, Ludmer, Molloy (*At Face Value*), Surtz, Weber.

5 For the early modern history of Spanish "sodomy" see Benassar, Carrasco, Perry ("The Nefarious Sin"), Tomás y Valiente, and Monter.

6 See the discussion in Li of "articulation" and postcolonial theory.

7 See Park for a critique of the "one-sex body" proposed by Laqueur. On the figure of the hermaphrodite, see Donoghue, Epstein, Jones and Stallybrass, Nugent, Silberman, and Daston and Park.

8 For a study of the transvestite as the "third" that upsets the ruling binary structure of gender, see Garber and Herdt.

9 See chapter 2 of Butler, *Bodies That Matter,* "The Lesbian Phallus and the Morphological Imaginary," 57–91, and the "phallicized dyke," 96.

10 See the discussion in Burshatin.

11 The corporeal motifs of "reterritorialization," Lacanian "fiction" and "locus of control," "having" versus "being the phallus," and "transfigurative wish" are all borrowed from Butler, *Bodies That Matter* 57–119.

12 "Ah! ah! Monsieur est Persan? Comment peut-on être Persan?" (Montesquieu 69). Also cited by Gilroy, who asserts that the question "remains stubbornly and wilfully unanswered" by "bourgeois humanism" (44).

Skirting the Question:

Lesbians and María de Zayas

~

Mary S. Gossy

¿Quién ha visto que una dama se enamore de otra? The English translation would be "Whoever heard of a lady falling in love with another woman?" But in her *Desengaño amoroso* "Amar sólo por vencer" [Loving only to conquer],[1] María de Zayas writes *¿Quién ha visto?* [who has seen]. I want to translate this because this article is for people working both within and without Hispanism—people who I can expect will know my languages and understand them, people who are not yet sure of themselves, and people who have not yet learned to understand. This position is like the position of the lesbian feminist theorist working in Golden Age Hispanism, the most traditional kind, because it is the one that makes myths about the texts that are the central myths of all other Hispanisms. Many Golden Age scholars would rather not see or hear from lesbians, and many lesbian and queer theorists have never heard anything about the Golden Age, so doing lesbian feminism and Golden Age Hispanism requires a lot of translation.

In 1647 María de Zayas published the question, "¿Quién ha visto que una dama se enamore de otra?" A few decades before, Sebastián de Covarrubias said in his dictionary that "Algunas vezes llamamos ver lo que es propio de otro sentido" [Sometimes we call "seeing" that which really pertains to another sense]—such as hearing. A little later in his definition, he says, "Ver y creer" [Seeing is believing] (Covarrubias Orozco 1000b). Or is it? If not, why not? Why is it so hard to answer the literal question, "Who has seen a lady fall in love with another?"

In seventeenth-century Spain, where Zayas's story is set, we know from archives and legal documents that sex between women was a punishable and punished offense. Both Mary Elizabeth Perry's analysis of the situation in early modern Seville (125) and Valerie Traub's discussion of contemporaneous French and English cases (62–83) assert that neither a woman's "*desire* for another woman, nor any non-penetrative acts she might commit were crimes, but the prosthetic supplementation of her body was grounds for execution" (66). I refer to Traub's excellent essay, with which I both agree and disagree, because it is one of the most theoretically sophisticated pieces on the topic of lesbian desire in the early modern period. Later she adds: "[A]lthough 'tribades' and 'sodomites' supplementing their bodies necessarily performed a certain amount of what Judith Butler terms 'gender trouble,' the absence of outcry against 'feminine' homoeroticism suggests that it posed very little gender trouble at all" (78). "Feminine" homoeroticism in Traub's formulation means sex between two women who are not supplementing their femininity with any appliances or trappings of masculinity. Here I would like to suggest that the lack of an outcry or punishment of this feminine erotic expression does not mean that it was not a source of gender trouble. Sometimes very troubling facts produce very little outcry, and the lack of outcry in fact frequently signals big trouble; this whole process is called repression. Faced with this silence (whoever heard of?) and invisibility (whoever saw?) around the possibility of women having sex with each other without imitating heterosexual roles, Traub says two things: First (in her first sentence), that in the early modern period, "lesbian desire doesn't exist. Not at least, as such" (62). Second, at the end of the essay, since "as such" leaves a lot of room, Traub says that she "find[s] it inconceivable that within the vast array of erotic choices reported by early modern culture, 'feminine' bodies did not meet, touch, and pleasure one another" (79). This is like the conclusion that Terry Castle reaches in the introduction to *The Apparitional Lesbian:* that "Western civilization, it seems, has always known on some level about lesbians" (9). In Traub's case, common sense, and in Castle's the literary record as *part* of the historical record, make it possible to access awareness of lesbian expression in the past.

    Lesbian is for some an anachronistic word for a woman who falls in love with another woman—before 1900. So I will recur to Castle again: "I still maintain, if in ordinary speech I say 'I am a lesbian,' the meaning is instantly (even dangerously) clear" (15). Castle says that the word makes sense, and that saying it produces certain political and personal effects.

Also, the statement "if I say I am a lesbian, the meaning is clear" has a specific narrative structure. When I say I am a lesbian, I am putting my sexuality into discourse—I am saying it *to* someone else, who may or may not be a lesbian, and who may or may not understand, and both of those possibilities can be dangerous. I can make trouble and get into it by publicly announcing my erotic love for another woman. This trouble is evident in Western texts from Juvenal and the New Testament up to popular representations of lesbians today, and everybody knows it. Why then, do many critics and historians strain so at the question "Whoever saw a lady fall in love with another woman?" There is an explanation, if not an answer, in "Amar sólo por vencer."

The explanation has to do with the fact that the question is asked at all. "Amar sólo por vencer" is the sixth story in María de Zayas's second collection of stories, the *Desengaños amorosos*. Both this and her first collection, *Novelas amorosas y ejemplares*, are framed narratives told by upper-class people engaged in a contest of storytelling on successive evenings. In the first collection, both men and women tell stories; in the second, published ten years later, there are only female narrators. Male homosexuality is directly represented in one story, "Mal presagio casar lejos" [It's a bad omen to marry far from home]. Female homoeroticism is represented in at least one story from each collection: "La burlada Aminta" [Aminta deceived], in which a woman helps to seduce another woman for the sake of her boyfriend, and "Amar sólo por vencer." Both of the stories with lesbian trajectories, although appearing in different collections, have the same narrator in the frame tale, a lady named Matilde. The story she tells in "Amar sólo por vencer" has a relatively simple plot. A rogue named Esteban develops a passion for Laurela, who is almost too young for marriage, and much too rich and noble for Esteban to ever hope to marry anyway. His lust, however, is so compelling that he feels that he must get her somehow, so he decides to dress up as a woman and become one of her ladies-in-waiting. From the second the character puts on a dress, the narrator resolutely refers to him as Estefanía, using only feminine forms. Because of her charm and her musical talent, Estefanía is instantly admitted to the house. She proclaims her love for Laurela, has fits of jealousy whenever the possibility of Laurela's marriage to a man is raised, and defiantly insists on her amorous rights to Laurela. This love of one lady for another is judged by the other maids to be a hilarious form of madness and is the cause of much mirth in the house. But more than a year later, the day comes when Laurela's father arranges his daughter's marriage, and the fun ends. On hearing the news, Estefanía has a fainting fit that frightens everyone, especially Laurela, who has no idea how she will be able to explain "tal amor y tal sentimiento" [such a love and such a feeling] to the rest of the household (319). Later that night, Estefanía confesses that she is Esteban (Zayas maintains the feminine pronouns just like this), and Laurela cannot believe her. During this conversation, Estefanía asks Laurela, "¿no has conocido que soy lo que digo y no lo que parezco? Porque quién ha visto que una dama se enamore de otra?" [Haven't you known that I am what I say and not what I seem? For who has ever seen a lady fall in love with another woman?] (320). Laurela still cannot fathom what Estefanía is saying to her and goes to bed in a room with her three sisters; "Laurela se aseguró de que Estefanía no se pondría en ningún atrevimiento, caso de que fuera don Esteban" [so that she would be sure that Estefanía would not be able to try anything, in case she was really Don Esteban] (321).

That night, Laurela decides that if Estefanía is Esteban, she would still have some charming characteristics, and so for this reason and as an attempt to preserve her honor, Laurela decides to take up Esteban's offer of marriage. The two sneak away from her father's house and consummate their relationship in the back room of the house of one of Esteban's friends. Early the next morning, Esteban wakes a surprised Laurela, takes her to church, and tells her that he cannot marry her because he is already married to another woman in another town. At this point, he disappears from the story, never to be heard from again—which means that he is never punished.

Laurela is not so lucky, though. Her father, having understood what has happened, will not see her, so for more than a year she stays in her aunt's house nearby, waiting for him to forgive her. Her relatives grow tired of having her around the house, though, and so arrange one day to cause a wall to topple on Laurela and her serving girl. In a death typical of Zayas's stories, Laurela's head is broken open, and she suffocates under the debris. Everyone laments the terrible accident, the aunt and uncle are happy to be rid of their houseguest, and the story ends. Matilde, the narrator of the frame tale, sees Esteban's behavior as an extreme example of perseverance in evil but in her conclusion makes no mention of the operation of gender in Esteban's deceit. All she says is that men are willing to put themselves through "más transformaciones que Prometeo" [more transformations than Prometheus] in order to dishonor women (331–32). Of course, Prometheus is not known for his amorous transformations; there are no stories of him to compare with what Zeus, for example, did for love. But the word *transformation* does point back to the key moment of the text, which is the story of Estefanía.

In one of her last articles, Ruth El Saffar wrote about the narrative structure of Zayas's novellas. There is conflict and action in the frame tale as well as in the framed stories, and the content of the framed stories is meant to influence the outcome of events in the frame tale. Further, the prose narratives of both the frame tale and the framed stories are interrupted by frequent songs and poems that carry veiled messages whose meaning is clear only to certain listeners. El Saffar says that "Zayas leaves a large gap between sender and fictional recipient in many of Lysis's [the frame tales' organizing narrator] poems. The presence, in Golden Age drama, of the misperceiving recipient (usually the deceived husband), always implies another destinary for whom the hidden message is intended" (18). Thus the narrative structure of Zayas's collections has many layers: characters in a framed story tell stories to influence each other; the framed story's meaning influences action and meaning in the frame tale; and the meanings produced by way of the reflection and refraction between framing and framed tales carry hidden meanings to the readers to whom María de Zayas is writing: the women to whom she is describing the trap of patriarchy, and to whom she ultimately suggests the all-female world of the convent as a redemptive home. Like the poems in other stories and in the frame tale, the Estefanía story is a self-contained narrative unit that influences the reception of the stories that contain it. An example of this is that when Lisis, the protagonist of the frame tale, finally decides to forget about marriage and enter a convent, one of the two women accompanying her is named nothing other than Estefanía. The Estefanía story is a current that carries a specific meaning within the context of Zayas's writing about how women can survive or escape from compulsory relationships with men.

This meaning is about gender and desire. Spanish, like other Romance languages, makes it harder, in some ways, to be oblique about a person's gender than English does. Most adjectives in Spanish are marked as masculine or feminine, and their use makes clear the gender of their referent. The narrator relentlessly calls Estefanía Estefanía, and once the character says her name in the presence of Laurela, there is no doubt as to her written gender. I think that the consistency of the femininity of Estefanía has a meaning for Zayas's readers. Goytisolo's famous article "El mundo erótico de María de Zayas" finds the action of "Amar sólo por vencer" hopelessly lacking in verisimilitude because of the text's insistence that the idea that Estefanía might be a man never even occurred to Laurela. What I would argue here is that Zayas's first concern is not to tell a good Aristotelian story, but rather simply to represent a possibility. For as long as Laurela believes that Estefanía is a woman who loves her erotically, the love of one woman for another is accomplished in writing. The reader knows that this love of a woman for another woman is a fiction, but that fiction also sustains the acknowledgment that such a love can be put into discourse, that language can speak and write it. What little critical attention has been directed toward this story has been focused on Esteban's cross-dressing; I would like to suggest that for lesbians, and for historians of female homoeroticism, Laurela's reception of a discourse of erotic love from a person who she believes is a woman in love with her is of primary importance. As hard as it may be for some readers to face, Laurela believes that Estefanía is a woman in love with her, and within that fiction, we may read what María de Zayas wrote about ladies who fall in love with each other.

At the beginning of the Estefanía story, Zayas writes that Estefanía was so charming that she was immediately made part of the household, and then adds:

Porque si a todas agradó, a Laurela enamoró: tanto era el agrado de la doncella. (299)

[Because if she pleased all the women, she made Laurela enamored, so great was the pleasure of the young woman.]

This sentence, at the outset of the encounter between Laurela and Estefanía, immediately makes a distinction between the way that the other women of the house reacted to Estefanía and the way that Laurela did. *Agradar* is "to please or to charm," but *enamorar*, usually a reflexive rather than a transitive verb, has only erotic meanings. *Enamorarse* means "to fall in love," with all the attendant carnal implications. For Covarrubias, interestingly, *enamorar* is something a woman does to a man: "Enamorar: poner codicia a otro alguna mujer para que la quiera con sus atavíos y halagos." Here it is something that Estefanía does to Laurela—it is on the order of "you made me love you." What is crucial is that Laurela's response differs from that of the other women. It is explicitly erotic.

The sentence that follows the one I have just cited goes:

No fue este amor de calidad del² de don Esteban; porque Laurela, sin advertir engaño, creyó que era mujer. (299)

[This love was not of the quality of that of Don Esteban, because Laurela, without knowing of the deceit, believed that he was a woman.]

What exactly is the quality of the love of Don Esteban, and how does Laurela's differ from it? The difference, according to the sentence, is conditioned on Laurela's belief that Esteban is Estefanía. The quality of Esteban's love for Laurela is that of a man for a woman. Laurela, we know from the first sentence, is in love with Estefanía, not with Esteban. Her love's quality is not that of a man for a woman. It is that of a woman for a woman. Zayas's Spanish is actually more transformative than the English, because when she writes "creyó que era mujer," the masculine pronoun drops out entirely. It could as well be translated, "Laurela believed *she* was a woman." Zayas here is defining the possibility of a love that is erotic but not heterosexual, of one woman for another—what shall we call it?

A little later Estefanía says to Laurela:

Estoy tan enamorada (poco digo: tan perdida) que maldigo mi mala suerte en no haberme hecho hombre.
—Y a serlo—dijo Laurela—que hicieras?
—Amarte y servirte hasta merecerte, como lo haré mientras viviere; que el poder de amor también se extiende de mujer a mujer, como de galán a dama.

[I am so in love (that's not enough: I am so lost) that I curse my fate for not making me a man.

—And if you were—said Laurela—what would you do?
—I would love and serve you until I was worthy of you, as I will do
as long as I live; because the power of love extends from woman to
woman, as well as from gallant to lady.]

It is clear that from Esteban's perspective, all of this talk is just another way
to eventually get Laurela into bed, but Laurela receives it homoerotically.
Laurela's reception of the message shows that Zayas's text literally makes
room for a lesbian reading.

Laughter is another response to this discourse. Both Laurela and the
other girls react to Estefanía's protestations of love with giggles, that well-
known escape valve for unwelcome sexual tension. Their laughter is proof
that the serving girls, too, have gotten the message. At one point, they and
Estefanía refers to Neoplatonism and the genderlessness of the soul. But
Estefanía recurs ro Neoplatonism and the genderlessness of the soul. But
her theorizing is unsatisfying to the girls, who cannot conceive of the
embodiment of the idea of a woman loving another woman. Seeking a
more concrete resolution to their questions, "entre burlas y veras, jugando
unas con otras, procuraban ver si era mujer o hombre" [half-jokingly,
half-seriously, playing with each other, they tried to see whether [s/he]
was a woman or a man] (318).

Zayas does not specify what form these explorations take, but the scene
presented is that of the girls touching Estefanía or lifting her skirts. They
cannot fully accept that a woman could love another woman, and so keep
looking for a male body to resolve their doubt. But it is hard to imagine
that the scene presented would not be homoerotically titillating to the
female reader. Another earlier episode also puts the reader in a voyeuristic
position. After the text announces that Laurela is in love with Estefanía, we
are told that Laurela invites Estefanía to help her undress, and that Estefanía judges Laurela to be "aún más linda desnuda que vestida" [even
more beautiful naked than clothed] (309). This scene puts the female
reader in Estefanía's position, sharing her pleasure at seeing Laurela's
naked and unambiguously female body—perhaps with the more prudish
reader announcing, "Isn't that terrible," before turning to the next page.

The girls' game with Estefanía, "procurando ver si era mujer o hombre"
[trying to see if she was a woman or a man], articulates the problem of
seeing lesbians in writing. As analysts of gender, the girls are limited in

their investigative possibilities because they play with the textile of the skirt to see the marker of sexual difference, the penis. When the text says, "ver si era mujer o hombre," it alludes to the presence or absence of a penis, or what Freudian terminology calls castration. But "lesbian" is by definition not visible to the gaze that looks for castration. Lesbian is about something more than castration; looking for castration or the lack of it misses the lesbian point. In regard to this, in specifically Golden Age terms, it is important to note that the interest in what is under the skirts within her text extended to contemporary critics of Zayas's work and person. In 1643 the Catalan writer Francesc Fontanella published a satire in which he said that Zayas "Semblava a algun cavaller, / mes jas' vindra a descubrir / que una espasa mal se amaga / baix las 'sayas' feminils" [looked like a gentleman, / but it will be discovered, / that a sword is hard to hide / under feminine skirts] (Fontanella 231). Sayas, with an S, means "skirts" in Spanish; Fontanella's pun makes our author's name Mary of the Skirts. The alternation between S and Z calls to mind Barthes's study of cross-dressing, and cross-spelling, in Balzac's story *Sarrasine*. Barthes says that in that story, in which a man loves a man dressed as a woman, there is an S where a Z should be; Barthes's whole book explains how the missing Z is a sign of gender trouble. For Fontanella, in Zayas's name there is a Z where an S should be—Zayas doesn't fit in the skirts he would like her to squeeze into. His verses oppose sword and skirt as emblems of masculinity and femininity; they seek to fix María de Zayas in a heterosexual order as a way of discrediting her writing. But there is more to and under the skirts, and in lesbian desire, than meets the phallocentric eye, and it takes a certain kind of gaze to spot it.

The heterosexual order outside Laurela's rooms puts an end to the story of Estefanía. When Laurela's engagement is announced, and Estefanía insists that she is Esteban, Laurela can neither perceive nor believe it. Estefanía asks why Laurela has not understood that she is what she says and not what she seems, but it has never occurred to Laurela to split discourse and performance into separate categories; she isn't thinking in terms of men and women. In utter frustration, Estefanía asks Laurela, "¿Quién ha visto que una dama se enamore de otra?" It is an odd question to pose given that the story begins with the declaration that Laurela is enamored of Estefanía. Because we have just read the story of a woman who is in love with a person who she thinks is a woman in love with her, the answer to the question "Whoever heard of a woman falling in love with another woman?" is "We all have." A better question is, why is it so hard to admit it? Zayas's story simply enunciates, in writing, that erotic love between women, in the seventeenth century and today, is *conceivable*. The question is its own answer, because it contains the very possibility it seeks to deny.

Notes

1   In Zayas y Sotomayor. "Amar sólo por vencer" is the sixth story in this collection. There are seventeenth-century translations into English under the name of P. Scarron. H. Patsy Boyer has recently translated the first volume of Zayas's novellas, *The Enchantments of Love: Amorous and Exemplary Novels* (Berkeley: University of California Press, 1990). Translations from the *Disen-chantments* [*Desengaños*], the second collection, in this article are my own.

2   An early edition of the *Desengaños* that Alicia Yllera names *C* deletes the word *del* here, making the line run "No fue este amor de calidad del Don Esteban." The two earliest editions of the *Desengaños* have *del* (Zayas y Sotomayor 101–2).

The Legend of Jorge Cuesta:

The Perils of Alchemy and the Paranoia of Gender

~

Robert McKee Irwin

. . . the states of sexual confusion, on a scale of infinite gradations which range from scandalous hermaphroditism to those forms which are so attenuated that they might be confused with normality itself, are so numerous that there is scarcely a human being whose sex is not blurred by a concrete doubt or a shadow of doubt. —Gregorio Marañón

No fixed form will contain you,
no durable contour will imprison you
and while the light is at its most intense your shadows attain a greater depth.
Your movement assembles a fictitious statue
that is the armor with which love
covers your vulnerable weariness;
but behind its lying wall
secret orgies vanquish you
and your face is corroded from within
by your intimate disorders
—Jorge Cuesta

As a recent issue of the journal *GLQ* makes abundantly clear, it is debatable whether Freud has been more friend or foe to homosexuals in the course of the twentieth century (Fuss, *Pink Freud* 1). It is often seen that psychoanalysis, following the tradition of turn-of-the-century sexology, simultaneously pathologized homosexuals while providing a theoretical challenge to cultural stereotypes of gender and sexuality. However, besides some fascinating inquiries into turn-of-the-century Argentina, little work has been done to trace out the precise effects of the advent of sexology and psychoanalysis on sexuality in Latin America.[1] Certainly, no such work exists in Mexico, a culture whose attitudes toward homosexuality have been oddly ambivalent throughout the century.

Carlos Monsiváis describes Mexican sexuality in the early twentieth century as a "panorama de repressiones manejadas desde el confesionario, de prácticas ridículas y mitos oprobiosos" [panorama of repressions managed through the rite of confession, of ridiculous practices and opprobrious myths] ("Ortodoxia" 187), the central one being that of male heterosexual desire, never directed toward the wife, but directed toward extramarital affairs. In other words, sexual pleasure was limited to the forbidden. Thus, Eduardo Castrejón, the author of Mexico's first (anti-)gay novel, *Los 41: Novela crítico-social,* often seems confused in his attempts to portray male homosexual desire. His task, according to his editors, is to "flagela[r] de una manera terrible un vicio execrable, sobre el cual escupe la misma sociedad, como el corruptor de las generaciones" [flagellate in a terrible way an execrable vice, which society itself spits upon, as the corrupter of generations] (vi). Accordingly, his descriptions of a feminized male (homo)sexuality include the requisite terms such as "bestial degeneración" [bestial degeneration], "nefandas aberraciones" [nefarious aberrations], "triste degradación" [sad degradation], and "envilecimiento increíble" [incredible vilification], yet they are unexpectedly interspersed among phrases such as "grandiosa dicha" [grandiose bliss], "soberano placer" [supreme pleasure], "mundo de placeres sensibles y de nuevos goces" [world of sensual pleasures and new delights], and "país de la eterna felicidad" [land of eternal happiness] (9–10).

This culturally construed association of the pleasurable with the forbidden may explain Mexico's simultaneous rejection of, and fascination with, homosexuality in the early part of the century, but what was understood by the term *homosexuality* then? The events on which *Los 41* was based, a police raid on a transvestite ball and the ensuing scandal, inaugurated the first major public discussion of Mexican homosexuality since colonial times.[2] This discussion did not posit any lucid theory of homosexuality; however, it did aid in the formation of a stereotype whose presence has become so ingrained in Mexican culture that it is still the subject of study today. As Monsiváis puts it: "Desde entonces y hasta fechas recientes en la cultura popular el *gay* es el travesti, y sólo hay una especie de homosexual: el afeminado" [From that time and until quite recently in popular culture gay male equals transvestite, and there is only one kind of homosexual: the effeminate/feminized man] ("Ortodoxia" 199).

This "Latin" gender-based system of sexuality in which homosexuals must be categorized (or are impelled to categorize themselves) as "active" (male) or "passive" (female) is often contrasted with an opposing system (sometimes designated as "modern" and usually associated with U.S. gay culture) in which sexual object (male desiring male) is more important than sexual aim (male desiring to play the designated female role). Whether or not we believe that such systems dominate sexual culture in Mexico or the United States, there is no doubt that at least since Octavio Paz famously introduced homosexuality into mainstream intellectual discourse in Mexico in his discussion of *albures* (*El laberinto* 35), Mexican male homosexuality has been routinely discussed as a function of active/passive.[3]

Following the revolution, virility came to be *the* metonym of Mexicanness, leading to the advent of an often strident homophobia in Mexico: "En los años veintes y treintas la homofobia es actitud tan generalizada que no necesita singularizarse. Nadie, en rigor, es homófobo porque todos, en algún grado, detestan o desprecian o compadecen a los homosexuales" [In the twenties and thirties homophobia becomes such a universal attitude that it is not necessary to single anyone out. No one, strictly speaking, is homophobic because everyone, to some degree, detests or looks down on or pities homosexuals] ("Ortodoxia" 201). In particular, the so-called *Contemporáneos,* a cenacle of young poets, some of whom were known to be homosexuals and others who were presumed guilty by association, were vigorously attacked for decades. These attacks by rival writers and artists and politicians and literary critics appeared within newspaper debates on national culture, under the guise of literary criticism or even art, and as organized plots to expel these poets from their bureaucratic posts in the federal government. For example, a 1934 petition to the Public Health Commission, an organization established to rid the public sector of "counterrevolutionaries," signed by numerous prominent intellectuals, called for the defense of "las virtudes viriles" [virile virtues] by combating "la presencia del hermafrodita" [the presence of the hermaphrodite] ("Ortodoxia" 201). That same year, a campaign against Jorge

Cuesta's journal *Examen,* including charges of "pornography," led to the forced resignation of Cuesta and other *Contemporáneos* from their public posts (they were eventually legally exonerated) (Sheridan, *Contemporáneos* 388–90). Or, in perhaps a lighter vein, Antonio Ruiz el Corzo painted a group of "preciosas ridículas" [*précieuses ridicules*] under a huge 41—a symbol of Mexican homosexuality throughout the century—including likenesses of *Contemporáneos* Salvador Novo, Xavier Villaurrutia, and others (notably, Lupe Marín, wife of Jorge Cuesta) ("Ortodoxia" 201).

However, the ways in which this homophobia in Mexico in the first half of the twentieth century was influenced by the widening dissemination of psychoanalytic discourse remain uninvestigated. Monsiváis notes that Freudian psychoanalysis was taken up by the state as a partial replacement for Roman Catholic dogma, giving a scientific basis for traditional systems of social control. "De hecho, el machismo que conocemos es un invento cultural, un primer producto de la 'freudianización' del país" [In fact, machismo as we know it is a cultural construct, one of the first products of the "Freudianization" of the country] ("Ortodoxia" 193). In other words, Monsiváis's position is that psychoanalysis was not innocently applied in Mexico but rather cynically misread to rationalize existing thinking, at least politically speaking. I will argue that in the case of Jorge Cuesta's life and legend, such an attitude toward Freud (as much a Mexicanization of Freud as a Freudianization of Mexico) would seem to have occurred within the realm of psychoanalysis itself in Mexico, and that its influence lives on in contemporary literary criticism and biography.

Cuesta's life, it should be stated up front, has not been examined in any great detail. He had written no overtly autobiographical texts before his death, and although he does play an important role in the autobiographical novel of his (ex-)wife, Lupe Marín, *La única,* her vitriolic descriptions of him reflect more accurately on the bitterness of their divorce than on what we might imagine to be his genuine character or behavior. Thus, to a large extent, we are dealing here less with the biography of a person than with the rumors that have helped constitute a legend. Nonetheless, as will become apparent, it is the legend, the public image of Cuesta (during his lifetime and posthumously), along with that of his contemporaries, that is of interest here.

Recent attempts to investigate Cuesta's life have ranged from Louis

Panabière's meticulous literary biography, which is simultaneously aided and compromised by the cooperation obtained from Cuesta's sister, Natalia, and his son, Antonio, to the amusing attempt by Victor del Valle and Cristina Múgica to better understand Cuesta through his astrological chart, a project they undertook despite the uncertainty about his birth date, which might have been anywhere between 21 and 23 September 1903, thus not even permitting them to ascertain for certain whether he was a Virgo or a Libra (they assume he was born 21 September under the sign of Virgo).[4] We do know that he was born in September 1903 in Córdoba, Veracruz, to a wealthy family that suffered great financial losses during the revolution. Cuesta came to Mexico City to study chemistry and engineering as a teenager. Although he maintained these interests throughout his life, he also became attracted to a bohemian lifestyle of late-night cafés and literature. He befriended Xavier Villaurrutia around 1920 and eventually began to publish poems and essays, integrating himself into the group of young writers who would become known as the *Contemporáneos* in the late twenties. In 1927 Cuesta met Lupe Marín (who had just been abandoned by Diego Rivera, who had decided to return to his ex-wife, Frida Kahlo). Cuesta's family rejected Lupe Marín as "depraved," but he married her a year later. In 1930 they had a son, Antonio, and shortly thereafter went through an ugly divorce. He won custody of his son, who ended up being raised by Cuesta's mother and his sister, Natalia.

Many of the more lurid rumors regarding Cuesta were generated, it seems, by Marín, both by word of mouth and then later via her autobiographical novel, *La única*, published in 1938. Marín claimed, for example, that Cuesta was driven out of his hometown of Córdoba after trying to rape his sister. Marín also accused him, in later years, of committing incest (again with Natalia), of homosexual desire for a friend of hers, and of incestuous homosexual desire for their young son. Such rumors, of course, were eaten up by the *Contemporáneos'* enemies, who always did the most damage to the group not through intellectual debate but through scandalous accusations and name-calling. In Cuesta's case, it didn't help that he was something of an iconoclast who, unlike many of his cohorts who tried to stay out of politics, became notorious for his articulate and biting attacks on traditional institutions. His attitudes have earned him the designation of both "moralist" and "immoralist."

Cuesta would probably have preferred the latter term. His admiration for Gide is well-known, but it is Julian Benda who is thought to have influenced Cuesta most. Over the years, Cuesta's anti-institutional, anti-traditional stance was directed against the nationalist movement in Mexico that affected both government policy and artistic modes, traditional sexual morality in Mexico (he was an early advocate of sex education in public schools), the leftist ideology that was becoming dominant in Mexican politics during the twenties and thirties (a famous, irreverent essay was entitled "Marx no era inteligente, ni científico, revolucionario, ni socialista, sino contrarevolucionario y místico" [Marx was not intelligent, nor scientific, nor revolutionary, nor socialist, but counterrevolutionary and mystical]), and even the science of psychiatry, his position on which we will look at a bit later.

As a social critic, Cuesta was often not highly regarded in his day and was largely forgotten for several decades after his death, but beginning around the late seventies, his work was revived in tandem with the rise of poststructuralist theory, which Cuesta's thinking would seem to have foreshadowed. On the other hand, as a poet, Cuesta is less highly regarded. His inward-looking sonnets and love poems lack the masterful style and fluidity of his contemporaries Xavier Villaurrutia and José Gorostiza. In fact, Cuesta is perhaps most famous in the realm of poetry for having edited an anthology of Mexican poetry (along with his fellow *Contemporáneos,* but in his name) that notoriously excluded several canonized poets and proposed a rebellious new national aesthetic (which clearly had nothing to do with the rebellious new nationalist aesthetic promulgated by the government).[5] Only in recent years has his final poem, "Canto a un dios mineral" [Chant to a Mineral God], published just a month after his death in 1942, gained the admiration of critics.

Besides being a critic and poet, Cuesta was a scientist. He not only worked as a chemist and engineer throughout most of his adult life but also worked constantly on his own experiments and inventions, a practice that gained him the affectionate nickname among his friends of "el alquimista" [the alchemist] (Villaurrutia, *Obras* 847–49). Cuesta's experiments are not well documented, and as with his personal life, what we know about them is perhaps as much legend as fact, but the general thrust of his interests is clear. Like his criticism, which is dominated by a recalcitrant distrust of institutions, Cuesta's "alchemy" seems directed toward undoing inevitabilities of time and nature. Preservation is a key theme in his work: preservation of art (he sought to concoct a substance that would preserve paintings), preservation of food (it is said that he had come up with a powder that would prevent fruit, especially oranges, from rotting for a time), preservation of life (he studied the curative properties of marijuana, sought a cure for cancer in enzymes, and is rumored to have been at work on a panacea based on his fruit preservation concoction). Perhaps this theme in his work has helped spawn the rumor that he had been in search of "the elixir of life." Furthermore, he was interested in metamorphosing substances (in a truer tradition of alchemy). For example, it is said that he could change water to wine (or at least that he had produced something tasting something like wine by adding certain substances to water); it is also claimed that he was able to fabricate the scent of English lavender in his laboratory. He had, additionally, invented, they say, a serum that would allow one to drink liters of alcohol without getting drunk. Finally, according to testimony from both Cuesta and his son, Antonio, he was in the habit of experimenting on himself, on his own body, a deed that was to have ramifications for our legendary hero later on.

It is difficult to ascertain the extent to which Cuesta was a substance abuser. It is known that he liked to drink, and that he experimented with marijuana, but there is no evidence that, like his cohorts Salvador Novo and Xavier Villaurrutia, Cuesta ever used other recreational drugs such as cocaine (Novo, "Memoirs," 27–28). Moreover, although Octavio Paz implies that Cuesta hung out in downtown cafés with Antonin Artaud during his stay in Mexico City before his expedition to the land of the Tarahumara in search of peyote and greater truths (Paz, "Hieroglyphs" 98), there is nothing to indicate that Cuesta, despite suffering from migraines, ever tried any of the painkilling opiates to which Artaud was addicted, although Cuesta is rumored to have had an interest in hallucinogenic plants (Capistrán 144, n.1). What is known is that Cuesta ingested certain substances he was working on; specifically, he is known to have injected himself with the substance he was using to preserve the freshness of oranges.

Although he was a scientist, his respect for the branch of science known as psychiatry was slim. In his famous essay on the poet-killer Salvador Díaz Mirón,[6] Cuesta becomes incensed at the labeling of Díaz Mirón as a pathologically antisocial being. Instead, Cuesta argues that Díaz Mirón's acts of violence are not pathological; such acts may damage society, in which case society can be viewed as becoming ill through them (and perhaps this would justify punishment of the criminal). However, such crimes *for the criminal* might have "las consecuencias fisiológicas más saludables" [the most healthy of physiological consequences] (*Poesía y crítica* 331). In an argument that might have appeared in a book by Michel Foucault or Gilles Deleuze, Cuesta protests, "cuando un alienista define las características de un temperamento antisocial, la sociedad que toma como referencia es un ser exento de anormalidad en virtud de la misma definición" [when an alienist defines the characteristics of an antisocial temperament, the society that is taken as a reference is an entity exempt from abnormality by virtue of the same definition] (330).

Why was Cuesta concerned with psychiatric institutions? The question posed in January 1940 (when he published his essay on Díaz Mirón) would have been answered by most, even Cuesta's closest friends (except, of course, for his ex-wife), with a shrug of the shoulders. However, a few months later, this was not to be the case. In September 1940, at the urging of his friend Eduardo Villaseñor and Natalia Cuesta, Jorge made an appointment to meet with Spanish exile Dr. Gonzalo Lafora, a prominent medical doctor. Cuesta's migraines were getting worse, and he also had a seemingly chronic hemorrhoidal condition that worried him.

The incident that occurred in the office of Dr. Lafora and Cuesta's response, both documented in an undelivered letter addressed to the doctor,[7] nowadays constitute an important, though often ignored, chapter in the legend of Cuesta. In the letter (worth quoting here at length), Cuesta reports the following:

> Yo le expuse a usted que el carácter que habían tomado unas hemorroides que me afligen desde hace diez y seis años me habían dado el temor de que se tratara de una modificación *anatómica,* que tuviera caracteres de androginismo, como se acostumbra llamar a estas modificaciones, o de estado intersexual, como también se acostumbra llamarle. Ahora bien, *sin hacerme un examen anatómico,* usted calificó que *la exposición* de mi padecimiento, y no *mi padecimiento mismo,* era lo que constituía mi enfermedad, la cual era una obsesión o manía, y por consecuencia tenía un carácter nervioso o mental. Pues (juzgó usted), lo que yo pretendía era *absurdo.* (Capistrán 146, emphasis in original)

[I explained to you that changes in the character of some hemorrhoids that had been afflicting me for sixteen years had made me fear that I might have been undergoing an *anatomical* modification, with qualities of androgyny, as such modifications are usually known, or of an intersexual state, as they are also commonly known. Then, *without giving me an anatomical examination,* you determined that *the exposition* of my ailment, and not *my ailment* itself, was what constituted my illness, which was an obsession or mania, and consequently nervous or mental in nature. Thus (you judged), what I tried to say was *absurd.*]

Specifically, Cuesta was afraid that some of his experiments that involved ingesting enzymes had been exacerbating these somatic symptoms. In fact, he was in the process of drafting a study on enzymatic processes and wanted Dr. Lafora to give him an educated opinion on it. Lafora's reaction to Cuesta's ideas, however, was swift to the point of rashness. Cuesta writes:

Usted encontró dos cosas: 1°. Que era un nuevo absurdo (revelador también de la obsesión mental) que yo atribuyera a esas substancias una acción anatómica. . . . 2°. Encontró usted que el efecto que pudieron tener las substancias que ingerí debería localizarse en el sistema nervioso. . . . Así, pues, concluyo, en general, que usted desechó la observación del padecimiento que me aflige, y por cuyas manifestaciones fisiológicas no se interesó usted, después de considerar que ya era absurdo en lo anatómico, para atender a un padecimiento *mental o nervioso,* constituido probablemente por una obsesión sexual, originada en una homosexualidad reprimida, y acompañado de un hipertiroidismo que (en caso de comprobarse) para usted tiene también una importancia neurológica en este caso, y no morfogenética, como podría serlo tratándose de un padecimiento "hormonal." (148–49)

[You found two things: 1st. That it was another absurdity (pointing also to the mental obsession) that I attributed an anatomical effect to these substances. . . . 2nd. You found that the effect that the substances I ingested might have ought to be located in the nervous system. . . . Thus, I conclude, in general, that you cast aside the observation of the ailment which afflicts me, and whose physiological manifestations do not interest you, after considering that it was anatomically absurd to begin with, in order to attend to a *mental or nervous* ailment, probably constituted by a sexual obsession, originating from a repressed homosexuality, and accompanied by a hyperthyroidism that (if verified) has, for you, a neurological—and not morphogenetic, as would be the case with a "hormonal ailment"—importance as well in this case.]

Clearly, Dr. Lafora, at least according to Cuesta's letter—another element of the Cuesta legend, perhaps no more reliable than Lupe Marín's novel or Natalia's reminiscences, as there is no way of verifying whether Cuesta's interpretation of the meeting was accurate, or whether Cuesta indeed had any of the symptoms from which he claimed to suffer—had jumped to conclusions. Cuesta was judged mentally ill based on the fact that he insisted on speaking about intersexuality, and *not* on whether his statements reflected reality. His body, it seems, made no difference to the doctor.

However, that Dr. Lafora never examined Cuesta's body perhaps indicates that it was actually of major significance. It was, after all, rumored to be a homosexual body. Perhaps Dr. Lafora felt threatened by this locus of (repressed?) homosexual desire, now claiming to be, even more frighteningly, an intersexual body. If hemorrhoids did not perhaps seem the most logical indication of androgyny, the prospect of examining Cuesta's sphincter to verify this may have been too much for Dr. Lafora, compelling him to diagnose Cuesta's words alone. And it was Lafora's diagnosis of Cuesta's words that allowed him to justify not submitting Cuesta's homosexual body to an intimate examination.

This case would seem to confirm the opinion of Monsiváis that Freudian psychoanalysis, despite the frequent tentativeness and even ambivalence of Freud's writing, quickly (certainly by 1940) became, in many places, a mystified, totalizing, normative system, an ideology in a sense, which, through such tropes as the Oedipal myth and penis envy, was mobilized to calcify norms of gender and sexuality. Here, Cuesta's references to intersexuality were immediately deemed absurd and the result of "a sexual obsession originating from repressed homosexuality." Even a physical challenge to gender could be contained through psychoanalytic authority.

At this point, it is worthwhile to take another look at Freud's notion of paranoia. It is ironic that Freud's famous study of paranoia has undoubtedly constructed its own legend of a man whom Freud never met during his illness, but whose case he interpreted only by reading his autobiography: Daniel Paul Schreber.

There were certain tropes of paranoia (Freud, we often forget, was not the first to write on the subject and in fact did not present such a radically new position on the subject as he is given credit for) that Freud recognized in Schreber. Most pointedly, his delusions of persecution and sexual metamorphosis had been discussed decades earlier by Richard von Krafft-Ebing under the heading "metamorphosis sexualis paranoia" in his catalogue of the many types of "antipathic sexuality." In Krafft-Ebing's discussion of homosexual neuroses, "[t]he determining factor . . . is the demonstration of perverse feeling for the same sex; not the proof of sexual acts with the same sex" (247). Thus, Freud's diagnosis of Schreber's paranoia as being the result of repressed homosexual desire was not exactly revolutionary. However, what Freud ignores in his analysis of a patient whom he had never met is the physical, an aspect that *was* considered by Krafft-Ebing, who recognized what he called "organic taint," or physical anomalies distorting gender and contributing to "cerebral neuroses" of the "antipathic" variety (294). Still, assuming that Schreber's transsexuality/hermaphroditism was delusionary, perhaps the only clear difference between Freud and Krafft-Ebing on the Schreber case was that the homosexuality inferred by both was seen as "moral decay" and "perversion" by the Krafft-Ebing and was viewed more sympathetically as a universal, if not unproblematic, part of everyday life by Freud (Freud, "Three Essays" 242, 253, 258)—a rather ironic difference at that, given that only Krafft-Ebing considered morphological aspects of sexuality.

The Cuesta case bears many eerie similarities to that of Schreber, similarities of which Dr. Lafora was perhaps aware. Cuesta feared he was becoming a woman. Lafora, unlike Freud, did not infer homosexuality in his patient because Lafora already knew that Cuesta was one of the publicly vilified *Contemporáneos*. Ironically, of the eight or so poets most central to the publication of the literary and cultural journal that gave the group its name, only two, Salvador Novo and Xavier Villaurrutia, were widely known to be homosexuals. However, even today, in casual conversation, Mexican literary scholars, when asked about the sexuality of the *Contemporáneos,* are likely to respond, "Oh, they were all queer," but when pressed are forced to admit, "Well, we only really know about Novo and Villaurrutia."

It is not surprising, then, that Lafora assumed Cuesta to be homosexual. And although, at least in Cuesta's letter, the term *paranoia* was not used, the similarities to the Schreber case are quite strong. Considering that Freudian psychoanalysis was already becoming popular in Mexico,[8] it is quite possible that Lafora had Freud in mind during his consultation with Cuesta. Also not mentioned in the letter was Schreber's other major symptom, delusions of persecution. However, this case clearly recalls not Freudian persecutory paranoia so much as Guy Hocquenghem's recasting of persecutory paranoia not as a fear of one's own homosexuality but as "a paranoia that seeks to persecute" homosexuality (56). Cuesta's case would seem to reflect not only a paranoia about homosexuality but a paranoia with respect to gender. Certainly some discourse on sexuality did deal with biological intersexuality, including Krafft-Ebing; Spaniard Gregorio Marañón's *La evolución de la sexualidad y los estados intersexuales* [Evolution of sexuality and intersexual states] experienced fairly wide diffusion in both Spain and Latin America in the 1930s. On the other hand, Latin American cultures in general and postrevolution Mexico in particular are famous for making rigid gender difference part of national ideology. In a country where even writing was supposed to be "virile," how could a male body be permitted to turn female?[9]

It is particularly interesting to note that although Paz and others have assumed passive homosexuality to be somehow equated with male effeminacy, this well-defined male homosexuality—which, defined by gender identification in sex roles, posed minimal threat to hegemonic ideology of gender—was apparently acceptable as something that may not have been sanctioned and perhaps needed to be eradicated but did exist in Mexico. It may have been a mental illness, a biological tragedy, a joke to be played out in popular culture and the arts, a secret vice, or a nasty foreign influence brought to Mexico by lovers of Wilde and Gide, but the existence of autochthonous homosexuality was not denied in Mexico as vehemently as it was in some other Latin American countries during this era. On the other hand, challenges to biological principles of gender difference were inadmissible: for Dr. Lafora, for (as we shall see) Cuesta's literary biographers, and even for Cuesta himself. Nancy Chodorow asserts: "On several statistical variables, there may be more difference within each sex than between the sexes. Moreover, the extent of between-sex variation varies among societies, and variation among cultures is often greater than that between the sexes of any particular culture" (15). The element of ideology in views of gender and gender difference are more than we may realize, as the legend of Cuesta demonstrates.

We return, then, to Cuesta's legend. Lupe Marín was the first to predict his downfall in retrospect; she claims he told her that owing to his migraines, he expected to go insane by age thirty-five. Natalia Cuesta recalled decades later that he had been dropped and had cracked his head against a marble table as an infant. She also remembered that later in his life, he became troubled with hallucinations of snakes.[10] Biographer Nigel Grant Sylvester invites a certain Dr. Guevara Oropeza to give his own diagnosis (much like Freud's diagnosis of Schreber, based on Schreber's book, Guevara Oropeza must base his diagnosis on Cuesta's letter): "Cuesta era un paranoico esquizofrénico que padecía de complejo de persecución y de extensa ansiedad. Jorge tenía un concepto irreal de auto-evaluación que le producía dudas e inseguridades con sentimiento de inferioridad compensados con delirio de grandeza" [Cuesta was a paranoid schizophrenic who suffered from a persecution complex and extensive anxiety. Jorge had an unreal concept of self-evaluation that produced in him doubts and insecurities with a sentiment of inferiority compensated by a delirium of grandeur] (Panabière 84).

Other recent scholars prefer to cite Foucault to trace an etiology of Cuesta's fall into "insanity." Louis Panabière denies the possibility of repressed homosexuality being a cause of Cuesta's ills: "[n]o se ve por qué habría reprimido esas presuntas tendencias homosexuales (ni siquiera se preocupa de negarlas en su carta), pues no tenía a ese respecto ningún prejuicio; además algunos de sus amigos, piénsese tan sólo en Villaurrutia, tampoco tenían problemas para dar pleno curso a sus tendencias" [it cannot be seen why Cuesta would have repressed these presumed homosexual tendencies (he doesn't even bother denying them in his letter), since he had no prejudices in this regard; moreover none of his friends, think only of Villaurrutia, had any problems either in giving full rein to their tendencies] (82). For Panabière, Cuesta's lifelong questioning of conventional reason and traditional institutions defined him as "anormal por exceso de razón, uno de esos seres que la sociedad acostumbra llamar locos" [abnormal for [his] excess of reason, one of those beings whom society is used to calling crazy] (76).

References to Foucault would undoubtedly have been appreciated by Cuesta himself. His letter to Lafora opens with a rather chilling description of a doctor-patient relationship to which Cuesta refers not as a consultation but as an "interrogatorio" [interrogation]. He points out in the first paragraph "el cohibimiento natural que aflige al paciente ante el examen del médico (sobre todo cuando se trata de un médico tan consciente de su propia autoridad como usted, y como debe de serlo todo médico eminente, y de un paciente tan poco consciente de su propia enfermedad como yo)" [the natural inhibition that afflicts a patient upon being examined by a doctor (especially when it concerns a doctor as conscious of his own authority as you are, and as should be the case with every eminent doctor, and a patient as little conscious of his own illness as I am)] (145). Thus, when Cuesta goes to the doctor to complain of a physical "affliction," Dr. Lafora finds only a mental one. Later in the letter, Cuesta uses the same word to describe the diagnosis: he is "afflicted" with inhibition.[11]

Alejandro Katz, one of the most recent scholars who has undertaken the legend of Cuesta, arrives at conclusions similar to those of Panabière, again citing Foucault, but with a non-Foucauldian twist that leads one to believe that we are not much better off with respect to homophobia and sexual repression than we were in Freud's or Cuesta's day. Katz imagines a sort of tacit conspiracy to lynch Cuesta. As a voice of dissidence, an iconoclast who questioned everything, and often vociferously, his "*secuestro psiquiátrico*" [psychiatric sequestering] was inevitable. "[E]l loco, el alienado, es el que no se posee. Así se resuelve el problema. . . . Cuesta no es ya Cuesta, está desposeído de sí mismo" [The crazy person, the madman is the one who does not possess himself. In this way the problem is resolved. . . . Cuesta is no longer Cuesta, he is dispossessed of himself] (104). It is a case of sinister depropriation. The question is by whom: Dr. Lafora? The government? Society at large? The Katzian Cuesta, then, is a sort of tragic postmodern subject.

But if Katz had read Foucault's *Mental Illness and Psychology* or *Madness and Civilization*, he clearly had not read *The History of Sexuality*. Katz goes on to say that "[d]e hecho, Cuesta nunca fue acusado de homosexualidad, salvo por extensión de acusaciones hechas a otros miembros del grupo [*Contemporáneos*]" [in fact, Cuesta was never accused of homosexuality, except by extension of accusations made concerning other members of the group] (105). Katz sees Cuesta as wanting to become a woman. His incest (which Katz takes as a fact) indicates a desire to become his sister. Furthermore, his ingestion of enzymes (which Cuesta suspected of having somatic effects), to Katz, points to a desire for transsexual metamorphosis. He goes on to clarify, speaking to an imaginary Platonic interlocutor, "No me importa la homosexualidad. Es usted quien me lleva siempre al tema de lo patológico. . . . A Cuesta no le interesaba ser mujer: eso es la homosexualidad, no una metamorfosis. Metamorfosearse en mujer, en cambio, es mantenerse en tensión entre dos estados contrarios y, en consecuencia, es no ser ninguna de las dos cosas" [I don't care about homosexuality. It's you who keeps bringing me into the realm of the pathological. . . . Cuesta was not interested in being a woman: that is homosexuality, not a metamorphosis. To turn into a woman, on the other hand, is to maintain a tension between two contrary states and, in consequence, is to not be either of the two things] (107).

So, what are we left with? We are left with the same confusion with regard to transsexual desire and homosexuality that existed for Freud. We are left with homosexuality, even for a scholar who cites Foucault dozens of times, as pathology. Moreover, we are left with an androgyny that remains in the realm of the imaginary and not the real, a real that appears to have been forgotten by Freud as well. Cuesta's body, it must be remembered, according to the letter, did not begin transforming owing to his recent experimentation with enzymes. It had presumably been in a state of androgynous flux since his adolescence. In other words, we are left with analyses of Cuesta that, even when they do not designate him a madman, refuse to even acknowledge the possibility of a non-self-induced, non-imaginary state of intersexuality.

At a recent lesbian, gay, and bisexual conference in Los Angeles, a panelist spoke of her own troubling experience.[12] She was born with both male and female genitalia. In her early childhood, her parents, horrified at the monster they had borne, permitted her doctor (as is the common practice in such cases in North America—she was Canadian) to sever her male genitalia, leaving her with a single gender, but without the ability to experience sexual pleasure, and with deep psychological wounds. Whether

Jorge Cuesta was indeed a hermaphrodite to any degree, or merely delu-
sional, we shall never know. However, what is clear is that Dr. Lafora did
not want to know. Nor have any of Cuesta's critics to date, some of whom
fume at "gossipy" studies such as that of Panabière for even mentioning
the incident with Lafora (León Caicedo 9–11). Like the parents and doctor
of the emasculated panelist, for such critics the notion that gender might
not be fixed would be unthinkable, and certainly not something worthy of
critical inquiry. An ironic aside is appropriate here: in Jacques Lacan's
studies of the psychoses, one of his key observations is that for paranoiacs,
certainty is more important than reality (*Psychoses*, 75), and it is not
repression (Freud's repressed homosexuality) that characterizes psychoses
such as paranoia, but foreclosure (81, 321). In this case, the foreclosure of
the possibility of gender nonconformity for Lafora and for later inter-
preters of the Cuesta legend points to a paranoia lurking largely unnoticed
in the realm of psychoanalysis and, frequently, in academic discourse on
gender.

The legend of Cuesta concludes in a tragedy not dissimilar to that of the
panelist. Two years after Lafora's diagnosis, Cuesta, confined in a house of
friends, emasculated himself. Soon after that, he was to be institutionalized. According to the legend, he made the paramedics (or whoever
came to take him away) wait outside while he finished the last stanzas of
his final poem, "Canto a un dios mineral." Then there is a disputed story
in which in the hospital, Cuesta tried to poke out his eyes. The final scene
depends on whether or not you believe this Oedipal inspiration: either
using the arms of the straitjacket in which he was confined to prevent him
from poking out his eyes, or using his bedsheets, on 13 August 1942, Jorge
Cuesta hanged himself.[13] If, as Deleuze and Guattarí state, "Judge Schreber's destiny was not merely that of being sodomized, while still alive, by
the rays from heaven, but also that of being posthumously oedipalized by
Freud" (57), what can we say was Cuesta's destiny? That he was Oedipalized, castrated, and hanged by Freud would seem to be the answer, and
all for the preservation of an overdetermined gender binary.

Appendix: *Carta al Doctor Lafora [Letter to Doctor Lafora]*

México, 19 de septiembre de 1940

Sr. Gonzalo R. Lafora
Paseo de la Reforma 27
México, D.F.

Muy señor mío:

Como he encontrado, seguro por el cohibimiento natural que aflige al paciente ante el examen del médico (sobre todo cuando se trata de un médico tan consciente de su propia autoridad como usted, y como debe de serlo todo médico eminente, y de un paciente tan poco consciente de su propia enfermedad como yo), que el reconocimiento que tuvo usted la bondad de hacerme se deslizó por un camino que fue una sorpresa para mí, y que fue trazando usted mismo con su interrogatorio, y por el cual, como debe hacerlo el paciente respetuoso de su médico, me dejé llevar con la mejor voluntad, me parece pertinente, y espero que para el más claro dibujo de los síntomas así lo encuentre usted, precisar por escrito lo que pudo quedar confuso en una plática en la que me sentí con muy poca libertad.

Me expresó usted que seguramente padecía yo de una inclinación homosexual reprimida, y que esta inclinación y su represión consiguiente eran causa de una manía u obsesión mental, que usted pretendió poner de manifiesto con sus preguntas, *desde el principo del reconocimiento.* Yo reconozco el derecho de un médico, si se trata de un médico eminente como usted, con una larga experiencia, de diagnosticar *a priori,* por una pura intuición. Así pues, he considerado con seriedad este diagnóstico hipotético con que guió usted el interrogatorio que se sirvió hacerme, y sin objetar yo, también *a priori,* una opinión que ni usted ni yo todavía tenemos la buena o la mala suerte de comprobar, me parece que, por lo nuevo y sorprendente que resultó la enfermedad que usted puso a la luz, quedaron completamente en la sombra los hechos relacionados con la enfermedad de que yo estaba consciente.

Yo le expuse a usted que el carácter que habían tomado unas hemorroides que me afligen desde hace diez y seis años me habían dado el temor de que se tratara de una modificatión *anatómica,* que tuviera caracteres de androginismo, como se acostumbra llamar a estas modificaciones, o de estado intersexual, como también se acostumbra llamarle. Ahora bien, *sin hacerme un examen anatómico,* usted calificó que *la exposición* de mi padecimiento, y no *mi padecimiento mismo,* era lo que constituía mi enfermedad, la cual era una obsesión o manía, y por consecuencia tenía un carácter nervioso o mental. Pues (juzgó usted), lo que yo pretendía era *absurdo.*

Quiero admitir que el solo hecho de pensar y expresar un absurdo pueda ya ser la manifestación de una obsesión mental, a los ojos de un médico tan experto como usted. Pero encuentro, doctor, que este *absurdo* no deriva de una imaginación *mía*. No soy yo quien imagina que hay estados intersexuales, que se manifiestan *anatómicamente*. Ni soy yo quien expresa que la forma de esta manifestación anatómica puede ser, en unos casos, una desviación o degeneración de la próstata. Me parece impertinente que un enfermo le cite a un médico los autores, aunque no si se trata de un libro que tiene un carácter de vulgarización científica, como es el de Remy Collin, *Las hormonas,* y que un enfermo sin concocimientos médicos encuentra placer en consultar, sobre todo si tiene el propósito, no de curarse él a sí mismo, sino de tomar una conciencia más clara de sus propios síntomas, cosa que le permite expresarlos con más claridad al médico en cuyas manos se pone. Pues bien, este libro, entre otros, justifica el *absurdo* en que usted ve el síntoma de una obsesión. De modo que me parece conveniente poner en claro que, si la opinión es realmente absurda, ni soy yo el autor exclusivo de ella, y ni siquiera la apoyo. Sólo me permití exponerla ante usted como una orientación, a fin de que usted la juzgara de un modo objetivo, bien aceptándola, para hacerme un reconocimiento anatómico y de este modo verificarla, o bien rechazándola, como se rechaza una opinión infundada *de otro médico*.

También recuerdo que encontró usted otro *absurdo* (revelador del mismo padecimiento *mental* que usted sospechó) en la opinión que le expresé de que *las funciones enzimáticas* son químicamente *funciones sexuales,* o viceversa. Tal parece que observó usted una obsesión sexual en el hecho de que *viera* yo una sexualidad en las funciones enzimáticas. Me parece conveniente hacer notar que no hay en realidad autor de química biológica, de diez años a esta fecha, que no sostenga que las *funciones hormonales son funciones enzimáticas,* y que no sostenga, además que *la unidad enzimática* de un organimso vivo (sin exeptuar el hombre) radica en *la funcíon reproductiva,* como se pone de manifiesto en el embrión. Ahora bien, yo, personalmente, he efectuado investigaciones químicas sobre los procesos enzimáticos y en un terreno puramente químico he observado que se comprueban las observaciones y las teorías biológicas que reconocen en la sexualidad o en la reproducción el centro funcional de las unidades enzimáticas vivas, esto es de los organismos vegetales y animales. Puse en manos de usted, una relación sobre este particular, con todo desinterés, y es una relación que cualquier químico biólogo puede sujetar a una verificación objetiva, tanto experimental como teoréticamente. Y le ofrecí a usted, cosa que cumpliré en su oportunidad, suministrarle copia de la relación complementaria que me propongo redactar en los próximos días. En la parte que le entregué a usted, se explica (de un modo superficial, per. con una fiel referencia a los hechos experimentales de laboratorio) lo que puede llamarse el aspecto *digestivo,* de las funciones enzimáticas. Lo que estoy por redactar es lo que tiene que ver con el aspecto sexual o reproductivo. Verá usted, pues que también concibo las funciones enzimáticas como procesos digestivos, y que en la relación en que expongo el resultado de mis experiencias, en primer lugar me ocupo en *la digestión,* y dejo para uno posterior la reproducción.

Me parece conveniente precisar todo esto, a fin de que usted tenga a la vista de un modo claro, y los aprecie en su verdadero carácter, los hechos que en una conversación pudieran quedar obscuros y expuestos a no ser apreciados debidamente.

También le manifesté a usted que en los últimos meses estuve ingiriendo substancias enzimáticas que yo mismo preparaba por el procedimiento de síntesis que descubrí, con el objeto de experimentar en mí mismo su acción *desintoxicante.* Se lo manifesté a usted con el objeto de que usted pudiera considerar el efecto anatómico o morfológico que hubiera podido tener en mí la ingestión de esas substancias. Usted encontró dos cosas. 1°. Que era un nuevo absurdo (revelador también de la obsesión mental) que yo atribuyera a esas substancias una acción anatómica. Debo también precisar que yo en lo personal nunca he hecho observaciones ni teorías sobre las acciones morfológicas de las substancias enzimáticas y químicas en general, observaciones y teorías que ya son una disciplina científica a la que se llama morfogenética. Ahora bien, los que han observado las más sorprendentes acciones morfogenéticas en las substancias enzimáticas, son los especialistas en esa rama, algunos de los cuales yo sólo he tenido la curiosidad de leer. Pero debo notar que no he encontrado infundada en ninguna parte la convicción de que, por una acción química, se pueden producir o se hayan producido modificaciones anatómicas del tipo más *absurdo,* por *absurdo* que parezca que pudieran producirse; 2°. Encontró usted que el efecto que pudieron tener las substancias que ingerí debería localizarse en el sistema nervioso. Esto puede ser como usted lo sospecha; pero no creo que pueda comprobarse sino por la observación biológica, en otros organismos experimentales, de la acción de las substancias que yo ingerí, y que hasta ahora no son conocidas por nadie sino por mí mismo que las preparé.

Así, pues, concluyo, en general, que usted desechó la observación del padecimiento que me aflige, y por cuyas manifestaciones fisiológicas no se interesó usted, después de considerar que ya era absurdo en lo anatómico, para atender a un padecimiento *mental o nervioso,* constituido probablemente por una obsesión sexual, originada en una homosexualidad reprimida, y acompañado de un hipertiroidismo que (en caso de comprobarse) para usted tiene también una importancia neurológica en este caso, y no morfogenética, como podría serlo tratándose de un padecimiento "hormonal."

Ahora bien, doctor, todo esto puede ser, aunque no le veo más fundamento que la convicción de usted. Pues me parece que lo que aquí me preocupo en puntualizar debe tener la consecuencia de que, entre las representaciones que yo

mismo tengo de mi propio padecimiento, las que son susceptibles de una verificación objetiva, deben librarse, tanto, de la sospecha de que sean una pura forma
mental, patológicamente *tendenciosa.* Y de las en esta carta mencionadas encuentro que *todas* se pueden verificar objetivamente, a saber: primero, la forma
anatómica del padecimiento; segundo, su naturaleza de efecto enzimático u hormonal; tercero, la influencia que tuvieron en su evolución las substancias enzimáticas que estuve ingiriendo. Y lo que a mí personalmente me interesa es que
un médico con la competencia que usted tiene examine objetivamente mi padecimiento antes de valorizarlo, si le merece interés, o si no le quita un tiempo que le es
de más utilidad empleado en otras cosas.

Y el fin de esta carta no es otro, señor doctor, que preguntar a usted si quiere
interesarse, no en mi preocupación, sino en lo que constituye su objeto, o sea la
evolución anatómica y fisiológica que se ha verificado en mi organismo probablemente desde hace diez y seis años, y que también probablemente fue acelerada por
la ingestión de substancias enzimáticas, cuya naturaleza me he interesado en
mostrar a usted.

La impaciencia, la excitación que usted ha podido notar en mí no tienen otro
origen que el de ver desatendido, por considerarlo *a priori* falto de realidad más
físicamente viva. Y esta impaciencia no me deja espacio para interesarme en el
tratamiento *de otras* enfermedades, físicas o mentales, que pudiera yo padecer.

Y para que esta misma impaciencia no pueda dejar oculto el interés amistoso
que también en el fondo me mueve, me ha parecido oportuno hacerla llegar a
manos de usted por conducto de don Eduardo Villaseñor, nuestro común amigo,
y a quien no dudo en confiar lo íntimo y confidencial que, por su propia naturaleza, contiene el estado orgánico que me afecta y que he querido que merezca la
atención de usted.

Quedo un afectísimo y seguro servidor.

Jorge Cuesta

[Dear sir:

As I have found, surely due to the natural inhibition that afflicts a patient upon
being examined by a doctor (especially when it concerns a doctor as conscious of
his own authority as you are, and as should be the case with every eminent doctor,
and a patient as little conscious of his own illness as I am), that the meeting that
you had the kindness to grant me slid onto a path that was a surprise for me, and
that you yourself were drawing out with your interrogation, and along which, as
should be the case with a respectful patient towards his doctor, I let myself be led

in good faith, it seems pertinent to me, and I hope, through the clearest description of my symptoms which you find herein, to explain in writing what might have remained confusing in a conversation in which I felt quite restrained.

You expressed to me that I most assuredly was suffering from a repressed homosexual inclination, and that this inclination and its consequent repression were the cause of a mania or mental obsession, which you attempted to reveal through your questions, *from the beginning of the meeting*. I recognize the right of a doctor, if it concerns a doctor as eminent as yourself, with substantial experience, to diagnose *a priori*, by pure intuition. Therefore, I have taken quite seriously both this hypothetical diagnosis with which you led the interrogation that you took it upon yourself to subject me to, as well as, without any objections on my part, an opinion, also *a priori*, which neither you nor I yet have had the good or bad luck to prove; it seems to me that, as new and surprising as the illness that you brought up turned out to be, the facts related to the illness of which I was aware have remained totally hidden.

I explained to you that changes in the character of some hemorrhoids that had been afflicting me for sixteen years had made me fear that I might have been undergoing an *anatomical* modification, with qualities of androgyny, as such modifications are usually known, or of an intersexual state, as they are also commonly known. Then, *without giving me an anatomical examination,* you determined that *the exposition* of my ailment, and not *my ailment itself,* was what constituted my illness, which was an obsession or mania, and consequently nervous or mental in nature. Thus (you judged), what I tried to say was *absurd.*

I want to admit that the sole fact of thinking and expressing an absurdity might very well be the manifestation of a mental obsession, in the eyes of as expert a doctor as yourself. But I find, doctor, that this *absurdity* does not derive from *my* imagination. I am not the one who imagines that there are intersexual states, which manifest themselves *anatomically.* Nor am I the one who explains that the form of such an anatomical manifestation can be, in some cases, a deviation or degeneration of the prostate. It seems impertinent to me for a patient to cite authors to a doctor, although not if it is a case of a book which has a quality of scientific vulgarization, as is that of Remy Collin's *Las hormonas* [Hormones], and for a patient without medical knowledge to derive pleasure from consulting, above all if his purpose is not to cure himself, but to become more clearly aware of his own symptoms, so as to permit him to express them with greater clarity to the doctor into whose hands he puts himself. In any case, this book, among others, justifies *the absurdity* in which you see the symptom of an obsession. So, it seems proper to me to make clear that, if the opinion really is absurd, neither am I the exclusive author of it, nor do I even support it. I only allowed myself to explain it to you as an orientation, so that you might judge it in an objective fashion, either accepting it, and giving me an anatomical examination to verify it, or rejecting it, as one rejects an unfounded opinion *of another doctor.*

I also recall that you found another *absurdity* (revealing of the same *mental* ailment that you suspected) in the opinion that I expressed to you in which *enzymatic functions* are chemically *sexual functions,* or vice versa. It seems that you observed a sexual obsession in the fact that I *saw* a sexual aspect to enzymatic functions. It seems useful to me to point out that there is not in reality any author in the field of biochemistry, within the past ten years, who does not believe that *hormonal functions are enzymatic functions,* and who does not believe, further-more, that *the enzymatic unity* of any live organism (without excepting man) is found in *the reproductive function,* as is revealed in the embryo. Now, I, personally, have carried out chemical research on the enzymatic processes and in purely chemical terrain I have noted that the biological observations and theories which recognize that the functional center of live enzymatic unities, i.e. of plant and animal life, lies in sexuality or reproduction can indeed be proven. I handed over to you a report on this topic, with total lack of self-interest, and it is a report that any biochemist can subject to an objective verification, both experimentally and theoretically. And I offered, and I will follow through at an appropriate time, to submit to you a copy of a complementary report which I propose to draft within a few days. The part which I gave you explains (albeit superficially, but with a faithful reference to the experimental laboratory results) what might be called the *digestive* aspect of enzymatic functions. What remains to be written is the part that has to do with the sexual or reproductive aspect. You will see, then, that I also conceive of enzymatic functions as digestive processes, and that in my report, I reveal the result of my experiments: I firstly concern myself with *digestion,* and leave reproduction for later.

It seems proper to specify all of this so that you might get a clear picture of it all, and appreciate, in their true character, the facts that in conversation might be left obscure and liable not to be duly appreciated.

Moreover I explained to you that in recent months I was ingesting enzymatic substances that I prepared myself for the procedure of synthesis that I had dis-covered, with the aim of experiencing their *detoxifying* effect myself. I told you this in order that you might consider the anatomical or morphological effect that the ingestion of these substances might have had. You found two things: 1st. That it was another absurdity (pointing also to the mental obsession) that I attributed an anatomic effect to these substances. I should also specify that I personally have never made any observations nor theories about the morphological effects of enzymatic and chemical substances in general, observations and theories that are already a scientific discipline known as morphogenetics. In any case, those that have observed the most shocking morphogenetic effects in enzymatic substances are the specialists in the field, only some of whom have I had the curiosity to read. But I should note that I have not in any way found unreasonable the conviction that, through a chemical effect, anatomical modifications of the most *absurd* type, *absurd* though it might appear that they could be produced, can be and have been produced. 2nd. You found that the effect the substances that I ingested might have ought to be located in the nervous system. This might be as you suspect; but I do not believe that it can be proven except by biological observation, in other experimental organisms, of the effects of the substances which I ingested, and which as of now are not known by anyone besides the one who prepared them: me.

Thus, I conclude, in general, that you cast aside the observation of the ailment which afflicts me, and whose physiological manifestations do not interest you, after considering that it was anatomically absurd to begin with, in order to attend to a *mental or nervous* ailment, probably constituted by a sexual obsession, originating from a repressed homosexuality, and accompanied by a hyperthyroidism that (if verified) has, for you, a neurological—and not morphogenetic, as would be the case with a "hormonal" ailment—importance as well in this case.

While all this might be true, doctor, I do not see in it any further foundation beyond your conviction. It seems to me that what I am concerned with detailing ought to have the consequence that among the representations that I myself have of my own ailment, those that are susceptible to an objective verification ought to be freed from the suspicion that they are purely *mental,* pathologically *tendentious,* in form. And regarding those mentioned in this letter, I find *all* of them to be objectively verifiable. To find out: first, the anatomical form of the ailment; second, the nature, enzymatic or hormonal, of its effect; third, the influence that the enzymatic substances that I was ingesting had on its development. And what interests me personally is that a doctor with your competence might objectively examine my ailment before appraising it, if it merits interest, or if it does not waste time that is more usefully spent in another way.

And the aim of this letter is none other, my esteemed doctor, than to ask you if you are willing to take an interest not in my preoccupation, but in that which constitutes its object, i.e. the anatomical and physiological development that has been taking place in my organism since probably sixteen years ago, and which has also most likely been accelerated by the ingestion of enzymatic substances whose nature I have taken care to show you.

The impatience and agitation which you might have noted in me have no origin other than in seeing myself neglected, by your having considered my ailment an *a priori* lack of *physically* live reality. And this impatience leaves me no space to interest myself in the treatment *of other* illnesses, physical or mental, which I might suffer.

And in order that this impatience not leave hidden the friendly interest that also moves me deeply within, it has seemed opportune to get this letter into your hands via Don Eduardo Villaseñor, our mutual friend, and to whom I do not hesitate to entrust with the intimate and confidential information that, by its own nature, is contained in the organic state which affects me and which I have wished might secure your attention.

I remain your devoted and faithful servant,
Jorge Cuesta]

Notes

An earlier and briefer version of this essay appeared as "El más triste de los alquimistas mexicanos: Jorge Cuesta y la tragedia del género" in Rosaura Hernández Monroy and Manuel F. Medina, coords., *La seducción de la escritura* (Mexico, 1997). All translations, unless otherwise noted, are my own. The second epigraph, an untitled poem by Jorge Cuesta, was written around 1938 but published for the first time in *Zaguán* 6 (winter 1978): 3; it was reprinted in *Poesía y crítica* 44. The source for the appendix is from Capistrán 145–50.

1 See Salessi; Molloy, "The Politics of Posing."

2 For a fairly thorough summary of early colonial discourse on Mesoamerican homosexuality, see Guilhem Olivier; for some insights into the persecution of homosexuals in New Spain during the Inquisition, including public burnings, see Salvador Novo, *Las locas, el sexo, los burdeles,* especially pages 14–15.

3 For example, see Maldonado Vázquez, Carrier, Murray, Gutmann.

4 This study appears in Cuesta, *Sonetos* 95–103.

5 See Guillermo Sheridan's introductory presentation to Cuesta, *Antología de la poesía mexicana moderna* 7–35.

6 Díaz Mirón (1853–1918) is remembered as one of the most important poets of his day, and also as a prominent politician; however, his biography is marred by scandals of violence and even killings. As a teenager in Veracruz, he spoke fluent English and French and yet was sent abroad by his parents, not for a better education but because he had become the leader of a *pandilla juvenil* (street gang). His left arm disabled in an "incident of violence" at age twenty-five, he became convinced that "un arma al menos es indispensable para la protección del honor de un individuo" [at least one weapon is necessary for an individual to protect his honor] (José Luis Martínez 254). Soon after this, he ignited his first national scandal by, in a fit of rage, challenging the governor of Veracruz to a duel. However, Díaz Mirón is not credited with his first

killing for another four years. His second followed nine years later. In both cases, he was jailed, then acquitted after claiming to have acted in self-defense. This pattern of violence continued throughout his life: at age seventy-four, he got in trouble in his job as high school teacher for hitting a student in the head with his revolver. But, according to José Luis Martínez, "[a]quellas reglas frenéticas que dominaron y arruinaron su vida fueron también las que impuso a su obra" [that frenetic order that dominated and ruined his life was also what inspired his work] (253–57).

7   The letter was published for the first time in *Vuelta* in 1977 and was recently republished by Miguel Capistrán in *Los Contemporáneos por sí mismos*. It appears here in its entirety as an appendix to this article.

8   Monsiváis writes of the decades prior to the 1950s that "es la moda colonizada la que transforma angustias y neurosis de la clase media norteamericana en utopía prestigiosa de un sector considerable del país" [it is colonized fashion that transforms North American middle-class angst and neurosis into a prestigious utopia for a sizable sector of the country] ("Ortodoxia" 191).

9   See Díaz Arciniega, Balderston.

10   Panabière (79) cites an interview by Elena Poniatowska with Marín, and another conducted by himself with Natalia Cuesta, both in the 1970s.

11   It should be noted that Lafora was not a psychoanalyst but a medical doctor, "una de las figuras científicas más destacadas que integraron la emigración republicana de fines de los treinta" [one of the most outstanding figures of the Spanish republican immigration of the late 1930s] (Capistrán 144).

12   Holmes, "Queer Cut Bodies."

13   For different versions of this story, see Panabière 83 and Capistrán 145.

II

~

NATIONALISM

AND

DESIRE

Poetry, Revolution, Homophobia:

Polemics from the Mexican Revolution

‿

Daniel Balderston

Los individuos de moralidad dudosa que están detentando puestos oficiales . . . con sus actos afeminados, además de constituir un ejemplo punible, crean una atmósfera de corrupción que llega hasta el extremo de impedir el arraigo de las virtudes viriles en la juventud. . . . Si se combate la presencia del fanático, del reaccionario en las oficinas públicas, también debe combatirse la presencia del hermafrodita, incapaz de identificarse con los trabajadores de la reforma social. (Quoted in Monsiváis, "Salvador Novo" 277)

[Individuals of doubtful morals who are holding official posts . . . with their effeminate acts, besides constituting an example worthy of being condemned, create an atmosphere of corruption that reaches the extreme of preventing the maturing of virile qualities in our youth. . . . If the presence of fanatics and reactionaries is combated in public offices, so also should be the presence of the hermaphrodite, who is incapable of identifying with the workers in the social reforms.]

These fighting words, written by one group of Mexican intellectuals against another in 1934, define the ways in which the cultural nationalism of the Mexican Revolution was marked as masculinist and heterosexist.[1] I will be looking here at the conflicts between a revolutionary nationalism of this kind and expressions of homosexual desire in intellectual and artistic circles in Mexico City from the 1920s onward. For although the link between "nationalisms" and "sexualities" is of widespread interest to scholars of cultural studies and is even the title of a recent collection of essays, there has been little attention to the furious polemics that erupted in Mexico in the years after the revolution, polemics centered largely, but only tacitly, on the presence of homosexual artists and poets in the *Contemporáneos* group. After reviewing these polemics, I will look at some examples of homoerotic poetry by two of the *Contemporáneos,* Xavier Villaurrutia and Salvador Novo, whose jobs in the civil service were at stake in the cultural wars, interesting examples of the literature of gay resistance.[2]

The first of the polemics erupted in 1924. An article entitled "La influencia de la Revolución en nuestra literatura," signed with the pseudonym of José Corral Rigán (and probably written by Febronio Ortega, Carlos Noriega Hope, and Arqueles Vela), described some avant-garde writers, Tablada, Novo, Taniya, and Villaurrutia, as the "producto literario subconsciente del movimiento literario" [the subconscious literary product of the literary movement] (Schneider, *Ruptura* 161); the word *subconsciente* apparently means "to be derogatory," thanks to its association with psychoanalysis (and hence with sexuality). This article was followed a month later by a more explicit attack: Julio Jiménez Rueda, in an essay entitled "El afeminamiento en la literatura mexicana" [Effeminacy in Mexican literature] states that earlier literary schools, including symbolism and naturalism, possessed

> chispazos de genio, pasiones turbulentas, aciertos indudables y frecuentes y ponían en la obra un no sé qué, comprensión de la naturaleza circundante, amor, elegancia, pensamiento original, que la distinguía del modelo que imitaba. . . . Pero hoy . . . hasta el tipo del hombre que piensa ha degenerado. Ya no somos gallardos, altivos, toscos . . . es que ahora suele encontrarse el éxito, más que en los puntos de la pluma, en las complicadas artes del tocador. (Schneider, *Ruptura* 162)

> [sparks of talent, turbulent passions, undeniable and frequent successes and put a certain "je ne sais quoi" into the work, understanding of surrounding nature, love, elegance, original feeling, that distinguishes it from the model being imitated. . . . But today . . . even the sort of man who thinks has degenerated. We are no longer striking, proud, rough . . . instead, now it is more frequent to find success not in the points made by the pen, but in the complicated arts of the boudoir.]

The blanket character on this attack, which seems to include anyone and everyone, led to responses such as Francisco Monterde's article "Existe una literatura mexicana viril" [A virile Mexican literature exists] (Schneider, *Ruptura* 163–67), in which he celebrates the work of Mariano Azuela and of certain "poetas de calidad—no afeminados" [poets of quality—not effeminate] (165). A series of other articles on the topic appeared in late 1924 and early 1925, most notably a survey on modern Mexican writing in *El Universal Ilustrado* that appeared at the same time that the newspaper was publishing *Los de abajo* in serial form.

The same concern with avoiding effeminacy marks the second manifesto of the *Estridentistas,* dated 1 January 1923 and signed by Manuel Maples Arce, Germán List Arzubide, and some two hundred others. The last paragraph of the manifesto reads in part: "Ser estridentista es ser hombre. Sólo los eunucos no estarán con nosotros" [To be a stridentist is to be a man. Only eunuchs are not with us] (Schneider, *Estridentismo* 50). The "eunuchs" in question would be those Mexican poets who did not sign; because Ramón López Velarde was already dead, these would include some from the previous generation (Amado Nervo, Enrique González Martínez, and José Juan Tablada, most notably) and such emerging poets as Villaurrutia, Novo, Pellicer, and Torres Bodet.

The *Estridentistas* had such power in the state of Veracruz that its capital, Xalapa, was known as "Estridentópolis." Governor Jara of Veracruz was a loyal supporter of Germán List Arzubide, who said that the governor

comprendió que en nuestra protesta lírica y nuestra actitud combativa contra lo apolillado y lo falaz, había una actitud de violenta repulsa a todo lo inútil, lo ruin, lo parasitario o mendaz, en conjunto, la imagen de un mundo que había engendrado la miseria, el dolor, la angustia, la desilusión y el desencanto que iban infiltrándose en la savia viril de nuestra juventud y nuestro pueblo. (Schneider, *Estridentismo* 24)

[understood that in our poetic protest and our combative attitude against what is moth-eaten and false, there was an attitude of violent rejection against everything useless, bad, parasitic or mendacious, in sum, the image of a world that had been engendered by the misery, suffering, anguish, disillusion and disenchantment that was infiltrating into the virile sap of our youth and our people.]

Thus, a close alliance between a revolutionary governor and the incendiary literary movement was built out of a common opposition to a bogeyman constructed of the *ancien régime* and the homosexual vampire interested in stealing the "virile sap" of the revolutionary allies.

The *Estridentistas,* like the Italian futurists, sought an aggressive masculinist aesthetic based on warfare, technology, the subjugation of women, and the bashing of effeminate males. The gay bashing was part of an aesthetic program and appears over and over again in the writings of the movement. List Arzubide, in his 1927 history of the movement, *El movimiento estridentista,* wrote:

> El Estridentismo anclaba el triunfo: ellas se derretían sin cautela en sus frases . . . los verseros consuetudinarios habían sido descubiertos en la Alameda, en juntas con probabilidades femeninas y habían sido obligados por la Inspección General de Policía a declarar su sexo y comprobarlo, acusado de un chantage [*sic*] de virilidades en caída. (Schneider, *Estridentismo* 281)

> [Stridentism was anchored in triumph: they melted carelessly in their phrases . . . the confirmed versifiers had been discovered on the Alameda, in the company of presumed feminine persons, and had been forced by the Police Chief to declare what sex they were and to prove it, accused with blackmail on their fallen manhood.]

Note that by now the "enemy" of the *Estridentistas,* who in their turn are "amurallado[s] de masculinidad" [fortified in masculinity], had narrowed. The focus of List Arzubide's wrath is the *Contemporáneos* group, many of whom were gay. Two men in particular would be the targets of repeated attack for the next several decades: Salvador Novo and Xavier Villaurrutia. And there was guilt by association in this witch-hunt: the Cuban critic Jorge Mañach would accuse the painter Agustín Lazo of having published some short stories that were "escritos llenos de molicie" [writings full of softness] (Sheridan, *Contemporáneos* 243) and would assert that this "softness" was an ideological softness.[3] Revolutionary nationalism, here as elsewhere, had to be constructed by expelling all traces of sexual dissonance.

The irony of the *Estridentista* position, of course, was that it depended on a return to the very bourgeois values the group claimed to have broken with. As Guillermo Sheridan has noted: "La militancia vanguardista de Maples Arce no tardó en ser sustituida por la militancia anti-homosexual; enfurecido con los Contemporáneos recurre a la moral de los mismos burgueses que denostaba en sus poemarios juveniles" [The avant-garde militancy of Maples Arce was not long in turning into an anti-homosexual militancy; infuriated by the Contemporáneos he turns to the morality of the very bourgeoisie that he had attacked in the poetry of his youth] (Contemporáneos 132) Maples Arce's attacks on the poetry of the Contemporáneos accuse the poets of being "semiinclinados por los mismos complejos y tendencias" [semi-inclined by the same complexes and tendencies] (133). Novo's poetry, for instance, "resalta por una intención de trivialidad que no disimula los deseos bajo ningún eufemismo sexual, como en sus otros compañeros de tribu" [is notable for its trivial intentions that do not conceal his desire with any sort of sexual euphemism, as in the other members of his tribe] (133), and Villaurrutia's writing "se ofrece por las fatalidades del sexo bajo un arreglo de palabras que apenas encubre los artificios de una falsa elaboración . . . que se sirve de la inversión como método poético" [is offered by the fatalities of sex in an arrangement of words that barely covers the artifices of a false process of elaboration . . . making use of inversion as a poetic method] (133).

The attack on the Contemporáneos had by 1925 united a series of rather disparate threads: a suspicion that they were not sufficiently nationalist at a time when the Obregón, and then the Calles, governments were under attack;[4] a suspicion that their writing was not sufficiently "virile" in a context still marked by the memory of armed struggle (soon to break out again in the Cristero revolt); a suspicion that their aesthetic was not that of the emerging revolutionary party (Sheridan, Contemporáneos 181). Of particular interest vis-à-vis this last is the relation of the Contemporáneos group to the muralist movement. In the early twenties, Novo wrote an article in defense of Diego Rivera, but by the later twenties, when Villaurrutia had begun to write the articles that would make him Mexico's most eminent art critic, relations with Rivera and company had soured. Villaurrutia's friendship with Agustín Lazo began in 1925, and Lazo's art was decidedly apolitical (Debroise 127–38). Rivera would soon accuse Lazo and his friends of a lack of virility in similar terms to those used earlier by Maples Arce and List Arzubide. As Sheridan has noted, the "nationalists" accused the *Contemporáneos* of having stayed outside of the "proyecto nacional de cultura" [national project of culture]:

> Por si fuera poco, se les comenzará a identificar a partir de la polémica con una militancia vergonzosa: los "afeminados." Curiosa conclusión: mientras el nacionalismo y la voluntad social poseen un sexo definido y orgullosamente erecto, los "otros" titubean en una indefinición ideológica que, por metonimia, lo es también sexual. (259)

> [As if this were not enough, they were soon identified in the polemic with a shameful militancy: the "effeminate." Strange conclusion: while nationalism and social power possessed a sexual organ that was well-defined and proudly erect, the "others" vacillated in an ideological lack of definition that was always, by metonymy, sexual in nature.]

The document I quoted part of at the beginning of this essay, a petition from a group of intellectuals (José Rubén Romero, Mauricio Magdaleno, Rafael Muñoz, Francisco L. Urquizo, Ermilo Abreu Gómez, Humberto Tejera, Jesús Silva Herzog, Héctor Pérez Martínez, and Julio Jiménez Rueda), dated 31 October 1934, was addressed to the *Comité de Salud Pública* asking for a purge of government workers, obviously with Novo and Villaurrutia in mind. At about the same period, Rivera caricatured the two in his murals at the *Secretaría de Educación Pública* (Monsiváis, "Salvador Novo" 277). Similarly, the group of realist painters called "30-30" called for the firing of government functionaries for the following reason:

> Y estamos contra el homosexualismo, imitado a la burguesía francesa actual; y entre ellos, favorecidos ahora, y nosotros, luchadores incansables, existe el abismo de nuestra honradez que no se vende por un puesto. El gobierno no debe sostener en sus secretarías a los de dudosa condición psicológica. (Monsiváis, "Salvador Novo" 213)

> [And we are against homosexuality, an imitation of the present bourgeoisie of France; and among those who are favorites at present and ourselves, indefatigable fighters, there exists the abyss of our honesty, not sold for a job. The government should not employ in its ministries persons of dubious psychological condition.]

The full story of the 1925 polemics is told in Víctor Díaz Arciniega's *Querella por la cultura "revolucionaria,"* which constantly mentions the homophobic and sexual content of the polemics yet oddly never focuses directly on the issues of sexuality itself or considers how the invocation of homophobia relates to the question of the creation of a national, "revolutionary" culture.[5]

And yet Villaurrutia was no doubt one of the inventors of a new national project that—for better or for worse—was to go in a straight—and I suppose I should underline *straight*—line from Samuel Ramos to Octavio Paz. The meditation on death in *El laberinto de la soledad* circles endlessly around Villaurrutia's *Nocturnos,* with their insistent meditation on death in life. And Novo would go on to become the chronicler of decades of Mexican life, near the end even achieving the status of television celebrity, as José Joaquín Blanco has recalled:

Ciertamente, Novo fingió ante el público toda su vida: escribió cosas sobre la patria, las buenas costumbres, la moral familiar, etc., y cobró caro por sus servicios, no sólo en dinero: sus patrones y la sociedad tuvieron que aceptarlo con su facha "maldita" de homosexual evidente, depilado, maquillado, con anillos y pelucas, diciendo en sus crónicas periodísticas cosas a las que nunca otros que carecieran de su vocación de amargura y suicidio emocional se habrían atrevido. Cuando, en el régimen de Díaz Ordaz, Novo doctoraba en televisión sobre virtud patriótica se entablaba entre él y el público una clara confrontación de mentiras *asumiendo la farsa:* el sexagenario maquillado, acicalado, amanerado y con joyas aparentaba educar (¡el Maestro de la Juventud en travesti!) a una sociedad mojigata que, a su vez, fingía—comedia de histriones—dejarse educar por él. (168–69)

[Novo, to be sure, feigned for the public all of his life: he wrote things about the fatherland, good manners, family values, and so forth, and charged a high price for his services, and not only in monetary form: his patrons and society had to accept him in his "damned" aspect of a flaming homosexual, his eyebrows plucked, wearing makeup, rings and wigs, saying things in his journalistic chronicles that others who lacked his vocation for bitterness and emotional suicide would never have dared to say. During the regime of Díaz Ordaz, when Novo pontificated on television about patriotic virtues, a clear affinity for lies lay between him and his public *making evident the farce:* the sexagenarian, made up, dressed in style, affected and covered with jewels, pretending to educate (the Teacher of the Young in drag!) a hypocritical society that, in turn, pretended—as if in some clown act—to let itself be educated by him.]

That tragicomic finale is another side of the same story of institutionalized revolution: the new revolutionary government of the 1920s sought to protect the "virile sap" of radical youth from contamination by effeminate *extranjerizantes,* and the tottering regime of Díaz Ordaz used the homosexual vampire or bogeyman—and the bullets and helicopters and nightsticks at Tlatelolco—to discipline the wayward youth of 1968.

Despite the attacks—or perhaps because of them—Villaurrutia and Novo published a number of homoerotic texts, not perhaps as bold as the poems that Antônio Botto was publishing in Portugal or Luis Cernuda in Spain, but as bold as anyone was at that point in Latin America. Unlike that of Botto or Cernuda, this is not a homosexual poetry that specifies the gender of the beloved; instead, the gender of the beloved is carefully *not* specified, and the love is associated with danger, silence, and self-censorship. Although these may sound mostly like negative qualities fifty or sixty years later, this is nonetheless a poetry that expresses homosexual passion and is still powerfully sensual. And there is none of the self-hatred that marks Federico García Lorca's most explicit gay poem, the ode to Walt Whitman in *Poeta en Nueva York.*

The most gay-affirmative of the works of Villaurrutia and Novo (apart from Novo's posthumous sonnets) are published within a few years of the *Estridentista* attacks: Novo's *Nuevo amor* and *Seamen Rhymes* in 1933, Villaurrutia's "Nocturno de los ángeles" in 1936. Gay themes are also present in both poets' prose writings, as in Novo's memoir of a trip to the United States, "Return Ticket" (1928), or the 1928 essay by Villaurrutia on the art of his friend Agustín Lazo, which includes such phrases as: "Agustín Lazo es un pintor de niños comestibles, maduros como duraznos maduros. Pintor de niños de más de veinte años, de niños de edad madura" [Agustín Lazo is a painter of delectable boys, mature as ripe peaches. A painter of boys more than twenty years old, of mature boys] (*Obras* 1044). In the same article, which Merlin H. Forster terms Villaurrutia's most interesting and most unorthodox work of criticism (*Contemporáneos* 90), the poet says that Lazo was to Rivera as Cocteau was to Mayakovsky (*Obras* 1044), a phrase that knowingly refers to a sexuality as well as to an aesthetic program.

An early example of this poetry is Novo's "Amor," a poem later imitated by Villaurrutia in his "Amar conduisse noi ad una morte." Novo writes:

> Amar es este tímido silencio
> cerca de ti, sin que lo sepas,
> y recordar tu voz cuando te marchas
> y sentir el calor de tu saludo.
>
> Amar es aguardarte
> como si fueras parte del ocaso,
> ni antes ni después, para que estemos solos
> entre los juegos y los cuentos
> sobre la tierra seca.
>
> Amar es percibir, cuando te ausentas,
> tu perfume en el aire que respiro,
> y contemplar la estrella en que te alejas
> cuando cierro la puerta de la noche.
> (*Poesía* 75)

[To love is this timid silence / near you, without your knowing it, / and remembering your voice when you leave / and feeling the warmth of your greeting. // To love is waiting for you / as if you were part of the sunset, / neither before nor after, so that we be alone / amidst the games and stories / on the dry earth. // To love is to perceive, when you are absent, / your smell in the very air I breathe, / and to contemplate the star in which you depart / when I close the door of the night.]

Villaurrutia, sometimes the less bold of the two in expressing same-sex love, when he rewrites this poem comes no closer to specifying the gender of the lovers but bends gender roles nonetheless:

> Amar es absorber tu joven savia
> y juntar nuestras bocas en un cauce

hasta que de la brisa de tu aliento
se impregnen para siempre mis entrañas.
(*Obras* 77)

[To love is to absorb your young sap / and to join our mouths in a
river-bed / until my innards are impregnated forever / by the wind of
your breath.]

The references to sap, innards, and impregnation clearly connote anal
intercourse when written (as here) by a male poet. The poem is explicit in
its references, though without specifying the gender of the partners.

Yet most of Villaurrutia and Novo's critics will go to any lengths to deny
the homoerotic elements of these poems. For instance, in his discussion of
"Nocturno amor," Moretta invents a beloved woman nowhere mentioned
in the poem (94). Villaurrutia is careful here and in almost all of his other
love poetry not to disclose the gender of the beloved—a difficult feat in
Spanish—by referring instead to parts of the body (some with the masculine grammatical gender, some with the feminine), to emotions and
actions, in short, to what the beloved does, feels, expresses, but never to
the beloved him- or herself. The poem, however, explicitly raises the question of gender, even as it refuses to specify the gender of the object:

Ya sé cuál es el sexo de tu boca
y lo que guarda la avaricia de tu axila
y maldigo el rumor que inunda el laberinto de tu oreja
sobre la almohada de espuma
sobre la dura página de nieve
(50)

[I know what the sex of your mouth is / and what the greed of your
armpit conceals / and I curse the noise that floods the labyrinth of
your ear / on the pillow of foam / on the hard page of snow]

The most explicitly homoerotic of Villaurrutia's poems, "Nocturno de
los ángeles" [Nocturne of the angels/Los Angeles nocturne] refers to highly
sexed male angels, hanging around the downtown Los Angeles cruising
grounds made famous later in John Rechy's *City of Night*. The manuscript

of the poem, which Villaurrutia gave to Carlos Pellicer, has been published in a facsimile edition, with marginal illustrations by the poet showing sailors embracing, kissing, and stroking one another's thighs. The poem is divided into two sections; the first describes the nocturnal fauna of Los Angeles, the second the visit of the angels to that place. The second stanza reads:

Si cada uno dijera en un momento dado,
en sólo una palabra, lo que piensa,
las cinco letras del DESEO formarían una enorme cicatriz luminosa,
una constelación más antigua, más viva aún que las otras.
Y esa constelación sería como un ardiente sexo
en el profundo cuerpo de la noche,
o mejor, como los Gemelos que por vez primera en la vida
se miraran de frente, a los ojos, y se abrazaran ya para
siempre.
(*Obras* 55)

[If every one were to say at a given moment, / in a single word, what he is thinking, / the six letters of the word DESIRE would form a huge neon scar, / a constellation older, more alive than any of the others. / And that constellation would be like a burning sexual organ / in the deep body of the night, / or better still, like the Twins who for the first time in their lives / look at one another face to face, eye to eye, and embrace once and forever.]

In both halves of the poem, three lines appear:

Caminan, se detienen, prosiguen.
Cambian miradas, atreven sonrisas.
Forman imprevistas parejas.
(55–56, 57)

[They walk, stop, continue. / They exchange looks, dare to smile. / They form unexpected couples.]

In the first half of the poem, this unproblematically refers to the men cruising in the square. In the second half, after the angels have come down to earth on invisible ladders, it also refers to cruising, though the angels (who assume names such as Dick and John and Marvin and Louis) are curiously passive, letting others touch their bodies feverishly, letting themselves be kissed, the objects of the human trinity of "la carne, la sangre y el deseo" [flesh, blood and desire] (56). The poem ends:

> Sonríen maliciosamente al subir en los ascensores de los hoteles
> donde aún se practica el vuelo lento y vertical.
> En sus cuerpos desnudos hay huellas celestiales;
> signos, estrellas y letras azules.
> Se dejan caer en la [sic] camas, se hunden en las almohadas
> que los hacen pensar todavía un momento en las nubes.
> Pero cierran los ojos para entregarse mejor a los goces de su
>   encarnación misteriosa,
> y, cuando duermen, sueñan no con los ángeles sino con los mortales.
> (57)

[They smile mischievously when they go up the hotel elevators / where slow vertical flight is still practiced. / On their naked bodies there are celestial tracks; / signs, stars and blue letters. / They let themselves fall into bed, sinking into the pillows / that make them think for a moment of clouds. / But they close their eyes to give themselves up more fully to the pleasures of their mysterious incarnation, / and when they sleep they dream not of angels but of mortals.]

The angels are said to come "del mar, que es el espejo del cielo" [from the sea, that is the mirror of the sky] (56), and the celestial marks on their bodies are of course tattoos: Villaurrutia is writing of the persistent gay fantasy about sailors on shore leave. The gentle inversion of the common instruction to Hispanic children, "sueña con los angelitos" [dream of the little angels], reveals that the angels think more about their mortal companions than Rechy's hustlers would readily admit of themselves.

But there are many other Villaurrutia poems that have fairly obvious gay content, many of them published in his late book *Canto a la primavera* (1948). The first poem of "Décimas de nuestro amor," reads, for instance:

A mí mismo me prohibo
revelar nuestro secreto,
decir tu nombre completo
o escribirlo cuando escribo.
Prisionero de ti, vivo
buscándote en la sombría
caverna de mi agonía.
Y cuando a solas te invoco,
en la oscura piedra toco
tu impasible compañía.
(*Obras* 79)

[I forbid myself / to reveal our secret, / to utter your full name / or to write it when I write. / Your prisoner, I live / looking for you in the dark / cave of my agony. / And when alone I invoke you, / I touch in the dark stone / your impassive company.]

The subject of the poem is the need for care in guarding a dangerous secret, a secret that seems to be the homosexual nature of the relationship. The same theme is expressed in several other poems in the collection, including "Nuestro amor," "Inventar la verdad," and "Amor condusse noi ad una morte." Yet in his reading of these poems, Eugene Moretta invents a wholly imaginary biography to justify this love: the poet, he says, is speaking to a woman whose prisoner he is, a woman both present and absent (182). A few pages later, Moretta, still speaking of the "Décimas," writes that they are occasioned by "la mujer cuya ausencia, *según el poeta,* intensifica el dolor de su soledad en razón directa a la distancia que la separa de él, a pesar de que la presencia de ella también lo 'hiere' " (194, emphasis added) [the woman whose absence, *according to the poet,* intensifies the pain of solitude in exact proportion to the distance between them, despite the fact that when she is present she "wounds" him].[6] It should be noted, however, that Merlin H. Forster, when talking about these same poems, is careful to refer to a "beloved person" whose gender is not specified (*Fire and Ice* 122, 128, and passim).[7]

Novo, meanwhile, published his best homoerotic poems in the collection *Nuevo amor* (1933). One of the finest poems in the book is the fourth:

Junto a tu cuerpo totalmente entregado al mío
junto a tus hombros tersos de que nacen las rutas de tu abrazo,
de que nacen tu voz y tus miradas, claras y remotas,
sentí de pronto el infinito vacío de tu ausencia.
Si todos estos años que me falta
como una planta trepadora que se coge del viento
he sentido que llega o que regresa en cada contacto
y ávidamente rasgo todos los días un mensaje que nada contiene sino
    una fecha
y su nombre se agranda y vibra cada vez más profundamente
porque su voz no era más que para mi oído,
porque cegó mis ojos cuando apartó los suyos
y mi alma es como un gran templo deshabitado.
Pero este cuerpo tuyo es un dios extraño
forjado en mis recuerdos, reflejo de mí mismo,
suave de mi tersura, grande por mis deseos,
máscara
estatua que he erigido a su memoria.
(86)

[Beside your body totally surrendered to mine / beside your taut
shoulders from which are born the routes of your embrace, / from
which your voice is born and your clear, remote glances, / I suddenly
felt the infinite emptiness of his absence. / If all of these years he has
been lacking to me, / like a climbing vine that hangs onto the wind, / I
have felt that he arrives or returns in each contact / and I avidly tear
every day at a message that contains nothing but a date / and his name
grows larger and vibrates ever more deeply / because his voice spoke
only to my ear, / because he blinded my eyes when he turned his own
aside / and my soul is like a great uninhabited temple. / But this body
of yours is a strange god / forged in my memories, a reflection of
myself, / smooth in my tautness, great from my desires, / a mask / a
statue I have erected in his memory.]

This poem depends on a strange displacement from the lover's body in the
bed next to him to a former lover's body: from "tu cuerpo" to "su ausen-

cia." Although neither the present nor the past lover's gender is specified, the same adjectives are used to describe the speaker's body and desires (taut, large, deep) as the lovers' bodies. In the last line, Novo uses a word that Villaurrutia uses famously in a number of his best-known nocturnes, *estatua,* which is revealed in this context to be a reference to the eroticized memory of a male lover's body.

Another poem published in the same year, "Romance de Angelillo y Adela" (1933), is a playful narrative ballad of Novo's encounter in Buenos Aires with Federico García Lorca. "Angelillo," an Andalusian bullfighter, meets "Adela," a dark Mexican beauty, in a silvery city (the city, that is, on the River Plate, Buenos Aires):

Porque la Virgen lo quiso,
Adela y Angel se encuentran
en una ciudad de plata
para sus almas desiertas.
Porque la Virgen dispuso
que se juntaran sus penas
para que de nuevo el mundo
entre sus bocas naciera,
palabra de malagueño
—canción de mujer morena—,
torso grácil, muslos blancos
—boca de sangre sedienta.
(*Poesía* 105–6)

[Because the Virgin so desired, / Adela and Angel met / in a silvery city / for their deserted souls. / Because the Virgin so decreed / that they should unite their sorrows / so that once again the world / would be born between their mouths, / the word of the man from Málaga, / the song of the dark woman, / graceful torso, white thighs / a mouth of thirsty blood.]

As José Joaquín Blanco notes (170), Novo provided the clues to the deciphering of this poem in his travel memoir of Buenos Aires in *Continente vacío* (in *Toda la prosa* 301–8). In this narrative of Novo's meeting with

Lorca, Novo is at first apprehensive about meeting the celebrated poet and playwright: "Ante tamaña popularidad yo vacilo en mi deseo de conocerlo. Lo admiro mucho, pero no querría ser simplemente un admirador suyo más, y quizá no habrá medio de ser su amigo" [In face of such celebrity I waver in my desire to meet him. I admire him greatly, but would not want to be simply one more of his admirers, and perhaps there would be no way of becoming his friend] (301). But a few pages later the reader is treated to a sight of Lorca in bed, wearing white-and-black striped pajamas and surrounded by his admirers (305). After referring to Lorca's ode to Walt Whitman, which Novo finds "virile, brave, beautiful" (307), Lorca treats Novo to a rendition of the Mexican revolutionary song "Adelita" (308), the name recalling, of course, the alias Novo assumes in his campy ballad.[8]

Novo's most explicit gay texts are posthumous, however: his eighteen pornographic sonnets and his memoirs of his—and Villaurrutia's—scandalous youth.[9] The sonnets have been published in a limited edition of five hundred copies; two fragments from the memoirs appeared in the late 1970s in the ephemeral magazine *Política sexual,* published by the first major gay liberation group in Mexico, the Frente Homosexual de Acción Revolucionaria, and in English in Leyland's *Now the Volcano,* an anthology of gay Latin American literature. It is now up to readers and critics to recover these texts, memoirs that can tell us much about gay life in Mexico City in the first decades of revolutionary Mexico.[10]

One of the posthumous sonnets reads:

Si yo tuviera tiempo, escribiría
mis Memorias en libros minuciosos;
retratos de políticos famosos,
gente encumbrada, sabia y de valía.

¡Un Proust que vive en México! Y haría
por sus hojas pasar los deliciosos
y prohibidos idilios silenciosos
de un chofer, de un ladrón, de un policía.

Pero no puede ser, porque juiciosa—
mente pasa la doble vida mía
en su sitio poniendo cada cosa.

Que los sabios disponen de mi día,
y me aguarda en la noche clamorosa
la renovada sed de un policía.
(*XVIII sonetos* no. 2)

[If I had time, I would write / my Memoirs in detailed books; / portraits of famous politicians, / important people, wise and worthy. // A Proust who lives in Mexico! And I would let / pass through my pages the delicious / and forbidden silent idylls / of a driver, a thief, a policeman. // But it cannot be, because / my double life wisely goes on / putting each thing in its place. / Because the wise take my time during my day, / and in the clamorous night / the renewed thirst of a policeman awaits me.]

These forbidden sonnets, not published until 1986, are scarcely more explicit than "Nocturno de los ángeles," published in 1936. The few published fragments of Novo's memoirs are campy accounts of sexual adventures, apparently still considered too racy for Mexican readers. The continuing suppression of discussion of gay themes in the writing of these two poets and their contemporaries would seem to be due to an "anxiety of (queer) influence," because these writers are the unacknowledged gay fathers of Octavio Paz and of modern Mexican poetry.[11]

Notes

1   Schneider asserts that the Contemporáneos were "nationalists without the demagoguery or exaggerated rhetoric of their antagonists. They loved their country critically and without flag-waving" ("Introducción" 5).

2   A fine paper that in many ways parallels what I will have to say here, "Outsiders at the Center: The Contemporáneos and the Construction of Culture in Post-Revolutionary Mexico," was presented by Tamra Suslow-Ortiz at the MLA meetings in Chicago in December 1995.

3   Similarly, in 1923 Julio Torri complained to Alfonso Reyes that Pedro Henríquez Ureña had surrounded himself with a group of "muchachos petulantes y ambiguos como Salomón de la Selva" [petulant and ambiguous young men like Salomón de la Selva] (Díaz Arciniega 36), showing the presence of this

homophobic rhetoric even in contexts that have nothing to do with revolutionary nationalism.

4 Díaz Arciniega notes repeatedly that the ferocity of the attack increased when Calles came to power in 1925, and after Vasconcelos had left the Ministry of Education (30–38, 123).

5 An example of Díaz Arciniega's limited focus: "Lo más sorprendente es que con los dos conceptos ['afeminado' y 'viril'] y tal relación, algunos polemistas pretenden formar las 'categorías' estéticas y el 'esquema' analítico suficientes para ponderar y encauzar a la literatura mexicana" [The most surprising thing is that with the two concepts ("effeminate" and "virile"), some polemicists try to form esthetic "categories" and the analytic "scheme" sufficient to consider and channel Mexican literature itself] (56). He never really considers why these terms in particular are invoked, though he mentions them on 53–62, 66, 86–92, 142, and elsewhere. I am grateful to Robert Irwin for pointing out the Díaz Arciniega book and for his remarks on an earlier version of this essay.

6 Suslow-Ortiz refers in terms similar to mine to "the tortured misreadings made by earlier critics, who refused to see (and perhaps refused to discuss) the possibility of a homoerotic interpretation of the poems" (9).

7 Earlier, Ramón Xirau had spoken of "the poet himself as an absence in the face of the beloved" (30), using the masculine form *amado,* which in this context could be gender-specific as a male lover or non–gender specific.

8 In *Los Contemporáneos en el laberinto de la crítica,* a collection of essays on the group that is otherwise devoid of extended commentary on the sexuality that marked and united most of its members, the out gay Spanish poet Luis Antonio de Villena comments on a late book of Novo's, *Sátira* (1970), noting that Novo assumed a final position of defiance: "Dandi al fin, hombre altivo, deseoso de epatar, se autoproclama viejo bujarrón, se ríe, se acaricia, se exhibe y gime a la par que goza" [A dandy to the last, a proud man, desiring to shock, he proclaims himself an old queer, laughs, strokes and exhibits himself, crying out as he comes] (212). For a recent biography of Novo, see Alderson.

9 One example of Novo's *desenfado,* or outrageousness, in his later writing that was published in his lifetime, just two years before his death, is the opening sentence of his book of journalistic chronicles, *Las locas, el sexo, los burdeles en México* [Queens, sex, bordellos in Mexico]: "Hubo siempre locas en México" [There were always queens in Mexico]. This declaration exceeds the import of the first chronicle in the book, "Las locas y la Inquisición" [Queens and the Inquisition], which reports on several Inquisition cases against "sod-

omites," and the placing of this first sentence at the beginning of the book is extraordinarily emphatic, as if to say, "There always were, there are, and there always will be . . ."

10 Monsiváis told me (in September 1992) that a fuller edition of the memoirs is to be published in Mexico City.

11 For all their noise about procreative sexuality, the *Estridentistas* have no progeny among contemporary Mexican poets.

Nationalism, Male Anxiety, and the Lesbian Body

in Puerto Rican Narrative

Agnes I. Lugo-Ortiz

In one of the first systematic efforts to institutionalize what in Puerto Rican literary historiography came to be known as the generation of 1940, René Marqués outlined the paradigmatic shifts that, in his view, accounted for the newly achieved "maturity" of the writers of his era. The prologue to his foundational anthology, *Cuentos puertorriqueños de hoy* (1959), organizes these changes along three main axes: the renovation of literary techniques through the appropriation of contemporary European and Anglo-American models (Faulkner, Joyce, Williams, Woolf, etc.); the development of new thematics linked to urban transformations occurring in the country by the mid–twentieth century, and interpreted within existentialist and psychoanalytic frameworks; and the reassessment of the relationships between literary endeavors and the process of national definition, an association already intensified in the country through the works of the generation of 1930.[1]

The anthology—which includes sixteen stories by eight young male writers—rather than being an account of the multiple literary practices taking place in Puerto Rico during the mid–twentieth century, may be read as Marqués's literary manifesto, a programmatic statement on the aesthetic and political path he envisioned for modernizing Puerto Rican national literature. As Arcadio Díaz Quiñones has seen it, if Marqués undertook a "conservative" and "nostalgic" position with regard to the process of socioeconomic modernization accelerating in the country by midcentury, this ideological position was articulated through a paradoxically modernizing literary practice. Literary modernity, according to Díaz Quiñones, was deployed by Marqués as a critical weapon against social modernity: "Entabló esa guerra [against modern sociocultural transformations] con las mismas armas de su enemigo, con las armas de la 'modernidad' técnica y estética" [He waged that war . . . with the same weapons as his enemies, with the weapons of technical and aesthetic "modernity"].[2] This will to literary modernization required the "opening" of Puerto Rican writing to the international literary marketplace as well as the importation of modern techniques of representation; the appropriation of the "present" as a primordial source for "literariness"; the organicity between the literary imagination and the forging of a national identity; and, not openly stated but nevertheless clearly prescribed, the need to consolidate a homosocial literary community, a virile community to direct and control the cultural future of the nation.[3]

If in the prologue to the anthology Marqués's literary project is made explicit, the selection and organization of the stories in the collection can be read as another level, less evident and more slippery, of those doctrinal formulations. Occupying a privileged—even foundational—position in that collection are two stories by Abelardo Díaz Alfaro, an author whom Marqués does not claim as a member of the new generation (that of 1940), but who nevertheless is assigned the role of its main precursor as a "transitional" figure. In particular, the placement of Alfaro's "El Josco" (1948) as the first in the book—at the threshold of the collection, in a liminal space, so to speak—retrospectively invites us to read the story as a sort of nucleus encoding some of the generative problematics of modern Puerto Rican literature, as Marqués conceived of it. The problematics encoded in "El Josco" (and which would be repeated and intensified in other stories of the collection, as will be seen shortly) can be divided along two interconnected lines: the first pertaining to a doctrinal proposition in which gender categories—framed as a polarization masculine/feminine—are entangled with issues of national definition, becoming the privileged language for the articulation of national identity; and the second concerning a system of literary figuration in which the "masculine body" was posed as a locus of metaphoric transpositions, metamorphoses, mutilations, and exchanges (not always, but more often than not) vis-à-vis the female body. This figurative system maps a site in which the "masculine body" is subject to incessant displacements and transformation and is, not incidentally, the receiver of the writer's libidinal energies—the subject of his anxieties and desires. Although on the thematic surfaces of the texts what becomes visible is the choreography of an apparently heterosexualized national identity, in the "cracks" of their signifying practice what can be identified is an intense homoerotic exercise. These figurations, inscribed in texts such as Emilio Díaz Valcárcel's "El sapo en el espejo" [The toad in the mirror] and Marqués's "En la popa hay un cuerpo reclinado" [There is a body lying in the stern]—both included in the anthology—constitute one of the most powerful and memorable lines of representation in the literature of the period.[4]

It is within this system of "masculine" representation that we may read the first ephemeral emergence of a lesbian character in Puerto Rican narrative: the "mannish lesbian" figured in Emilio Díaz Valcárcel's "El asedio" [The siege].[5] This "lesbian body" is another expression of the cultural anxieties ciphered around the figurations of the "masculine body." Moreover, these masculine figurations can be understood as the narrative conditions of possibility of that lesbian body.

It is significant that Marqués did not include "El asedio" in his *Cuentos puertorriqueños de hoy*, despite having judged that it "revealed to us an author with a great mastery of narrative techniques, deep stylistic preoccupation, a master's hand in psychological observation, and a poetic energy that dignifies the sordid themes that motivate most of his stories."[6] In "El asedio" the "sordid theme" in question, no doubt, was lesbianism, "the love that dare not speak its name." At the end of the 1950s, Marqués did not dare speak it either. By celebrating the exceptional literary qualities of "El asedio," but not including it in his anthology, Marqués departs from the pattern followed for the other authors in the collection. In all the other cases, Marqués celebrates only the texts he has decided to anthologize. According to Díaz Valcárcel himself, Marqués judged that "El asedio" was not publishable because Díaz Valcárcel had better stories.[7] Yet, it is "El asedio," and not the stories included in the collection, that receives the most extensive and celebratory comments by Marqués. Why was it excluded? Beyond biographical explanations that would suggest that Marqués was suppressing a text that personally implicated him (Marqués himself was homosexual), it is possible to formulate other reasons linked to the programmatic coherence of Marqués's literary project as it is articulated in the anthology and to the systems of representation that are privileged there. "El asedio" overflows, exceeds, one of the most important aesthetic and ideological lines of the collection. It closes the figurative system elaborated around the "masculine body," enacting a final dislocation of the cultural attributes of masculinity through their transference to the "female body." When the ontological attributes of "men" are transplanted to the "female body"—when "man" vanishes, so to speak—a border has been transgressed and boundaries have been dissolved. This transgression was going to signal, as well, the unavoidable exhaustion of some of Marqués's literary propositions at the dawn of the 1960s, with the progressive consolidation of new modern cultural subjects and the emergence of new social problematics. This essay will examine the programmatic emergence and intensification of the representational system articulated around the "masculine body" (as it is formulated in the anthologizing practice of René Marqués), taking it to its moment of closure in the lesbian figure of "El asedio."

Point of Emergence: The Liminal Location of "El Josco"

"El Josco" is one of the most strongly institutionalized texts in Puerto Rican literary history. The story has been anthologized numerous times and is part of the country's school curriculum; in and through "El Josco," many Puerto Ricans have learned to love la patria [the fatherland], internalizing the myths constructed in the text.[8] According to Marqués, Díaz Alfaro's literary symbology signifies "Puerto Rican man, harassed by forces aiming to disintegrate his personality and his human dignity, and finally succumbing to these forces in a self-destructive gesture" (51). "El Josco" is an allegorical narrative in which issues of anticolonial resistance are embodied in a fight between two bulls, one signifying United States imperialism, and the other (el Josco), Puerto Rican virile cultural forces under siege.

La cabeza erguida, las aspas filosas estoqueando el capote en sangre de un atardecer luminoso. Aindiado, moreno, la carrillada en sombras, el andar lento y rítmico. . . . Era hosco por el color y por su carácter reconcentrado, huraño, fobioso, de peleador incansable . . . lo veía descender la loma, majestuoso, doblar la cerviz, resoplar su aliento de toro macho sobre la tierra virgen y tirar un mugido largo y potente. . . .

—Toro macho, padrote como ése . . . no nació pa yugo. (57)

[The head erect, his sharp crossed horns piercing his cape in the blood of a luminous sundown. Indian-like, dark, a shadow of grease on his face, a slow and rhythmic walk. . . . He was "hosco" [which means both dark-colored and glum or sullen] because of his color and of his self-absorbed character, diffident, phobic, that of a tireless fighter . . . one could see him descending the hill, majestic, lowering his forehead, snorting his macho bull breath on the virgin soil and throwing out a long and powerful bellow. . . .

—Macho bull, a stud like that . . . was not born to be under the yoke.]

The animal is characterized as an "hosco" [aloof] bull, one who avoids the company of other animals, powerfully demarcating the borders of his own personality and territory in a dynamic of self-sufficiency and mastery (over the virgin soil). The allegory concentrates on the issue of paternity (stud bull) and the symbolic threat of castration through replacement. Don Leopoldo, the owner of the estate, decides that it is necessary to improve the stock of his cattle through breeding and brings a white American bull to replace el Josco as a stud. Codifying the resistance to castration—to lose the place of the father—in a fight between the two bulls, the story focuses on their encounter, "frolicking" on the physical description of the animals—which are allegorical signs that simultaneously inscribe and displace the human male figure:

Las cabezas pegadas, los ojos negros y refulgentes inyectados de sangre, los belfos dilatados, las pezuñas firmemente adheridas a la tierra, las patas traseras abiertas, los rabos leoninos erguidos, la trabazón rebullente de los músculos ondulando sobre las carnes macizas. . . . El toro blanco . . . avanzó egregio, imprimiéndole a la escultura imponente de su cuerpo toda la fuerza de sus arrobas . . . el Josco alargó el cuerpo estilizado, levantó la testa triunfal, las astas filosas doradas de sol. (60, 61, 62)

[Their heads locked together, black and shining eyes, injected with blood, their lips dilated, their hooves planted in the soil, their back-legs spread, the lion-like tails erect, the boiling entanglement of the muscles undulating under the massive flesh. . . . The white bull advanced egregiously, impressing on the powerful sculpture of his body all the strength of his weight . . . el Josco stretched his stylized body, lifted his triumphant head, his sharp horns bronzed by the sun.]

El Josco, despite being smaller, wins the fight, but Don Leopoldo decides anyhow that the white bull will be the stud, condemning el Josco to the yoke—to which he never actually submits. The story closes with the spiritual and physical suicide of el Josco, with death as the only virile option in front of castration: "[L]a cabeza sepultada sobre su cuerpo musculoso" [His head buried under the weight of his muscular body] (63). Marcelo, a peon on the estate, for whom el Josco was like a son ("his only son," the narrator tells us, intensifying "paternity" as one of the organizing principles of the allegory) pronounces in the last line of the text the inescapable moral: "Ese toro era padrote de nación; no nació pa yugo" [That bull was a native stud; he was not born to be under the yoke] (63).

The story, at its doctrinal surface, poses the question of political domination within an intensely gendered framework. National identity, it is more than suggested, is a matter of masculine identity, of patrilineal reproduction, and domination over "the virgin soil." Students of Puerto Rican literature have already remarked how this interpretative model is closely tied to a "nostalgia" (on the part of former landowning sectors and their ideologues) for an agrarian patrician order in the face of modern urban transformations undergone by the country after the 1940s.[9] Dependent modernity and the cultural shifts it generated, most notably the relocation of woman's role in society and concomitant changes in the process of gendered subjectification, were perceived as (and indeed, to a large degree, were) a continuum with structures of colonial domination. The equivalency established between gender dislocation, modernity, and colonialism is precisely one of the chains of meaning most obsessively taken up by René Marqués. In a paroxysm of anxiety, Marqués pinpoints in his well-known essay "El puertorriqueño dócil" (1960) what he viewed with anguish as the imposition of an "Anglosaxon—foreign—matriarchal pattern" in the country, at the expense of el último baluarte cultural desde donde podía aún combatirse, en parte, la docilidad colectiva: el *machismo,* versión criolla de la fusión y adaptación de dos conceptos seculares, la *honra* española y el *pater familiae* romano. (175)

[the last cultural bastion from which Puerto Rican collective docility could have been attacked: *machismo,* the Creole version and adaptation of two time-honored concepts, Spanish honor and the Roman *pater familiae.*]

Modernity and colonialism, or better an oxymoronic colonial modernity, was constructed as one indiscriminate and converging phenomenon: a process of disempowerment for Puerto Rican men, a process of national emasculation. In *Cuentos puertorriqueños de hoy,* "El Josco," in its foundational position, utters this doctrine proposed by Marqués as one of the generative sources of the Puerto Rican modern literary response.

More subtle, perhaps, and probably with greater literary implications for a significant portion of the narrative of the period, is the centrality of the body in the textual practice of Díaz Alfaro. "El Josco," as the passages quoted show, is a text of an intense corporeality, and more precisely, of an intense masculine corporeality. If, at a doctrinal level, issues of anticolonial resistance are framed as issues of gender identity, at the interconnected level of the textual signifying practice, it is a bodily matter—a masculine bodily matter inscribed in a game of allegorical displacements. It is a rhetorical figuration in which the (male human) body is intensely positioned but never fully present. This rhetorical operation, in which the masculine body primarily appears as a battleground crossed and structured by politics, is one of the generative nuclei of textual production to be revisited and intensified in two of the most traumatic texts of the Puerto Rican literary imagination during the 1950s, not incidentally included by Marqués in his anthology: Emilio Díaz Valcárcel's "Un sapo en el espejo" and René Marqués's "En la popa hay un cuerpo reclinado." Both texts take up the figurative system elaborated in the narrative of Díaz Alfaro and move it to a higher level of literary and ideological intensity. The next sections will discuss how these texts rearticulated the figurative obsession around the male body. They set the borderlines that will come to demarcate the representation of the "mannish lesbian" in "El asedio."

Point of Intensification: Mutilations, Castrations, and Transferences

Both in Díaz Valcárcel's "El sapo en el espejo," as well as in Marqués's "En la popa hay un cuerpo reclinado," masculine bodies become objects of incessant transfigurations on the basis of intense power struggles with and against female bodies and desires. In Díaz Valcárcel's text, these transfigurations take place through the metamorphosis of a man, a veteran of the Korean War, into a toad—a semantic inversion of the narrative structure of the fairy tale. The nameless protagonist of the story lost his legs in the war; his body is a mutilated one. To compensate for his sexual impotence—the impossibility of penetrating the body of his wife—the man insists on engaging in cunnilingus. She reacts with repugnance to his advances, dramatizing, more than the uselessness of his penis, his total lack of the phallus.[10] The climactic event in the story occurs when the man, alone in his bedroom, sees his own image in the mirror:

> En un chispazo de lucidez vióse en el espejo: los brazos tensos sosteniéndolo como dos patas, el tronco echado sobre los muñones, y la imagen de un sapo zigzagueó en su cerebro. . . . Se sintió inmundo y la imagen del animal se le grabó en el cerebro. Esa noche, bajo el bombillo, en el aire líquido y amarillento, el espejo había golpeado de muerte su esperanza. (262–63)

> [In a spark of lucidity he saw himself in the mirror: his tensed arms holding him up as if they were two legs, the torso on top of the stumps, and the image of a toad flashed in his brain. . . . He felt filthy and the image of the animal was engraved in his brain. That night, under the lightbulb, in the liquid and yellowish air, the mirror struck the death blow to his hope.]

The image reflected in the mirror (not that of a prince, certainly, but of a toad) is the turning point for the real metamorphosis. This is the moment in which the subject, in a Lacanian reversal, rather than encountering the fiction of his coherence, faces the truth of his incompleteness. It is an encounter with the impossibility of affirming himself as a masculine subject, or even more, as a human subject at all: he understood that "había comenzado a desmoronarse su último baluarte de hombre" [his last bastion as a man was starting to crumble] (265). At the end of the story—when his wife returns home, repentent at having abandoned him, assuring him that she will obey him completely and that, indeed, she wants to be his woman (that she will become the desired object of his possession)—the man cannot hold back his anguish, and "saltó dos veces hacia el frente, croando" [he jumped forward twice, croaking] (267).

In this story, the figuration of an incomplete, mutilated body is linked to, and appears as a signifier of, two interconnected power systems: first, the Korean war as an index of the United States' imperialist power over Puerto Rican men (an index of colonial politics that is destructively imposed on the real bodies of Puerto Rican men); and second, the sexual rejection performed by the wife as an extreme sign of the protagonist's impotence (an index of sexual politics that undermines his possession of the phallus). This dispossession, emblematic of a discontinuity between masculine body and social power, will reach its most violent degree of thematization in René Marqués's "En la popa hay un cuerpo reclinado."

If, in "El sapo en el espejo," the masculine body is figured through a mutilated and incomplete inscription, and through the metamorphosis of the man into an animal, in Marqués's "En la popa hay un cuerpo reclinado," the transfiguration of that body will reach a higher degree of intensity: the story is now, without any rhetorical ambiguities, a tale of castration. As a hateful response to a life of feeling besieged by women, the male protagonist (who also is nameless, and who is constructed in a counterpoint of stream of consciousness, inner monologues, and indirect free speeches) decides to poison his wife. The man places her corpse in a boat and rows far out to sea: "en el vientre del bote" [in the womb of the boat], as if it were a moment of rebirth free of the mother's body. Once away from the shore, when "la visión del mundo" [the view of the world] appears to be unfocussed (i.e., once he did away with "reality"), the male character undresses himself and cuts "el tejido esponjoso" [the spongy tissue]—which is never called by the word *penis*—and throws it, as an offering, at the corpse of the woman who is lying in the stern of the boat.

Throughout the story, the figuration of the male body is based on an economy of lack:

Sus músculos, en la flexión rítmica, apenas si formaban relieve en los bíceps; meras cañas de bambú, apenas nudosos, sin la forma envidiada de otros brazos. . . . Observó su pecho hundido. *Debo hacer ejercicio. Es una vergüenza.* La franja de vellos negros separando las tetillas . . . su propio vientre escuálido formaba arrugas más allá arriba del pantaloncito de lana. (136)

[His muscles, in a rhythmic contraction, barely marked any biceps; just thin, bamboo canes, barely knotted, without the envied form of other's arms. . . . He glanced at his flat chest. *I should exercise. It is a shame.* The narrow line of his black chest-hair separating his nipples . . . his own squalid abdomen, wrinkled over the wool shorts.]

Initially, the only place where the character does not seem to be physically lacking is between his legs, where the narrator tells us dwelled "an exaggerated bulk"—as if it were an object of "excess," and not of lack. But it is "excess," as the text will eventually reveal, because it should not be there, as if it were something surpassing and overflowing the natural boundaries of the male body.

The ultimate scene of castration with which the story closes becomes the final instance of emasculation and self-destruction, the moment when the protagonist becomes "real lack" by becoming a "woman." That act is the climactic point in a narration that organizes a complex network of emasculating forces. One of its most desperate registers can be read in passages structured by paranoid fantasies of besiegement:

La principal es mujer, y la alcaldesa es mujer, y la senadora es mujer, y mi madre fue mujer, y yo soy sólo maestro, y en la cama un hombre, y mi mujer lo sabe, pero no es feliz porque la felicidad la traen las cosas buenas que se hacen en las fábricas . . . y ella insiste en que lo eche afuera [el semen] para conservar el cuerpo bonito y lucir el traje nuevo. (143–44)

[The school principal is a woman, and the mayor is a woman, and the senator is a woman, and my mother was a woman, and I am only a simple school teacher and in bed a man, and my wife [mujer/woman] knows it, but she is not happy, because happiness is brought about by good things that are made in factories . . . and she insists that I throw it [the semen, it is implied] outside [of her] so that she can have a pretty body and show off the new dress.]

This stream of consciousness diatribe intermingles some of the elements that the character perceives to conspire against his masculinity. The most obvious among them is, of course, the placement of women in positions of social power. More subtle, perhaps, are the links established in the passage between the wife's rejection of maternity (of having his child, of making him a "father," which is reminiscent of "El Josco") and the critique of the commodification of experience in modernity (and more specifically, in colonial modernity). This commodification, according to the story, transforms the female body into an aesthetic object and a window of consumption (to "have a pretty body" to "show off the new dress"). It can be read as an emblem of the coitus interruptus that proscribes the experience of maternity, foreclosing, in consequence, the very permanence, preservation, and existence of the father. In the story, the incapacity of the male character to engage in human relationships mediated by structures of consumption (the wife desires a television set, a washing machine, a new house, etc., forcing him to take on financial commitments that later he will not be able to meet) is proposed as the cornerstone of his emasculation. It is significant that the wife's leitmotif throughout the story is "Un hombre de verdad le da a su mujer lo que ella no tiene" [A real man gives his woman what she does not have], a phrase that resounds with echoes of Freudian penis envy. What the woman does not have (and which is linked in the story to structures of consumption, to the possession of commodities) is a penis. This will be the final gift offered to her by the male character, closing the cycle of emasculation with a self-destructive gesture, with his own transfiguration into a woman: he is the phallus that the woman can possess only in death.

Central to the story, and entangled with the issue of the commodification of experience as an emasculating force, is the recurrence of the castrating mother throughout the character's intense stream of consciousness monologues. She is the one who begins the process of the character's feminization, undermining his vocation to become a writer and encouraging him to pursue a "practical life," that is a modern life (the life of the provider, as it is conceptualized by Marqués).

Pero exigen, piden, demandan de mí, de mí sólo. Eres tan niño. Y tienes ya cosas de hombre. Y no supe si lo decía porque escribía a escondidas. . . .

No te cases joven, hijito. *Y el sentido no estaba en el amor. . . . Y tampoco era en escribir:* Deja esas tonterías, hijito, *sino en una profesión, la que fuese, que no podía ser otra sino la de maestro, porque no siempre hay medios de estudiar lo que más se anhela. . . . Y no pasaría necesidades, teniendo una carrera, como había asegurado ella, ni escribiría jamás.* (137–38)

[*But they request, they ask, they demand a lot from me, only from me.* You are such a child. And you already have things of a man. *And I did not know if she said that because I used to write covertly. . . .* Do not marry young, my little son. *And meaning did not dwell in love. . . . Nor in writing:* Stop those silly, useless things, my little son, *but in a profession, whatever this may be, which could not be anything other than a teacher, because one cannot always study what one most desires. . . . And I would not suffer any needs, having a profession, as she had assured me, and I would not write ever again.*]

The mother figure not only inhibits his sexuality but also deprives him of his first phallus: the pen—which for Marqués, we recall, was the privileged instrument in the hands of the virile writer to counteract Puerto Rican docility, thus the seminal instrument for building the nation. In the story, the signifiers of castration are established in a chain of equivalencies: the interruption of writing (which in Marqués's system is synonymous with a cancellation of the nation), the difficulty in possessing the female body—with its consequent obstruction to paternity—and, last, the impossibilities of satisfying the laws of a consumerist society. The imbrication of all these signs conditions the final collapse of the male body, a transfiguration through which the morphology of lack is made visible.[11]

The masculine body: allegorical inscription and self-destruction in "El Josco"; mutilation and metamorphosis in "El sapo en el espejo"; castration, effeminization, and transference of the phallus to the female corpse in "En la popa hay un cuerpo reclinado." It is within this system of literary figurations that a last transformation of the masculine body would take place in mid-twentieth-century Puerto Rican narrative: the ephemeral emergence of the "mannish lesbian" in Emilio Díaz Valcárcel's "El asedio."

This story is the most extreme instance in a figurative system mobilized by anxiety and is simultaneously the system's moment of closure.

Point of Closure: The "Mannish Lesbian"

> Sintió subírsele a la garganta el confuso sentimiento de su ilegitimidad que permanecía anclado en ominoso acecho en el fondo de su espíritu. Un espíritu contrahecho, pensó, regocijándose en su propio flagelo. . . . La falda, que delataba unas caderas secas, no era lo suficientemente larga para cubrir las rodillas nudosas, casi masculinas . . . ojeó su cuerpo seco y anguloso, se arregló distraída el severo cuello de anchas solapas, abotonado casi hasta la asfixia. (11, 13)[12]

> [She felt going up her throat a confused feeling of illegitimacy that remained anchored in ominous wait at the bottom of her spirit. . . . A deformed spirit, she thought, rejoicing in her self-flagellation. . . . The skirt, which revealed her narrow hips, was not long enough to cover her knotty, almost masculine, knees . . . she observed her own dry and angular body, and distractedly fixed the severe collar of her shirt, buttoned up to the point of suffocation.]

It is tempting to suggest that in "El asedio," the penis ("the floating signifier") that the male character throws at the woman's corpse acquires new fictional life in Díaz Valcárcel's mannish lesbian. If in Marqués's story masculine anxieties about dislocation of gender categories are resolved in a paranoid fantasy of castration, in "El asedio," those anxieties would reach a new point of resolution in a narrative of punishment: punishment against those who dare to alter the naturalized sociocultural order ruled by laws of sexual differentiation. The threat to established norms, and the damnation it could entail, are represented in the character of the "mannish lesbian," a neurotically tormented figure—who not incidentally is also an intellectual. Through her, the story recycles what John d'Emilio has called "the myth of silence, invisibility, and isolation as the essential characteristics of gay life" ("Capitalism and Gay Identity" 101).

The representation of the "mannish lesbian" in "El asedio" is articulated along two axes corresponding to the construction of the body of the character and to the penetration of its subjectivity by an omniscient narrator. The character is, to a large degree, a reductionist reelaboration of Radclyffe Hall's Stephen Gordon—from *The Well of Loneliness*—and Jean-Paul Sartre's Ines—from *Huis Clos*.[13] The surfaces of this imagined lesbian body also selectively activate some sexological theories from the turn of the twentieth century about the visibility and legibility of lesbian identity—in particular those by Richard von Krafft-Ebing and Havelock Ellis. In addition, the fictionalization of a lesbian subjectivity is made in the context of a problematic appropriation of Sartre's existentialist predicate "Hell are the others." From this intertextual collage emerges a nameless figure around which would be exemplified not the universality of anguish produced by the disencounter between the desires of the one and the incommensurable reality of the others (as it is thematized by Sartre in *Huis Clos*), but the sad destiny of those anomalous beings who pretend to take exception to and alter the normative order of the world. Again, it is destiny that writes and disfigures the body.

The lesbian imagined in "El asedio" is an intensely homographetic figure, to use Lee Edelman's fruitful concept: a stereotypical figure that confirms the presupposition that the signs of homosexuality and lesbianism can be unequivocally identified on the surfaces of the body, and that, in consequence, the borders between heterosexuality and homosexuality are clearly, distinctively, and visibly marked (Edelman 163–64). The lesbian body in "El asedio" carries the signs of a deviation, an anomaly, a form against nature—"contrahecha" [counterfeit]. It is a "dry" body [*seco*], "angular" [*anguloso*], a masculine body. Moreover, the text appropriates the taxonomical system established by Richard von Krafft-Ebing at the end of the nineteenth century to classify different kinds of "lesbians" along a series of predetermined physiological and social characteristics. According to Krafft-Ebing, certain physiological features, established in terms of the degree of "masculine appearance" in a woman, corresponded to a specific set of social behaviors that could reach the point of completely altering cultural prescriptions about "the feminine." Carroll Smith-Rosenberg has pointed out how the definitions proposed by Krafft-Ebing about the lesbian "did not focus on the sexual behavior of the women categorized as lesbian but rather on their social behavior and physical appearance."[14] The kinds of lesbians in Krafft-Ebing's system "seemed to desire male privileges and power as ardently as, perhaps more ardently than, they sexually desired women" (270). In particular, Smith-Rosenberg notices how one of Krafft-Ebing's types, the "mannish lesbian,"

> linked women's rejection of traditional gender roles and their demands for social and economic equality to cross-dressing, sexual perversion, and borderline hermaphroditism. This new sexual subject assumed a critical role in the grand Edwardian social drama, which used physical disease to enact social disorder. (270)

It can be said, as well, that during the 1950s, Puerto Rican narrative represented physical deformity to enact social disorder and punish it. The portrayal of the "mannish lesbian" in "El asedio" invites us to read her as a figure in which changes in gendered prescriptions intensified in the country during the 1940s are disqualified. The story is a discursive intervention geared to classifying and mastering what was perceived as a threat. In this intervention, sociocultural changes are pathologized through the figuration of a denaturalized, hermaphrodite, deformed, almost monstrous body, and through a sick psyche. It is just this image that, by contrast, would reflect the striking and desired visage of normality.

Through a reworking of Sartre's existentialist predicate "Hell are the others," the lesbian of "El asedio" is represented as an antagonistic figure vis-à-vis the world. Her paranoid psyche perceives the existence of the others as "harassment." The "others," in her view, attack her with the spectacle of their joyful "normality," fostering in her—according to the omniscient narrator—a shameful sensation of "illegitimacy."

> Una familia normal y feliz, pensó apoyada sobre el volante. Un padre gordo y de apariencia próspera, recién afeitado, una bella pareja de niños, y una madre que alcanza ya los treinta años, mofletuda, satisfecha como toda mujer que siente colmados sus instintos cardinales. (11)

> Un matrimonio joven y dos niños ocuparon la mesa de al lado. Otra vez la imagen del matrimonio feliz, pensó. . . . Los odiaba. (13)

> [A normal and happy family, she thought resting on the steering wheel. A fat father, of prosperous appearance, recently shaven, a beautiful

couple of kids, and a mother, close to her thirties, chubby, satisfied like every woman who finds all her cardinal instincts fulfilled.

A young married couple and two children were sitting at the table in front of her. Again, the image of the happy marriage, she thought. . . . She hated them.]

The world becomes a projection of her neurotic and tortured subjectivity. In the face of what is felt as the other's happiness, the lesbian—resentful of her own solitude—is represented as a subject who constitutes herself by generating hatred.

Estaba sola en el fondo de una soledad sin nombre, sin esperanzas de salir alguna vez hacia un mundo cálido y deseado, el mundo de los otros. (13)

[She was alone, in the depth of a nameless solitude, without hopes of ever reaching a warm and desired world, the world of the others.]

Feeling rejected by the "warm" and "happy" world of normality, as well as by the woman she desires,[15] the nameless lesbian takes refuge in her apartment, in her "interior"—the trace of her ultimate separation from the world. Two visual images hanging from the walls of her apartment codify and hierarchically synthesize the poles of the conflict staged in the story: the tensions between the behavior of an anomalous, "unnatural" being, and the "natural," normative order of the law. The first of these images is a reproduction of a painting by Modigliani—bought in New York at Macy's—representing the stylized image of a naked woman. This image is presented as a sort of fetish of the unreachable object of her desire.

Tenía los ojos fijos en la primorosa reproducción de un Modigliani: una mujer en tonos ocres y rojizos, con un largo cuello estilizado. La copia fue comprada en Macy's el invierno pasado, luego de la visita al Museo de Arte Moderno, después de las largas charlas sobre Arte y Personalidad Contemporáneos. Neida [the woman she desires] se había reído mucho de ese cuadro, y se había dejado caer sobre el canapé descuidadamente mostrando una blanca rodilla. Esa noche ella descubrió la furia con que Neida subrayaba sus negativas. Y el cuadro quedó allí, testigo mudo e inútil de otra noche perdida. (17)

[She had her eyes fixed on the exquisite reproduction of a Modigliani: a woman of ocher and reddish tones, with a long stylized neck. The copy was bought at Macy's last winter, after the visit to the Museum of Modern Art, after the long talks on Contemporary Art and Personality. Neida [the desired woman] laughed a lot about this painting, and let herself fall carelessly onto the canapé, showing her white knee. That night she discovered the fury with which Neida underlined her refusals. And the painting remained there, mute and useless witness of another wasted night.]

Hanging next to this image—where the unattainable erotic object is melancholically encoded, along with the impoverishing experience of rejection and a vital loss ("otra noche perdida" [another wasted night])—is an engraving by Puerto Rican graphic artist Rafael Tufiño. It is significant that this image is placed next to the window, framing the exit to the outside world.[16] Tufiño's engraving represents a group of men working in the fields, in direct contact with nature. Although, strictly speaking, an engraving is also a "reproduction" (one made, though, through less modern, more artisanal means than photography), its value seems to be the inverse of Modigliani's reproduction. To a large extent, the artisanal technology of engraving and the difference between impressions—which are generally numbered—invest the end product with the aura of originality. The juxtaposition of both images (Tufiño's and Modigliani's, respectively) ciphers a strictly hierarchized system of binary oppositions: a work perceived as an original versus the copy (with its consequential connotations of authenticity and inauthenticity); the aura of the artisanal and unrepeatable versus the mechanically reproduced (linked to modernity as that which is artificial, industrial, and impoverished—as Walter Benjamin has discussed it); the presence of the real versus the fetish; the national versus the foreign; the realist image of men versus the stylized body of the woman. Furthermore, Tufiño's engraving, with its value of authenticity and autochthony, becomes a sort of catalyst for the anguished anagnorisis of the lesbian character: the recognition of her own "inauthenticity" and "counternaturality."

> Miró hacia la ventana, cerca de la cual colgaba un grabado de Rafael Tufiño. Un grupo de hombres desyerbando, trazados con vigorosas líneas. Esa puede ser la felicidad, meditó; en esos brazos nudosos y en esos rostros contraídos por la miseria hay un serio compromiso con la vida, una sinceridad de propósitos que tú, la *scholar,* la humanista, nunca has tenido. (17)

> [She looked toward the window, next to which hung an engraving by Rafael Tufiño. A group of men clearing the fields, traced with vigorous lines. That could be happiness, she thought; in those knotted arms, and in those faces contracted by misery, there is a serious commitment with life, a sincerity of purpose that you, the *scholar,* the humanist, have never had.]

The passage reinscribes some of the binary structures mentioned earlier, intensifying their immediacy: masculine versus feminine, manual labor versus intellectual pursuits, body versus mind, the "natural" versus the world of culture (the *scholar*), sincerity of purpose versus a lack of commitment to life, happiness versus unhappiness. The sequence comprising the terms "feminine," "intellectual work," "the mind," "the world of culture," "lack of commitment to life," and "unhappiness" juxtaposes some terms that within hegemonic cultural discourses do not belong together. The culturally dominant associations would link the feminine to nature and immanence while linking masculinity to the world of culture, to that which transcends itself—to use the existentialist framework that informs the narration. The relationship established between "abnormality," "feminine," and "culture" (as a sign of a renunciation to inhabit the plain order of the "natural") allows us to read the remaining terms in the sequence as effects of that association: a lack of commitment to life and unhappiness. These are the generators of the meaninglessness that traverses the life of the lesbian. The axes for the figuration of the lesbian subject—which are emblems of the transgression against the naturalized order ruled by the laws of gender—are posed as existential nonsense.

Se contempló en el espejo. Te estás poniendo vieja, murmuró; te estás poniendo vieja sin haber logrado nada de la vida, sin haber sido ni siquiera un poco sincera. (17)

[She contemplated herself in the mirror. You are getting old, she mumbled; you are getting old without having achieved anything in life, without having been even a little bit sincere.]

Furthermore, the story is constructed in a series of symmetrical structures because the pair Tufiño/Modigliani corresponds to another pair of clearly delimited images: the mirror image (as a false and impossible narcissism, an inverted narcissism in which one's own image becomes the image not of desire but of contempt) versus the image of an exterior, inaccessible world, framed—as if it were another painting—by the window. The text closes with the lesbian, almost detached from her own self, looking out of the window at the spectacle of the outside world. It is in that final moment that the character is subject to the textual punishment of solitude and pain. Moreover, it is the moment in which the character ejects herself, abjectly, toward the outside.

Sacó la cabeza ventana afuera. La brisa caliente, bochornosa, que pesaba sobre el ruidoso tráfago de la ciudad, le produjo vértigo. Escupió hacia la noche, hacia la humanidad, hacia aquella multitud de seres altivos y bárbaramente normales que la asediaban con el alarde de la felicidad. Escupió una, dos, tres veces, hasta que sintió el llanto, un llanto duro que se negaba a humedecer su rostro, se cuajaba bajo sus párpados. (18)

[She stuck her head out of the window. The warm, shameful breeze, that weighed heavily on the noisy traffic of the city, gave her vertigo. She spat at the night, at humankind, at those masses of aloof and barbarically normal beings that besieged her with their happiness. She spat one, two, three times until she felt a cry, a hard cry that refused to wet her face, coagulating under her eyelids.]

"El asedio" brings to a point of closure the figurative system structured around the "masculine body," insofar as it takes the floating signifiers of masculinity and embodies them in a female figure. This is the most extreme inscription in the narrative of the period of the displacements of the phallus; it is a point where the phallus abandons its conventional sites of embodiment, attempting to traverse the feared borders of differentiation. But that transgression, that denaturalization of signs, implies for the character—in a punitive and vengeful textual resolution—the impossibility of relating to the outside world, her total disencounter with the reality of the others.

The "mannish lesbian" codifies the transgression of two prerogatives culturally associated with masculine desire and constitutive of the possession of the phallus: the desire to possess the female body, and the desire to possess knowledge and culture—thus, the reification of nature that is posed in the story. "El asedio" inscribes a desperate counterattack directed at recasting a particular cultural order through the discourse of "the natural," this discourse understood as an authoritative expression of what was desired as immutable. To defy the laws of gender and sexuality implied, according to this proposal, the grotesque deformation of the "natural order"—the alteration of the "feminine body" and the tremendous punishment of a monstrous "masculinization."[17]

"El asedio" is another twist of paranoid fantasy, a further eruption of cultural anxieties in the face of what was perceived as the "undermining of masculine power," which organizes a significant part of mid-twentieth-century Puerto Rican narrative. Nevertheless, this system was going to fade quite rapidly. The whirlwind of modernization quickly made it obsolete, requiring different forms and proposals capable of interpellating new social problems and cultural subjects. A few years after the publication of Marqués's anthology, Luis Rafael Sánchez published a text in his first collection of short stories, *En cuerpo de camisa,* in which a homosexual character would function as a deconstructive figure with regard to the repressive structures of community formation. In "¡Jum!" the community, in order to preserve its "homogeneity," does not hesitate to destroy those who attempt to deviate from the prescribed social order. Unlike "El asedio," in "¡Jum!" what is subjected to critical reflection is not the "deviant," no longer understood as a "problem," but the normativity of the world—the established cultural paradigms—now represented as a criminal activity.[18] Similarly, by the end of the sixties, a group of women writers would defy the assigned disassociation from the world of culture and contribute to some of the most important literary journals of the period (e.g., *Zona de carga y descarga, Guajana*), relativizing in the process the desired homosociality of the literary community promoted by Marqués. Later on, Manuel Ramos Otero would signal new figurative plots for the masculine body, and its homoerotic possibilities, making explicit what for the writers of the generation of 1940 was latent, contained fear. New literary and cultural projects took root, displacing a significant part of the aesthetics and the ideological guidelines established by René Marqués at the end of the 1950s.

In the meantime, the lesbian inscribed in Díaz Valcárcel's story still sits, looking out at the world through the window of her apartment. Caught between two literary generations—exceeding the figurative system elaborated around the "masculine body" and problematically announcing the emergence of new cultural and political subjects—she remains alone with a tear in her eye. She is waiting for the day when through other figurative exercises, she will be able to reenter the field of Puerto Rican narrative representations.

Notes

A slightly different version of this essay is forthcoming in Spanish in *Ibero-americana* (Frankfurt, Germany). I appreciate the comments and suggestions made by the participants at the conference Hispanisms and Homosexualities (NYU, April 1994), which have helped me to rethink some of the issues discussed in this paper. The end product is, of course, my sole responsibility. Diane Miliotes, once again, has given me the most generous intellectual and emotional support—to her my greatest gratitude.

1 *Cuentos puertorriqueños de hoy.* This collection includes the following authors and stories: Abelardo Díaz Alfaro ("El Josco" and "Los perros"), José Luis González ("La carta," "En el fondo del caño hay un negrito," and "El pasaje"), René Marqués ("Otro día nuestro" and "En la popa hay un cuerpo reclinado"), Pedro Juan Soto ("Los inocentes" and "La cautiva"), Edwin Figueroa ("Aguinaldo negro" and "Lolo Manco"), José Luis Vivas ("El fósforo quemado" and "Interludio"), Emilio Díaz Valcárcel ("Sol negro" and "El sapo en el espejo"), and Salvador M. de Jesús ("La llama del fósforo" and "Vertiente"). Each selection is preceded by an interpretive essay written by Marqués, a brief "autobiography" of each author, and answers provided by the authors to the questions "What is your concept of the short story?" and "Why

do you cultivate this genre?" Besides Marqués's introductory essay (entitled "The Puerto Rican Short Story in the Generation of 1940"), the anthology includes a bibliographic appendix of the works of each author. Quotations used in this essay refer to the eighth edition of the anthology (1985).

2　Díaz Quiñones, "Los desastres de la guerra" 160. Useful for the theoretical discussion of the tensions between economic modernity and literary modernity is Matei Calinescu's *Faces of Modernity: Avant-Garde, Decadence, Kitsch.* Another anthology contemporary to Marqués's but with a different literary and ideological program is Concha Meléndez's *Antología de autores puertorriqueños: El cuento.*

3　Important for the discussion on "homosociality" are Eve Kosofsky Sedgwick's *Between Men: English Literature and Male Homosocial Desire* and Wayne Koestenbaum's *Double Talk: The Erotics of Male Literary Collaboration.* Díaz Quiñones has observed, as well, how the prologue to *Cuentos puertorriqueños de hoy* is an exaltation of the writers of Marqués's own generation but, above all, a valorization of his own literary works. The deeply narcissistic edge of Marqués's literary essays is notable and carries through in his assessments of the writers of his generation. The implications of this narcissistic impulse for the constitution of a homosocial cultural space surpass the scope of this essay, but the subject undoubtedly deserves to be studied in detail elsewhere.

4　It is almost a commonplace of the literary criticism on Marqués to discuss his feminine characters and the author's overt misogyny in his portrayal of them (e.g., Barradas, Díaz Quiñones, Gelpí, J. L. González, Palmer, Solá). Marqués himself, in the prologue to *Cuentos puertorriqueños de hoy* and in "El puertorriqueño dócil," emphasized the centrality of the literary representation of "woman" for the modernizing impulse of the new generation. For Marqués, the "maturity" of the (always male) writer and of a national literature must be measured "by the degree of analytical capacity [the writer exhibits] with regard to the thrilling and exciting opposite sex." This capacity would allow the male writer "to explore, with cold lucidity, all the cracks of that other psychological world, evasive, mysterious and—without a doubt—for him, poor devil!, very dangerous" ("El puertorriqueño dócil" 174–75). According to Marqués, Puerto Rican literature—thanks to him and the members of his generation—has reached a high degree of maturity; it has reached "manhood" (to say it in terms akin to his interpretive system). It is not surprising that within this model, writers are the only ones in a position to defend national culture. Writers are not "docile" but virile defenders of the salvation of the fatherland: "machismo." This literary virility ("maturity") is closely linked to the symbolic possession of woman—to their capacity to penetrate her symbolically. Furthermore, through that symbolic traffic of female images, the writers of 1940 consolidate themselves as a literary generation. The symbolic possession of "women"—characteristic of the new narrative—is one of the meeting points of the new generation, a point where men encounter each other in a homosocial embrace that unifies them. This homosocial embrace, behind the scenes and concealed by an apparent obsession with "women," is one of the issues to be touched on in this paper. For a more detailed discussion of this issue, see my "Notas sobre el tráfico simbólico de mujeres: Homosocialidad y modernidad literaria en Puerto Rico" (forthcoming in *Revista de Crítica Literaria Latinoamericana*). Fundamental for the analysis of the traffic in women as a strategy to consolidate male alliances are Luce Irigaray ("Women on the Market" and "Commodities among Themselves" in her *This Sex Which Is Not One* 170–91), Sedgwick (*Between Men*) and Rubin ("Traffic").

5 There are several "homosexual" characters in contemporary Puerto Rican literature, starting with "el hijo de Trinidad" (Trinidad's son) in Luis Rafael Sánchez's "¡Jum!"; the insinuations in Rosario Ferré's *Papeles de Pandora* and the evident ambiguities in *Maldito Amor;* the openly homosexual voice in Manuel Ramos Otero; the "entendidos" with regard to uncle Sergio in Magaly García Ramis's *Felices días, tío Sergio;* and the homoerotic panic in René Marqués's last novel, *La mirada,* so intelligently analyzed by Arnaldo Cruz-Malavé, not to mention some of Marqués's dramas of the 1970s. The "lesbian" is remarkably absent from Puerto Rican narrative, except in Mayra Montero's recent novel *La última noche que pasé contigo.* Nonetheless, the "lesbian" has emerged as a poetic voice in texts such as Nemir Matos's *Las mujeres no hablan así* and, more recently, Lilliana Ramos's *Reróticas.*

6 These comments about "El asedio" appear in the introduction to the selections by Díaz Valcárcel in *Cuentos puertorriqueños de hoy* 242.

7 Personal communication. I thank my mother, Nilda Ortiz García, for conducting a brief interview with Díaz Valcárcel on my behalf, and the author for his kindness in answering my questions.

8 "El Josco" was originally published in *Terrazo* (1948), Abelardo Díaz Alfaro's first collection of short stories.

9 It is important that it is Marcelo, and not Don Leopoldo the landowner, who most strongly identifies with el Josco. The story articulates part of the populist ideology triumphant during this period. In 1948, the year when *Terrazo* was published, Luis Muñoz Marín became the first elected Puerto Rican governor of the country. The new political project posed national identity without presupposing the constitution of an independent national state. Its

rhetoric did not address the great economic interest in the island but rather the disenfranchised sectors of society, which gathered under the Partido Popular's motto "pan, tierra y libertad" [bread, land, and liberty]. Cf. Alvarez-Curbelo and Rodríguez-Castro, eds., *Del nacionalismo al populismo.*

10 Judith Butler has clarified, apropos Lacan's theory of the phallus, how women constitute the Phallus: "For women to 'be' the Phallus means . . . to reflect the power of the Phallus, to supply the site to which it penetrates, and to signify the Phallus through 'being' its 'Other,' its absence, its lack, the dialectical confirmation of its identity. By claiming that the Other that lacks the Phallus is the one who *is* the Phallus, Lacan clearly suggests that power is wielded by this feminine position of not-having, that the masculine subject who 'has' the Phallus requires this Other to confirm and, hence, be the Phallus in its extended sense." Women here are not absolute alterity but "the site of masculine self-elaboration" (*Gender Trouble* 44). Cf. Lacan, "La significación del falo."

11 Arnaldo Cruz has observed how the canonical texts of Puerto Rican literature have instituted the nation not through the exhibition of the phallus but through the testimony of its lack: "It is my contention that, in a brilliant Nietzschean-like reversal, Puerto Rican canonical texts have not ruled through potency but through impotence; that unlike those Latin American foundational texts that Doris Sommer has so passionately analyzed, Puerto Rican canonical texts have rallied us and bound us through failure and impotence. It has been an exhibited impotence, such as the protagonist's self-castration in ["En la popa hay un cuerpo reclinado"]. An impotence that has cunningly incited us to close ranks around the father, with righteous indignation or with rage" ("Toward an Art" 140–41).

12 Díaz Valcárcel.

13 Compare the passage quoted at the beginning of this segment with section 6, chapter 24, of *The Well of Loneliness*, in which Stephen Gordon contemplates with anguish and hatred the image of her own body reflected in the mirror: "That night she stared at herself in the glass; and even as she did so she hated her body with its muscular shoulders, its small compact breasts, and its slender flanks of an athlete. All her life she must drag this body of hers like a monstrous fetter imposed on her spirit" (186–87). Radclyffe Hall's novel, as Catharine Stimpson has pointed out, is a "parable of damnation" (quoted in de Lauretis, "Lure of the Mannish Lesbian" 211) to be reworked in "El asedio." For two lucid discussions of *The Well of Loneliness*, see de Lauretis and Newton.

14 Smith-Rosenberg 269. In my discussion of Krafft-Ebing's and Havelock Ellis's theories, I follow Smith-Rosenberg's analysis.

15 Different from Krafft-Ebing's lesbians, and closer to Havelock Ellis's specula-

tions, Díaz Valcárcel's lesbian is a sexualized figure—similar to Stephen Gordon in *The Well of Loneliness*. Her sexualization takes place insofar as it allows the representation of lesbian sexuality as frustration, as a nonreciprocated desire. Again, it is another instance where the total disencounter of the lesbian with the world is thematized, intensifying the representation of her complete solitude. For a discussion of Ellis, see Smith-Rosenberg 270–72.

16 Rafael Tufiño was one of the graphic artists contemporaneous with the writers of 1940. It may be worthwhile to remember that Tufiño also designed the cover for the first collection of short stories published by René Marqués, *Otro día nuestro* (1955).

17 For an enlightening discussion of "sex" as a discursive construction and not as the "natural base" on which "gender" is superimposed, see Judith Butler, *Gender Trouble* 6–7.

18 For a detailed reading of Luis Rafael Sánchez's "¡Jum!" see my "Community at Its Limits: Orality, Law, Silence, and the Homosexual Body in Luis Rafael Sánchez's '¡Jum!' "

Caribbean Dislocations:

Arenas and Ramos Otero in New York

Rubén Ríos Avila

For Alberto Sandoval, who does not want to go back home

The Other I/Land

Reinaldo Arenas and Manuel Ramos Otero may or may not have enjoyed (or endured) a brief encounter in the streets of New York, but they had quite a few things in common in the city they shared for about ten years. Two openly homosexual men from the Caribbean—one Cuban, the other Puerto Rican—found in the City a way out of oppressive homophobia and pretty much declared themselves queer writers in exile. Ramos Otero distanced himself in the early seventies from what he felt was a hypocritical and provincial colonial domesticity, a dominating Puerto Rican *familia de todos nosotros,* and became instead a citizen of the Village, particularly the gay Village, which in those years defined itself around Stonewall, Christopher Street, and the old docks.[1] Arenas arrived in New York via Mariel in the early eighties, hoping to become finally free from a government that persecuted and imprisoned him for being gay. Although Ramos Otero lived in New York twice as long as Arenas, Arenas can also be called a New York writer as well as a Cuban writer, if only because it was in New York that he finally found a place to rewrite the novels that were destroyed or lost during his years as a homeless writer in Lenin Park and the *solares* of Centro Habana and La Habana Vieja. It was a decade of frantic writing and publishing for Arenas, compared to a more restrained and limited output by Ramos Otero. For Arenas, his exile was a radical decision, a point of no return. He knew he would never go back to Cuba. That, contrary to Ramos Otero, Arenas quickly became disillusioned with the city as well as with its gay culture actually gave his writings of those years the right amount of cynicism, urban angst, and jaded humor—so evident in *The Doorman,* for example—that one expects from a megapolitan writer. These qualities are perhaps what made him a true New Yorker.[2]

Ramos Otero, on the other hand, like many Puerto Ricans who live in the United States, visited the island often. Although his homosexuality is overtly thematized in his writings, it does not become a radical form of political dissent, as in Arenas.[3] In Arenas, homosexuality functions as a counterethics for the Cuban revolution. All revolutions are chaste, repressive of sexuality, he wants to stress in *Before Night Falls:* "It was logical for Fidel Castro to persecute us, not to let us fuck, and to try to suppress any public display of the life force" (93). Contrary to a system that for Arenas was governed by the chaste ideal of collective mobilization under the authoritarian leadership of a castrating father, Arenas flaunts the exhibition of untamed individual desire, particularly sexual desire, as the basis of freedom. If Castro is the castle, the rock, the castrating agent of the revolution as phallic signifier, then Arenas turns his name, the name of the writer, into the debunker of the name of the father; he writes in order to disintegrate the castle, to dissolve the rock, to rewrite the castle as a *Castro de arena,* as a sand castle.[4]

Ramos Otero has no nation to dismantle, no authoritarian father figure to debunk. Therefore, his writing is not tragic and heroic, like Arenas's, but farcical and decidedly avant-garde. He is also a debunker, but in his case the target is the literary canon of Puerto Rican letters. In Puerto Rico literature has usually been at the service of national identity, a claim made more urgent by what has been perceived as the unresolved political status of two successive stages of colonialism. Desire has therefore meant above all national desire. Writing revolves around this founding void, and the need to fill it up, usually through the resurrection or rehabilitation of an empowering unifying myth: the defense of the national language, the inseminating power of an originating race or the possible recollection of a broken memory. In the face of these cultural duties, the Puerto Rican writers, as Ana Lydia Vega aptly says, quickly discover that censorship has an "auto," that it drives itself home as self-censorship.[5] Conversely, Manuel Ramos Otero writes to uncensor his self. Never before in Puerto Rican literature do we witness a more overt, insolent, and unabashed exhibition of individuality as in Ramos Otero. His is a complex, strategic praxis of individuality. Its most revolutionary tactic is not confessionalism, although it is there. It is not even sexual exhibitionism, although it is also there. It is the tactic of style. Nation-forming writing is not supposed to call too much attention to its tics, its little idiosyncrasies, the disturbing signatures that obstruct the message, the transparent calling. He is not, by any means, a stylist, a master of style. Quite the contrary, his writing imposes style as aberration and distortion, as digression and noise, as cacophony and vulgarity. Style for him becomes a form of heavy breathing, a constant recalling of the voice of the writer uncomfortably proximate, too close for comfort.

It is not surprising that both writers ended up in exile. They are, to be sure, too much to handle. However, being separated from the homeland meant something different for each of them. For Arenas, exile was a radical decision. For Ramos Otero, it was a lifestyle. But the type of exile that ultimately interests me here is not measured really in terms of physical distance from the homeland. In this respect, Edward Said has a more accurate definition of the true state of exile for marginal artists and intellectuals:

> There is a popular but wholly mistaken assumption that being exiled is to be totally cut off, isolated, hopelessly separated from your place of origin. Would that surgically clean separation were true, because then, at least, you could have the consolation of knowing that what you have left behind is, in a sense, unthinkable and completely irrecoverable. The fact is that for most exiles the difficulty consists not simply in being forced to live away from home, but rather, given today's world, in living with the many reminders that you are in exile, that your home is not in fact so far away, and that the normal traffic of everyday contemporary life keeps you in constant but tantalizing and unfulfilled touch with the old place. (48–49)

It is this notion of exile as a kind of intermediate, purgatorial in-betweenness that I would like to address, the neither here nor there quality of a writing for which eccentricity means to be forever cast off from the center. Ultimately, what defines this kind of exile is not necessarily expatriation. It is rather a state of mind, a quality of thought that places you outside, in between places, constantly traveling and never quite arriving.

After he moved to Havana from Holguín and began to write novels and stories, Arenas quickly became an embarrassing foe of the revolution. The publication abroad of *The Ill-Fated Peregrinations of Fray Servando* very soon portrayed him as an author who could not get published in Cuba.[6] The novel itself is a clear defense of the writer as a dangerous enemy of any form of coercive authority, and ultimately as an enemy of the state. The state-appointed writer is for Arenas the worst kind of traitor, and he is characterized in *The Ill-Fated Peregrinations* as the secretary of the dictator, and as the author of a voluminous treatise called "El saco de las losas" [The bag of bricks]. The allusion to Carpentier's *El siglo de las luces* is not particularly subtle. *El mundo alucinante* is a decidedly anti-Carpenterian novel. The idea of writing as the ever-spiraling ascent toward the true discourse of revolution from the eighteenth-century European model toward the twentieth-century Cuban model, so central for Carpentier, is the opposite of Arenas's view of writing as peregrination, as compulsive repetition of the act of escape precisely from this very understanding of discourse as truth. To Carpentier's modern, eighteenth-century inherited concept of history as progressive illumination and progress, Arenas opposes an anti-modernist image of history as a set of repeated hallucinations.[7]

In Puerto Rico, Ramos Otero has not been regarded as a model writer either. Take, for example, the story "La otra isla de Puerto Rico." An old Puerto Rican man in his seventies dies in Athens next to the fourth volume of his memoirs, and notice is sent to his *hacienda* in Arecibo, where his twin sister is also dying the very same day at the very same hour.[8] She was also writing her memoirs, which are nothing less than a history of the island as told from the point of view of the dominating *criollos,* in this case descendants of immigrants from the Canary Islands, the brother and sister Olmo Olmo. There is, however, another story, the one told by the son of a baker from Manatí, who comes to the hacienda and discovers in the library the hidden life of a mulatto woman, Madame Cafole, who turns out to have been the lover and coconspirator of the illustrious ancestor of the twins. She is the family's skeleton in the closet. The son of the baker ends up living in Manhattan, the other island of Puerto Rico, and from there he (or is it sister Olmo Olmo?) attempts to finish the true version of his memoirs. But the reader does not know for sure who really writes "La otra isla de Puerto Rico." Each voice camouflages another one: the twin brother and sister disappear under the mask of the son of the baker from Manatí, a town that is known as the Athens of Puerto Rico, and Manuel Ramos Otero's place of birth. An inside joke thus discloses the true place where the aging criollo writer dies, not in the Athens of Greece, but in the Athens of Puerto Rico. The *hacendado* is evicted from the house of letters, or from the house of history, by the son of the working class. Finally, it becomes increasingly impossible to locate the author of the memoir or the place of the memoir. Therein lies the basic assumption of the story: Puerto Rico can only be conceived as an *otra isla,* ever shifting from the focus of the narrative to the same extent that the subject of the narrative shifts as well. "La otra isla de Puerto Rico" is about the impossibility of assigning ultimate authority for the writing of national memoir, or national memory. But the story can also be read as the perverse manipulation of the son of the baker of Manatí, the Athens of Puerto Rico, who writes from New York, from exile, where an island and an I, or the land of the I, can only be written as the other land, as the land of the other, as the other island of Puerto Rico. For Manuel Ramos Otero, writing about the island becomes indistinguishable from writing about the land of the I. He is the other I land.

José Luis González does not consider this good writing. Exiled, as well, in Mexico for being a declared and active Marxist, González has been an influential figure in the design of the canon of Puerto Rican literature as the privileged site for the disclosure of an inherent, although belated, will to nationhood. Every other dream must be abdicated when the Puerto Rican artist is confronted with the national imperative of self-realization. Therefore, it is not surprising that he deplores Manuel Ramos Otero's artistic project because González finds it dangerously narcissistic. In Arcadio Díaz Quiñones's "Conversación con José Luis González," he says the following when referring to Ramos Otero:

> It is undeniable that Puerto Rican writers are finally exploring the erotic dimension of their reality, with greater freedom than their elders. However, the case of Manuel Ramos Otero seems to me highly objectionable ["bastante discutible"]. I see in him an obviously talented writer who has not yet achieved the necessary artistic distance required for the transformation of experience into literature. (46)

For González, Ramos Otero is not a true writer but a narcissistic sexual demagogue.

A sort of mortifying discomfort becomes central and defining in this type of writer, and one senses that exile here is both forced and voluntary. What drives this type of writing and this type of writer out of the home, which is the literal definition of exile? What home are they dislocating themselves from? What is the role of discomfort as part of the reading experience of these texts? Can there be such a thing as a poetics of discomfort, a kind of writing that is founded not on empathy but on the contrary, and figures itself as radical eviction?[9] What seems apparent is that the very thing that renders these texts ideologically or ethically suspect is what also becomes the enabling mechanism of their rhetorical strategies. Discomfort is assumed and incorporated as a key element of the reading experience. The writer evicted beyond the canonical frontiers of the house of letters in turn evicts the reader, and seems to say, do not come here to tell this moment, stop, thou art so fair.

Exile, be it forced or voluntary, is almost a founding condition for a Latin American or a Caribbean writer, from Sarmiento, Bello, Hostos, and Betances to García Márquez, Roa Bastos, Cortázar, or José Luis González. To a certain extent, the New York of Arenas and Ramos Otero is also the New York of the Latin American writer in exile, and more particularly, the New York of Martí: the transitory shelter from which to envision a nation, or even more, from which to figure a nation.

Although the differences between Martí and our two writers need no excessive explanation, let us entertain the possibility that both Arenas and Ramos Otero are writers in exile under the sign of Martí. After all, it is precisely from afar, from the distance the city imposes and produces, that Martí was able to delineate a poetics of Cuban and American writing. Exile was, in the nineteenth century, the proper space from which to dream the nation, the enforced distance that mobilized desire toward the horizon of that foundational image. Martí invokes a "Nuestra América" from New York, and one feels that the potential crystallization of this longed-for consensus, of this fictional *nosotros* where the *otros* are subsumed by the utopian magnetism of the *nos*, is precisely empowered or fueled by its being uttered in the no-man's-land of urban exile. The acceleration, noise, and illegibility of the city become the negative stimuli against which to envisage the *patria* as the land of stasis, rhythm, and readability. For this kind of writing, displacement is a provisional detour, the eccentric loop back to the center as origin and sense. Exile is a necessary evil, the unsettling and transitory space from which to ground the nation as vision.

In his famous May 1895 letter to Manuel Mercado, Martí makes clear that it was his duty "de impedir a tiempo con la independencia de Cuba que se extiendan por las Antillas los Estados Unidos y caigan, con esa fuerza más, sobre nuestras tierras de América. Cuanto hice hasta hoy, y haré, es para eso. . . . Viví en el monstruo, y le conozco las entrañas:—y mi honda es la de David" [to prevent, by the independence of Cuba, the United States from spreading over the West Indies and falling, with that added weight, upon other lands of our America. All I have done up to now, and shall do hereafter, is to that end. . . . I have lived inside the monster and know its entrails—and my weapon is only the slingshot of David] (*Epistolario* 357). The poet writes from the entrails of the monster. Like Jonah inside the whale, he endures being swallowed up by a monstrous other in order to educate his prophetic voice, the voice that will enable him to say the truth; for example, the truth about the United States, which is the title of one of his articles for the political journal *Patria*. Although in his poetry Martí struggles with the darker aspects of desire and dares to take a look at the turmoil of his heart, the overriding nationalist ethos that controls his public life is also what shapes and structures meaning in his poems. "Envilece, devora, enferma, embriaga / la vida de ciudad: se come el ruido, / como un corcel la yerba, la poesía" (*Poesía mayor* 236). Poetry is the opposite of the city: the neutralizer of the evils of city noise. The city corrupts, devours, sickens, and intoxicates; poetry is the grazing horse that swallows noise; it exists to restore rhyme and meaning in the world. The city is a chaotic desiring machine. Its untamable plurality becomes for Martí a sort of dirty laboratory, or the improbable womb for the pure body of the nation. A nation, yes, is conceived always as an aggregate of different sectors and interests but is made coherent only by the founding power of a common enemy.

Walk on the Wild Side

A hundred years later, at the end of another century, Reinaldo Arenas and Manuel Ramos Otero are the improbable heirs of Martí's dreamed nation, and also of Martí's New York. But these two overtly homosexual writers, for whom writing works to a great extent as an acting up of their sexuality, are also in a radically different place. Their detour is anything but temporary, and the patria they envisage from afar is as disfigured as it is figured. Martí wrote in exile, but from the standpoint of the dreamed home. Mobility was only the necessary condition for the eventual return to the promised fatherland. What gives a book such as *Flores del destierro* its governing tension is the struggle to tame and domesticate desire, to chastise it, and in so doing to make it chaste: "La casta soledad, madre del verso" [chaste solitude, mother of verse], he says at the ending of "La noche es la propicia." For Arenas and Ramos Otero, *la noche* is also "la propicia." Writing occurs to dare night to visit the solitary poet, right before it falls as the mantle of death. Night is the proper time for the *Book of Death*, for the *Invitation to Dust*.[10] But solitude here is far from chaste. The overt sexualization of desire expresses itself as an extreme form of temerity.

If anything, Arenas and Ramos Otero flee from home precisely because the Martían, and in a general sense the modern, idea of the nation as such is too narrowly defined by the governing principle of an imagined community as the homogeneous product of consensus. Such a nation leaves no space for those who do not fit within the prescribed universality of the prevailing rhetoric of unity and harmony. If Martí dreamed in New York of the eventual foundation of the father's house as a place of harmony, it is precisely against that harmony that these two writers envision their exile. They were the *otros* that could not fit and did not want to fit within his *nosotros*.

In *Black Skin, White Masks*, Frantz Fanon says:

> There are close connections between the structure of the family and the structure of the nation. Militarization and the centralization of authority in a country automatically entail a resurgence of the authority of the father. In Europe and in every country characterized as *civilized* or *civilizing*, the family is a miniature of the nation. (141–42)

This kind of gay writing expresses itself through the script of homosexual desire as exile from the nation-family, and in so doing it becomes radically uncivilized; it becomes wild. In much the same way that, for Fanon, the black man is the other of white man's culture—the white man's phallus and the object of his bio-phobia—the gay man, by virtue of the overt sexualization of his desire, also becomes a genitalized pariah, a marked body in exile.

But then exile functions here as a mode of being; it is a way of being ill at ease with the world. The fundamental in-betweenness that Said considers an essential trait of intellectual exile—a trait that is ultimately interior to the condition itself of art and criticism as radical forms of dissidence—is, for the queer, also the condition of provocation and discomfort. Exile is what forever distorts the harmony of the home. In "Domus and the Megalopolis," Lyotard talks about the language of the Domus, the language of the Home, and he says that "Domestic language is rhythmic. There are stories: the generations, the locality, the seasons, wisdom and madness. The story makes beginning and end rhyme, scars over the interruptions" (*The Inhuman* 192).[11] Let us say, following Lyotard, that a writing that foregrounds homosexual desire provokes a kind of interruption that can not be obliterated. It instills a sort of cacophony that cannot be made rhythmic or euphonic. It produces a location that usurps home as locality, and most of all, it inscribes itself against the grain of the notion of generation.

From a classical national perspective, literature has been, as an institution, one of the preferred sites for the nation as home. This becomes clear in the opening verse of Borges's sonnet "Al hijo": "No soy yo quien te engendra. Son los muertos" [I am not the one who engenders you. It's the dead]. The sonnet is about writing and progeny, or the notion of writing as metaphysical insemination, where the writing I is a shadow of the Platonic idea as origin and telos. Home is the place where progeny is secured.

One does not think immediately of Borges when tracing the nationalist lineage of Latin American writing, but he has become, ironically, its most eccentric guardian. Perhaps Latin America today is, above all, a community of nations gathered under the enabling coherence of a shared house of letters. Writers such as Fuentes and Vargas Llosa have become its most prestigious ambassadors, and many believe that these last hundred years since Martí's founding, propitious night of exile are indeed one hundred years of *casta soledad,* of chaste solitude, governed by the ruling madness of a hidden father tied to the firm trunk of an enormous, labyrinthine genealogical tree. Ultimately, Borges's literary library is not qualitatively different from García Márquez's tree in Macondo, because they are both homeward bound. One is at home within the family of successive, echoing generations, whereas the other is at home within the family of successive, echoing metaphors.[12] But writing outside the domus, exiled from the domus, is also writing outside progeny and insemination. It is writing against the ruling authority of domestication. It becomes a kind of productivity without the domestic responsibility of reproductivity, or what Lyotard would call repeated domestication. It is writing outside the preconceived lineage of fathers and sons.

The queer, we must admit, are no easy homecoming queens.[13] They are what Bhabha would refer to as the unhomely, those for whom writing functions as a radical form of *abgrund.* Therefore, their beyond is not the netherland of utopian crystallization, but the frontier of a differentiating limit, the threshold that marks their irreducible liminality. Bhabha talks about "the intervention of the beyond that establishes a boundary: a 'bridge' where presencing begins because it captures something of the estranging sense of the relocation of the home and the world—the unhomeliness—that is the condition of extra territorial and cross cultural initiations" (9). In a way, then, the unhomely Arenas and Ramos Otero are in perpetual exile, and they write from and within exile: New York is only the preferred synecdoche of exodus, and not its utopian grounding. Their writing, more than unhomely, is ultimately homeless: it can envisage home, but it does not want to go back. It might entertain the melancholy nostalgia of return, but mainly as a pose, for it knows beforehand that once out of the closet, there is no turning back.

Camping Out

In a story titled "Ceremonia de bienes y raíces," which can be loosely translated as "Real estate ritual," Ramos Otero describes the passion of a gay couple for empty houses. They moved constantly from place to place for the pleasure, or perhaps for the pain, or briefly inhabiting a new and strange place. Each new moving confronted them with the unwelcome emptiness of the house, which actually felt jealous of their love and wanted to expel them away and far from its virginal white walls. "Because we had a taste for empty houses, we turned our monthly moving into the habit of our lives," the story says. Further on, we read: "We liked the house for its emptiness, for its ever nothing nothingness. Once we covered its feet with the emerald green carpet and softened the noise, the house then attacked us with its vicious temerity. It made us feel like murderers of its small body."

How can one write never to feel at home? How can one possibly write with nothing to write home about? How can we not at least try to turn the empty house into a home and make it love us or want us? For Ramos Otero, the dream of domesticity is illusory, always endangered by the menacing nothingness that is the true habitat of writing in exile, and even more so by the utter irreality of love, that binding pact on which the togetherness of domesticity is supposed to rely: "It must be dawn, because when I open my eyes and now it is no longer night, John is no longer sleeping with me, his body next to mine, one can no longer hear nor feel his presence, he no longer talks or writes next to me in this room. This room where I remain alone, barely waking up, sleepwalking with these legs which attempt a steady step and almost melt under my weight but finally return to me and let me walk in this empty room which is a part of this empty house" (*Cuentos de buena tinta* 119).

What is the ritual of real estate? It seems to be the ritual of repeated foreclosure and eviction of a lonely tenant. It is, in many respects, the ritual of abjection. The abjected is the one who is a castoff from the family of the home and also from the family of the nation. But for someone like Judith Butler, abjection can concomitantly be the site of persecution and liberation insofar as the exclusion effected by the normalizing heterosexual I triggers a process of resignification of the signifier, turning the exile and the unhomeliness of abjection into an adventurous *camping out.* Butler shows that the assumption of a normative heterosexuality relegates homosexuality to the realm of the impossible, or the domain of the imaginary, always rendered illegitimate through the force of the law. One is culturally viable inasmuch as the other one is imaginary and transient (*Bodies* 111). Let us say then that abject homosexual identities happen beyond prescribed impossibility, in the realm of imagination, precisely as the experience of transience itself.

For Bhabha the location of culture is always a relocation: the subject has to reposition itself in order to avoid domestication by homogenizing nationalist, political, or sexual pieties. The postcolonial subject that he is mainly interested in, therefore, is located at the borderline, his or her identity marked by the frontier, by the limit as an unsurpassable site of difference. His or her time is therefore that of the beyond, always escaping the naming of the limit, even so, or perhaps precisely more so when the name giver (the self-appointed baptizer/interpreter) claims to have the authority of naming difference as the Other, an Other that enables a sort of Western deconstructive comfort. Bhabha is suspicious of an all too easy eccentricity for the Other that denies it its power to signify and turns it into the West's docile body of difference.

It is out of this contention that I would like to speak of an *unmanageable* body of difference in Arenas and Ramos Otero. In my view, subjects are positioned in this type of writing through a series of *dislocations,* rather than relocations, of culture. A dislocated body of difference is violently relocated, a fractured body, a body made up of different types of body parts, some of them pertaining to the body politic and some of them pertaining to the body sexual. In Arenas the primal scenario of homo-erotic negotiation cannot be neatly separated from the equally primal scenario of the Cuban Revolution. Notions such as passivity and activity, role playing, and the body language of the hard binary oppositions that articulate sexual performance as the drama of the penetrator and the penetrated cannot be divorced from the central theatrical antagonism of Arenas and Fidel. It is Fidel whom Arenas in his memoir holds responsible for his death, and it is against Fidel that Arenas commits suicide, in much the same way a desperate lover reacts to the indifference of the supreme object of desire, with death as the ultimate gesture of difference. It is, ironically, for Fidel that Arenas saves his last and highest fidelity.

It is equally impossible to disregard the colonial reality of contempo-rary life in Puerto Rico, and that particular subaltern experience when we face the extreme positionality of sexual activity that we find in Ramos Otero. "Do it to be the way I tell you or don't do it at all," the masochist narrator tells the sadist in Ramos Otero's story "The Exemplary Life of the Slave and the Master" (*Cuentos de buena tinta* 175). The notion of the reversibility of power and its vectorial, de-centered economy, a notion so actively at work in this story, reflects as much the body as the country and their intersecting laws of desire. That is why it is impossible to read either author entirely in terms of the politics of queer performativity or, con-versely, in terms of the politics of antitotalitarianism or anticolonialism.

These margins converge and dissect each other, producing an aggregate of dissonant contestations.

What is dislocated difference? It is a difference that refuses to comfort the reader, a difference that insists in its irresoluteness. The writer in perpetual exile, the writer as abject, thrives in discomfort. One can read these texts only as dislocated bodies, and I mean the term in its physical, medical sense of fracture of the bones. The cast-off body is a broken, suffering body, humiliated precisely as body. There is a comic and horrifying moment in Arenas's memoir that captures the drama of abjection. One of Arenas's friends, in the darkness of a theater, thinks that he is being touched and caressed by an anonymous lover but is really being smeared with shit:

> It was an incredible scene to watch; a queer full of shit from head to toe, right on Prado Boulevard, in the midst of the Carnival and surrounded by thousands of people. Actually, he had no trouble making his way through the crowd; the stench coming from him was so bad that as he ran, a breach opened up to make way for him. He got to the Malecón and plunged, fully clothed, into the Ocean. (*Before Night Falls* 96)

The dislocated body is the body that runs in the midst of the Carnival along Prado Boulevard; it is the body that runs to the ocean, and the stench coming from it does not ever seem to go away. For Arenas, writing as dislocation takes the form of constant "peregrination": a moving away from any form of authority, not only the patriarchal authority of dictatorial totalitarianism but also the marginal authority of "correct" homosexual democratization. The reader of Arenas is, as it were, assaulted by his insistent bodily smell. Discomfort is the response to an assault. The abject I takes the reader hostage and forces an encounter face-to-face.

In *The Assault*, perhaps Arenas's most horrifying novel, about a character who searches for his mother in order to kill her only to find out that she is none other than the Totalitarian Dictator himself or herself, the *Reprimerísimo*, or the Represident, the notion of domus becomes a nightmare of hyper-normative enforced togetherness. The government, presented as a nightmarish dystopia of absolute control, has created the concept of the *multifamilias*, a place where everybody lives and eats and works and copulates in the same room. The domus becomes the prison of harmony, the hell of enforced rhyme. By killing the phallic couple embodied in the mother as *Reprimerísimo,* Arenas enacts the fantasy of overcoming the source of his abjection, the possibility of killing the ambiguous objects of desire who simultaneously lure him into the house and cast him off from it.

If for Ramos Otero the house is still a potential dwelling place, for Arenas living and writing occur outside, in the heart of darkness of Lenin Park before night falls. Lenin Park, a large, woodsy park on the outskirts of Havana, became Arenas's hiding place, one of his favorite hunting grounds for sexual cruising, and also his office, where he wrote many of his texts. The park is a primal scene. The state may claim to name it Lenin and digest it within its ideological project, but Reinaldo lives to preserve the park's sacred wilderness and its radical alterity as the site of nature and imagination. The park is the living quarter of the writer in exile, the insisting nature to the state's culture.

Homeless peregrination becomes in Arenas the sign of abjection as radical exile, and in Ramos Otero hyperbolic narcissism becomes a dislocating, destabilizing counterauthority. "I am god," the narrator says in "Hollywood Memorabilia," and he goes on to say, "And I will invent a character whose name will be Angel. His name will be John. His name will be Paul" (*Cuentos de buena tinta* 95). In Ramos Otero there are practically no characters beyond the all-consuming and proliferating central subjectivity that turns the writing experience into a repeated spectacle of confession, disclosure of secrecy, and exhibition of eccentricity. This is writing as radical attitude. Yes, the dislocated, homeless body of the abjected one in exile has attitude. Attitude is the abjected one's way to appropriate and perform the script of the outsider. A subject whose claim to existence has been so radically put into question by the double abjection of colonialism and homosexuality, which is the case of Ramos Otero, finds in erotic and promiscuous solipsism a disquieting and provocative site of utterance.

The final question is, of course, the question about the privileging of a subject-position that is so precisely empowered through its unquestioned foregrounding. The "outside" of abjection, which in turn becomes the ground for an aggressive sexual heroism, eventually becomes a domesticated outside, the site of an ideologically hardened "real." It is undeniable that there is a kind of activism in this sort of radical sexual performance that eventually becomes the blind site for the truth of the subject. The narrating I of "Hollywood Memorabilia" is, of course, not Ramos Otero. Neither is Arenas Fray Servando, nor even the I of his memoir. But these are poetics of the self from which a certain kind of writing is enabled, the writing that reappropriates and performs the "literary" exile of the abject. And here we arrive at a problematic impasse: To what extent is this dislocated I put into question? How empty is the self as master evictor? How truly radical is the project of exile? Does it include the possibility of exile from exile?

It does not. Exile is an improbable, solitary, but nevertheless secure, home, one that is ultimately safe within its protective outside. The writing that evicts does not evict itself. It is self-righteously alone, heroically alone. Lovers and enemies come and go in these stories, and what remains is the repeated strategy of a solitary hunter. But for that hunter, it is true; the forest becomes a nest. Butler has very high moral stakes for the queer positioning of subjects in the world when she warns her reader:

It is one of the ambivalent implications of the decentering of the subject to have one's writing be the site of a necessary and inevitable expropriation. But this yielding of ownership over what one writes has an important set of political corollaries, for the taking up, reforming of one's words does open up a difficult future terrain of community, one in which the hope of ever fully recognizing oneself in the terms by which one signifies is sure to be disappointed. (*Bodies* 242)

But writing in Arenas and Ramos Otero is not community oriented. They never yield ownership of their abjected selves, especially once they become reconstituted through the performance of reverse eviction. In a way, the avant-garde heroism of the writing that produces these fractured selves forbids that sort of generosity. That ultimate expropriation of the last center, the improbable center of the margin as focus, does not happen. But perhaps heroes, like saints and martyrs, are meant to be alone, staring at us from the distance of their attitude, with the empty, nonreflective stare of a wild animal. That is their beyond, the shrine at the end of their peregrination: the unquestioned placing of their dislocated selves. This blind outside constitutes the field of authority of this type of writing, its enabling condition. Instead of providing a hermeneutics for its indocility, the one that could turn this unruly, wild self into a properly distanced

Other, it insists in camping out, and in staring at us, with the blank stare that promises only the allure of discomfort.

Notes

1   The allusion here is to a 1976 collection of short stories by Magaly García Ramis, *La familia de todos nosotros*. Ramos Otero, together with García Ramis, Ana Lydia Vega, Rosario Ferré, and Edgardo Sanabria Santaliz, among others, belongs to a group of writers who started publishing in the seventies from a radically urban perspective, questioning a series of deep-rooted national pieties, such as the family, the home, the *"casa de estudios"* (a name given to the University of Puerto Rico by chancellor Jaime Benítez), and a series of metaphors of national unity conceived as an unproblematic, unifying domesticity. For an insightful interpretation of this metaphor, see Rodríguez Castro.

2   For a bibliography of articles and critical essays about Arenas, see Ette.

3   Ramos Otero's writing is not a manifesto of a dissenting position, but it is, however, political: "My generation is the result of our disillusionment and the debacle of the Puerto Rican Commonwealth, a result of mass migration to the United States, of exile as a way out of the prison house of colonialism, it is a result of the civil rights movement of the sixties and of its struggle against the dated values of fake democracy and capitalism. Migration and the creation of a newly discovered and somewhat schizophrenic urban culture dismantles institutions such as family, church and feudalism." This is taken from an interview with Jan Martínez. This and all subsequent translations are mine. For a comprehensive and illuminating reading of the place of the city and of exile in Ramos Otero, see Gelpí, "La escritura transeúnte de Manuel Ramos Otero."

4   For a Lacanian reading of the place of the name in Arenas, see Bradley Epps's excellent article "Proper Conduct: Reinaldo Arenas, Fidel Castro, and the Politics of Homosexuality."

5   Vega's contagious sense of humor barely hides the dominant anxiety of self-censorship, which is truly a censorship of the place of the self in nation-forming writing: "From Manuel Alonso on, passing through the generations of the forties and the fifties and continuing on to the seventies, our literature—and I say this without any intention to belittle its quality—is constituted as a variation of the same, obsessive theme: the symphony of national identity, with its two melodic lines of anti-imperialism on the one hand and class struggle on the other" (85).

6   For this article, I am using Andrew Hurley's translation for the Penguin edition of 1987. The novel was originally published in Mexico in 1966 with the title *El mundo alucinante*. In the previous English translation of 1971, the title is rendered as *Hallucinations*.

7   See Barrientos. Also see Ette, "La obra de Reinaldo Arenas: una visión de conjunto" in *Escritura de la memoria*.

8   The story appears in *Página en blanco y staccato*.

9   The issue here is, of course, ethical. In Ramos Otero's story from *Página en blanco y staccato* titled "La heredera" (The heiress), the epigraph from Lawrence Durrell's *Justine* is quite telling: "I suppose that we writers are cruel people." Among other things, "La heredera" is an act of vengeance against another writer, Rosario Ferré (formerly a close friend of the author and the cofounder of a magazine where Ramos Otero collaborated, *Zona de carga y descarga*, which is mentioned in the story under the name *Puerto*), thinly disguised as the character Socorro Averasturi. The character, who wants to become a writer and writes admiring letters to an author named Manuel, is a parody of a bourgeois woman trying to find herself through literature. What renders Socorro's literary quest ultimately illegitimate is that the narrative voice does not trust her. Cruelty here is invoked as a sort of privilege of "true" literature. By parodying Socorro's literary vocation, the story claims to steal away from her a superior, more literary space and a kind of legitimacy that transcends her quest for authenticity. Vengeance here is aimed ultimately against the class she represents, a Puerto Rican bourgeoisie (Ferré, a renowned writer, also happens to be the daughter of a former governor, like Socorro) that has performed for too long an emblematic, ennobling literary destiny that needs to be revoked by a different and contrary project, embodied in Ramos Otero's writing. Arenas also enacts equally disturbing evictions, particularly in his memoir. The quest for homosexual pleasure is often achieved at the expense of meaningful relationships. Oftentimes lovers become shadows for a predatorial sort of conquest that blurs, diminishes, and ultimately trivializes anything other than an overwhelming, self-feeding compulsion. Blacks are stereotypically genitalized, and women are either suspicious witches, perverse phallic mothers, or simply invisible next to an all-consuming sexual quest. What is the ethical standpoint of this kind of writing? Solipsism can at times acquire the semblance of the inhuman. But perhaps the inhuman here is a cruel strategy of demolition, if one thinks that the edifice of literature, of art and its relation to the state, is founded to such a great extent on the morality of abnegation, and the disappearance of the I for the sake of the common good. Queer here becomes a poetics for the suspi-

cion of the authenticity of the idea of a common good. Queer here foregrounds the literary as the production of a disquieting and disturbing self.

10   Death wish, along with its traditional nocturnal invocation, becomes a central theme for Ramos Otero. In *El libro de la muerte,* his first book of poems, death is seen as the enabling limit of the monumental. Burials, graves, and cemeteries become triumphant theaters for the spectacle of death and decay. A series of elegies to dead homosexual poets is also imbued with this triumphant tone, as if that most scandalous of limits—death—were the appropriate edge from which to assess the radical otherness of their desire. In *Invitación al polvo,* his last book (a posthumous collection of stories, *Cuentos de buena tinta,* appeared a year after his death from an AIDS-related disease), death becomes the beyond of sexuality. Like the Bataille of *L'erotisme,* and more specifically like the Quevedo of Baroque stoicism, Ramos Otero equates the *polvo* (dust) of death with the *polvo* (seed) of sex.

11   For Lyotard a certain restoration of the avant-garde is needed if art is to function as a radical way of being in the world. The possibility that artistic endeavors are not founded on docile acts of communication is precisely what keeps them from being systematically "humanized." Quoting Apollinaire, Lyotard says that artists are people who want to become inhuman. The book is a diatribe against the pedagogies of humanism, particularly against the way education functions as the domestication of the child. Art is wild, uncivilized, from this point of view. It is childish, it gives in to desire, and it insists on inhabiting or performing the nature of culture. One could read Arenas and Ramos Otero as writers of interruption, in this sense, where a certain restoration of an avant-garde indocility is at stake. Such a rhetoric is, in both cases, articulated against a normative realism (social realism or enlightened modernism in Arenas, and programmatic nationalism in Ramos Otero) that reduces the literary within the framework of pedagogy. Sexuality would function here as the agent of interruption, the marker of difference. This would imply a foregrounding of the sexual, to the point where it is reified as the outside of norm, as the real of an oppressive symbolic. Sexuality then becomes the wild real of exile.

12   The "Nota de agradecimientos" at the end of García Márquez's *El general en su laberinto* is a telling sign of this project of legitimation. The author thanks everybody who helped him "unearth" the figure of Bolívar from the grave of oblivion, facile allegorization, and political piety. The list encompasses a veritable army of writers, critics, and well-intentioned readers all over Latin America, including Paris, perhaps the project's founding ur-city. The irony is that the novel is very much an elegy for Bolívar's dream of continental unity, shattered by rivalry and a repeated history of inevitable fragmentations. The

only contemporary agents of coherence echoing Bolívar's dream are pathetically parodic: the drug culture and the respective national debts to North American banks. And then there is Literature. It is the old *querelle* of arms versus letters, and if Bolívar was the failed soldier, then García Márquez might just be the successful writer, the carrier of the torch. In the English translation of *The Ill-Fated Peregrinations,* Arenas laughs at some critics who found an influence of *One Hundred Years of Solitude* in his book. His book was, of course, published earlier. But more important is that Arenas's novel is in so many ways the opposite of Macondo's allegory. For him history is antigenerational and antichronological. It is closer to José Lezama Lima's notion of *eras imaginarias:* a series of poetic collisions or imagistic intoxications, intonations of the avant-garde understanding of *poesis* as the agency of imagination.

13   The term *queer* itself is most useful when deployed from within its radical instability. Judith Butler says: "If the term 'queer' is to be a site of collective contestation, the point of departure for a set of historical reflections and futural imaginings, it will have to remain that which is, in the present, never fully owned, but always and only redeployed, twisted, queered from a prior usage and in the direction of urgent and expanding political purposes" (*Bodies* 228).

III

~

QUEERS

AND/IN

PERFORMANCE

The Swishing of Gender:

Homographetic Marks in *Lazarillo de Tormes*

~

B. Sifuentes Jáuregui

In the function of speech, we are concerned with the *Other.*—Jacques Lacan, *The Seminar of Jacques Lacan II*

I was dreaming, then of a bull's horn. I found it hard to resign myself to being nothing more than a *littérateur.* The matador who transforms danger into an occasion to be more brilliant than ever and reveals the whole quality of his style just when he is most threatened: that is what enthralled me, that is what I wanted to be.—Michel Leiris, "The Autobiographer as *Torero*"

Lazarillo de Tormes is, perhaps, too familiar. Its familiarity lies not only in the fact that all Hispanists must inevitably read the text and that it has been placed, whether consciously or unconsciously, at the origin of the novel, but the text's "familiarity" might be located also in the author-protagonist's very obsession with representing and maintaining the integrity of the family romance. This double articulation of the "familiar" (if you like, the question of genealogy) presents us with a complicated situation: On the one hand, because of Hispanists' familiarity with this masterpiece, we often ask ourselves if there is anything new that can be said about the *Lazarillo*—there are so many evaluations and reconstructions of the text that they provoke an anxiety about speaking; it is difficult to be original with respect to this small text. On the other hand, does the narrator's, Lázaro's, imposition of, and desire for, the perfect family restrict the kinds of readings that have been made about the text? By suspending—if only momentarily—the different, more known readings of the life of the rogue,

I hope to bring out something new in rereading (or queering) this classic.[1] I may not be able to reveal the author's name, but we may get closer to understanding why he hides it. This essay seeks to plot out and hint at some directions for my work on issues regarding the structuration of masculinity and its relation to trauma in narrative. I am interested in developing a theoretical apparatus for understanding Spanish and Spanish-American literature, through a theory of the novel that focuses on sexualities, psychoanalysis, and performativity.

The Case

The *Lazarillo* involves the famous "case" wherein he defends himself against accusations of his and his wife's affair with the Arçipreste (a ménage à trois) and tries to explain the misadventures that educated him and led to his relative success. From the very beginning, the text is setup as an exculpation; indeed, as Albert Sicroff has suggested, it is an explanation given by Lazarillo to uncover that which motivates sixteenth-century men's actions: their desire for honor and fame. It is also a text in which— following again Sicroff—"Lázaro habrá de reclamar sus derechos ('por que se tenga entera noticia de mi persona') [mediante] esta nonada, en que este grossero estilo escriuo" [Lázaro will reclaim his rights ("so that you have entire notice of my persona") [through] this throwaway [*nonada*], which I write in this vulgar style] (159).[2] I find this explanation fairly straightforward. An interesting element that the critic seems to overlook— actually, in the way he articulates Lazarillo's claims—would be how self-conscious the boy really is: "en . . . este grossero estilo escriuo" illustrates that Lazarillo is writing as someone else, that he is using a language that is not his own.[3] "Esta nonada," this throwaway statement that Lazarillo calls his text, is an erasure, not only of the author but of language or of any system of signs used in self-representation. "Esta nonada" aims in a double direction: the effacement of the author and the destabilizing of language. In effect, "esta nonada" presents a radical and original form of writing and self-figuration. The boy's self-imposed style further signifies on the critic's reading; notice that Sicroff doesn't change the subject in his quoting of Lázaro: "este grossero estilo *escriuo*" (italics mine). It is taken for granted among critics that the signature of picaresque discourse would be its autobiographical voice; the *Lazarillo* introduces an awareness of a *grossero estilo*, which calls into question any pretense of autobiography, insofar as the subject being represented is a studied version of the subject, a studied performance with the intent to "clean up" any defamation of character.

Any approach that seeks to categorize this text in a particular genre would be destined to fail: the inscription of a self-consciousness, self-effacement, and play in language itself makes it terribly difficult to grasp the polysemic—almost deconstructive—nature of the picaresque. Any exercise of textual framing must account for the excess that it cannot capture. The most convincing and boldest theoretical interpretation (with respect to its far-reaching consequences) that has taken advantage of this framing has been put forth in general terms by Roberto González Echevarría; he notes that

> the novel, having no fixed form of its own, assumes that of a given document endowed with truth bearing power by society at specific moments in time. The novel, or what is called the novel at various points in history, mimics such documents to show their conventionality, their subjection to rules of textual engenderment similar to those governing literature, which in turn reflect those of language itself. It is through this simulacrum of legitimacy that the novel makes its contradictory and veiled claim to literariness. (*Myth and Archive* 8)

González Echevarría specifically comments on how the picaresque and its relation to notorial legal arts (*relaciones*)[4] display quite literally this act of mimicry and enact the paradigm; then he adds that this project of textual and discursive mimesis, which is reproduced time and time again and gets collected in a kind of narratological unconscious that he calls the Archive, is at the heart of the literary creation in Latin America.[5] Although the framing (read: "disciplining") of the text is felicitous in this instance, we must ask ourselves the degree to which the textual framing of the legal "case" impedes our reading of the text. I am not dismissing the legal aspect of the *Lazarillo*, but I would like to broaden the notion of "case" into the realm of psychoanalysis. I insist on this because I am not fully convinced that a mimetic act is as powerful in revealing the legal text's ordinariness as the critic would claim. As a matter of fact, mimetic acts are not always subversive but rather contribute to the myth of originality or the ordinary through assimilation—I welcome any political dimension in reading this.

A vulgar, though efficient, counterexample to comprehending mimesis as an effective manner to reveal another's conventionality is embodied in the "wanna-be." Already Lazarillo's mother had pronounced this function of mimicry when she determined "arrimarse a los buenos, por ser uno dellos" [to get close to good people, in order to be one of them] (15). Lazarillo could be described as a wanna-be; more precisely, the self-consciousness that hovers throughout his text would only show that he *wants to be* a wanna-be; he is usurping the role of the usurper, performing a performance.[6] Giving another turn of the screw to Lázaro's mother's statement, "arrimarse a los buenos" can be literalized: *arrimarse* means more than coming close to others, but also *arrimar*, to ventriloquize, to rhyme, to speak the language of the Other. This Lacanian imperative *avant la lettre* heightens again the complexity of language in the *Lazarillo*.

I agree that the *Lazarillo* is subversive, that it takes on the master narrative of the law and denaturalizes and shows its literary rank and foibles. What is it, then, that destabilizes the status of the law? How?

One of the first shifts that I would like to perform in reading otherwise the famous "case" involves rethinking the structural relation between literature and the law. Another way to reread González Echevarría's intervention would be to understand the novel—here the *Lazarillo* specifically—as a textual performative; that is to say, on an intertextual level, the text performs as another document, consequently using the prestige that may be found therein as a means of self-authorizing yet fully subverting the "original" text's discursive pretension. My departure from his theory happens in replacing the mimetic act with a theory of performativity.[7] Judith Butler says that

> [p]erformativity is . . . not a singular "act," for it is always a reiteration of a norm or set of norms, and to the extent that it acquires an act-like status in the present, it conceals or dissimulates the conventions of which it is a repetition. (*Gender Trouble* 12)

Performativity is not an incessant mimicry or enactment of a pose, not an obsessive compulsion gone astray. Rather, performativity is a display or repetition of the conceptualization and construction of the event. It is this performative process that reveals the discursive contours and slips of the law (as an unprecedented, primal utterance) that permits the picaresque

to become subversive; this happens, as Butler notes, when "a kind of cita-
tionality, the acquisition of being through the citing of power, a citing . . .
establishes an originary complicity with power in the formation of the
'I.'" The citing of power is not done without the deliberate awareness that
the law has already constructed the subject that speaks,[8] and that

> [p]erformativity describes [a] relation of being implicated in that
> which one opposes, this turning of power against itself to produce
> alternative modalities of power, to establish a kind of political contesta-
> tion that is not a "pure" opposition, a "transcendence" of contempo-
> rary relations of power, but a difficult labor of forging a future from
> resources inevitably impure. (241)

So when I say that the picaresque text *performs* as another document, I am
highlighting the process by which the text hinges on a specific, (hidden)
structure or epistemology that gives the "original" text its facticity and
authority.

Now, however appealing I may find this re-presentation of González
Echevarría's theory of the novel, theories of performativity have seldom or
never been assigned to *grands récits* but have been used to explain the
interrelation between language and subjectivity—the formation of the
"I"—specifically questions of gender and sexualities. The superimposition
and comparison of the mimesis of the Archive and theories of performativity is an uneasy one. Assigning the notion of performativity to entire
texts is rather problematic insofar as the *specific* means of self-figuration or
the constructions of subjectivity—intellectual, sexual, or national—get
lost or, at least, displaced. I do not want to say that performativity is not
present in the *Lazarillo*, but rather that there is a strategic locality involved
in articulating the different instances of performance.

Along these lines, a special criticism that I have of González Echevarría's conceptualization of the novel is his lack of attention to the question
of subjectivity, especially sexuality in picaresque texts. The *Lazarillo* or
Quevedo's *Buscón* or, more recently, Luis Zapata's *Adonis García* contains a
strong presence of sexual desire—at times, violent in its affirmation or
repression. It was precisely the "sexual" element found in the picaresque
that interrupted, if not overhauled, the formulaic nature of the *relación* on
which it is based. What happened later to the discussion of sexuality in

writing a "theory of the narrative" that is founded in a reading of the picaresque?

If I have gone on too long with this question, it is because I would like to recontextualize the *Lazarillo*, not only as a *relación*, but also as a "case history." I imagine that some sexual underpinnings of the text are what give it its subversive power. It may seem rather uncanny to read the *Lazarillo* as a case history: nonetheless, I feel that in the text there emerges the voice of the patient and the silence of the analyst:

> Y pues Vuestra Merced escribe se le escriba y relate el caso muy por estenso, parescióme no tomalle por el medio, sino del principio, porque se tenga entera noticia de mi persona. (10–11)

> [And since Your Lordship writes that I write to you and relate the case very extensively, I thought I should not begin in the middle of things, but from the beginning so that you would have entire notice of my person.]

The "*caso*" that goes back to the beginning is a case history; it is *within* the confines of this special "case" that I hope to discuss some of the sexual performances and their significance that have been lost. Again, I would like to insist that what I am trying to do here is simply to release the text from the legal underpinnings that have been previously suggested and examine it in other contexts.

Trauma

The *Lazarillo* is the story of an abandoned child. His mother, unable to care for him, accepts the offer of a blind man who wants the child to join him and serve as his guide. Thus begins the boy's odyssey and education, thanks to the kindness of strangers—to use John Boswell's term. We quickly learn that the blind man is not kind at all but rather constantly beats and starves the boy. A horrible moment where we see the old man's treatment of Lázaro happens when the boy takes to drinking and devises a plan to drink the man's wine. He punctures a tiny hole in the jug and sucks what seeps out; afterward, he covers his hole with a piece of wax.[9] How-

ever, Lazarillo's good fortune does not last long because the old man finds
the hole and decides to punish the boy:

> Y luego otra día, teniendo yo rezumando mi jarro como solía, no pen-
> sando el daño que me estaba aparejado ni que el mal ciego me sentía,
> sentéme como solía [entre las piernas del ciego]; estando recibiendo
> aquellos dulces tragos, mi cara puesta hacia el cielo, un poco cerrados
> los ojos por mejor gustar el sabroso licuor, sintió el desesperado ciego
> que agora tenía tiempo de tomar de mi venganza, y con toda su fuerza,
> alzando con dos manos aquel dulce y amargo jarro, le dejó caer sobre mi
> boca, ayudándose, como digo, con todo su poder, de manera que el
> pobre Lázaro, que de nada desto se guardaba, antes, como otras veces,
> estaba descuidado y gozoso, verdaderamente me pareció que el cielo,
> con todo lo que en él hay, me había caído encima. (32–33)

> [And then another day, having gone back to my jug as I used to do, not
> thinking about the harm that was waiting for me nor that the blind
> man could sense me, I sat myself as I used to [between the legs of the old
> man]; while receiving those sweet gulps, my face facing the sky, my eyes
> half-closed so that I might enjoy better the tasty liquor, the desperate
> blind man felt that he now had an opportunity to take revenge against
> me, and with all his might, raising with both hands that sweet and
> bitter jug, he let it fall on my mouth, helping himself, as I say, with all
> his strength, in such a manner that the poor Lázaro, who did not expect
> any of this, rather, like other times, was carefree and joyful, truly it
> seemed to me that the heavens, with everything that is in them, had
> fallen on top of me.]

I would like to suggest that this particular scene represents an event of
trauma—in the broadest sense of the word. The trauma takes place on at
least three separate levels: First, the obvious manifestation is the physical
breaking of the jug on the face (of course, the cutting of the face); Lazarillo
adds that "[f]ue tal el golpecillo, que me desatinó y sacó de sentido, y el
jarrazo tan grande, que los pedazos dél se me metieron por la cara, rom-
piéndomela por muchas partes" [the little blow was such that it shook me
up and made me lose my senses, and the "jugging" was so great, that pieces

of it cut through my face, breaking it throughout] (33). Pieces of the jug actually become encrusted on the body of the boy. Second, the trauma happens on a grammatical and syntactical level in the text: after the blow, Lazarillo's narrative is broken: "[T]he poor Lázaro, who did not expect any of this, rather, like other times, was carefree and joyful, truly it seemed to me that the heavens, with everything that is in them, had fallen on top of me." The commas in this passage are like pieces of the jug encrusted in the text. The narrative suffers or performs the trauma caused to the boy. I should be explicit here that the process of narrative or textual performative occurs at this juncture as a linguistic crisis; that is, language and speech are broken. Third, the subject "I" becomes split or traumatized and becomes "el pobre Lázaro"; he loses his sense of self ("shook me up and made me lose my senses"). Thus, if we are to understand the picaresque, even at its etymological level, "*picar,*" a puncture, a cut, we must also translate the picaresque as a "trauma." These different valences of trauma disrupt not only the integrity of the subject but also language.[10]

At this specific moment in the *Lazarillo,* we see how the text suffers the fortune of the subject. How both text and subject function in sync could be explained by the problematics of autobiography, which de Man explains as "not a genre or a mode, but a figure of reading or of understanding that occurs, to some degree, in all texts" (70). Autobiography is a *figure* of reading that requires the *splitting* of the subject to read itself. The textual representation of the trauma mirrors quite literally, then, that autobiographical moment as a *figure of reading.* The subject reads/writes himself; in so doing, he may even illustrate or perform those moments of trauma as textual inscriptions or grapheses. What is also significant about this beating is that it is the second time that the blind man mistreats the boy so violently—the first time beating his head against a stone bull. What I find so important is that this repetition signals the unmistakably masochistic fantasy of "a child is being beaten."[11] Paradoxically, the beatings of Lazarillo are a spectacle or fantasy of masculinity, insofar as masculinity is here set up as containment and valor, the embodiment of the notion of "*aguantarse,*" as I have shown elsewhere.[12] This spectacle to some degree reminds us of Leiris's *torero:* "I found it hard to resign myself to being nothing more than a *littérateur.* The matador who transforms danger into an occasion to be more brilliant than ever and reveals the whole quality of his style just when he is most threatened" (155). What the *Lazarillo* shows us is that the citing of the legal *relación* offers the anonymous author the possibility of rehearsing other subjectivities, his masculinity for example.

What other inscriptions are contained in the text that mark or call attention to the autobiographical process of reading, of subject formation?

Homographesis or Unmarked Trauma

There are many such textual inscriptions that would capture that "brilliant . . . style" of masculinity in the *Lazarillo,* inscriptions that illustrate how the boy conceptualizes himself and the world around him. One of the most fascinating moments in the text is the fourth *tractado,* in which our hero meets the Mercedarian friar. As opposed to the earlier chapters, in which the narrator goes to extreme pains to explain beatings, cheating practices, and other things his masters did, here he barely says anything. Why silence? Why this gap in reading? What is performed by this silence?

I cite it in its entirety:

> *Cómo Lázaro se asentó con un fraile de la Merced, y de lo que le acaesció con él*
> Hube de buscar el cuarto, y éste fue el fraile de la Merced, que las mujercillas que digo me encaminaron, al cual ellas le llamaban pariente. Gran enemigo del coro y de comer en el convento, perdido por andar fuera, amicísimo de negocios seglares y visitar: tanto, que pienso que rompía él más zapatos que todo el convento. Éste me dio los primeros zapatos que rompí en mi vida; pero no me duraron ocho días, ni yo pude con su trote durar más. Y por esto y por otras cosillas que no digo, salí dél. (110–11)

> [*How Lazarillo met the Mercedarian friar, and of what happened with him*
> I was to find the fourth [master], and this was the Mercedarian friar, whom those little women that I mention led me to, [and] whom they called family. A great enemy of the daily routine and of eating in the convent, crazy to walk around outside, a great friend of secular affairs and of visiting: so much so, that I believe that he broke more shoes than the entire convent. He gave me the first pair of shoes that I ever broke in my life; but they didn't last me eight days, nor could I keep up with this

meandering [*trote*] anymore. And because of this and other little things that I don't say, I left him.]

Reading the question of homosexuality in(to) this chapter is nothing new. Bataillon appears to be the first to suggest that the phrase "[y] por esto y por otras cosillas que no digo" "pourrait laisser supposer le pire quant aux relations de ce maître avec le jeune garçon" [allows us to imagine the worst regarding the master's relation with the young boy] (55). In 1968 Márquez Villanueva, following Bataillon's lead, thought that these "cosillas" "alud[en] *a lo peor,* a pecados nefandos" [allude *to the very worst,* to nefarious sins] (79; emphasis mine); that same year, Molho wrote that the "cosillas" was something that "semble pedérastrie" [looks like pederasty] (xxix)—this being the most explicit reading of a possible homosexuality in the fourth tractado. It was not until 1978 that Sieber finally used the word: "The secret crime to which Lázaro refers—the friar's homosexuality— remains at the level of implicit communication, permitting only an interpretation based on insinuation and its effects" (58). Sieber's fine reading of the sexual connotations of the shoes, a signifier of sexuality, allows him to read the homosexual question. The earlier *tentative* discussions of the possibility of a homosexual presence remind us that homosexuality presents us with the problem of naming the body. This problem is articulated as a negation: *peccatum illud horribile, inter christianos non nominandum.*[13] Or, "otras cosillas que no digo." More recently, Thompson and Walsh have found confirmation that proves almost without a doubt that the friar was, indeed, engaging in sodomite practices. Citing from the trials of the Inquisition—"varios mercedarios del convento de la Merced de Valencia, que evidentemente se convirtió en una guarida de sodomitas, etc." [several Mercedarians from the convent of the Merced of Valencia, which has evidently turned into a den of sodomites, etc.] (444)—as well as looking at a joke-proverb from the period—"[c]uando vieres a un fraile de la Merced, / arrima tu culo a la pared" [when you see a Mercedarian friar, bring your ass to a wall]—that suggests the proclivities of the Mercedarian friars, Thompson and Walsh show different examples of the stereotypical perception of the Mercedarian's sexual desire or perversions. I believe that there is another place of evidence that sexualizes the friar: his endless meandering, his *trote.* In Covarrubias, "*Trotar* las mujeres es andar de priesa divagando por todas partes del lugar" [*Trotar* for women is going around quickly walking aimlessly throughout some place]. *Trotar* is thus referred to as a feminine act; by referring to the friar's *trote,* Lazarillo is indeed feminizing the friar, marking the friar's body as a woman's, a homosexual. Given all of these examples that point to the homosexuality of the friar, it is almost laughable to see how Rico protests that "casi toda la crítica ha querido ver aquí la alusión eufemística a unas relaciones nefandas entre el mozo y el fraile. En la vida de Lázaro, sin embargo, no hay el menor indicio para suponer tal escabrosidad, y del fraile se dice que es amigo de las 'mujercillas' " [almost all critics have wanted to see here a euphemistic allusion to nefarious relations between the boy and the friar. In the life of Lázaro, however, there isn't the slightest sign to suppose such an awful thing, and about the friar, it is said that he is a friend of 'little women' "] (*Lazarillo,* introduction 112, n. 9). What Rico overlooks is that these "little women" call the friar "pariente," family. This would seem to suggest that Lazarillo is conjuring up a new form of domesticity. Rico protests so much as to want to discipline (that is, normalize) the text; he wants to maintain the narrative within the traditional, familiar narrative— or what Michael Warner calls repro-sexuality and repro-narrativity. All the while that the Spanish critic seeks to correct the text's family lineages by imposing a repro-narrative, he loses sight of the more complex family romances that Lazarillo is constructing, almost as if to make his own triangle at the end seem more amenable, less threatening to the status quo. If anything, what this reference to family and domesticity of the friar and his little women does is signify on the perversion of the family by the very bodies (the church, in this instance) that purport to protect it.

Warner states that "[r]eprosexuality involves more than reproducing, more than compulsive heterosexuality; it involves a relation to self that finds its proper temporality and fulfillment in generational transmission" (9). In using the term *repro-narrativity,* I want to underline the normalizing discourse that accompanies the pretension of compulsive heterosexuality: to wit, I am talking about the expectations and, indeed, the assurance of happiness and narrative closure that "marriage" brings. Repro-narrativity is the graphetic inscription of heterosexuality in the *Lazarillo.* The other face of the coin—which is to say, the silence of the homosexual—is not an easily readable inscription, but rather a repression or "closeting" or an "untold story"—a term introduced by Mary Gossy. If an assumption of sexuality as "hetero-normal" can be manifestly expressed by repro-narrativity (*not* an innocent assumption, but one that can be conveniently attributed to any text or event), the homo-repressed inscription can be best defined by what Edelman calls homographesis, not readily available signs, codes in the closet. Edelman defines "homographesis" as

> the process by which homosexuality is put into writing through a rhetorical or tropological articulation that raises the question of writing as difference by constituting the homosexual as text. The process whereby the homosexual as subject of discourse, and therefore a subject on which one may write, coincides with the process whereby the homosexual as subject is conceived of as being, even more than as inhabiting, a body on which his sexuality is written. (xx)

Edelman displaces the question of the "homosexual character" in writing, an essentialist question that seeks points of reference to uncover or identify what is homosexual—indeed, a checklist that will answer, "¿quién es más macho?"; instead he asks whether or not it is more fruitful to look at how the process of writing constructs the homosexual. The notion of the "body" that Edelman puts forth is more complex than just the physical but includes the textual, political, and sexual as well. I would then argue that "whether the friar 'is' or 'isn't' " is really beside the point, but what matters is how the possibility or impossibility of homosexuality is written or marked in/on the text and, more important for us as Hispanists, what matters is how that homographetic marking in the *Lazarillo* has been *read* by our colleagues Bataillon and Rico as something that is morally wrong.

Coming out from under the Archive

If the fourth *tractado* has been constructed as Lazarillo's encounter with the sodomite friar, what does that say about our hero? Notice that when the critics mention the question of sodomy, it is alway pertaining to the friar. I want to suggest that Lázaro's not being more explicit had to do very much with being directly accused as a sodomite himself.

In the *Séptima Partida* of Alfonso X, el Sabio. Titulo. XXI. *De los que fazen de luxuria contra natura* [Of those who have lust against nature], we learn the following:

¶*Ley. II. Quien puede acusar a los que fazen el pecado sodomitico, e ante quien, e que pena merecen auer los fazedores del, e los consentidores.*
Cada uno del pueblo puese acusar a los omes que fiziessen pecado contra natura, e este acusamie[n]to puese ser delante del judgador do fiziessen tal yerro. E si le fuere pruado deue morir porende: tambien el que lo faze, com el que lo consiente. Fueras ende, si alguno dellos lo ouiere a fazer por fuerça, o fuesse menor de catorze años. Ca entonces non deue recibir pena, porque los que son forçados non son en culpa, otrosi los menores non entienden que es tan gra[n] yerro como el aquel que fazen.

[*Law II. Who can accuse those who commit the sodomitic sin, and before whom, and what punishment the doers of this sin deserve, as well as those who consent.*
Each one in the town can accuse the men who commit sins *contra natura*, and this accusation can be done before the judge [of the place] where such crime was committed. And if it is proven, he must die for it: the one who commits it as well as the one who consents. Except, however, if one of them has done it by force or was under the age of fourteen. Because then, he should not receive punishment, because those who are forced are not guilty, and the minors do not understand how great a crime they commit.]

According to Rico—interestingly enough—at the time of the fourth *tractado*, Lazarillo would be around fourteen years old.[14] I am tempted to say that he might already be fifteen. If Lazarillo defers telling us about those "cosillas," it is because he might be accused of sodomy as well, which would be counterproductive for someone who is defending at that moment the integrity of the family romance.

Now the question remains why Lázaro would even mention this event at all. I propose that the answer may be found in the last word of the *tractado*: "salí dél"—"I came out from under him or his influence," or more literally, "I pulled out of him." Both translations offer us something interesting: the first—I came out from under him—leaves the impression of a moral choice made by the narrator; the second—"I pulled out of him"—gives the impression of a coitus interruptus. It could say that a *coitus interruptus* or an interrupted discourse or interrupted repro-narrative is what Lazarillo is trying to explain throughout the fourth chapter. The slippery ambiguity of the final phrase, "salí dél," permits another reading: in "salí dél," "él" is not necessarily or solely "él," the friar, but also "él," Lázaro. The possibility of homosexuality is included also in the splitting that we saw earlier. I would like to read this splitting of Lázaro's (masculine) subjectivity as an instance of a crisis, fragmentation, or breakup of the subject. These faults and their concealment left behind by this critical moment in writing and self-figuration could be referred to in this case as a sexual and textual trauma as well as an instance of hysteria.[15]

Mitchell proposes that "hysteria sometimes presents not the negative of the sexual perversion but the negative of a perverse knowledge" ("King Lear" 104). Lazarillo's words and action negate not the "homosexual" as a category—even in his obliqueness, he manages to mention the subject of the friar's sodomitic practice—but rather his own homosexual tendencies, a perverse knowledge. Indeed, sexuality is manipulated over and over in this seminal text. Lazarillo's resorting to the family romance (to the *grand récit*) as a safe haven represents a regression to a "safer" textuality (the law) and sexuality (compulsory heterosexuality). I do not want to conclude necessarily that Lazarillo was a homosexual—the term may be inopportune. Besides, it would be too facile a conclusion. Nevertheless, it would not be too much to assert that the *Lazarillo* needs no "queering"; it is already a queer text. And as such we must ask, what are the critical and literary historical consequences of bringing out this fact? That is the question. The conclusion we can draw from this reading is that male *heterosexuality* has its limits, limits that we must constantly question, that we must always define. Those limits are the product of the inevitable breakup of the law.

Broken Pieces Together

Allow me to sketch some conclusions. Often, in writing this essay, I sensed that literary history obeys a similar impulse to straighten out what is unwieldy, what is queer. This is very much like the overall project of Alfonsine law to draw up a national subject clean of nefarious sin.[16] Even literary historical projects as progressive as González Echevarría's place the query (and queerness) of the sexual subject in the back file of his Archive. For that reason, I began this essay criticizing the limits of González Echevarría's theory of the novel, suggesting that the paradigmatic rewriting that he proposes leaves something out, and that that something is sexuality. Ironically, it is the sexual subject that brings about the subversion of the master text. The strategies for putting into practice this subversion are many (from parody to negation). I chose to focus on performativity because it appears to be one of the more provocative critical moves and seems to work well in allowing us to understand that conjunction between Hispanisms and homosexualities. Along these lines, a question that needs more exploration is not just what impact theories such as Butler's have on Hispanisms, but, as important, what contributions and correctives Hispanists can bring to queer theory and gender studies.[17]

I propose that we rethink how performativity can be used to describe literary history and genre, not just subjectivity and gender. In this evaluation, we are met with a different question: *How* is literary history "sexed"? The conception of homographesis seems helpful in looking at sexual demarcations in texts and narrative. Finally, we can begin to notice how the Mercedarian friar's *trote*—and, let us not forget implicating, Lazarillo's rhythmic imitation—is more than an aimless meandering; his *trote* is a switching of sexual codes; it is a swishing that is difficult for literary and legal histories to control and accept.

Notes

1 For a comprehensive collection on the *Lazarillo* and the picaresque, refer to Pellón and Rodríguez-Luis, *Upstarts, Wanderers, or Swindlers: Anatomy of the Picaro.* For my general understanding of the picaresque and of the *Lazarillo,* in particular, I have relied on Peter Dunn's excellent work, on González Echevarría's review article "The Life and Adventures of Cipión: Cervantes and the Picaresque," as well as on Sieber's *Language and Society in "La vida de Lazarillo de Tormes."*

2 Unless otherwise noted, all translations of the texts are mine.

3 For an excellent analysis that shows the rhetorical turns taken by Lázaro in writing Lazarillo—both text and person—see Shipley, "Critic as Witness" esp. 183–85.

4 "[I]n the patrimonial bureaucracy [of fifteenth- and sixteenth-century

Spain] legitimization is granted through the alienated political codes that have become a simulacrum of seigneurial power. The individual who can and does err, writes to the embodiment of natural law . . . to plead for exculpation and to recapture his or her legitimacy. . . . Out of this relationship between the individual and the state the novel will emerge, as the writer protagonist of the picaresque writes a report about his life to an absent authority." (54–55). Thus González Echevarría explains the originality of the *Lazarillo* and the picaresque. Along those lines, my opinion on the status of the picaresque as a genre is that it is not one. I rather think of the picaresque as a positionality, the situation of an oppositional narrative voice with the intent to disrupt the sequence of canonical intertextual relations, not parodic or carnivalesque (in the world-upside-down sense), not simply a minus sign before an event, but a linguistic awareness that presents the event and its perversion.

5   For a summary of González Echevarría's theory of Latin American narrative, refer to *Myth and Archive* 8–18.

6   In this way, Lazarillo anticipates and deconstructs Luna's *La segunda parte del Lazarillo de Tormes*. The anonymous author of the Lazarillo represents (or doubles) in his silence the role of the wanna-be; by claiming authority, by giving a name and a face to the anonymous, Luna reduces the complexity and revolution of the subject of the "original" Lazarillo.

7   I am using the term *performativity* to mean a "citational and reiterative practice" as introduced by Judith Butler in her *Gender Trouble* and later elaborated in *Bodies That Matter*.

8   For a discussion of the question of the subject as produced and judged by the law, see Butler, *Gender Trouble* 2–3.

9   "Yo, como estaba hecho al vino, moría por él, . . . acordé en el suelo del jarro hacerle una fuentecilla y agujero sotil, y delicadamente, con una delgada tortilla de cera, taparlo; y al tiempo de comer, fingiendo haber frío, entrábame entre las piernas del triste ciego a calentarme en la pobrecilla lumbre que teníamos, y al calor della, luego derretida la cera, por ser muy poca, comenzaba la fuentecilla a destilarme en la boca, la cual yo de tal manera ponía, que maldita la gota se perdía" (31–32).

10 Paul Julian Smith reminded me that there is an obvious homoerotic reading in this passage; I will not address it here because I want to focus on the conflation of the body of the subject and of the text itself. It is worthwhile, though, to refer to Javier Herrero's essays on iconography. He insists that "wine is an image of woman": first as "the paradise of motherly love," then as "the degradation of the cuckolded husband." He sees the role of wine to be "its structural value as a unifying element . . . of the book" ("The Ending" 314). I am afraid that I can't agree with his archetypal reading. For starters, to

reduce wine to the image of woman is quite problematic; we need only think of the classically problematic role of wine as pharmakon and pharmakos, exemplified by Bacchus, an androgynous god. But, more important, what I would like to stress about Herrero's reading is its heteronormative stance that ignores the homoerotics of the boy lying and sucking between the old man's legs. Herrero writes that "[i]t is very difficult imagining him in that position, and indeed, a well-known critic has used this description as an argument against the 'realism' of the novel, etc." ("The Great Icons" 9–10). Yikes, why is it difficult to imagine Lazarillo in that "position"? Second, why resort to a "well-known critic" to substantiate such a banal point? What I see happening here is a clear example of homosexual panic ("it is very difficult imagining him") as well as a critical homosocial adjustment ("a well-known critic")— calling on tradition and authority to defy the queerness of the text.

11   By this, I do not want to demean real child abuse by saying that it is a fantasy. I am alluding to Freud's essay "A Child Is Being Beaten," in which he discusses the relationship of beating fantasies and the identification with a gender; Freud suggests that behind the fantasy of "a child is being beaten" is a repression: "I am being beaten by my father." This fantasy lies at the center of the Oedipal complex, specifically the primal scene. Gender identification happens as the subject is caught up in this spectral relation; the subject positions himself or herself in the fantasy to identify gender and power.

12   In my study of the performance of masculinity in *Kiss of the Spiderwoman*, I elaborate that "what defines a 'man' most . . . is his cunning and valor to 'take it all,' (*aguantarse*) whether that 'all' is torture or humiliation. Without fail, the greatest humiliation that a 'man' can suffer is becoming a 'woman'—the possibility of castration can be matched with the threat of sodomy [to become a homosexual or 'like a woman']. Hence, accepting sodomy can be read as a shifting sign for masculinity" ("Scars" 113). For a fuller discussion of the concept of *aguantarse* as it relates to gender identification, see chapter 3 of my "Scars of Decisions."

13   I use this expression, which Lee Edelman discusses in his book *Homographesis* 5.

14   See Rico's introductory essay in which he discusses time period of the text (13–30) and the age of the boy (15).

15   My hypothesis is that trauma/splitting is necessary for writing on the subject as other and that splitting destabilizes the claim to gender (and genre) uniformity. On the question of male subjectivity, trauma reveals the "male hysteric." I leave this idea dangling because I am still uncertain of the overall impact that it has in the development of Spanish narrative. I am speculating that the fourth *tractado* of the *Lazarillo* is but an early instance where the author

breaks up to reveal his subjectivity. I am thinking about other early male hysterics: the Arçipreste de Hita lamenting the death of his *trotaconventos*, Calisto's courtly melancholia; and, of course, the hysteric Don Quijote and Don Juan will later become the paradigms of male hysterics in their full-fledged splendor.

16 The most comprehensive study that addresses how gay subjects became scapegoats for larger social, cultural, and national subjects is Boswell's *Christianity, Social Tolerance, and Homosexuality.*

17 In this essay, I was interested in showing ways in which Hispanists can contribute to the growing scholarship on performativity. Most of the texts and scholarship on performance and performativity ignore the contribution made by Hispanists and Latin Americanists. I am thinking about the recent work by Sylvia Molloy on the "pose": to what degree is her discussion on posing in nineteenth-century Latin American texts counter to notions of performativity? What are the historic specifics that might shape performances differently?

The Politics of Posing

Sylvia Molloy

Now, once I feel myself observed by the lens, everything changes: I constitute myself in the process of "posing," I instantaneously make another body for myself, I transform myself in advance into an image.—Roland Barthes, *Camera Lucida*

At a conference held a few years back in Brazil, I read a paper in which I reflected on the ambivalence and general disquiet awakened by Oscar Wilde in certain turn-of-the-century Latin American writers involved in the joint venture of constructing national identities and renewing literature. My paper attempted to capture the way in which José Martí's gaze, for one utopian moment, gathered Wilde the exemplary rebel and Wilde the problematic deviant (a *raro,* a *queer,* a fop) in one image; a conflictive one, to be sure, but still *one* image. I attempted to reconstruct the moment when both "sides" of Wilde *could be thought of together* before giving in to the pressure of ideology that would, first, tear them asunder and, second, retain one to the detriment of the other. Judging from the reaction of one of my respondents, the ambivalence and reader disquiet of the past century had carried onto this one. He proceeded to consider the relation between Wilde and Latin America as a "mere" case of imitation, mainly sartorial, a matter of fashion, an exercise in mimetic frivolity. Latin Americans had simply "played at" being Wilde, as one puts on a flashy costume that catches the eye, a green carnation on one's lapel. As such the relation was declared inconsequential and, moreover, insignificant. Decadence was, above all, a question of *pose.*

This reaction did not differ essentially from the way in which decadent Latin American literature had been read for years, that is, as frivolous, and therefore reprehensible, posturing. Indeed, when discussing the literary renewal effected by turn-of-the-century *modernismo* in Latin America, Max Henríquez Ureña wrote of Rubén Darío, "Rubén asume una *pose,* no siempre de buen gusto: habla de su espíritu aristocrático y de sus manos de marqués. . . . Todo esto es *pose* que desaparecerá más tarde, cuando Darío asuma la voz del Continente y sea el intérprete de sus inquietudes e ideales" [Rubén adopts a *pose,* not always in good taste; he flaunts his aristocratic attitudes and his nobleman's hands. . . . All this is a *pose* that he will overcome later, when he takes on the voice of the continent and becomes the interpreter of its anxieties and ideals] (97). Disdained for its levity or ridiculed for its effeteness and its extravagance, *posing* as a cultural gesture, whether in society or in literature, is considered, at best, a fleeting malady, a "passing stage." A genteel fluttering of hands, an affected oddity, an *acting out,* it is reassuringly replaced by the authority of group ideology, the "voice of the continent." I want to think about *posing* in Latin America differently, not as the vapid posturing of some ghostly *fête galante,* a set of bodily or textual affectations at odds with national and continental discourses and concerns from which Latin America ultimately recovers, but as an oppositional practice and a decisive cultural statement whose political import and destabilizing energy I will try to recuperate and assess.

Posing in Latin America occurs (and becomes cause for concern) in a diversity of discourses, more precisely, in the intersection of those discourses, where the aesthetic, the political, the legal, and the medical converge. To trace the way in which posing constructs itself and to detect its points of tension, I shall look closely at a series of turn-of-the-century Latin American texts—articles, poems, social essays, case histories—and will consider them as they simultaneously converse and disagree with European constructions of posing.

Bodies on Display

Countries are read like bodies in the nineteenth century, in Latin America as well as elsewhere. Bodies, in turn, are read (and are offered up for reading) like cultural statements. To reflect on posing, I want to rescue that body, that posing body, in its intersection with nation and culture, stress its physical aspects even as it appears in texts, consider its inevitable theatrical projections and its pictorial connotations; I want to consider what gestures accompany, or rather determine, the conduct of the Latin American *poseur*, how a field of visibility is constructed within which a pose is recognized as such and finds a coherent reading.

Exhibitions, as cultural forms, are the nineteenth century's genre of choice, scopophilia its guiding passion. Nationalities are displayed in world fairs, diseases in hospitals, art in museums, sex in *tableaux vivants*, goods in department stores, the quotidian as well as the exotic in photography, dioramas, panoramas. There are exhibitions; there is also exhibitionism. The latter word is first used to describe a pathology in 1866; the word for the individual—the exhibitionist—is coined in 1880. To exhibit is not only to show, of course, but also to render more visible. Charcot, that great exhibitionist of pathologized others, is described by Freud as "un visuel, un homme qui voit" (Didi-Huberman 30). When the resident photographers at the Salpêtrière (resident because they had to be on hand to seize the "right" moment of pathology) photographed hysterics, they had to make sure that the disease would be seen. The touching up of photographs—cavernous eyes, darkened circles, grimacing mouths—was not uncommon; but, more important, the posing of patients themselves, eager to collaborate in the exhibition and repossess their disease, rendered the condition manifest (Huberman 46). I am particularly interested in that heightened visibility as it affects posing. Controlled by the poseur, exaggeration (i.e., the reinforcement of the visible) is a strategy of provocation, a challenge forcing a gaze, a reading, a framing. Posing is always an act of "being for" and, not infrequently, of "being against." Like Baudelaire's *maquillage*, "it should not hide nor should it avoid discovery; it must exhibit itself, if not with affectation, at least with a kind of innocence" (Baudelaire 914)—the very innocence that renders it threatening.

The fin de siècle reacts to the heightened visibility of the body, that is, to the pose, in different ways. The street, the clinic, and the text are three of the pose's choice spaces of production; diagnostics, denunciation, and "private recognition scenes," as Wayne Koestenbaum has called them (45), are three of the responses the pose elicits. All three, from denunciation through identification, are intensely scopophilic. Excess always prompts what Uruguayan writer Felisberto Hernández would much later call "la lujuria de ver" [the lust of looking].

Playing the Ghost

On two occasions, when referring to a nineteenth-century poet of inordinate, even scandalous, visibility, Rubén Darío cites an epigraph from Villiers de l'Isle Adam's *L'Eve future:* "Prends garde! En jouant au fantôme on le devient" (Villiers 103). In an essay on Lautréamont published in *Los raros* (a collection of literary portraits, in the manner of Gourmont's *Livres des masques,* which I can't help but translate as *The Queers*), Darío writes: "No sería prudente a los espíritus jóvenes conversar mucho con ese hombre espectral, siquiera fuese por bizarría literaria o gusto de un manjar nuevo. Hay un juicioso consejo de la Kábala: No hay que jugar al espectro, porque se llega a serlo" [It would not be prudent for young minds to converse at any length with this spectral man, not even for the sake of literary curiosity or the pleasure of trying new delicacies. There is a judicious saying in the Kabbala: One should not play at being a ghost for one ends up being one] (2:436). Then, in a second piece, "Purificaciones de la piedad" [Purifications of pity], the notably ambivalent article on Oscar Wilde's death, Darío again writes: "[D]esdeñando el consejo de la cábala, ese triste Wilde *jugó al fantasma y llegó a serlo*" [neglecting the advice of the Kabbala, that pitiful Wilde *played at being a ghost and ended up being one*] (3: 471; my emphasis). In both cases the phrase is used in a cautionary way, to call attention to the extravagant character of both writers and to the dangers of "playing at" things in general. But Darío gives the phrase an odd interpretive twist. To play the ghost and end up being one, if taken literally, would seem to point to a loss of substance, of tangible appearance—in sum, to a disappearing act.[1] Yet Darío seems to point to the opposite as the end result of so much "playing," to an excess of visibility, of *presence.* The contradiction is only apparent, of course. Wilde's excessive visibility, Darío implies, is precisely what leads to his ruin: to play the (excessively visible) ghost is, ultimately, to play with death. Indeed, Darío calls Wilde a "mártir de su propia excentricidad y de la honorable Inglaterra" [martyr of his own eccentricity and of honorable England] (3: 471), the order of the terms implying that he brought his end upon himself. I would like to add a twist to Darío's phrase, suggest that the ghost be seen as the phantasmatic construct of what cannot be said, what lacks visibility because it lacks a name. In Rubén Darío's reading, Wilde plays at being something that is not named and by playing at it—by *posing* as that something—*is* that something. Posing is the representation of invisibility. The play's the thing—the rest, as Wilde might say, mere leather and prunella.

One should not forget the dense semantic texture acquired by the verb *to pose* in the context of Wilde's trials, closely followed in Latin America as, indeed, throughout the world. In a letter of 1 April 1894, the Marquess of Queensberry writes to his son: "I am not going to try and analyze this intimacy, and I make no charge; but to my mind to pose as a thing is as bad as to be it. With my own eyes I saw you both in the most loathsome and disgusting relationship, as expressed by your manner and expression. Never in my experience have I seen such a sight as that in your horrible features" (Hyde 71). A few weeks later, confronting Wilde in his own home, Queensberry says: "I do not say you are it but you look it, and you pose as it, which is just as bad" (73). In a letter to his father-in-law, written a few months later, Queensberry again writes, "If I was quite certain of the thing, I would shoot the fellow at first sight, but I can only accuse him of posing." We know how the story ends: on 18 February 1895, Queensberry leaves a card for Wilde at his club, a card on which is written: "For Oscar Wilde, posing as a somdomite" (76). The rest, as they say, is history.

The unnamed (the *thing*, the *it*) is of course Wilde-as-homosexual; what does not fit in words cannot be formulated as a subjectivity but is made manifest by Wilde's "manner," his "expression," his "horrible features," in a word, by a demeanor principally summed up in bodily attitudes and conforming an all too visible *pose*. As Moe Meyer writes, "It is important to remember that Wilde was initially entered into the legal process not for perverse sexual activity (sodomy), but for perverse signifying (*posing* as a sodomite). He was a semiotic criminal, not a sexual one" (98). Queensberry's cunning use of the verb *to pose*, calculated to avoid a countercharge of libel, ostensibly pointed to artifice, to deceit: Wilde was accused not of being a sodomite but of posing as one. Yet with equal cunning, and with a flair for paradox reminiscent of Wilde himself, Queensberry's accusation hints that *posing* and *being* may indeed be collapsed into each other, that one is what one poses. This hint, of course, was not lost on the prosecution. That the crown moved on to a second trial, in which charges were brought against Wilde not for posing but for being, shows indeed the identifying power of posing. The pose opened a space in which the male homosexual was seen; he became a subject and was represented and named.[2]

This excursus is not immaterial if one bears in mind the intense curiosity awakened by Wilde—most specifically, by Wilde's body and dress—in Latin American writers and, more generally, in writers of all the Spanish-speaking world. Wilde may well be cut down to mere particulars of fashion, but the impact of those particulars, as synechdoches for the individual, is undeniable. José Martí is obsessed by Wilde's hair, his clothing, his shoe buckles, his breeches, to the point that they threaten his whole-hearted acceptance of Wilde's aesthetic message (Molloy, "Too Wilde" 187–89). Enrique Gómez Carrillo, who knew Wilde in Paris, is also struck by "su cabellera, lisa y luciente, [que] hacía a su rostro enorme un marco rubio que me chocaba por lo femenino, o mejor dicho, por lo afeminado de sus *bandeaux*" [his smooth shiny hair, providing a golden frame for his huge face, [which] disturbed me because of its feminine quality, or better said, because it was parted in an effeminate way] (*Bohemia* 190). Carrillo also memorably evokes Wilde at home "vestido apenas con una camiseta descotada de lana roja" [scantily clothed in a scoop-necked, red woollen undershirt] (*Almas* 149), and in Spain Ramiro de Maeztu, who never laid eyes on Wilde, knew enough about him to imagine "un *dandy* que, aun después de muerto, se presentase ante el eterno Dios fumando con petulancia un cigarrillo de boquilla dorada y echando el humo en roscas" [a dandy who, even after death, would come before the eternal God petulantly smoking a cigarette in a gold cigarette-holder and blowing out the smoke in rings] (Pérez de Ayala 16). Darío, in the unforgettable article he writes about Wilde's death, compulsively brings up Wilde's dead body, the rot and decay of which Darío belabors, only to repress it at the end of the piece in favor of Wilde's everlasting work (Molloy, "Too Wilde" 189–91). Wilde is fetishized even before his work is read, recognized as standing in for that unnameable to which his posing points at every turn.

A Comedy of Mannerisms

Not all turn-of-the-century posing refers unequivocally to the homosexual, a subject yet to be defined and in whose formulation, both cultural and legal, Wilde's trials played such a large part. But I would argue that all turn-of-the-century posing does refer *equivocally* to the homosexual, for it refers to a theatricality, a dissipation, and a *manner* (the uncontrollable gesturing of excess) traditionally associated with the nonmasculine or, at the very least, with an increasingly *problematic* masculinity.[3] Posing makes evident the elusiveness of all constructions of identity, their fundamentally performative nature. It increasingly problematizes gender, its formulation and its divisions: it subverts categories, questions reproductive models, proposes new modes of identification based on recognition of desire more than on cultural pacts, and offers (and plays at) new sexual identities. It also resorts to an exploitation of the public, in the form of self-advertisement and very visible self-fashioning, that appears to make the spectator very nervous about what goes on in private. Indeed, after Wilde, posing will become increasingly suspect, will be read more and more as advertising sexual deviance.[4] In Latin America, this is particularly true in those cases in which posing—and decadence in general—are considered in relation to hypervirile constructions of nationhood.[5] Posing invites new formulations of desire at once disturbing and attractive. That is why—in order to defuse its transgressive and, at the very least, homoerotic charge—it is usually reduced through caricature or dismissed as "mere imitation." It is accepted as a cultural detail, not as a practice, cut down to sissy proportions: it is "una fastidiosa cháchara de *snobs* que van a nuestras selvas vírgenes con polainas en los zapatos, monóculo impertinente en el ojo, y crisantemo en el ojal" [the gossip of snobs who go into our virgin jungles wearing spats, a monocle, and a chrysanthemum on their lapel] (Ulner 207).[6]

In the context of Latin American cultures, such disparaging remarks could be deadly. Indeed, in literatures whose very foundational gesture is ironic mimicry and deviant citation—"Qui pourrai-je imiter pour être original?" writes Darío (in French, of course)—to dispatch posing as imitation, belittling it as a frivolous dressing-up, is a pernicious move: it is to get only half the picture, and the least-interesting half at that. In fact, one of the most striking scenes of posing (in that it gives rich new meaning, precisely, to the notion of "dressing up") is to be found in "Kakemono," an Orientalist piece by the Cuban poet Julián del Casal. In the poem, a voyeuristic narrator enumerates the very deliberate gestures of a female subject who, "Hastiada de reinar con la hermosura / Que te dio el cielo por nativo dote" [Weary of ruling with the beauty / which Heaven naturally bestowed on you] (Casal 173), ritually transforms herself into a Japanese empress. The near religious character imparted to the ceremony, in which every detail of dress signifies and every gesture constitutes a pose; the drastic erasure of "nature" and "self" that the transformation presupposes (so reminiscent, in fact, of a drag queen's routine); and, most important, the interpellative stance adopted by the text—in lieu of a third-person description, a voyeuristic "I" forcefully addresses a "you," becomes that "you" in the very act of reproducing each gesture, as would a mirror—all attest to an intensity of transformative *action* that goes far beyond the chrysanthemum on the lapel, the monocle and spats in the jungle. Casal's transformist knows, as did Wilde, that "a climax may depend on a crinoline" and that "attitude is everything" (Wilde 1065, 1078): in constructing her pose, s/he is the Japanese queen.

It is obvious that I am referring here more to the dynamics of posing than to the self-containment of isolated gestures. The latter can no doubt sum up, in one blow, the disruptive potential of posing, offering a bodily metaphor that will linger, uneasily, in memory: say Julián del Casal's Helen, stroking a lily as she gazes on the ruins of Troy, or his Petronius, calmly inhaling the smell of his blood, one last time, as it ebbs from his severed veins, or for that matter the proud drag queen "posing as an Honest Woman" that Jorge Salessi has rescued from turn-of-the-century police files (Salessi 346). Here I am interested in posing as narrative; a fitful narrative to be sure, of which one might say, as Arthur Symons did of Mallarmé's syntax, that it is "something irregular, unquiet, expressive, with sudden surprising felicities, with nervous starts and lapses, with new capacities for the exact noting of sensation" (Dowling 134). Only within a sequence does posing, either as a way of life or as a way of writing, *make sense.*

Few recognized the transgressive potential of posing as a way of writing better than the Uruguayan José Enrique Rodó in his essay on Rubén Darío. Rodó offers a remarkably sympathetic reading of Darío's poetry in which he literally takes on Darío's voice, incorporating his manner in an act of poetic ventriloquism while attempting to curb the excess that he assimilates, once again significantly, to affectation in dress:

Nunca el áspero grito de la pasión devoradora e intensa se abre paso al través de los versos de este artista poéticamente calculador, del que se diría que tiene el cerebro macerado en aromas y el corazón vestido de piel de Suecia. También sobre la expresión del sentimiento personal triunfa la preocupación suprema del arte, que subyuga a ese sentimiento y lo imita; y se prefiere—antes que los arrebatados ímpetus de la pasión, antes que las actitudes trágicas, antes que los movimientos que desordenan en la línea la esbelta y pura limpidez—los mórbidos e indolentes escorzos, las serenidades ideales, las languideces pensativas todo lo que hace que la túnica del actor pueda caer constantemente, sobre su cuerpo flexible, en pliegues llenos de gracia. (172)

[Never has the rough cry of intense, devouring passion shot through the verses of this poetically calculating artist. One would say that his brain is steeped in perfumes and his heart enveloped in suede. The supreme preoccupation of art triumphs over personal feeling, masters that feeling by imitating it. Over the impetuous bursts of passion, over tragic attitudes, over movements that may disturb the elegant, untroubled purity of the line, [this poetry] prefers morbid and indolent obliqueness, serene idealizations, pensive languishing, all that makes the actor's robe drape over his supple body in ample, exquisite folds.]

This pensive languishing (akin to the "tender, caressing, voluptuous effects" that Leavis condemned in Shelley (Sinfield, *Cultural Politics* 34), these ample, draping robes, are overt signs of artifice for Rodó. That they are perceived as noxious, evirating, and possibly homoerotic, is shown by Rodó's caveat when referring concretely to Darío's poems: "Versos golosos, versos tentadores y finos, versos capaces de hacer languidecer a una legión de Esparta. . . . Si se tratase de ir a la guerra, yo los proscribiría" [Inviting verses, tempting and delicate verses, verses capable of making a Spartan legion swoon. . . . If there were an oncoming war, I would ban them] (179). Indeed, Rodó inscribes his attraction for, and fear of, the morbid, his preoccupation with virility and eviration, in a Latin American context that is defensively political. In that respect, the ideological framework of this essay on Darío is not insignificant. Over a period of several years, Rodó wrote a three-volume reflection on Latin American culture pointedly titled *La vida nueva*. The first volume, bearing the messianic title of "El que vendrá" [He Who Must Come], was a call for a spiritual leader, a *revelador* (literally, he who reveals) for Latin America.

The second volume, containing the long, ambivalent essay on Darío from which I have quoted, answered the summons of the first book in the negative: Darío's poetry was a poetry of affectation, of pose; as Rodó famously asserted, "no es el poeta de América" [he is not the poet of America]. The third volume of *La vida nueva* gave closure to the series, providing both the positive spiritual guidance for which the first volume yearned and a corrective to Darío's pernicious posing denounced in the second: an antidote to decadent artifice, the final volume contained Rodó's celebrated essay *Ariel*. So in an ideological scenario of his own making, Rodó, the cultural diagnostician, first identified a need, then analyzed the "wrong" remedy—Darío's poetry of pose—and then triumphantly, barely one year after his piece on Darío, proposed his own solution.

Dedicated to the youth of America, *Ariel* proposed a programmatic Latin American identity. It persuasively argued for self-improvement through renewed contact with Latin America's "strong" European forebears, Greece and early Christianity. A blend of evangelical *caritas* and Renanian Hellenism, whose sentimentalized virility would successfully glue together a male intellectual community for years to come, *Ariel* was the pedagogue's victory. Yet it would not be inappropriate to see this essay more connected to posing than it would at first seem. Indeed, I would argue that *Ariel* could be read as an act of posing *pro patria*, a model of homosociability that, although attempting to purify itself of the "morbid and indolent obliqueness" associated with posing, is no less an exercise in posing, and homoerotic posing at that, with its own brand of serene idealization and pensive languishing. Let me point to one telling example. This is an essay that shuns the visual with passion, an essay in which only one voice is heard, that of the master Prospero, speaking for the last time to an undifferentiated group of male students. Not only do these students lack voice (thus deviating from the Socratic model that obviously inspires the scene) but they remarkably lack bodies and lack gestures—not to mention pensive languishing and draping robes. The only visual reference, the only physical detail contained in this essay is therefore all the more striking: gazing at his young disciples gathered one last time in his study, as if seeking inspiration before speaking, Prospero pauses one moment to caress the winged statue of Ariel. That studied gesture, *the only one in the whole book*—the older man stroking the bronze ephebe—that *pose*, on the brink, as it were, of an essay that sublimates physicality at every turn, contains Rodó's homoerotic *paideia* in its entirety. Although Rodó may decry posing in Darío's poetry, the posing of his alter ego, Prospero, finds Rodó out.

Pose and Pathology

I now want not to think of posing as a mannerism or as the expression of nonmasculinity but to think of mannerism and the visibilization of nonmasculinity—and, more concretely here, of homosexuality—as posing. What I propose is more than a mere reversal of terms: I want to argue that the terms are not equivalent to begin with, and that very noncoincidence complicates the work of posing in Latin America. The double movement would be as follows: (1) Posing refers to the unnamed, to the *it* or the *thing* the inscription of which, as Wilde's case made clear, is posing itself; thus posing *represents*, is a significant posture. But (2) the unnamed, once named and rendered visible, may be now dismissed, in a specific Latin American context, as "just posing"; thus posing once again represents, but this time as a masquerade, as a significant *imposture*. To put it more simply: posing points to a fleeting identity, states that one is something; however, to state that one is that something is "to pose," that is, to pretend to be that something while not really being it.

It is in this context that I wish to take a look now at posing as pathology. As such, it appears in the complex, painstaking taxonomy devised by the Argentine psychiatrist, sociologist, and criminologist José Ingenieros at the turn of the century. A disciple of Nordau, Ingenieros, who also dabbled in poetry,[7] seems not to have disliked posing himself. As Aníbal Ponce writes, "Su vestidura detonante de refinado y de esteta, sus *boutades* inverosímiles, sus paradojas inagotables, habían hecho de él, en la opinión liviana de los cenáculos, un curioso diletante de la ciencia y del arte: mezcla extraña de Charcot y D'Annunzio con Lombroso y Nietzsche" [His costume, striking in its aesthetic refinement, his incredible epigrams, his unending taste for paradox, had turned him, in the frivolous opinion of the litterati, into a strange dabbler in science and in art; an odd mixture of Charcot and D'Annunzio with Lombroso and Nietzsche] (38).[8]

Like so many practitioners of forensic psychiatry at the turn of the century, wielding medical authority to force out "the truth" from their resisting patients, Ingenieros is interested in studying (i.e., exposing) pathologies and is particularly concerned (again like many psychiatrists of the period) with simulation, which he follows from its purely biological manifestations (animal mimetism, for example) to those cases in which extreme altered states are simulated as compensatory strategies for basically utilitarian, often criminal, purposes—as "*un medio fraudulento de lucha por la vida*" [a fraudulent means of succeeding in life] (*Simulación* 114; emphasis in the original). Although the main goal of his study is the simulation of madness in criminals (the subject of his very popular doctoral dissertation), he strives to classify simulation of a more general kind, from the benign to the extreme, in an incredibly detailed system. Simulation, for Ingenieros, is born of a flaw, a maladjustment, a weakness. A strategy from the margins toward the center defined by the author as "pathomimicry," it allows the simulator to pretend to be what he or she is not in order to pass, to be successful, to achieve a goal. The criminal pretends to be mad to escape punishment; the fabricator pretends to be someone else to achieve prestige; the proletarian immigrant pretends to be middle-class to achieve acceptance. For Ingenieros, one cannot, like Oscar Wilde, simulate (pose as) what one is: to pose, for Ingenieros, is necessarily to lie.

To illustrate the pathology of simulation, that is, the pathology of posing, Ingenieros gives examples:

> El ambiente impone la fraudulencia: vivir, para el común de los mortales, es someterse a esa imposición, adaptarse a ella.
>
> Quien lo dude, imagínese por un momento que el astuto especulador no simule honestidad financiera; que el funcionario no simule defender los intereses del pueblo; que el literato adocenado no simula las cualidades de los que triunfan; que el comerciante no simule interesarse por sus clientes; que el examinando no simule conocimientos de que carece y el profesor una profundidad inconmensurable; . . . que el pícaro no simule la tontería y el superior la inferioridad, según los casos; el niño una enfermedad, el maricón el afeminamiento, el propagandista la pasión, la esposa astuta el histerismo. (*Simulación* 185)

> [The environment demands fraudulence: to live, for most human beings, is to submit to that demand, to adapt to it.
>
> Whosoever doubts this should just imagine, for a moment, a wily

speculator not simulating honesty in his financial dealings; a politician not simulating to uphold the interests of the people; a mediocre writer not simulating the qualities of those who succeed; a merchant not simulating concern for his clients; a student in an exam not simulating the knowledge he lacks and the professor not simulating infinite wisdom; . . . a trickster not simulating stupidity, a superior not simulating inferiority, according to the situation; a child not simulating sickness, a faggot not simulating effeminacy, a hack not simulating writerly passion, a cunning wife not simulating hysteria.]

If I am not mistaken, the faggot marks a break in the series of "fraudulent simulations." The faggot, one might argue, does not pretend to be what he is not (like the wily speculator pretending to be honest, or the healthy child pretending to be sick) but what in a sense he is—effeminacy, *afeminamiento,* the exhibition of the feminine. Posing, in this case, is not a compensatory gesture (as in the case of the trickster simulating honesty); it is a way of highlighting a performance, rendering it more visible. The example disrupts Ingenieros's neat taxonomy unless a more drastic interpretive turn is effected. In that reading (which I venture is the one Ingenieros had in mind), a *man* poses as what he is not—a *woman*—because, Ingenieros tells us, he is *really* a man. This brutal reduction to an essentialist binarism would of course present a great advantage for the good doctor: it eliminates effeminacy from his equation—that is, a certain *performance* of gender—and it eliminates the problematic homosexual as subject.

Ingenieros is well aware of the manner in which simulation draws attention to itself, with its excessive, theatrical visibility. That he is concerned with its socially disruptive potential, as well as its creative possibilities, is obvious from his references to his mentor, José María Ramos Mejía, himself author of a treatise on simulation. For the author of *Los simuladores de talento,* a book whose political projections Ingenieros very much admires (*Simulación* 220), simulators are guilty of "histrionismo desvergonzado" [shameless histrionics]; they rely on "todos los elementos da la ilusión y un dispositivo teatral, por medio del cual, combinando simples *manchas,* dan en el lienzo la sensación completa" [all the elements of illusion and a theatrical constitution thanks to which, combining a few simple *blotches,* they achieve on canvas the impression of a whole] (220). The mixed reference to the visual arts—simulation, and by extension pos-

ing, are simultaneously theatrics *and* depiction, embodiment and surface—is, I think, of interest here. Simulation and posing may be "pa-
thomimicries" but they are also, above all, art forms.

Ingenieros's vigilant attitude toward poseurs, his self-described zeal at
"unmasking" them, so reminiscent of Queensberry's epistemological tizzy
(was Wilde or wasn't he?), often leads, in the case of perceived sexual
deviance, as in the case of the faggot simulating effeminacy, not to a
pressing of charges but to a displacement in pathologies: "He's not really
one (whatever *one* is), he's just pretending." This displacement, I suggest,
produces something like a great cultural relief, similar to the "we don't
have that here" of certain anxious constructions of nationality. Take the
following case history of a "patient" whom Ingenieros "cures":

> Un joven literato, sugestionado por los fumistas franceses, creyóse
> obligado a simular los refinamientos y vicios fingidos por éstos, con-
> ceptuándolos verdaderos. Simulaba ser maricón [*pederasta pasivo,* in
> a previous version], haschichista, morfinómano y alcoholista; vestía
> trajes raros; trasnochaba en los cafés, simulando estar ebrio, aunque
> sentía repulsión orgánica por las bebidas alcohólicas. . . . Todo era
> producto de sus pueriles sugestiones, fruto de las fumisterías de los
> estetas y superhombres cuyas obras leía de preferencia y bajo cuya
> influencia vivía. (241)

> [A young writer, influenced by French *fumistes* [imposters], felt
> obliged to simulate the refinements and vices the latter pretended to
> have, believing them to be authentic. He pretended to be a faggot
> [*passive pederast,* in a previous version]; pretended to be addicted to
> hashish, to morphine, to alcohol; he wore bizarre clothes; he stayed up
> all night in cafés, pretending to be drunk, even when he felt a physical
> repulsion for alcohol. . . . This was all a product of his puerile imagina-
> tion, resulting from the impostures of aesthetes and supermen whom
> he read avidly and who influenced his life.]

In yet another version of the same case, worthy of being cited at length,
Ingenieros gives additional details about the case and, more generally,
about the process of posing:

En uno de nuestros círculos intelectuales conocimos a un joven inteligente e ilustrado, bastante sugestionable. Dedicado a la literatura, provisto de dotes poco comunes y de cierto refinamiento del sentido artístico, enfermó de estetismo decadentista, sugestionado por ingeniosos fumistas. . . . Con tales maestros, e influenciado, acaso, por otros fumistas locales, el joven creyó que para igualarlos era necesario *tener o simular* sus manifestaciones psicopáticas. . . . Emprendió luego, en sus conversaciones privadas, una campaña contra la normalidad de las relaciones amorosas. Los intereses del individuo eran, en su decir, antagonistas de la reproducción. . . . De ahí que el esteta debía encontrar en sí mismo su propia voluptuosidad, lejos de toda idea de reproducción.

De esta apoteosis del placer solitario, pasó, poco después, a la de otras perversiones. . . . Al poco tiempo manifestó profunda aversión por el sexo femenino, enalteciendo la conducta de Oscar Wilde, el poeta inglés [*sic*] que en aquel entonces acababa de ser condenado en Londres, sufriendo en la cárcel de Reading las consecuencias de sus relaciones homosexuales con Lord Douglas. Escribió y publicó una "Oda a la belleza masculina" y llegó a manifestar que sólo hallaba placer en la intimidad masculina.

Algunas personas creyeron verdaderas esas simulaciones, alejándose prudentemente de su compañía; por fortuna, sus amigos le hicieron comprender que si ella podía servir para sobresalir literariamente entre sus congéneres modernistas, en cambio le perjudicarían cuando abandonara esos estetismos juveniles.

El simulador protestó que nadie tenía derecho de censurarle sus gustos, ni aun so pretexto de considerarlos simulados. Mas, comprendiendo que, al fin de cuentas, nadie creería en ellos, renunció a sus fingidas psicopatías. (*Locura* 24–25; my emphasis)

[In one of our intellectual circles, we met an intelligent, cultivated young man who was quite suggestible. Devoted to literature, endowed with uncommon talents and a certain refinement of the artistic sensibility, and influenced by clever *fumistes,* he fell sick with decadent aestheticism. . . . Inspired by those masters—and possibly by other local *fumistes*—the young man believed that, in order to emulate them, it was necessary *to have or to simulate* their psychopathic symptoms [my emphasis]. . . . Then, in private conversations, he started a campaign against normal love relations. The interests of the individual were, to his mind, opposed to those of reproduction. . . . That is why the aesthete should find in himself his own voluptuousness, removed from all notions of procreation.

From this apotheosis of onanism he went on, later, to other perversions. . . . After a time, he displayed a deep and total aversion for the female sex, extolling the conduct of Oscar Wilde, the English [*sic*] poet who had just been found guilty in London and was paying the consequences of his homosexual relations with Lord Douglas in Reading Gaol. He wrote and published an "Ode to Masculine Beauty," and went so far as to declare that he only found pleasure in male intimacy.

Some people believed these simulations to be true, and prudently avoided his company. Fortunately, his friends made him understand that if these simulations might serve to enhance him from a literary point of view in the eyes of his *modernista* colleagues, they would harm him after a while when he gave up his youthful aestheticism.

The simulator protested that no one had the right to censure his inclinations, even if others thought them feigned. However, understanding that in the long run no one would believe those inclinations to be true, he renounced his feigned psychopathies.]

That the possibility of being considered queer in any form (either as a "passive pederast" or as a "faggot") should be deemed desirable, indeed considered a sign of literary prestige, is hard to imagine. *Modernismo*—the literary movement in which, according to Ingenieros, such a reputation would be considered a plus—was already defending itself anxiously (perhaps too anxiously) from intimations of sexual dissidence and avoiding implications of nonmanliness. Rodó distanced himself from Darío's *mollitia;* Darío castigated Wilde for his excesses, censured Rachilde's gender bending, and informed his readers that Verlaine's homosexuality was (again!) mere posing;[9] Martí busied himself with the task of heterosexualizing Whitman: it is difficult to imagine that in such an atmosphere, a simulation of passive pederasty should add distinction, or even enviable notoriety, to anyone's position. To anyone's *literary* position, that is, since it is clear that the appearance of sexual dissidence outside literature, in whatever form, had adverse effects not only on reputations but on personal lives. Thanks in part to the dogged investigative efforts of Ingenieros himself, these appearances, detected by the diagnostician's sharp eye and eagerly constructed as narratives of deviance, usually landed suspects in jail, in psychiatric wards, in police files, or in medical literature.[10]

The tenacity and the resourcefulness with which Ingenieros's medical narratives strive to establish the mendacious nature of posing is striking. In this particular case, he peppers the case history with words such as *simulate, feign, emulate,* and *fumiste.* Additionally, to confirm the ultimately illusory, and therefore inconsequential, qualities of posing, he strips the poseur of full responsibility: the young writer is puerile, easily suggestible, naive, too "refined." He affects poses he has read in books (the topos of the "poisonous book" is revived here) and is gullible enough to think that his models are "true" when in fact, Ingenieros authoritatively tells us, they are all "false." In other words, the pathological poseur is modeling his conduct on models, taken either from literature or from life, that are, already, impostures and therefore, according to Ingenieros, not to be taken seriously. D'Annunzio, Ingenieros observes elsewhere, is an "italiano que ha sufrido contagios psicológicos franceses [y] ha simulado ser partidario del amor sororal y del homosexualismo; es verosimil considerar simulados tales 'refinamientos' del instinto sexual. Se comprende que . . . [no] copuló con sus hermanas o con otros hombres" [an Italian who has suffered French psychological contagion [and] has pretended to be in favor of sororal love and homosexuality: it is fitting to consider those "refinements" of the sexual instinct as simulations. It is obvious that . . . he did not copulate with his sisters or with other men] (*Archivos* 477).[11] In the case history I have cited, the defensive zeal, the need to establish lack of authenticity, is only compounded by the fact that the young man is not a more or less distant European aesthete but "ours"; he belongs to "one of our intellectual circles" and thus threatens the very fabric of "our" culture.

This case history leaves unanswered questions that may be unanswerable; their very unanswerability makes them crucial to a reflection on turn-of-the-century posing. For example: In what manner does one simulate being a passive pederast? What are the words, the declarations, the conduct—surely nongenital—that allow for such a reading? What are the gestures, the bodily metaphors, the artifices that would express an as yet unformulated (but nonetheless visible) identity? Additionally: Where is the locus of simulation? Where, but in the panicked discursive reiteration of the diagnostician, that is, in ideology, is the simulation detected? What is the pose, or series of poses, that would on the one hand allow the diagnostician to detect a pathology, this particular pathology (he *is* a passive pederast, a faggot), and on the other exhibit that pathology as a simulation (he *is posing* as a passive pederast, a faggot). The disquieting last paragraph of Ingenieros's narrative abounds in hiatus. The poseur "protests" the censoring of his inclinations, then "understands," and then "renounces." Although the verb, with its echoes of more formal recantations or abjurations of belief, is strong, what exactly the young man renounces remains unclear. For Ingenieros it is a simulation. For the poseur it is "his inclinations," inclinations to which he believes he has every right "even if others think them feigned." Note that even Ingenieros (in a rare moment of professional caution?) does not have him say: "Because they are feigned." For the poseur, as for us, the difference matters little. For turn-of-the-century Latin American culture, it mattered a lot. It too "renounced" its poses, those poses that, during the briefest of moments, *signified* beyond their own simulation. Emptied out of meaning, emptied out of bodies, those Latin American poses hang in the closet of representation, not to mention the closet of criticism. It is time to return to them, if only ephemerally, the dashing visibility they once had.

Notes

1   For a provocative approach to ghosting, and spectral metaphors in connection with homosexuality, specifically with lesbianism, see Castle.

2   As Jeffrey Weeks writes, "The Wilde trials were not only the most dramatic, but also the most significant events, for they created a public image for the homosexual" (21).

3   On the complex readings of effeminacy at the turn of the century, see Sinfield, *Wilde Century*, especially chapter 2, "Uses of Effeminacy," 25–51.

4   What Alan Sinfield writes of the dandy might be extended, synechdochically, to the pose: "The dandy figure served Wilde's project because he had a secure

cross-sex image, yet might anticipate, on occasion and in the main implicitly, an emergent same-sex identity. . . . Wilde is exploiting the capacity of the image of the dandy to commute, without explicit commitment, between diverse sexualities" (*Wilde Century* 73).

5   There are a few notable exceptions. In connection with nationalism and homophobia, Lisa E. Davis interprets Puerto Rican Miguel Guerra Mondragón's late translation of *Salome* in 1914 (at a time when there were already three Spanish translations available) as a renewed gesture of political resistance. Davis suggests that this new translation of Wilde's play, performed to mixed reviews and repeatedly banned from theatres in Spain and Latin America, should be read as a revolutionary gesture. For Guerra Mondragón, a politician and distinguished statesman, *Salome* symbolizes, according to Davis, the antagonism between a minority of politically resistant aesthetes and a new social class influenced by U.S. pragmatism ("Traducción" 36–37).

6   Recourse to metaphors of dress to deride poetry and poets persists well into the twentieth century. When comparing Darío's poetry to that of his Spanish predecessor Bécquer, José Bergamín writes: "La castidad de la desnudez es prueba de virilidad: poesía de Bécquer; la sensualidad de los ropajes, de afeminamiento: poesía de Rubén Darío" [Chaste nudity is proof of virility: witness the poetry of Bécquer. Sensuality of attire is proof of effeminacy: witness the poetry of Rubén Darío] (Rodríguez Monegal 12).

7   For a discussion on the role of literature in Ingenieros's medical diagnoses, see my "Diagnósticos del fin de siglo."

8   For further analysis of the intersection of art and science in Ingenieros's writing and in his clinical diagnoses, see my "Diagnósticos de fin de siglo."

9   When reviewing Edmond Lepelletier's biography of Verlaine for his Latin American readers, Darío dismisses Verlaine's homosexuality as "mere" posing: "Los amigos de asuntos tortuosos se encontrarán desilusionados al ver que lo referente a la famosa cuestión Rimbaud se precisa [en Lepelletier] con documentos en que toda perspicacia y malicia quedan en derrota, hallándose, en último resultado, que tales o cuales afirmaciones o alusiones en prosa o verso no representan sino aspectos de simulación, tan bien estudiados clínicamente por Ingegnieros [*sic*]" [Those enamored of twisted matters will be disappointed to learn that the famous Rimbaud question is documented here [in Lepelletier] in a way to dismiss all malicious fabrication, and it is ultimately proved that such and such declarations or allusions in verse or prose are mere aspects of simulation, so proficiently studied, from a clinical point of view, by Ingegnieros] (2: 718).

10 For an excellent overview of the obsession, on the part of the medico-legal establishment in Argentina, to classify homosexuals, and the prurient curiosity that guided that classification, see Salessi.

11 In a later version of this paragraph, all reference to homosexuality disappears, and D'Annunzio is left simulating only incest—presumably, by then, a safer affectation (*Simulación* 232).

The Signifying Queen:

Critical Notes from a Latino Queer

~

Oscar Montero

"We are everywhere" was the motto of our march in Washington a few years ago. Not only are "we everywhere," "we" are so different that the homosexual desire that brought us together in the first place is criss-crossed by other, not always easily compatible, identities. Issues of race, class, and national origins have enriched, and at the same time fragmented, the utopian face of that joyful "we" in the fleetingly queered streets of the nation's capital.

The possibilities and limitations of identity politics for gays and lesbians are currently the field of a complex debate in which a range of disciplines converge, questioning and recasting the very assumptions that led to the debate in the first place. As Suzanne Oboler suggests, not all labels are created equal, and the histories of their making must be taken into account, even when it is expedient to use them as empowering signals of identity or to discard them as spent, limiting rubrics. "Gay" and "lesbian" are edged out by "queer," while transgendered folk demand a proper inflection of their own, militantly in meetings and rallies, as well as critically.

The term "Latino" is at once the macaronic shorthand of media talking heads and an empowering tool for those caught in the politics of border identities. On both the political and the intellectual fronts, Puerto Ricans and Chicanos have been traditionally identified with progressive policies, whereas the white middle-class success of many Cubans, not to mention the hard line of anti-Castro exile politics, has put us sons and daughters of "the Pearl of the Antilles" on the other side of the fence, so to speak, an unfortunate polarization that has dogged every thinking Cuban on both sides of the Florida Straits for nearly forty years, by now biblical in their resonance. In part, my aim is to cast a shadow on the myth of the much-touted "Cuban success story," largely white, square, straight, and triumphantly bourgeois, by deflecting it in my queer gaze. I am aware of the anachronistic nature of antibourgeois stances, but I inhabit the cliché not in a futile confrontational mode but rather out of a desire to be included in a cultural arena where queers of any stripe shine by their absence, to paraphrase a Castilian cliché. These pages offer a counterpoint between Henry Louis Gates's "Signifying Monkey" and our own Severo Sarduy, Latin American queer theorist *avant la lettre*. I aim for a position that is less *theoretical* than *theatrical* and rejoice in the shared etymology of the terms: a space to see and be seen.

Basing his comments on a sharp reading of Pérez-Firmat's witty deconstruction of Cuban American identity, Antonio Vera proposes a "sujeto divertido," awkwardly translated as a "subject of fun/diversion" and also a "diverted subject." I take advantage of the linguistic impasse to suggest an "inverted subject," "un sujeto invertido," which may in turn be translated back as a "queer subject." "Invertido/a" is an old, nearly discarded standby for "homosexual," inflected for male or female, as the case might be. The term has an almost quaint resonance, ripe for recycling.

"Gay" circulates in the Spanish-speaking world, but the complexities of its imported status are impossible to edit, and something of its original celebratory mode is lost in the translation. The uses of "queer" are even more circumscribed to the imperial metropolis. Perhaps "invertido/a" can serve as a provisional term. The Latino subject of inversion is of course a hybrid subject, both "the supreme crosser of cultures," in Anzaldúa's happy phrase, and a doubter of such celebratory moves, as José E. Muñoz points out in "*Choteo*/Camp Style Politics," his lucid reading of Carmelita Tropicana, nom de guerre of performer Alina Troyano (48).[1]

My point of departure is a tenuous, though hopeful, and decidedly queer look at the possible uses of Henry Louis Gates's *The Signifying Monkey: A Theory of African-American Literary Criticism*. My rather untidy misreading of Gates produces "The Signifying Queen," and she, as tutelary deity, leads the way in a search for an autochthonous queer reading of Latin American identities and cultures via the fiction of Severo Sarduy, mock autochthon, Signifying Queen extraordinaire.

The subtitle of *The Signifying Monkey, A Theory of African-American Literary Criticism,* affirms the construction of an enabling theory for African American writing. The aims of these pages must be more modest; at best they will open a zone of inquiry that is distant from Gates's masterful affirmation and perhaps envious of it. The two-headed hydra of constructionism versus essentialism no doubt lurks in the interstices, but useful as the debate has been, it "may now seem something of a blind alley," writes Paul Julian Smith (*Representing* 14). The Latino queer critic, not entirely at ease in the ill-fitting language of the debate, heads down that alley toward an alien philosophical aporia. The way out is not to restate the terms of the debate but to sidestep the debate, shifting to another register, to trope on the troper, turning Signifying Monkey into Signifying Queen.

The abject sign of deviance in a gay man, effeminacy, is reconsidered as a possible source of theory, which also means "spectacle," in turn related to "appearance" and "type." If butchness, which critic Alisa Solomon calls "learned behavior that feels natural" (37), may be empowering to lesbian women, effeminacy, or more specifically the notions of artifice and guile associated with it, may be usefully recast, even if a fuller discussion of "a Butch-Femme Aesthetic" in gay men and their productions is deferred.[2]

Gates's theory of African American criticism is an enabling way of reading texts that may have been ignored or dismissed by a Euro-centric reading. It is also a way of incorporating those texts into later expressions of African American writing. Gates's theory is grounded on the division between a white vernacular, so-called standard English, seamless in its production with the discourses of power, and black English, belittled as a product of cultural marginality or affirmed in the essentialist politics of ethnic identity. For Gates, the African American English vernacular is the source of the ruling trope of his theory, namely Signifyin(g), with a capital *S* and a bracketed final *g*. Signifyin(g) is a foregrounding of the signifier, a figurative misreading in order to get the upper hand, to mock the white establishment and define hierarchies within the black community that are invisible to a white gaze and therefore impervious to its policing. Signifyin(g) is "an intentional deviation from the ordinary form or syntactical relation to words" (80).

Deviation from the "ordinary form" has figured prominently in the modern construction of homosexuality, and in the representations of same-sex desire that have been culturally available, but whereas the role of the African American critic is to read Signifyin(g) as an empowering legacy, sexual deviation is another story, currently being reconsidered on so many fronts.

A pause and a double take on the trope of "deviation from the ordinary form" are in order. If it is empowering for African American culture and its readers, what can it do for Latino queers? Deviation has been defined from the outside by what the straight gaze has viewed as deviant, resulting in "the homosexual as the abject, as the contaminated and expurgated insides of the heterosexual subject" (Fuss 3). Cultural representations by homosexual men and women have sought not only to deconstruct those signs of deviance but also to incorporate them and use them for a different purpose. Gays and lesbians have long dealt with stereotypes of identity: femme, butch, lipstick lesbian, nelly queen, macho man. The novelty of queer politics is taking these terms, which are oppressive in the wrong hands, and turning them into affirmations of identity, however provisional or contingent such identities might be. The significance of this naming is not so easily dismissed in the name of a principle of homosexual desire somehow cleansed of feared binarisms. What is at stake is the question of who calls the shots in the performance of these representations, and whether they empower or produce, to cite Ed Cohen, "historically specific, asymmetrical patterns of privilege and oppression" (75).

By the end of the nineteenth century, one of Latin America's strongest— more "virile," they would have said then—foundational discourses of national affirmation was centered in New York, where José Martí's oratorical power distilled a sense of Pan-American solidarity and differentiation in the face of the aggressive values of the new metropolis. A representative moment in the foundation of a Latino subject in the United States is surely the moment when the observer in Martí's Coney Island faces the music and, powerfully placed between Baudelaire and Benjamin, joins the rowdy crowd the better to see himself and the better to distinguish himself from it.[3] But as Sylvia Molloy has shown, there is also the Martí ambiguously positioned before Oscar Wilde and Walt Whitman, the very writers who in the Anglo-speaking world mark the origins of an aesthetic sensibility and of a cultural production where same-sex desire is cast in a new, influential light.

Significantly, Oscar Wilde and Walt Whitman are popular heroes of the gay liberation movement. Their names are unconditional banners of gay identity. At the same time, the texts identified by those names are being read in complex ways by contemporary queer critics. On both counts, those names and texts have no counterpart for the Latino queer critic who would seek a Hispanic equivalent, a founding image and a text whose very ambiguities would lead to an empowering discourse. The Latino queer critic must then read differently. On the one hand, he or she reads the lacuna, the innuendo, the very omissions and absences that are constitutive of foundational texts; on the other, he or she must turn to marginal or eccentric texts and bring to light their fictions of homosexuality. Like African Americans, Latino queers seek fables of origin, on which and against which to write, fables that may be rejected or rewritten but whose absence turns the work of the critic into a tentative, erratic pursuit, one without the privilege of the tutelary figure masterfully evoked by Gates in his anatomy of the African American Signifyin(g) tradition.

The Yoruba deity Esu, cast from Africa during the diaspora and recast in Cuba as Echu-Eleguá, a prominent figure in the pantheon of Cuban santería, becomes Gates's empowering figure of origin, the prototype of the Signifyin(g) Monkey, the emblem of African American Signification and of African American criticism. "One of the many Yoruba creation myths," writes Gates, "lists Esu as the primal form, the very first form to exist. Before Esu assumed form, only air and water existed" (37). Esu is the will itself and is beyond the will as "the power of sheer plurality or multiplicity" (37). Almost Dionysian in its powers, Esu is before any differentiation and at the same time is the ruler of all differences. Esu is kin to Hermes and therefore an agent of hermeneutics. For Gates, it is the ruling deity, the *orisha,* "the muse of the critic" (35), and more explicitly, "the indigenous black metaphor for the literary critic" (9).

Esu is not restricted to human distinctions of gender or sex, writes Gates, quoting Robert Farris Thompson's description, which adds that Esu "is at once both male and female. Although his masculinity is depicted as visually and graphically overwhelming, his equally expressive femininity renders his enormous sexuality ambiguous, contrary, and genderless" (29). What is not clear is that whatever gender Esu adopts, its characteristically voracious sexual appetite is satisfied heterosexually, that is, by coupling with whatever sex is opposite. Gates suggests that Esu, as a figure of origins, is beyond such binarisms: "Each time I have used the masculine

pronoun for the referent *Esu,* I could just have properly used the feminine" (29). He goes on to say that "Fon and Yoruba discourse is truly
genderless, offering feminist literary critics a unique opportunity to examine a field of texts, a discursive universe, that escaped the trap of sexism in
Western discourse. This is not an attempt to argue that African men and
women are not sexist, but to argue that the Yoruba discursive and herme-
neutical universes are not" (30). Sexism and sexual difference itself are
avoided through the action of doubling the double, the number four
being sacred in Yoruba metaphysics, Gates explains.

Thus Gates accomplishes the empowering differentiation of African
American culture by evoking a deity whose very nature implies the incorporation of both sexes and the ability to cross genders with impunity. The
move works, yet the possibilities of same-sex desire, and the cultural
representations it may provoke, are neatly obviated. Gates bypasses the
poststructuralist critique of identity to construct an African American
critical idiom in which questions about the construction of "race" itself
are deferred. The inflection of ethnicity by gender, age, and sexual orientation is erased in the evocation of the tutelary deity of Esu, and the correla-
tive doubling of the double in Yoruba metaphysics. In this context, the
queer is neither rejected, thus at least giving rise to the representation of
that banishment, nor silenced, for the queer has never spoken.

It is ironic for a Latino queer that one of Gates's sources is Cuban writer
Lydia Cabrera. Cabrera, one of the pioneers of Afro-Cuban studies, is also
an important source of Sarduy's uses, or misuses, of Afro-Cuban lore.
Although Cabrera's homosexuality was the classic "open secret," in Eve
Sedgwick's phrase, it has no relevance in the context of Gates's discussion.
However, as Sylvia Molloy has suggested, the topic of Cabrera's homosexuality need not be irrelevant but rather needs to be read as a not atypical
"disappearing act" in literary relationships in Latin America.[4] Benefiting
from the freewheeling Paris of the sixties and at the same time from the
radical point of view of a perennial outsider, Sarduy's disappearing act is a
drag of a different feather. Fortunately, there is somewhere else to turn, for
the expulsion of the queer from the doubling of Yoruba metaphysics has
been extravagantly and queerly represented by Severo Sarduy. In the "Curriculum Cubense" of Sarduy's *De donde son los cantantes,* Gates's Echu-
Eleguá becomes a drag queen.[5]

Severo Sarduy's *De donde son los cantantes* is written under the sign of four. The doubles Auxilio and Socorro double themselves to produce the main characters in the novel, the three representatives of Cuban culture and a fourth element, the slippery writing subject. The famous coda at the end of the novel says that "three cultures have been superimposed to construct Cuban culture, Spain's, Africa's, China's; three fictions that allude to those three constitute this book" (151). Early readings of Sarduy's novel took this statement to the letter, pointing to the presence in Cuba of those three cultures. More lucid readings of the novel, by Roberto González Echevarría and Enrico Mario Santí among others, were quick to point out that it is "three fictions," to be read as such. The fourth fiction in the "Curriculum Cubense," the one apparently missing from the final coda, is that of the writing subject and his pale double, the reader.

Historically speaking, the presence of Chinese culture in Cuba is certainly important, but its impact can hardly compare with that of the defining legacies of African and Hispanic traditions. Chinese culture, however, is important in Sarduy's own fable of identity, where it fights for equal footing with the other more dominant traditions. During a stint as performers and streetwalkers in Havana's Chinatown, Sarduy's characters become Auxilio Chong and Socorro Si-Yuen. Dressed in the manner of a Ming empress, or so they say, "the Bald Divinities" star in a sort of mock Chinese opera. Subsequently, the pair become *babalaos*, priests in santería. Finally, in the fable of "Dolores Rondón," the protagonist proclaims: "Hija legítima soy de Ochum, la reina del río y del cielo" [I am the legitimate daughter of Ochum, queen of the river and of the sky] (61). Dolores is a devotee of Ochum. As we shall see, she is also an early deconstructionist, Cuban style.

In radically different ways, of course, both Sarduy and Gates delve into fables of origins. Their works offer distinct, idiosyncratic echoes of Derrida's writing on the archi-trace: "La trace, qui devient ainsi l'origine de l'origine" [the trace, which thus becomes the origin of the origin] (90). Gates's pansexual Esu, who deftly overcomes objections about the role of gender, centers a fable of origins that allows the critic to deploy his own writing within, yet against, the grain of so-called Western culture. Esu is the enabling agent of the critic's writing. But where is Sarduy coming from?

Sarduy permanently settled in Paris in 1960 and first published in *Tel Quel* in 1965. Even as Derrida was putting the final touches on *De la grammatologie,* Sarduy was reworking his radio play "Dolores Rondón" into his second novel, *De donde son los cantantes,* published in Mexico in 1967, the same year Minuit brought out Derrida's book. Derrida's influential reading of Rousseau and Lévi-Strauss, sharply focused on the complex slippage between nature and culture, echoes weirdly in Sarduy's fiction.

In more ways than one, Sarduy's slim novel is light-years away from Derrida's heavy tome, but there is more than a difference in genres, and heft, between the two. Derrida's essay opens with an unabashed royal "we": "Nous aurons à expliquer la place" (7). By contrast, Sarduy's displaced fiction, and fiction of displacement, is (trans)gendered, or at least heavily made up, from the start. No pronoun, certainly not "I" and not "we," may have a lasting claim to authority. In Sarduy's writing, faces, traditional mirrors of identity, appear only to be disguised or fragmented, as in this version of an elusive character's drag disguise: "En su rostro navegan peces, huyen mariposas negras sobre sus párpados" [On her face, crossed by sailing fish, black butterflies flee over her eyelids] (50). In *La ruta de Severo Sarduy,* González Echevarría writes that Sarduy's Cuban way with words is a literary (de)construction of French theories, precisely a transformation of theory into spectacle, a hybrid, willfully grotesque, yet passionate anatomy of identity, wrought on the fringes of the new theoretical pantheon then being erected in the shadow of the old one.

One of the narrators says that Dolores "[d]esprecia lo esencial, el lugar de su origen" [She despises what is essential, her place of origin] (60). Dolores is Ochum's "legitimate" daughter, and she is also a composite of Tongolele and Rosita Fornés, popular Caribbean divas.[6] A yearning for authenticity and a penchant for artifice not only coexist in the same body but become its driving force. In her efforts to turn herself into a blond, to achieve her fantasy of a lady, Dolores loses her hair, but her battle cry rings out: "¡Calva, coja, pero a La Habana!" [Baldie, limping, but Havana here I come!] (75).

By the time Dolores sets out for Havana's Presidential Palace, she is a tropical chimera, a construction of "woman," an ambitious "mulata," at once a critique of the essentializing of "race" in Nicolás Guillén, Cuba's most famous poet laureate, and of Cuba's cultural dependence on the United States, or certainly on Miami. Dolores's costume sums it up: "Traigan la peluca, el corset más estrecho, la lentejuela, la orquídea que llegó esta mañana de Miami. ¡Voy a Palacio!" [Bring me the wig, the tightest corset, the sequin, the orchid arrived this morning from Miami. I'm going to the Presidential Palace!] (75). In *De donde son los cantantes, mestizaje,* Latin America's original blending of races recast as powerful cultural and political metaphor, is parodically removed from its role as a fable of racial and ethnic identity and read as pure surface, as rhetoric and gesture. Dolores is a walking misreading of Cuban and Latin American notions of identity. Dolores Rondón is Nicolás Guillén in Carmen Miranda drag.

At the same time, the fourth and missing element in the picture, the writing subject, signals his presence through quotation and misreading of different cultures, layers whose superimposition make up (construct and paint) the text. Auxilio and Socorro are the Signifyin(g) Queens of the subject, whose queerness is historical, ontological, as well as sexual, whose "being" literally squirms within the binary labels of nineteenth-century pseudosciences, "homosexual," "heterosexual." Ultimately, Sarduy's queer reading of Latin American culture and his deconstruction of fables of origin and identity contrast with Gates's use of African mythology as a founding element of African American identity and as empowering critical conceit. Violently exiled from his place of origin, from his mother's place, racially "impure," queer, even bald like Dolores, Sarduy and his text do not have access to the good offices of a primal Signifier. The faggot writer's only recourse, literally his only "Succor," is Auxilio and Socorro, the Signifyin(g) Queens, the Bald Divinities, leather boys, drag queens, *las Cejudas* (those of the heavy eyebrows), *las Culito* (the tiny asses), the Fatties.

In the mock medieval allegory of the final section of the novel, Auxilio and Socorro represent Faith and Practice, and here Sarduy's parody bites its own tail, undoing all irony to affirm a cosmology ruled not by exclusions and labels but by the aesthetic in its strictest sense: a sense that passes through the body, that registers its passage there before becoming inexorably dialectic. Sarduy's Signifyin(g), to quote Gates once again, his "intentional deviation from the ordinary form" of narrative is also an anatomy of identity, where fables of nationalism, ethnicity, and gender are played against each other. In fact, their very play against each other, as represented by the Faithful Pair, makes up the narrative. Cosmetic becomes cosmology: "Pasión cosmética," Sarduy writes in *La simulación,* "pero a condición de dar a esa palabra el sentido que tenía entre los griegos: derivada de *cosmos,"* [Cosmetic passion, but under the condition that the word retain the meaning it had among the Greeks: derived from *cosmos*] (64).

In Sarduy, the received duality between "body" and "language" yields to the logic of the Signifying Queens, whose aim is to rescue the banished body, not in its specular totality but as fragment, the bits and pieces gathered by the pair at the end of *De donde son los cantantes.* The subject thus produced is neither psychological nor clinical. It is a by-product, a residue, of writing, less Lacan than Bataille, whose list of "wastes" one must recall: "[L]uxury, mourning, wars, rituals, the construction of sumptuous monuments, games, spectacles, art, perverse sexual activity" (28).

In Sarduy's writing, the support of the text is not the masked body of Renaissance theater but the performing body of the drag queen. Without the ontological intensity of Artaud, the performance of the drag queen questions the limits of representations and initiates a pact with the audience. Only a naive or uninitiated drag queen, or a similar reading of her, would regard drag as a misogynist imitation of "woman," for the "woman" displayed by drag is pure construction, essentially so. Drag does not cover the signs of the masculine, nor does it reveal them in a wink at the viewer, as in Hollywood's parade of mostly heterosexual "scare," or parodic, drags. Whatever her antics, or the outrageousness of her costumes, the drag act does not work unless there is in it something implicit and essential, namely, the drag queen's faith in her beauty and in her ability, and at once her failure, to project it. The drag, at least the drag that *signifies* to me, displays her entrapment in a binarism that no amount of theory can wave away, and that is her pathos, which is literally at the root of a shared sympathy. That is the pact of drag, its uselessness and its aura. It is the structure of that pact, and not the repetitive trappings of crossdressing, that is the model of writing and reading culture—Cuban cultures, Latin American cultures, Latino cultures—in Sarduy's novels. It is not an ideology of inversion, gayness, homosexuality, or queerness, but a style, an attitude at once pragmatic and derisive, a movement that overflows the very subject it has aimed to constitute. Dolores may mock her origins, but in the writing subject, there is mockery, or Cuban *choteo,* and nostalgia all at once. Like Auxilio and Socorro, the two-headed bat on the Bacardi bottle, the subject looks both ways, writing in the nostalgia of a lost orality that yields something of its aura only in the drag of symbolic representation.

Gates's theory of African American criticism finds in the figure of Esu both a writing muse and a myth of origin. Gates successfully combines Derrida's deconstructive strategies with the more pragmatic—that is to say, social, cultural, and political—needs of African Americans. Esu is the ancestor of the Signifying Monkey. Esu, writes Gates, is "the great trope of Afro-American discourse, and the trope of tropes, his language of Signi-fyin(g), is his verbal sign in the Afro-American tradition." More subjec-tively put, Gates as critic is the Signifying Monkey, who turns the epithet of white racism on its head by the intellectual efficacy of his own critical rhetoric. Having redefined the rules of the game, the critic may then reread in the confidence that "the black tradition has inscribed within it the very principles by which it can be read" (xxiii–xxiv). By con-trast, Latinos can only envy or desire the cultural and critical coherence achieved by Gates and superimposed as a healing balm on the violence of the African diaspora and its African American aftermath. In a different register, Gates does for African American criticism what Alex Haley's *Roots* did for a popular perception of African American origins, counter-balancing as it did slavery, dispersion, and, precisely, rootlessness with a vision of Africa as the source of an enabling, unifying fable for the many peoples forcibly brought to these shores to be lumped under the violent rubrics of "Negro," "colored," or "black."

For Latinos in the United States, the African American critic's fable of origin and identity would be difficult, if not impossible, to cast, for our places of provenance are as diverse as the "racial" metaphors used to classify us. "Latino" is no less macaronic than "homosexual." Both terms are shifters of identity, whereas "queer" is the troping of sexual identity. All labels are damning when handed down by others, but their very traffic in a culture can be slippery and thereby potentially empowering. Thus, with no pretensions to a false myth of origins, a queer Latino attitude of critical interpretation might emerge from such a slippage, at once recasting Gates's implicit sense of community and appropriating Sarduy's fable of identities as the crisis of the Latino queer subject. Sarduy's Double Signify-ing Queens, however, cannot claim the tutelage of Esu as deity of origins and muse of critical writing.

In *De donde son los cantantes,* Auxilio and Socorro deal in images, the series of photographs that they hand out at the Self-Service; yet the only "service" they can render the "self" is to dress it in a utopically endless metonymy, whose subject, on the metaphoric side of the equation, is absent, though alluded to in the one photograph that they keep to themselves: "Así reparte todas las fotos. Menos una. Se queda con la de carnet, tamaño seis por ocho, en la cual se ve de frente, mirando ligeramente hacia un lado, apenas seria, tal cual es" [She hands out all the photos. Except one. She keeps her i.d. picture, six by eight [centimeters], where she is seen full face, looking slightly to the side, barely serious, just as she is] (18–19). The photograph on an identity card is, after all, the subject's pale self, "tal cual es." The rest, to invert the sense of Verlaine's famous phrase, is literature. In other words, the identity of the self, "tal cual es," is a gray reduction, an impoverished representation, an identity card. By contrast, the costumes that Auxilio and Socorro rig for themselves are the proper signals of identity, its true theater, in the sense of space and performance.

Like Auxilio and Socorro, and like the French psychiatrist G. G. de Clérambault, the Signifying Queen has a passion for fabric and drapery. Clérambault's course on photographs of draped Moroccans at the Ecole des Beaux-Arts was canceled because the authorities feared the splitting of his project "into a consideration of cloth's usefulness and his fetishization of its useless, overbearing presence" (Copjec 95). Teaching in Paris in 1926, Clérambault described national identity on the basis of clothing types, clashing with the utilitarian, and imperialist, aesthetics of high modernism. For the Signifying Queen, clothing and gesture, and their literary representations, are essential elements in fables of national identity.

The Signifying Queen's penchant for drapery, for what may be called the drag of identity, now echoes in the antics of savvy drag queens and in the performances of Cuban American New Yorker Carmelita Tropicana, whose project reclaims lost queer energies from solid, often stolid and historically heterosexual, modes of Cuban American identities.[7] As mentioned earlier, critic Diana Fuss has written about homosexuality and the "the specter of abjection." Queer critics and performers now must turn homosexuality inside out, "exposing not the homosexual's abjected insides," as Fuss writes, "but the homosexual as the abject, as the contaminated and expurgated insides of the heterosexual subject" ("Inside" 3). Fuss goes on to say that "homosexual production emerges under these inhospitable conditions" (4), but emerge it does, whether "under the sign of Saturn," as it did for Verlaine, or under the sign of drag, as it does almost weekly in bars from Roanoke to Biloxi, not in abjection but in celebration. Marked by other borders, unstable or rigid as the case might be, the Signifying Queen reads those signs, bracketing abjection, or sealing it in her purse like a tiny fetish.

A kindly uncle once warned me not to dangle my shoe, a suspicious loafer, from the tip of my toe because "only faggots do that." Such homophobic attention to details of manner and dress is common in Latino and Latin American cultures, but rather than cry "Castration! You hegemonic patriarch!" I internalized loafers and other accouterments as signs of faggotry, using such knowledge to recognize my future accomplices and to make myself visible to them. Was the dangling loafer threateningly phallic? Would a tasteful pump be a mere fetish? At any rate, it should be noted that what is judged in the dangling loafer is not sexual orientation, much less homosexual identity, but a sartorial sign and a particular gesture.

For my unsuspecting uncle, appearance was identity, and a wispy ten year old should be informed of the signs of queerness so that he could suppress them, wherever his sexual orientation might take him. Needless to say, the queer rereading of Latino identity and its foundational texts will not let this pass. Latino queer criticism tropes on that sartorial advice, inverting it and thus foregrounding the signifiers of queerness. My uncle did teach me a lesson, which carried me through the perils of queer fashion. Long ago, for about three days, my unruly curls waxed and molded into a skull cap, I was a clone on Castro Street. Now Olga Guillot's greatest hits and an old pair of high-heel sandals turn vacuuming into an unsuspected pleasure. The drag of identity can thus coexist with, and certainly enrich, Cuban, Latin American, and Latino identities whose construction may be as precarious, as provisional, and yet as absolutely necessary as the costumes in my closet or the books in my library.

Notes

1 In addition to the works already cited, Mario García's discussion of dialogic identities has been especially helpful, as has the work of Juan Flores. Unpublished work by Iraida López and discussions with her on these topics have been invaluable during the preparation of this article. I also thank Jorge Brioso for his reading of this paper and his suggestions and insights.

2 Sue-Ellen Case, "Toward a Butch-Femme Aesthetic." On the "sissy origins" of colonial subjects, see Piedra 370–409.

3   Martí wrote his account of a visit to newly opened Coney Island in 1881, one year after his arrival in New York City for what would be a stay of fifteen years. His chronicle of the amusement park, precursor of our "entertainment complex," was published in Bogotá's *La Pluma,* 3 December 1881. Martí was awed by the electric lights and by the crowds in New York's famous beach towns, but he also took note of evident signs of poverty and racism. The notion of mass amusement was particularly puzzling, and troubling, to him. With characteristic insight, Martí wrote of Coney Island as a microcosm representing a new city and a new nation: "[E]sa inmensa válvula de placer abierta a un pueblo inmenso" [that immense pleasure valve opened for an immense populace] (*Obras completas* 9: 125).

4   For recent queer readings of Latin American literature and culture, see Bergmann and Smith, *¿Entiendes?* On homosexuality in Lezama, see Arnaldo Cruz, *El primitivo implorante.* On Arenas, see the recent articles in *Apuntes Postmodernos,* especially Fowler's and Zayas's. On Senel Paz, author of the story that became the script of *Strawberry and Chocolate,* see Bejel.

5   *De donde son los cantantes* (1967; Barcelona: Barral, 1980). Translated as *From Cuba with a Song* in *Triple Cross* (New York: Dutton, 1972). I have also consulted the critical edition of the novel by González Echevarría (1993). All references are to the Barral edition; all translations are mine.

6   Although Tongolele was from Mexico, she triumphed as the quintessential Cuban *rumbera.* Her trademark, besides the grasshopper skirts with yards of ruffles, was a dramatic white streak in her long black mane. An international star, still active in show business, Cuba's Rosita Fornés recently had to cancel a performance in Miami Beach because of fears that protests by a group of anti-Castro exiles would require costly security measures.

7   In "Flaming Latinas," José Muñoz comments on the process of reclaiming lost queer energies and quotes from Michael Moon's article on performer Jack Smith ("Flaming Closets," *October* 51 [winter 1989]: 37–55).

Pedro Zamora's *Real World* of Counterpublicity:

Performing an Ethics of the Self

~

José Esteban Muñoz

In *The Care of the Self,* the third volume of his *History of Sexuality,* Michel Foucault advocated, through a tour of antiquity and its philosophical underpinnings, an ethics of the self—a working on the self for others.[1] The care of the self emphasizes an ethics around nourishing and sustaining a self within civil society. To work on oneself is to veer away from models of the self that correlate with socially prescribed identity narratives. The rejection of these notions of the self is not simply an individualistic rebellion: resisting dominant modes of subjection entails not only contesting dominant modalities of government and state power but also opening up a space for new social formations. The performance of Latina/o, queer, and other minoritarian ontologies—which is to say the theatricalization of such ethics of the self—conjures the possibility of social agency within a world bent on the negation of such selves. My project here is to map and document a minoritarian ethics of the self and, more important, the ways in which representations of and (simultaneously) by that self signal new spaces within the social. I also suggest that the televisual dissemination of such performances allows for the possibility of counterpublics—communities and relational chains of resistance that contest the dominant public sphere.

My focus on a nexus of identity markers that circulate around queer and Latino is of importance for various reasons. The AIDS emergency has become a painful habit of being for many of us. Those of us who live inside and around Latino communities and queer communities know the ways in which so much has been lost, indeed that the present and far too many futures have been robbed. The necessity of publicizing such ethics of the self, of moving these ethics beyond the privatized zones of individual identities, is great during our contemporary health crisis.

But AIDS is only one of the reasons why publicizing and performing an ethics of self seems so essential for Latina/o and queer politics. The disjunctures between queer and Latino communities are many. The mainstream gay community ignores or exoticizes Latino bodies, and many Latino communities promote homophobia. Yet as of November 1994, the linkages between queerness and *latinidad* have never seemed so poignant. The 4 November 1994 election, nicknamed "the Republican revolution" by some news media pundits, made the headlines by establishing the New Right's majority status in the U.S. Senate and the House of Representatives. This reactionary tidal wave also included legislation that was calibrated to legislate against certain identities. Although two antigay amendments were barely defeated in Idaho and Colorado, Proposition 187 in California, a measure that further erodes the nation's civil rights by denying health care and education to immigrants who have been classified as "illegal" by the state apparatus, was passed. The targeted immigrant communities are non-Europeans, especially Latinos. An anti-lesbian and -gay amendment passed in Colorado in 1992—which reads very much like the barely defeated ordinances in Idaho and Oregon—proposed that lesbians and gays be stripped of any basic civil rights that would acknowledge and protect their minority status. The 1992 Colorado proposition was eventually overruled by the Supreme Court. Nonetheless, the popularity of such initiatives tells us something about the national body: homophobia, racism, and xenophobia are being codified as legislation. It can certainly be argued that these hate discourses have always been the law of the land, yet there is something *particularly* disturbing about the fact that the majoritarian public sphere announces these prohibitions and discriminatory practices as sites to rally around. Indeed, homo-hatred and Latino bashing are two of the New Right's most popular agenda issues. The 1992 Republican convention made all of this quite clear as countless speakers at the podium and delegates interviewed on the floor voiced their anti-immigrant and "pro-family" (which is always anti-queer) rhetoric. The 1996 GOP convention choose to remove ultraright zealots such as Pat Buchanan and Pat Robertson from roles of visibility, thus allowing much of these politics of exclusion to be relocated right below the surface of the televisual proceedings. Despite this prime-time camouflage, the New Right's agenda, spelled out in the GOP plank, still promised a repeal of civil rights legislation, further attacks on immigrants, xenophobic welfare reform, and more family values.

In this essay, I am interested in unveiling moments in which the majoritarian public sphere's publicity—its public discourse and reproduction of that discourse—is challenged by performances of counterpublicity that defy its discriminatory ideology. Counterpublicity is disseminated through acts that are representational *and* political, interventions in the service of subaltern counterpublics. The philosopher Nancy Fraser, following the work of other writers, has critiqued Jürgen Habermas's account of the public sphere for focusing primarily on the constitution of one monolithic bourgeois public sphere at the expense of considering other possibilities for publicity. Even though Habermas's work is essentially a critique of the bourgeois public sphere, his lack of recourse to counterpublics essentially reinscribes the exclusionary logic and universalism of the bourgeois public sphere. Counterpublics, for Fraser, "contest[ed] the exclusionary norms of the 'official' bourgeois public sphere, elaborating alternative styles of political behavior and alternative norms of public speech" (Fraser 4). Fraser goes on to point out the significance of subaltern counterpublics for women, people of color, gays and lesbians, and other subordinated groups. Oskar Negt and Alexander Kluge describe the public sphere as comprising various forms of publicity that are connected to different communities and modalities of publicity. Negt and Kluge's work maintains that counterpublics often emerge out of already existing industrial and commercial channels of publicity, especially the electronic media.

The act of performing counterpublicity in and through electronic/ televisual sites controlled by the dominant public sphere is risky. Many representations of counterpublicity are robbed of any force by what Miriam Hansen has called the "marketplace of multicultural pluralism" (xxxvii). The practices of queer and Latino counterpublicity, acts that publicize and theatricalize an ethics of the self, that I will be mapping present strategies that resist, often through performances that insist on local specificities and historicity, the pull of reductive multicultural pluralism.

The best way we can understand the categories "queer" and Latina/o or

latinidad is as counterpublics that are in opposition to other social movements—movements that are embodied in the hate legislation I have discussed. What is primarily at stake is space. The mode of counterpublicity I
am discussing makes an intervention in public life that defies the white
normativity *and* heteronormativity of the majoritarian public sphere.
Thus I am proposing that these terms be conceptualized as social movements that are contested by, and contest, the public sphere for the purposes of political efficacy—movements that not only "remap" but also
produce minoritarian space.

In what follows, I outline the activism and cultural interventions of
televisual activist Pedro Zamora. I will describe the way in which Zamora
understood the need to perform a Foucauldian ethics of the self and,
furthermore, to take a *next* step: a leap into the social through the public
performance of ethics of the self. I also call attention to the ways in which
this Cuban American cultural worker's performances accomplished tasks
that enabled the enactment of queer and Latino identity practices in a
phobic public sphere. These tasks include the denouncement of the dominant public sphere's publicity that fixes images and understandings of
queerness and *latinidad;* the enactment of resistance to the reductive multicultural pluralism that is deployed against them; the production of an
intervention within the majoritarian public sphere that confronts phobic
ideology; and the production of counterpublicity that allows *the possibility*
of subaltern counterpublics.

The theoretical schools I am blending here, social theory influenced by
Habermas and Foucault's discourse analysis, are more often than not
pitted *against* each other. Habermas's thinking appeals to, and attempts to
reconstruct, rationality. Foucault's, in its very premise, is a critique of
rationality. The mappings that public sphere social theory provides are
extremely generative ones. Yet as I leave the work of social theorists such as
Negt and Kluge, Hansen, and Fraser and return to the major source of
these paradigms, Habermas, I find myself having various misgivings with
his project's philosophical tenets: namely his use of, and investment in,
communicative reason.[2] Habermassian communicative reason presupposes that within all communicative gestures there exists an appeal to an
undeniable "good" that would alleviate all disagreements within the social. Foucauldians and others find the category of a universally defined
good to be an exceedingly easy target. For my own part, I am not inter-

ested in the exercise of dismantling Habermassian reason because such an endeavor would be of little use to my project.

My use of the public sphere is primarily indebted to Negt and Kluge's critique of Habermas, especially their move to critique the underlying concepts of universal reason that they identify in his project. Their critique uses Kant's critical philosophy (which resonates with Foucault's) to problematize the category of an abstract principle of generality. Their work then opens up space to conceptualize multiple publics, complete with their own particularities.

Jon Simmons has explained that it is indeed difficult to locate Foucault on any map of politics that we inherit from nineteenth-century philosophy. But he goes on to add that

> Foucault does belong to a "we," though this "we" is not easily classifiable according to traditional categories. How does one define the gay movement, feminism, youth protests, the movements of ethnic and national minorities, and the diffuse discontents of clients of educational, health and welfare systems who are identified as single mothers, unemployed, or delinquent? His transgressive practices of self with writing, drugs, gay friendship and S/M operate in the space opened by these movements. Those whose designated desires, genders, ethnic identities, or welfare categorizations do not seem to fit in this space. It is in this space where some women refuse to be feminine and become feminists; in which black-skinned people refuse to be Negroes and become African-Americans; and in which men who desire other men might refuse to be homosexuals and become gay. Like Foucault, they practice politics of those who refuse to be who they are and strive to become other. (103)

The space that Simmons describes is what I consider the transformative political space of disidentification.[3] Here is where Negt and Kluge function for me as valuable supplements to Foucault's mappings of the social. This space, what Simmons calls Foucault's "we," can be given a new materiality and substance when transcoded as counterpublics. Fredric Jameson, in a fascinating essay on Negt and Kluge, sees this connection between the German writers and Foucault, despite the fact that Jameson is ultimately opposed to Foucault and valorizes Negt and Kluge:

The originality of Negt and Kluge, therefore, lies in the way in which the hitherto critical and analytical force of what is widely known as "discourse analysis" (as in Foucault's descriptions of the restrictions and exclusions at work in a range of so called discursive formations) is now augmented, not to say completed, by the utopian effort to create space of a new type. (49)

The definition of counterpublics that I am invoking here is intended to describe different subaltern groupings that are defined as falling outside the majoritarian public sphere; it is influenced by a mode of discourse theory that critiques universalities and favors particularities, yet it insists on a Marxian materialist impulse that *regrids* transgressive subjects and their actions as identifiable social movements. Thus my notion of a counterpublic resonates alongside Simmons's description of "[t]hose whose designated desires, genders, ethnic identities, or welfare categorizations do not seem to fit." The object of my study, Pedro Zamora, was, from the purview of the dominant public sphere, one of those who did not seem to fit. In this way, his work can be understood as a counterpublic response to dominant publicity.

The young Cuban American activist disidentified with that dominant publicity, working with *and* on one of its "channels," MTV. Habermas, following the example of Frankfurt school predecessor Theodor Adorno, would probably see MTV as the providence of monopoly capitalism, locked into a pattern of sameness that was only calibrated to reproduce the consumer. He could never see MTV as a stage where radical work could be executed. Negt and Kluge understand that in this postmodern moment, the electronic media is essential to the reproduction of state capitalism and counterpublicity. Zamora also understood this. Using his keen sense of counterpublicity, he spotted *The Real World*'s potential as an exemplary stage. One only need consider the cover letter he sent MTV when he was applying for the show to understand how the young activist immediately saw the political potential of the medium. His pitch challenges the producers to consider the possibility of having a person living with AIDS on the show:

So why should I be on *The Real World*? Because in the real world there are people living productive lives who just happen to be HIV+. I think it is important for people my age to see a young person who looks and feels healthy, can party and have fun but at the same time needs to take five pills daily to stay healthy.

On one of your episodes this season [season 2] you had an HIV+ guy come in and talk about AIDS/HIV with the group. He was there a few hours and he left. I wonder what kind of issues would have come up if that HIV+ guy would be living with the group, sharing the bathroom, the refrigerator, the bedroom, eating together? Everyday for six months. Things that make you go hmmmm. (Johnson and Rommelmann 158)

Here Zamora describes the dramatic and televisual energy his inclusion in the show would generate. He does not pitch his project in all its political urgencies. He understands that one needs to disidentify with the application process to be given access to the stage that cable program provided him. His disidentification with the act of applying permits to him play up that fact that his inclusion would make for good TV as well as an important political intervention. He next speaks to his willingness to sacrifice his own privacy for the sake of his activism:

I know that being on *The Real World* would mean exposing the most intimate details of my life on national television. How comfortable am I with that? Well, I do that through my job every day.

If I can answer the questions of an auditorium full of fifth graders with inquiring minds, I am sure I could do it on national television.

He is willing to sacrifice his right to privacy because he understands that subjects like himself never have full access to privacy. Although the dominant public sphere would like to cast him in the zone of private illness, it is clear that his access to any real privacy, as *Bower v. Hardwick* signals, is always illusory. In this statement, the young activist understands that his desires, gender identifications, health, and national and ethnic minority status keep him from having any recourse to the national fantasy of privacy that other subjects in the public sphere cling to.

Magic Johnson, though he achieved celebrity before he tested positive for the virus, used his celebrity and the mass media in ways that are similar to those of Zamora, who came into celebrity through *The Real World.*

Hansen offers a reading of Magic Johnson's case that is so relevant here that it is worth citing at length.

> When basketball player Magic Johnson used his resignation upon having tested positive to advocate safe sex he did more than put his star status in the service of a political cause; he made a connection, albeit a highly personalized one, between the industrial-commercial public sphere of sports, its local reappropriation within the African-American community, and the counter-public struggle surrounding AIDS. While the latter is by now organized on an international scale, it continues to be marginalized domestically as a "special interest," to be denied public status with reference to its roots in gay subculture. Johnson's gesture not only made a public concern that the neoconservative lobby has been trying to delegitimize as private; it also, if only temporarily, opened-up a discursive arena, in both mainstream publicity and within the African-American community, in which sexual practices could be discussed and negotiated, rather than merely sensationalized or rendered taboo. Not least, it provided a way to return sex education to schools from which it had disappeared under Reagan. (Hansen xxxviii–xxxix)

While there is much to say about the vastly divergent strategies of negotiating that Johnson and Zamora employed, I want to suggest that it is useful to consider how the two men's examples are similar. Both used the power of celebrity to make counterpublic interventions using the mainstream media, a mode of publicity that is usually hostile to counterpublic politics. Both used their national stages to appear to various publics, including a mass public and the minoritized counterpublics from which they locate their own identities. They also decided to combat the neoconservative strategy of relegating public health emergency to privatized and individual illness. Both men, practicing a public ethics of the self, thematized and theatricalized their illness as public spectacles. The New Right is bent on removing AIDS from the public agenda, nourishing ignorance through the suppression of safe sex pedagogy, and, finally, cutting off federal support to PWAS and medical research. To better understand Zamora's example, it is useful to review the show's five-season run, noting shifts in each incarnation of the show.

Since its inception in 1991, MTV's *The Real World* has included queers in its "real-life" ensemble cinema vérité–style melodrama. The show's premise is simple: seven videogenic young people, all strangers, are chosen to live in a house together. The twenty-something group is usually somewhat racially diverse. Its gender breakdown is usually four men and three women. It has had five different "casts" and five different incarnations, in five different cities: New York, Los Angeles, San Francisco, London, and Miami. Every season has included a gay or lesbian character. The New York cast included Norman, a white man who sometimes identified himself as bisexual and sometimes as gay. Although he was rather charismatic, Norman was something of a minor character on the show; most of that season focused on the contrived sexual tension between innocent country girl Julie and Eric, a New Jerseyan Herb Ritts model who was nominally straight and went on to host the illustrious MTV dance party show *The Grind*. Much steam was lost in the show's second season. The queer came in as a midseason replacement. Beth was a white lesbian who worked in B horror movie production. Beth received probably less screen time than any other character in the show's five seasons. Both Norman and Beth dated, but their sexual lives were relegated to "special episodes." The way in which these two characters were contained and rendered narratively subordinate to the show's straight characters is a succinct example of the inane multicultural pluralism that Hansen has described. It also clearly displays some of the ways in which queers and the counterpublicity they might be able to disseminate are rendered harmless with the channels of the electronic media and the majoritarian public sphere. Zamora was the third season's house queer. Pedro did not fall into obscurity in the way his queer predecessors had. Rather, Pedro managed to offer valuable counterpublicity for various subaltern counterpublics that included U.S. Latinos, queers, and people living with AIDS.

For five months, Pedro was one of the only out gay men appearing regularly on television.[4] He was also one of the only Latinos seen regularly on national television. Furthermore, he was one of the only out people living with AIDS on television. Zamora was more than simply represented; he used MTV as an opportunity to continue his life's work of HIV/AIDS pedagogy, queer education, and human rights activism. Unlike his queer predecessors, he exploited MTV in politically efficacious ways; he used MTV more than it used him.

The fourth season of the show was set in London. At this point, the show broke from its pattern of having a house queer. The *Real World* London was less contentious than the San Francisco show. It included only one ethnic minority, a black British jazz singer, and no out lesbians, gays, bisexuals, or transgendered people. It would seem that the ethnic, racial, and sex diversity that had characterized the show's first three seasons was put on hiatus after the explosive San Francisco season that I will be discussing here. I will argue that the soft multicultural pluralism that characterized the series was exploited and undermined by Zamora and some of his peers. I am suggesting that the fourth season of *The Real World* can be read as a backlash of sorts. Which is to say it was an escape from North American politics and social tensions to a storybook England, a fantasy Europe that had none of its own ethnic or sexual strife. (The roommates actually lived in an apartment that was made up to look like a castle.)

The fifth season, set in Miami, represents a back-to-basics approach in which the tried-and-true formula of nominal racial and sexual diversity was reestablished. That show's cast included two women of color: Cynthia, an African American waitress from Oakland, California, and Melissa, "the local girl," a Cuban American woman from the Miami area. The house queer spot went once again to a white man, as it did in its classic first season. Dan, a college student from Rutgers University, was raised in the Midwest, where he grew up watching the show like many queer kids in the United States. In a feature article in *OUT* magazine, Dan spoke about the way in which he, as a pre-out youth, marveled at seeing an out Norman on the show's first season. In that article, Dan expresses his understanding that he was now, thanks to the show, going to be the most famous gay man in America. The young Real Worlder's statement testifies to the counterpublic making properties of the program. Dan aspires to be a model and a writer for flashy fashion magazines. His interviews on the program and in the print media indicate that he was cognizant of a need to be a public "role model" for queers, but his performances fell short of the radical interventions that Zamora produced.

Dan understood the need to project a positive image; Zamora, on the other hand, was conscious of the need to take the show's title seriously and be radically real. A coffee-table fan book that MTV published in 1995 while the fourth season was airing prints sound bites by many of the show's stars, producers, and crew; the book's revenues go, in part, to the

Pedro Zamora foundation. In that book, story editor Gordon Cassidy comments:

The one thing I feel best about in this show is what Pedro enabled us to present to the rest of the country, and not just about AIDS, but about who he was as a person, things that networks can't get away with. You think of the problems networks have portraying gay relationships, interracial relationships, and he was all of those. (Johnson and Rommelmann 90)

That Zamora was indeed all of these things is especially important. The "realness" of Pedro and the efficacy and power of his interventions have as much to do with the manner in which he insisted on being a complicated and intersectional subject: not only gay but a sexual person; a person of color actively living with another person of color in an interracial relationship; a person living with AIDS. Although Cassidy's comments could be read as an example of MTV slapping itself on the back, much of what he is saying is accurate. As of this moment, broadcast network television is unable and unwilling to represent queers who are sexual yet not pathological, interracial relationships, and stories about AIDS that portray the fullness and vibrancy of such a life narrative.

It would be a mistake to elide the representational significance of Zamora's work on the mainstream. Pedro, as Bill Clinton put it, gave AIDS a very "human face." Beyond that, he gave it a vibrant, attractive, politicized, and brown face. He showed an ignorant and phobic national body that within the bourgeois public's fantasy of privacy, the binarism of public health and private illness could no longer hold. That the epidemic was no longer an abstract and privatized concern. He willfully embodied and called attention to all those things that are devastating and ennobling about possessing a minority subjectivity within an epidemic. And although MTV gave Zamora a stage to do this work of education and embodiment, MTV should not be too valorized for this contribution because they often attempted to undercut it. In what follows, I offer a quick synopsis of Pedro's role and work on *The Real World*. I skip episodes that are not pertinent to Pedro's story or the story I am telling in this essay. I then consider the show's nineteenth episode in more elaborate detail.

The show begins with Cory, a college student from California who rendezvouses with Pedro[5] on a train. The young Anglo woman is very taken with Pedro, and Pedro, for his part, in a voice-over, explains that he was expecting to meet a woman who would be very much like Cory, very "all-American." Soon all of the roommates appear, including Judd, a Jewish cartoonist from Long Island; Pam, an Asian-American medical student; Mohammed, an African American Bay Area musician and writer; Puck, a white man who was a supposed bicycle messenger; and Rachel, a Republican Mexican American[6] from Arizona applying to graduate school. (I am aware that the preceding descriptions seem to be somewhat stock, but these were the primary identity accounts that the program offered.) That first episode concluded with Pedro sharing his scrapbook with his roommates. The scrapbook consisted of newspaper clippings from around the nation of his activist work. This outed him to the rest of the cast not only as queer but also as a person living with AIDS. Rachel was put off by this display and proceeded, during an interview in the confessional,[7] to voice her AIDS-phobic and homophobic concerns about cohabitating with Pedro. Thus the first episode began with the "all-American girl" meeting the handsome young stranger on a train and concluded with a conservative Latina expressing a phobic position against the young AIDS educator. This episode framed Pedro as one of the show's "star" presences, unlike the queers from previous seasons.

Episode 2 presents an early confrontation between Pedro and the show's other star presence, Puck. Pedro objects to Puck's postpunk hygiene in the kitchen and throughout the living space. Although the show hoped to frame this confrontation as a sort of odd-couple dilemma, it ignored the very material fact that Puck's lack of hygiene was nothing short of a medical risk for a person living with a compromised immune system. While Rachel goes to an "Empower America" fund-raiser and meets the New Right's beloved Jack Kemp, one of her personal heroes, Pedro goes on a first date with Sean, an HIV-positive pastry chef with a disarming smile. Sean and Pedro's relationship advances, and the couple fall in love by episode 6. Puck makes homophobic jokes about Pedro during this episode. According to interviews with the cast after the series was completed, these comments from Puck were a regular household occurrence and were, through editing strategies, downplayed by the producers.

In episode 8, Pedro goes for a checkup. He discovers that his T cell count has dropped significantly. This moment represents an important moment in TV history: a painful aspect of a PWA's quotidian reality is represented like never before. This sequence is followed by one where Pedro gives a seminar on safe sex and risk prevention at Stanford University. Puck, always vying for the house's attention, schedules a beachcombing expedition at the same time. Pam and Judd choose to watch and support Pedro while Cory and Rachel join Puck. The show crosscuts both sequences, emphasizing the divisions in the house. Tensions mount during episode 9. Pedro and Sean become engaged, and Puck reacts with what is by now predictable homophobia. The house confronts Puck on his behavioral problems in episode 11. Puck won't listen, and Pedro delivers an ultimatum to the house: it is either him or Puck. The members vote, and Puck is unanimously ejected from the house.

In episode 11 Pedro travels with Rachel to Arizona to meet her Catholic and Republican family. Pedro is exceedingly diplomatic with the family and connects with them as Latinos. Rachel's parents, both educators at a local school, invite Pedro to talk about AIDS at their workplace. One student asks if Pedro still has sex and whether or not he had a girlfriend. There is a tight shot of Rachel's mother looking worried and seemingly holding her breath. Pedro pauses and then answers that he is in "a relationship" and continues to practice safe sex. Cut to a shot of Rachel's mother looking relieved. This maneuver shows what is for many anti-homophobic spectators a difficult and problematic moment. Deciding *not* to be out and *not* to perform and inhabit his queerness at that moment was a worthwhile compromise in the face of his professional work as an AIDS educator dealing with adolescents in a public school. It can also be understood, at least in part, as a moment of Latino allegiance, where queerness is displaced by the mark of ethnicity. I want to suggest that understanding this disidentification with his queerness as a disservice to queers or his own queer identity would be erroneous insofar as these shuttlings and displacements are survival strategies that intersectional subjects, subjects who are caught and live between different minoritarian communities, must practice frequently if they are to keep their residencies in different subcultural spheres.

Episode 13 is focused on Pedro—as he returns home to Miami—and his best friend, Alex. The homecoming is cut short when Pedro becomes sick. In a post–*Real World* interview, Zamora explained that he wanted to show it all, the good days and the bad days (Rubenstein 38–41, 79–81). Representing as much as possible of the totality of living with AIDS was very important for his ethics of the self, his performance of being a self *for* others. That episode gives a family history and background. Pedro emigrated to the United States through the Mariel boat lift at the end of the Carter administration. He lost his mother to cancer when he was fifteen, a tragedy that rocked his family. His family is represented as a very typical blue-collar Cuban American family. Cuban Americans, especially Miami Cubans, are associated with right-wing politics and values. It is thus important to see this family embrace their son with no hesitation. The image of Cuban Americans loving, accepting, and being proud of a gay son complicates the map of *latinidad* that is most available within U.S. media. The better-known map positions Cubans on the far right and Chicanos on the far left, which, although demographically founded, is a nonetheless reductive depiction of *latinidad*.

Episode 16 depicts Pedro's bout with pneumonia, which eventually leaves him hospitalized. The housemates experience a feeling of helplessness that is common in support communities of people with AIDS. By the next episode, Pedro is out of the hospital and accompanies the rest of the cast on a trip to Hawaii. By the twentieth and final episode, Pedro has become very close to Cory, Pam, and Judd. The cast is shown moving out of their Lombard street flat.

By reading the second-to-last episode, episode 19, I want to point out the restraints that the show's producers put on Zamora's performances and the way in which the young Cuban American responded to those restraints. Pedro's romance became the major romance of the show; Sean never fell out of the picture like Norman and Beth's partners and flirtations. Sean became part of Pedro's quotidian reality. Both made their presence continuously known in the San Francisco flat. A few weeks into their relationship, Sean proposed marriage to Pedro, and Pedro accepted. In response, the show's other "star" presence, Puck, decided to one-up the queer couple by proposing marriage to his new girlfriend, Toni. Puck stands as proof that not all counterpublics challenge the way in which the social is organized by dominant culture. Puck's counterpublic is a juvenile version of rugged individualism; it represents a sort of soft anarchism that views all political struggles as equivalent to his own exhaustive self-absorption. The competing modes of counterpublicity between Pedro and

Puck eventually contributed to the breakdown in the domestic space that concluded with Puck being asked to leave.

The episode I want to consider tracks Pedro's and Puck's respective romances. Pedro's queerness is played against Puck's heterosexuality. The episode crosscuts between the two pairings. One questions the producer's rationale for juxtaposing Puck's romantic relationship with Toni with Pedro and Sean's commitment ceremony. Since Puck was ejected from the house, producers continued to film his encounters with his former housemates Cory, Rachel, and Judd. But except for this penultimate episode there was no presentation of Puck independent of his housemates.

Early in the episode, Sean and Pedro are shown in bed together as they lie on top of each other and plan their commitment ceremony. To MTV's credit, there has never been any scene of queer sociality like it on television. The scene of two gay men of color, both HIV positive, in bed together as they plan what is the equivalent of a marriage is like none that was then or now imaginable on television. The transmission of this image throughout the nation and the world is a valuable instance of counterpublicity. Edited within this scene are individual video bites by both participants. Sean explains:

Being with Pedro, someone who is so willing to trust and love and sort of be honest with is refreshing. I think that knowing that Pedro does have an AIDS diagnosis and has been getting sick makes me recognize the need to be here right now. I know that one of us may get sick at some time but the underlying understanding or this underlying feeling makes it a lot easier.

Sean's statement and his performance in front of the video camera explain their choice of having a formal bonding ceremony as being a response to a radically refigured temporality in the face of AIDS. This too is an important instance of nationally broadcast counterpublic theater that provides an important opportunity for the mass public to glimpse different life worlds than the one endorsed by dominant ideology.

Yet the power of this image and Sean's statement is dulled when the program cuts to its next scene. The previous scene of coupling is followed by Puck and Toni's coupling ritual. Puck, in a voice-over, announces that he and Toni are made for each other, that they are, in fact, "a matched pair." They go window-shopping for a wedding ring, and Toni eyes a ring that she likes; Puck scolds her and tells her that the window item is a cocktail ring, not a traditional wedding ring. He then offers to buy her a tie clip instead. (It should be noted that this footage is merely window-shopping; the show later shows the other couple actually selecting bands.) Sean's voice-over is narratively matched with the playful Toni, who explains that "[w]hen I first met Puck he was stinking and looking for a mate. I think we're in love. I know we're in love."

While Sean and Pedro are preparing for an actual ceremony, Toni and Puck are shown hanging out. Toni and Puck are not planning any sort of ceremony. The producer's strategy of matching the story lines and making them seem equivalent is resolved by a strategy of crosscutting the commitment ceremony with one of Puck's soap box derby races. Toni is shown cheering on Puck as he races his green box car. Since the show's inception, the producers of *The Real World* have always hoped for a romance to erupt on the set between cast members. That has yet to happen.[8] In lieu of such a relationship, the producers hope for an interesting relationship between a cast member and outsider. Sean and Pedro's romance emerged early on as the show's most significant relationship. I am arguing that the series producers were unable to let a queer coupling, especially one as radical as Sean and Pedro's, stand as the show's actual romance. Pedro and Sean's relationship and individual performances were narratively undermined by a strategy of weak multicultural crosscutting that was calibrated to dampen the radical charge that Pedro and Sean gave *The Real World*.

Despite these efforts by the show's producers to diminish the importance of Pedro and Sean's relationship, the ceremony itself stands as an amazingly powerful example of publicly performing an ethics of the self while simultaneously theatricalizing a queer counterpublic sphere. The ceremony begins with a shot of a densely populated flat. Sean and Pedro are toasted by Eric, a friend of the couple who has not appeared in any previous episode, and he delivers an extremely touching toast:

> It gives me a lot of pleasure and I see it as a real pleasure to speak on behalf of Sean and Pedro and to them. In your love you remind us that life is about now and love is about being there for one another. It is with real bravery that you open your hearts *to each other* and I think it's with

real hope that you promise your lives to each other. *We stand with you defiantly and bravely and with real hope.* To the adorable couple. (Emphasis mine)

This toast is followed by equally elegant statements by both Pedro and Sean. Eric's statement is significant because it marks the way in which Pedro and Sean's being for themselves ("to each other") is, at a simultaneous moment, a being for others ("we stand with you"). This ceremony is like none that has ever been viewed on commercial television. It is a moment of counterpublic theater. The commitment ceremony not only inspires the gathering of spectators at the ceremony to stand together bravely, defiantly and with hope, but, beyond the walls of the Lombard street flat and beyond the relatively progressive parameters of San Francisco, inspires a world of televisual spectators.

The Real World is overrun by queers. Queer bonds are made manifest in ways that have never been available on cable or broadcast television. Pedro's insistence on mastering the show's format through his monologues, domestic interventions, and continuous pedagogy are relaxed in this sequence I have just described. Here the public sphere is reimagined by bringing a subaltern counterpublic into representation. The real world is overrun by queers. Queers who speak about those things that are terrifying and ennobling about a queer and racialized life world. The commitment ceremony sequence in many ways sets up the show's closure. Puck's antics, crosscut and stacked next to the commitment ceremony, are narratively positioned to lessen the queer spin put on *The Real World* by Pedro. Such a strategy is concurrent with the show's pluralist ethos. Queer commitments, energies, and politics are never quite left to stand alone.

The way in which Puck's relationship is used to relativize and diminish the emotional and political impact of Pedro and Sean's relationship is reminiscent of Pedro's selection to be included in the cast *with and in contrast to* Rachel, a young Republican Latina. Again, the ideologically bold move of representing an activist like Pedro as a representative of *latinidad* is counterbalanced by a reactionary Latina. That Rachel and Pedro later bond as Latinos, despite their ideological differences, is narratively satisfying, producing a sense of hope for the spectator invested in pan-Latino politics.

The performance of a commitment ceremony itself might be read as an aping of heterosexual relationships. Such a reading would miss some important points. In a voice-over before the ceremony, Pedro discusses the need to "risk" being with Sean. He points to the ways in which this relationship, within the confines of his tragically abbreviated temporality, forms a new space of self, identity, and relationality; it is, in Foucault's terms, a new form. The couple form, crystallized as bourgeois heterosexual dyad, is shattered and reconfigured. Indeed, this is a disidentification with the couple form. When one is queer and knows that he or his loved one is dying, the act of "giving oneself" to another represents an ethics of the self that does not cohere with the prescribed and normative coupling practices that make heterosexuals and some lesbians and gay men want to marry. I want to suggest that Pedro and Sean's ceremonial bonding is *not* about aping bourgeois heterosexuality; rather, it is the enacting of a new mode of sociality. Foucault, in an often cited interview on friendship, suggested that we understand homosexuality not so much as a desire as something that is *desirable*. He explains that we must "work at becoming homosexual and not be obstinate in recognizing that we are" (*Foucault Live* 204). Homosexuality is desirable because a homosexual mode of life lets us reimagine sociality. The homosexual needs to "invent from A to Z a relationship that is formless" and, eventually, to arrive at a "multiplicity of relations" (204). Becoming homosexual, for Foucault, would then be a political project, a social movement of sorts, that would ultimately help us challenge repressive gender hierarchies and the structural underpinnings of institutions. Thus I want to mark Sean and Pedro's union as something new, a new form that is at the same time formless from the vantage point of established state power hierarchies.

I understood Pedro Zamora's life work as having surpassed MTV's and the show's producers' dubious politics. Pedro Zamora died on 11 November 1994. He was twenty-two. The day after his death, a front-page story appeared in the *Wall Street Journal*. The article explained that Pedro received thousands of fan letters a week. It quoted one letter from a South Carolina woman who wrote: "I never thought anyone could change my opinion of homosexuals and AIDS. Because of you I saw the human side of something that once seemed so unreal to me." The letter speaks to Pedro's intervention in the public sphere. It bears witness to the difference this young Latino's life work made. Perhaps even more important than this intervention in the public sphere is the way Pedro's work helped further consolidate a counterpublic, a sphere that stands in opposition to the racisms and homophobia of the dominant public sphere. We thus begin to view a new horizon of experience and perceive a real world of possibility.

Notes

1 See also "The Ethic of the Care of the Self as a Practice of Freedom" in *The Final Foucault.*

2 For an excellent reading of the political and philosophical disjunctures between Foucault and Habermas, see Jon Simmons, *Foucault and the Political.*

3 By disidentification I am referring to practices and spaces where identities are negotiated through a series of tactical and partial identifications within the majoritarian public sphere. I elaborate this project in my forthcoming study *Disidentifications.*

4 He has continued, even after his death, to be a beacon of queer possibility thanks to MTV's policy on running *Real World* reruns, from all five seasons, continuously.

5 The show itself used only first names. Thus when I discuss the narratives of actual episodes I employ Pedro, and I mostly refer to the man and cultural worker outside of the show's narrative as Zamora.

6 I use the term *Mexican American* to describe Rachel because I imagine her political ideology would not be aligned with the politics of the Chicana/o movement.

7 The confessional is a room where house occupants perform a personal monologue for a stationary camera. The confessional footage is later intercut with the show's narrative.

8 Judd and Pam did eventually begin dating, but only after the show stopped filming. Failed on-the-set couplings include Eric and Julie in season 1, Puck and Rachel in season 3, and Kat and Neil in season 4.

IV

~

DESIRE

AND

REPRESENTATION

Sexual Terror: Identity and Fragmentation
in Juan Goytisolo's *Paisajes después de la batalla*

~

Brad Epps

[El] terrorismo es la eliminación de un jugador del juego que se juega con él [Terrorism is the elimination of a player from the game that is played with him]. —Jesús Ibáñez

The Red Fags, *los Maricas Rojos,* are at the door. They knock with their knuckles and ask for the man of the house. Their voices, high-pitched and queerly accented, imitate, or strive to imitate, the sulky, somewhat shrill speech of little girls. They tap their heels and giggle disarmingly. Though they cannot be seen from the peephole, they sound like perfectly normal lasses, a bit too provocative perhaps, but certainly not too dangerous, the type that some men might imagine dressing up, or down, and photographing. And yet, regardless of how they might be imagined, they are waiting only for that moment of carelessness or simpleminded trust that allows them real entry. For once the door opens, once the master peeks out from his home, they launch their attack and, in attacking, expose themselves for what they truly are: ruthless, wily terrorists, experts in karate and high-tech weaponry, in the ways of the hand and the voice, in martial, modern, and mimetic arts.

So exposed, they quickly subdue the man, their man, and attach a bomb to his naked chest. They are effective militants, and as such, they are hierarchical. The leader, "*la jefa,*" is a hysterical Lacanian with dyed hair who makes psychoanalytic pronouncements; the main follower, or disciple, calls to mind an ignorant, ugly cousin from the provinces and parrots the leader's words, enriching them with a strong Catalan accent. As their dazed, gagged, and impotent hostage looks on, they rifle through his

library, scattering papers, letters, and photographs, and ruining everything that he has collected and copied. A bit later, with their search apparently concluded, they go to the bathroom, where they doll themselves up,
putting on perfume and cologne and washing their private parts in the
bidet: they may be wily and ruthless, but they are also clean and attractive.
Dressed to kill, they then depart, but not before leaving their hapless
victim written instructions concerning his fate. With the bomb still binding his body, he reads that he has exactly twenty-four hours to write the
complete story of his vices, fantasies, and weaknesses, to put down on
paper everything most sinful and sordid about himself. He reads, under
the threat of death, that he must write his self-critique, his confession, his
ever-so-grotesque autobiography. He must tell the truth, straight and sincere, without falsity or fiction, if he is to save himself from destruction.
The Red Fags have, so to speak, their fingers on the trigger.

   This scenario is not, I confess, of my imagination alone. Rather, it is a
paraphrased account, a translated, transcribed copy, of a scene in Juan
Goytisolo's *Paisajes después de la batalla* [*Landscapes after the battle*]. The
scene is titled, quite emphatically, "¡Raptado por los Maricas Rojos!" [Ab-
ducted by the Red Fags!], and is one of the last of seventy-seven fragments
in a text where fragmentation is of the essence. To borrow from Julián
Ríos, it is one of so many gags, or comic blows ["golpe de efecto cómico"],
that constitute the text's structural unity ["unidad estructural"] (Ríos 36).
Funny as all of this may seem, it also points to something quite serious.
Unity, or identity and integrity, and fragmentation, or dispersion and
difference, are the terms of one of the most serious and significant dilemmas of *Paisajes,* a dilemma dramatized, however comically, in the
attack of the Red Fags.[1] This attack is directed, as I have indicated, toward
a male subject at home, but it is situated, more amply, within the contemporary city, where subjects proliferate and dissolve, cohere and clash,
where they are scripted, erased, and rescripted anew. It is thus an attack at
once personal and public, "familiar" and "strange."

   But there is something more. Among the personal and public signs of
this attack, indeed chief among them, are homosexuality and communism, tied together and tied, in turn, to terrorism. Together, homosexuality, communism, and terrorism suggest something transgressive, or
subversive, that Goytisolo's text exploits parodically. The problem, at least
as it is styled here, is not so much that homosexuality and communism are

bound, one as much as the other, to terrorism, but rather that they are bound to a form of terrorism that aims, symbolically speaking, not for disruption, fragmentation, and dispersion, but for such things as order, truth, integrity, identity, and collective action. Beneath the wild and crazy appearances of the Red Fags lies a dogmatic and uncompromising will to unity (workers of the world, queers of all colors, unite!) that is at odds with what is here depicted as the free, creative play of the imagination. This "problem" is in turn problematic. For beneath the text's parodic excesses, its comic blows, its wild and crazy fragmentariness, its plays of irony and ambiguity, its professions of literary autonomy *and* social concern, lies a story, itself often dogmatic in its implications, in which communist and homosexual activism, presented as virtually identical, are the menacing other of storytelling, indeed of creativity, in general. Political and social reality motivates and informs the text, but it also threatens to spoil its game. In the pages that follow, I want to consider this double bind; I want to consider, among other things, how a work of "creative writing" can steel itself against criticism; how an author can safeguard the authority of authorship by preempting its destruction; how literary activity can be styled in such an ostensibly free and open way that it forecloses certain modes of *organized* activity, or activism, beyond it.

Set in a vibrantly babelesque Paris, "el París alógeno, poscolonial, barbarizado de Belleville o Barbès" [the allogenic, postcolonial, barbarized Paris of Belleville or Barbès] (*Paisajes* 147; *Landscapes* 85), *Paisajes* is rife with conflicting messages, competing languages, and colliding scripts: with contentious subjects and signs. Taking its inspiration from street graffiti, newspaper blurbs, scientific articles, personal ads, love letters, mystical poetry, advertisements, diaries, manifestos, and so on, it does its best to approximate its narrator's ideal of "un libro abierto al conjunto de voces y experiencias, construido como un rompecabezas" [a book open to the ensemble of voices and experiences, constructed like a puzzle] (*Paisajes* 229; *Landscapes* 153, translation altered). To this end, it cites and recites, imitates, satirizes, copies, translates, and transcribes the words of others: not so much repossessing them as disseminating and dispossessing them. It scatters, particularly at the beginning, non-European signs across the pages of a Spanish—but not *wholly* Spanish—text, thereby effecting a powerful critique of Western pretensions to universalism. What ensues is a puzzling openness, puzzling not just because openness enables, and is enabled by, global differences, but because openness can here seem so hermetic, public expression so personal and private.[2] Inasmuch as *Paisajes*, amid fragmentation, challenges confession, self-critique, autobiography, and other discourses of coherent identity, and yet at the same time champions the imagination of the autonomous individual, this puzzle is indeed compelling. For if the radically open book can be closed, then perhaps, just perhaps, the fragmented self can be the most self-sure.

I will return, in closing, to the *sure* slipping of identity; but for the moment I want to point out how the supposedly radical insecurity, uncertainty, and fragmentation of the self, like the openness of the book, involve a sense of lost or loosened form, of de-struction. Critics are quick to point out that *Paisajes* holds "no real plot" (Schwartz 477), "no real story line" (Braun 16), and that its reality, or irreality, is of its own making: autographic. A "structuralist exercise" or "burlesque" (Schwartz 477, 484) for some, it seems, for almost all, to be a text of self-generation, a text where discourse washes away both story and history to shimmer in its own eternal becoming. For José Manuel Martín Morán, this becoming is the literal, literary effect of excessive proximity and total instantaneousness, of time fragmented and fragmenting into a series of perpetual presents (Martín Morán 166); for Francisco Javier Blasco, it is the effect of an iterative verbal autonomy, a palimpsestic process without origin or end (Blasco 11, 23). For Martín Morán, it resembles the schizophrenia that Baudrillard associates with a state of terror; for Blasco, it resembles the polymorphism that Freud associates with an only partially socialized body. But among so many abstract resemblances, so many furious fragments of identity, terrorism, as Martín Morán suggests, stands out as a particularly dense phenomenon. This density is heightened, as I have indicated, by means of such identificatory markers as communism and homosexuality, but it is Goytisolo's configuration of terrorism, and its privileged place in the discourse of fragmentation, that I want to consider first.

Whatever its historical contours, terrorism is today most readily conjured up in such names and abbreviations as ETA, the IRA, the PLO, the Red Brigade, and the Shining Path, some of which are mentioned or evoked in *Paisajes*. No doubt something is lost in such a ready listing of names, but then again, it is not the specific character of the organizations they designate that interests Goytisolo as much as the symbolic power of terrorism in general. As Goytisolo presents it, terrorism is the irruption of the unexpected and the rupture of the routine, the insurrection of something violent and extreme. Although often associated in the West with the extreme Left, terrorism is also of the extreme Right and may even be a confusing amalgam of both: "[S]u militancia es múltiple, tentacular, polimorfa: abarca el espacio geográfico y cultural; el pasado, presente y futuro" [his militancy is multiple, tentacular, polymorphous: it encompasses geographical and cultural space; the past, the present, and the future] (*Paisajes* 209; *Landscapes* 138).³ The latter, "confused" and "confusing" terrorism is in fact the terrorism practiced, or imagined, by the narrator, author, or protagonist: a polyvalent terrorism whose only principle or end is the fragmentation of, and freedom from, identity (the *bond* between freedom and fragmentation is significant, and questionable, in its own right). Terrorism of the other, more conventionally extreme sort, be it of the Left or the Right, is practiced by an array of collectively identified groups, some historical but most fictional, that include the Red Fags.

It is important to keep the following distinction in mind: the terrorism that is valorized in *Paisajes* and sporadically and imaginatively practiced *by* the protagonist serves fragmentation and particularity, whereas the terrorism that is criticized, or resisted, in *Paisajes* and practiced *against* the protagonist by the Red Fags serves unity and totality. The latter terrorism is that of Terror itself, the terrorism, or terror, of totalitarianism. Jean-François Lyotard's declaration that "[w]e have paid dearly for our nostalgia for the all and the one, for a reconciliation of the concept and the sensible, for a transparent and communicable experience," rings strongly in this context (*The Postmodern Explained* 16). Like Lyotard, Goytisolo— or at least a textually inscribed "goytisolo"—calls for "war on totality" and "attest[s] to the unpresentable." The Red Fags, in contrast, struggle on behalf of totality and, threatening death, attest to total, and totally truthful, representation. Little wonder, then, that identity is here such a significant concern. For in making the concern of terrorism identity instead of, say, the nation-state, Goytisolo expands the violent potential of terrorism, brings it into writing. Terrorism is a real concern, punctuating social and historical existence outside the text, but it is also a rhetorical concern, tracing instability, uncertainty, and danger *in* the text. This is so even when, as in the queerly *inverted* case of the Red Fags, terrorism seeks to guarantee the certainty, stability, and security of identity by questioning uncertainty, destabilizing instability, and attacking insecurity. As with so much of Goytisolo, the relations between the world and the word, the whole and the part, are terribly involute. An effect of reality, terrorist violence is an effect, however weak, of the letter as well.

Playing with, or into, this violence, Goytisolo's text takes on what is arguably the most fantastically intimate site of social formation: the sexual body. Terrorism is rarely more terrorific than when it attacks the sexual body's fantasies of integrity, unicity, and individuality, when it brings home not merely the mortality of the body, but its anonymity and contingency as well. Sexual terror is thus a crucial project and problem of *Paisajes*, but here, unlike *Reivindicación del Conde don Julián* (*Count Julian*, 1970), it does not entail the violation of a hypersymbolic female body. Instead, it entails—and here *Paisajes* does resemble *Conde Julián*—acts of violence against an autobiographically inflected, highly symbolic male body. This does not mean that the role of women is insignificant or unproblematic in *Paisajes*, for among the text's most memorable characters are a number of little girls drawn from the photographic models of Charles Lutwidge Dodgson, otherwise known as Lewis Carroll.[4] These are the girls whose voices the Red Fags imitate in their assault on the home, girls who are themselves, in Goytisolo's rendition, willfully perverse dominatrices, gifted in the art of humiliating and subjugating grown men. Although Kessel Schwartz takes Goytisolo to task for what he describes as the writer's "childish schoolyard humor" (Schwartz 490), there is, I believe, something more serious in these childish games. The key partly lies, no doubt, in the figure of "un Reverendo profesor de la Escuela de Cristo oxoniana" [a reverend don of Christ College, Oxford] (*Paisajes* 92; *Landscapes* 44), in the figure of Lewis Carroll.

Writer, photographer, and admirer of little girls, Carroll is the principal alter ego of Goytisolo's protagonist.[5] Goytisolo makes much of Carroll's love of girls, presenting it as darkly comic, but it has still another side. As Gilles Deleuze puts it, "Lewis Carroll detests boys in general. They have too much depth, and false depth at that, false wisdom and animality" (10). Surface and depth, truth and falsity, love and hatred, femininity and masculinity, all are the coordinates of the childish schoolyard humor, as well as of the willful perversity, of Goytisolo's text. As part of Carroll's legacy, the love for little girls carries within it a hatred for little boys, including that of the lover himself as a little boy. And just as Carroll's attractions become pornographic under Goytisolo's pen, so do his aversions become violent, self-violent. This dynamic recalls the final section of *Conde Julián*, where the protagonist, imaginatively broken into two parts, viciously beats and sodomizes himself, or part of himself, as a little boy. In *Paisajes después de la batalla*, however, the hatred of little boys is not made explicit, but the hatred of the self is. The hatred that fuels sexual terror, or at least a form of sexual terror, does not issue in the rape of women and boys, as I have said, but rather is focused on the figure of the self of the adult author. The result may well be that *Paisajes* is less troubling than *Conde Julián*—Goytisolo calls *Paisajes* his first comic novel—but trouble nonetheless remains.[6] Some of the trouble hinges on the simultaneous calling and dismissal of the authorial self, "el remoto e invisible escritor 'Juan Goytisolo'" [the remote and invisible writer "Juan Goytisolo"] (*Paisajes* 42; *Landscapes* xi).[7] But some of the trouble lies, more specifically, in the fact that the fate of the self is bound to a version of sexual terrorism, or self-terrorism, that is ultimately more homo than hetero.

Carroll's little playmates may evoke a terrible mode of heterosexuality, but they are not presented as members of a terrorist group (like the Red Fags who *imitate* the little girls), and their most terrible act occurs, tellingly enough, when one of them "forces" the protagonist to sodomize himself with a carrot (*Paisajes* 176; *Landscapes* 109–10). In what amounts to a rawer, more tawdry version of *Venus in Furs*, a little girl, Agnès, calls the man her slave and humiliates him, threatening to expose him to his friends and ridiculing his inability to write (177; 110–11). While the little girl adds some particularly hurtful touches (she refuses to lubricate the carrot, and she takes photographs of the final product), the encounter is explicitly presented as one of the protagonist's masturbatory fantasies (102; 50): He has, as Agnès declares, invented her, written her, photographically imagined her, (for) himself (177; 110). Another of the protagonist's fantasies, this one directly tied to terrorism, occurs within a decidedly less girlish, less heterosexual, arena. Directing "un auténtico grito de angustia, una solicitud apremiante a los lectores de sexo masculino" [an authentic cry of anguish, an urgent appeal to readers of the masculine sex], the protagonist, narrator, and/or implied author begs to be strapped to a rack while three terrorists, here from the mysterious Oteka group, "proceden, con severidad implacable, a mi castigo y sodomización" [proceed, with relentless severity, to carry out my punishment and sodomization] (219; 146, translation altered). This fantasy, together with the protagonist's expressed desire elsewhere for the muscular bodies of Turkish and Arabic day laborers, situates the text within something ambivalently akin to homosexuality: albeit a homosexuality coded, somewhere between guilty stereotype and subversive parody, as ascetic, exoticizing, violent, and perverse.[8] I will have more to say about sexual ambivalence and ambiguity later (especially as they are related to, and "resolved" as, homosexuality), but for the moment, I simply want to note that the direct appeal to male readers, the obsession with the avatars of the self, and the linkage of punishment and sodomy, tie the text to a dominant myth of male homosexuality as masculinist, narcissistic, and masochistic.

The question of myth, whether dominant or not, is important. As with *Conde Julián,* storytelling itself appears suffused with myth. At least one of Goytisolo's critics, Annie Perrin, goes so far as to coin the term "sodomyth" ("El laberinto homotextual" 78). Mining the term more for its rhetorical than its ethical or political wealth, Perrin understands the sodomyth as a type of antimyth, parodying and fragmenting an oppressive status quo and its myths. As promising as this may seem, Perrin underestimates the fact that sodomy has been mythified in ways that support, instead of subvert, the heterosexist order. The most persistent of such myths centers on death, or more precisely on the willful death of the will itself. Sodomy has long been, as Lee Edelman notes, "the definitional act of de-generation" (9), by which the sexual body is collapsed into the anus, and the anus into a nihilistic vortex, a black hole of destruction, waste, and death. The annulment of the subject, the repudiation of the self, and the end of man, all of the postmodern turns played in *Paisajes,* not only are premodern (witness Goytisolo's appropriation of Sufism) but also have been coded, as Edelman points out, as the *dangers* embodied, symbolically, mythically, in sodomy. This complicates the often easy celebration of the decentering and fragmentation of identity by suggesting that decentering and fragmentation are themselves signs of identity, that they are functions of a narrative process in which the myths and the histories of "identity" are intertwined in quite specific ways: not all of them liberational.

The "sodomyth" entails, in other words, the history of sodomy, the story of law, morality, and the inscriptions, proscriptions, and prescriptions of the body. The sodomyth may indeed be subversive, as Perrin maintains, but it may also call for a subversion of its own, particularly insofar as it can function as a "negative" myth that *supports,* rather than undermines, "positive" myths of dominance and stability. Put simply, the sodomyth is not of Goytisolo's making alone but is *also* a product of the established order. Beyond any one person's control, the sodomyth, by representing the sodomite as dangerous, deadly, and destructive, as subversive, may serve to legitimate, yet again, an apparatus of control and punishment. Indeed, so mythified, subversion may itself actually shore up the dominant order. I say that it *may* do so, not that it *must* do so, in order to point out both an inevitable complicity and an undecidability that are often lost on many of Goytisolo's critics, for whom subversion (or revolution, or critique, or parody, or irony, or even ambiguity) is, at bottom, straight, simple, and self-evident. "All destructive discourses . . . must inhabit the structures they demolish" writes Jacques Derrida ("La parole" 194), which does not mean that these discourses always inhabit, or demolish, every structure in the same way or to the same degree. The structures inhabited and destroyed in Goytisolo's text are in fact quite varied, but the place of the "writer" is especially prominent. It is to the structure inhabited by the writing self, to a place called home, that the Red Fags hie with plans of destruction. They are by no means simple plans of destruction, for they are thick with strange inversions aimed at the (re)creation of the writer's life; they are aimed at forcing auto-graphy into auto-(bio)-graphy, at putting life back into the self and the self, once living, back into writing. Here, the Red Fags, despite their appearance, strive to generate a vital return and to uphold the law of moral accountability; they strive to produce a story that is, at bottom, straight, simple, and self-evident; they strive, that is, to undo—wildly, crazily, violently—the myth of sodomitic de-generation.

And yet the Red Fags are still scripted as the bearers of destruction, exploding the very self they would save through the script, through scripture. Like the missionaries of conquest, they destroy the subject who refuses to save himself *in their terms* or to see himself *in their image:* their restrictive, unimaginative image. They are, oddly enough, the bearers of an old death in new dress, the de-generates of postmodernism, holding on to retrograde, if not downright reactionary, notions of experience, identity, and responsibility. In all their campy extravagance, they mimic the conventions of the past. What is more, they reenact the sodomyth according to which they, as "fags," voraciously desire to know and to possess—

and in knowing and possessing to destroy—everything as their own. Edelman mentions "the allusive penumbra cast by Genesis" (99) over the
"mythology" of sodomy, the anti-Genesis. For Goytisolo, this allusion
may be shaded another way, in greater detail. I am thinking of the moment
in Genesis when "the men of the city, the men of Sodom, both young and
old, all the people to the last man, surrounded the house" of Lot. They had
seen two men—to Lot's more discerning eyes, two angels—enter Lot's
house, and they desired to know them: "Bring them out to us, that we may
know them," they cried. Knowledge was here of the carnal sort, bound to
possession and destruction, and Lot begged the Sodomites to "not act so
wickedly." So intent was he on protecting his guests, the two angelic men,
that he left his house, "shut the door after him," and offered his two
daughters, "who [had] not known man," in their stead. This is no small
offer, and yet, desiring to know men themselves, the Sodomites were not
appeased. "Then they pressed hard against the man Lot, and drew near to
break the door." At that moment, with Lot pushed up against the door, the
two guests pulled him inside and "struck with blindness the men who
were at the door of the house" (Gen. 19:4–11). The story, brief as it is, is
rich in resonance. In Abraham's time, long before the appearance of reds
and fags, the sodomites too were at the door: desiring knowledge, seeking
possession, and threatening destruction.[9]

   Tracing the biblical story into Goytisolo's is no doubt perilous business,
but it may serve as a caution against taking *Paisajes,* as Perrin seems to do,
as so surely "subversive" of dominant myths. Along with the oppressive
potential of sodomitic myths, Perrin also underestimates the problems
involved in reading Goytisolo's writing as homosexual and as politically
progressive. This is a problem shared, in varying degree, by a number of
Goytisolo's critics, all too ready to accept the *political* radicality of Goytisolo's work on the basis of style and structure and all too ready to delimit
radicality as always only "progressive" or "liberational." Radicality is, at its
most radical, disquieting and may include political positions that are far
from progressive. This itself is a disquieting assertion, which may explain
why it is so often eluded or ignored. Faithfully accepting the ambiguity,
dispersion, parody, and radical fragmentation of Goytisolo's text as being
in the service of the disenfranchised, Perrin, for one, glosses over the different, often contradictory, forms of disenfranchisement and reassembles
Goytisolo's text, indeed all of his texts since *Señas de identidad* (*Marks of*

Identity, 1966), within what she calls homotextuality. As Perrin styles it, "la homotextualidad, entendida como una escritura de la desviación, fundada sobre el autoengendramiento y la autonomía del texto cara a lo real . . . subvierte todas las instancias narrativas tradicionales" [Homotextuality, understood as the writing of deviation, based on self-elaboration and on textual autonomy in face of the real . . . subverts all traditional narrative situations] ("El laberinto" 75). Homotextuality, in other words, is devious and deviant, autonomous, subversive, and curiously self-engendering; it is, Perrin adds, labyrinthine, enigmatic, and given to such things as disguise, transvestism, the inversion of signs, and the search for pleasure (77). An appealing, if somewhat tired, parody of homosexual signs, Perrin's homotextuality, bound like her sodomyth to something radical, raises a number of problems. One problem in particular has to do with what is at stake in celebrating, without reservation, the so-called radical potential of fragmentation and parody.

My point is not that violent, comic, and parodic fragmentation should be resisted or rejected out of hand, but only that fragmentation as a general concept, strategy, and value should be critically interrogated. Fragmentation can only be *completely* "positive," politically, ethically, and aesthetically speaking, when it becomes coherent and unambiguous, when it ceases to be fragmentation. Whatever the liberational possibilities of fragmentation may be, I agree with N. Katherine Hayles when she says that "fragmentation and unpredictability are not . . . always cause for celebration" (27). As we shall see, something similar goes for ambiguity and, once again, for parody. After all, at least as it is presented by Perrin, parody *joins* fragmentation in acutely homotextual ways.[10] As mockery, mimicry, and ridicule, parody at once affirms and negates models and masters; as incompleteness, breakage, and detachment, fragmentation at once holds and loses identity and integrity: so far, so good. But what happens when parody and fragmentation are designated in specific sexual and political terms? What happens, more specifically still, when the Red Fags are privileged as the agents of parodic fragmentation? I say that they are privileged, however dubiously, because although there are other terrorist groups *in* the text, the Red Fags alone are implicated in the creation and destruction *of* the text (the Revolutionary Dykes are mentioned but do not engage in the attack). Unlike the group that struggles for the recognition of the lost Central Asian land of the Otekas, or the group that, under the name of Charles Martel, struggles for the conservation of an ultra-chauvinistic France, the *Maricas Rojos* set their sights not on some real or imagined nation but on the text itself. They are, in this, more radical and more contained than their counterparts: more radical because the terror-ist act they undertake aims at the authority of the author by whose very words they are, and more contained because their act, their aim, is, as Homi Bhabha might put it, abyssal: spiraling forever within the abyss of the text rather than projecting beyond it.[11]

The *mise en abîme*, spiraling queerly off center, may be sketched as follows: *Paisajes* begins and ends with references to a "Hecatombe" in which one form of writing, or *"grafía"* (*Paisajes* 236; *Landscapes* 159), is replaced by another; but lest this circle spin too neatly, toward the end of the text, the Red Fags are presented, as we have seen, as commanding a grotesque self-writing that turns out to be the very one that we have been reading. A few sections later, we read the impossible explosion, or heca-tomb, of both the writer and the writing: "[D]esmembrado y hecho trizas como tu propio relato alcanzas al fin el don de la ubicuidad te dispersas de país en país" [dismembered, torn to bits like your own story you finally attain the gift of ubiquity, scattered from country to country] (233; 156). The Oteka and Martel groups may scrawl graffiti on the walls of Paris, push unsuspecting commuters into the path of subway trains, and wreak public havoc, but the Red Fags are the ones who enter the privacy of the author's home, force him to scrawl the story of his life, and push him to destruction. They are inscribed as coercing inscription itself, an inscrip-tion in which creation is, in old sodomythic fashion, forever bound to destruction and generation to death. In this peculiar homotext, if the script remains, so does its eradication. The creative destruction and ter-rorist "privilege" of the Red Fags perhaps sound strange, but they are not, again, of my imagination. Andrés Sánchez Robayna, in a recent edition of the text, notes that it is with the fragment "¡Raptado por los Maricas Rojos!" that the text evinces "un progresivo *extrañamiento* de los planos del protagonista, el narrador y el autor empírico" [a progressive *extraña-miento* of the narrative planes of the protagonist, the narrator and the empirical author] (*Paisajes* 214). Moving beyond Sánchez Robayna, the progressive estrangement, or strangeness, of narrative planes may be read as a parody not only of the conventions of literary order, holism, and organicism, but also of the discursive ties between, on the one hand, communism and estrangement, and, on the other, homosexuality and strangeness. After all, they are not called the *Red* Fags for nothing.

There is, however, an imbalance here. For communists, estrangement is the unacceptably dispossessing price of capitalism, suffered most intimately by the proletariat but affecting the whole of humanity: Marxism, at least at its most humanist, posits a generalized (self)-estrangement, or (self)-alienation, that it criticizes and combats through the work, both theoretical and practical, of (re)unified consciousness.[12] But for homosexuals, estrangement has been styled more peculiarly, as strangeness: for homosexuals, that is, a quite specific strangeness is borne as the price of homophobia, under capitalism as well as under communism. As a result, the estranged proletariat is not of the same order as the strange homosexual, even though they may certainly coincide. This difference affects the play of parody as well. For, to signal the agents of narrative estrangement as reds, as communists, is to parody the communist claim to reverse or eliminate estrangement.[13] But to signal the agents of estrangement as fags, as homosexuals, is in a sense to replicate, rather than reverse, the homophobic rhetoric according to which gays and lesbians are themselves *already* estranged from the natural and the normal. Furthermore, the parody of communism is obviously more at home with capitalism, whereas the parody of homosexuality is at home, in many respects, with capitalism and communism both. This is not to say that a parody of homosexuality is not possible, nor that it cannot assume a variety of forms, but that it must contend with the drag of such related items as mockery, ridicule, and travesty and the context in which they are mobilized.

Queer and communist contexts are, whatever their overlaps and coincidences, separate in sovereignty. I mean simply that although there have been many globally acknowledged communist regimes or nations, there has never been a queer nation. There has never been a sovereign space for, dare I say it, queer ideology.[14] Indeed, if all communities are imagined, some seem to rely more on the imagination than others: this imaginativeness, depicted in Goytisolo's text as inimical to the aims, if not the acts, of certain types of activism, is worth keeping in mind. The gay and lesbian "community," in its most imaginative "national" projects, continually confronts the fragility and virtuality that are in certain respects its strongest reality. It confronts, that is, an intense diffuseness of space and time, a semiotics of invisible borders and unwritten histories shot through with often brilliantly coded bodies and stories. Outing and passing are only two of the more significant strategies of such intense diffuseness by which the "homosexual" goes in and out of focus, seems more or less strange. This last connection bears reasserting, for strangeness is here a function of defocalization and defamiliarization that never quite gives up the ghost of focalization and familiarity. In other words, strangeness, not unlike estrangement, conjures up images of a body, a home, a nation abandoned, made foreign, and yet still haunted by dreams of something natural and normal, something familiar in focus. Hence, the progressive extrañamiento of narrative planes that, for Sánchez Robayna, starts up in earnest in "¡Raptado por los Maricas Rojos" can only be measured, again and again, against a norm, standard, convention, or tradition with which the reader, presumably, is familiar. Parody and fragmentation are similarly measured. But here once more, against a familiar norm and established context, the communist and the homosexual are not balanced. The Red Fags are not only at odds with the protagonist, narrator, and author; they are also, as I have been suggesting, at odds with themselves.

Before I sound out the tensions between communism and homosexuality, I want to note briefly the ties between them. Context is again important, for such ties are most familiar to the citizens of nations such as the United States and Spain that have officially projected themselves, at some point or another in their history, as anticommunist and antihomosexual. Lee Edelman, in an excellent reading of the conflation of homosexuality and communism in the nationalistic discourse of the United States in the 1950s and 1960s, discusses "the national political identification of homosexuality with domestic subversion" (269). But if homosexuality and communism have been bound together as subversive in (and of) many Western nations, homosexuality and capitalism have been bound together as subversive in (and of) a number of communist nations. Because no historical nation has ever designated itself as homosexual, a double bind obtains: capitalist as well as communist nations have deployed, and in some cases continue to deploy, homosexuality as a sort of tactical weapon whose objective is to expose and explode the opposing (national or "international") ideology as already given to something strange, unnatural, abnormal, unstable, perverse, and deadly. The communist line, at least after Lenin, ties together capitalism and homosexuality as decadent, alienating, and unproductive, while the capitalist line ties together communism and homosexuality as, well, decadent, alienating, and unproductive. The rhetorical consistency reveals a shared anxiety that scripts homosexuality as a threat to national sovereignty. Subversive, sly, and seditious, homosexuality is *seen* as fracturing and fragmenting the integrity of society itself: a danger seen, but not seen, as coming from the *other* side.

Edelman underscores the significance of *seeing* homosexuality, of envisioning it as a social menace. "For when homosexuality enters the field of vision in each of [the] fragments of the social text," Edelman observes, "it occasions a powerful disruption of that field by virtue of its uncontrollably figuralizing effects; and that disruption of the field of vision is precisely what homosexuality comes to represent: so radical a rupture of the linguistic and epistemic order that it figures futurity imperilled, it figures history as apocalypse, by gesturing toward the precariousness of familial and national survival. . . . [I]t is seen as enacting the destabilization of borders, the subversion of masculine identity from within" (168). Noting that "[s]uch a reading of male homosexuality . . . is not unique to America in the early sixties" (168), Edelman's reading is apposite to Goytisolo's writing. Disruption, precariousness, destabilization, and peril run throughout *Paisajes*, where terrorism is accompanied by nuclear proliferation, ecological exhaustion, technological excess, and postcolonial dislocation. Indeed, it is as if the worst-case scenario of Edelman's anticommunist, antihomosexual ideologues had come true: the landscape of Goytisolo's postmodern Paris is, after the battle of strong ideologies, one of anarchy, terrorism, and apocalypse. Yet here too something is not quite right. Even as communism and homosexuality are conflated in and out of the text, they are, as I have already indicated, torn apart. From the communist perspective, anarchy, terrorism, and apocalypse are the dangers, not of communism, but of its resistance and rejection.[15] They are also, from the same perspective, among the dangers of homosexuality, its toleration and, even more, its acceptance. The fracturing and fragmenting that homosexuality figures in the eyes of the capitalist leaders hold, in short, for a good number of their communist counterparts as well.

This is, in and of itself, sufficient to fragment the parodic potential of the *Maricas Rojos*; but there is more. For if *Paisajes* parodies communist ideology, it also parodies the art that ideology inspires and, more strongly, demands. Crossing a landscape of ideological ruins, the narrator, protagonist, or author comes across people who still argue for a literature in the service of revolution, for "la literatura y el arte como arma o instrumento de combate" [art and literature as combat weapons or tools] (*Paisajes* 194; *Landscapes* 125). The literature of social realism, with all of its "héroes positivos, ingenieros de almas, centrales eléctricas, minas y zanjas, ecuaciones moralopolíticas resueltas en términos de progreso industrial" [positive heroes, engineers of souls, power stations, mines and trenches, moral-political equations solved in terms of industrial progress] (194; 125) is, within the ruinous space of Goytisolo's text, ridiculous. The allusions to works by Jesús Pacheco (*Central Eléctrica*, "Power Station"), Armando López Salinas (*La mina*, "The Mine"), and Alfonso Grosso (*La zanja*, "The Trench") are followed by allusions to the early works of Goytisolo himself, many of which obey the social (or socialist) realist doctrine of transparency, linearity, referential correspondence, and clear political engagement.[16] It is a doctrine that holds, that demands, that reality be represented faithfully and fully in art. In a sense, it is a doctrine that demands reality, and as Lyotard notes, "the demand for reality" is in effect a demand "for unity, simplicity, communicability, etc." (*The Postmodern Explained* 7). Lyotard also notes that this demand is, often as not, an attack on artistic experimentation and that "any attack on artistic experimentation is inherently reactionary" (7). Lyotard's assertion may be debatable (it is, among other things, too general and too vague), but it is germane to Goytisolo's text: wild as the Red Fags may seem, their attack on artistic experimentation—understood here as an attack on creative freedom—and their demand for reality reveal them to be the agents of reaction.

The repudiation of the realist aesthetic and the rejection of works written under its sign—works considered by the author to be, if not childish, at least immature—is part and parcel of Goytisolo's much-touted rejection of communism. Born of painful disillusionment, it is a rejection that Goytisolo has articulated in *Juan sin tierra* (*Juan the Landless*, 1975), *Makbara* (1980), and *Las virtudes del pájaro solitario* (*The Virtues of the Solitary Bird*, 1988), in numerous critical essays and newspaper articles, in his two-volume autobiography, in texts both before and after *Paisajes*. It constitutes, therefore, a kind of personal confession, one that tells the story, over and over, of a falling from faith, of a progressive estrangement from Marxist-Leninism. Goytisolo's contact with the Soviet Union is important, yet for a number of personal and cultural reasons, it is his contact with Cuba that is decisive. The notorious Padilla case, in which the Cuban writer Heberto Padilla was obliged by the revolutionary regime of Fidel Castro to make a devastating public self-critique, or "autocrítica," is at the center of Goytisolo's critique of communism and is echoed in the *Maricas Rojos'* demand for an "autocrítica" in *Paisajes.*[17] Interestingly, however, Goytisolo's disillusionment with communism, the almost confessional account of his estrangement from it, is motivated not just by communist restrictions on art, thought, and creativity, not just by the persecution of other writers. It is also motivated by the persecution of (other) homosexuals and other "improper subjects."

In *En los reinos de taifa* (*Realms of Strife,* 1986), Goytisolo addresses himself and writes, in explicitly fraternal terms, of "lo que estaba ocurriendo a tus hermanos de vicio nefando, de vilipendiado *crimine pessimo* y, junto a ellos, a santeros, poetas, ñáñigos, lumpens, ociosos y buscavidas, inadaptados e inadaptables a una lectura unicolor de la realidad, a la luz disciplinada, implacable, glacial de la ideología" [what was happening to your brothers in nefarious vice, the reviled *crimine pessimo,* and along with them, *santeros,* poets, *ñáñigos,* lumpens, idlers, and scroungers, unadapted or incapable of adaptation to a monochrome reading of reality, to the implacable, disciplined, icy glare of ideology] (175; 147).[18] Once more, Goytisolo describes communist ideology in terms of an unforgivably monochromatic realism, one that seems particularly unsuited to the presumably "multicolored reality" of homosexuals. And yet, as Edmund White notes, it is just this "reality" that Goytisolo tries perhaps to avoid by "throw[ing] himself into the revolutionary spirit" (19). With its promise of a new and better world, its faith in justice, dignity, and cooperation, its sense of being both historically necessary and humanly free, its demands for commitment and even sacrifice, with all this, the revolutionary spirit of communism may not only "raise" Goytisolo above the supposedly more personal and petty concerns of sexual desire but also set him up for a fall that reverberates in his work even today.

This, at any rate, is one of the trajectories recounted in his autobiography, where Goytisolo's disillusionment is with communism and realism, not with "homosexualism."[19] But there is more to this trajectory. If Goytisolo distances himself from communism in part by "identifying" with "homosexuals," if he pits one against the other, he subsequently confronts not homosexuals but gay activists: more demanding, critical, accusatory, and "reproachful" than his "brothers in nefarious vice." Discerning what he identifies as a similarly shrill sense of purpose, he comes to bind gay activists and communists together and to distance himself from both in the name of freedom and the creative imagination. The lag in this trajectory is in many respects the work of history. For although communists have long established their own models and institutions (institutions that could then entrap and models that could then collapse), "homosexuals" have not laid claim, until recently, to anything close to such cultural power. In the rise and fall of master narratives, communist and queer, all things are not equal.

My point is not by any means that homosexuality and communism are incompatible, let alone that they cannot coincide as the signs of identity: such is certainly, and fortunately, not the case. But Goytisolo's deployment of the two in *Paisajes* raises questions about the effect of the real on the written, questions, that is, about the place of the writer, the author. A self-styled "autobiografía grotesca," or grotesque autobiography, *Paisajes* presents a double-edged challenge. On the one hand, it challenges the reader to reduce the text to the life of the author, to read it as a grotesque expression or reflection of Goytisolo's own experiences, thoughts, and desires. On the other hand, it challenges the reader to resist such reduction as itself grotesque, as a simpleminded perversion of textuality. Goytisolo's narrative of political disillusionment, his fragmentary parody of communist ideology, plays off both hands, with autobiography grounding, as it were, the ungrounding of textuality. Goytisolo's narrative of erotic explosion, his fragmentary parody of sexual activism, however, plays a bit differently. The difference lies, as I have suggested, in the historical power of cultural models and institutions, in the contextual force of such factors as national sovereignty and aesthetic ideology.

The force of history and context: when the protagonist, narrator, or author writes of his sexuality, he invokes an isolation and estrangement that is less the effect of having once belonged, or of having once thought or claimed to have belonged, than of having never belonged: "he entrado en contacto con diversas agrupaciones, colectivos y unidades móviles de feministas, gayos, lesbianas, pedófilos, S & M, fist fuckers, etc., sin obtener de ellos el menor apoyo a mi causa. Ni los Maricas Rojos ni el Frente de Liberación Fetichista ni los Grupos de Choque de las Tortilleras Revolucionarias han querido aceptar y hacer suyos mis justas reivindicaciones y agravios" [I entered into contact with various associations, collectives, and mobile units of feminists, gays, lesbians, pedophiles, SMs, fist fuckers, etc., without obtaining from them the slightest support for my cause] (*Paisajes* 72; *Landscapes* 25). It is hard, not to say impossible, to read this somewhat libertarian passage in terms of an autobiographical real, no doubt because it centers on issues of sexual desire.[20] Sexuality has, of course, long been linked to the private and the personal whereas politics has been linked to the public and the collective: hence the history of surveillance, repression, and confession that Foucault, among others, has interrogated. Given this history, it is perhaps not surprising that in both volumes of his "true" or "real" autobiography (*Coto vedado* and *En los reinos de taifa*) as well as in a number of interviews, Goytisolo is more inclined to publicize, and contextualize, the details of his political relations than the details of his sexual relations, though the latter are by no means absent. What he does publicize, however, is his estrangement from *politically organized collectives* of gays and lesbians, an estrangement described, as we have just seen, in *Paisajes* as well. The effect is that although such things as voyeurism, pedophilia, masochism, and bestiality remain discreetly within the confines of this grotesquely open autobiography, that although the details of the "justas reivindicaciones y agravios" (i.e., his "just cause") remain faithfully in the realm of fiction, the problems with communists and gay activists do not. What makes the Red Fags so terrible is that they demand, it seems, all the details.

It is the demand for reality in all its details, bound to the imperative to confess, that is at the heart of Goytisolo's sexual terror. To a certain degree, Goytisolo seems to be in strong company. "The confession was, and still remains," as Michel Foucault observes, "the general standard governing the production of the true discourse of sex" (*Foucault Live* 63). Foucault's observation has itself been literalized into an imperative, an excruciating anticonfessional imperative governing the production of a counterdiscourse of sex. But the fact is that Foucault, like Goytisolo, like all discursive subjects, confesses even in refusing to confess.[21] Foucault, to be sure, intimates as much and becomes progressively more interested in the gay movement. Another gay writer, Samuel Delany, draws on Foucault and writes not just of confession and the refusal to confess but also of the coyness surrounding sexuality, a coyness that is itself "a huge and pervasive discourse" (176).[22] Goytisolo's writing hardly seems coy; in fact, it is often unabashedly pornographic, exploiting the figures of Lewis Carroll and his girlish models for what Gayle Rubin, in another context, calls the "erotic hysteria" that surrounds the sexuality of children ("Thinking Sex" 6). And yet Goytisolo's writing is coy in another, more reticular, sense. Its coyness lies in the self-parodic denial of the self, in the ecstatic fragmentation of personality in and as textuality, in the authorial destruction of the author, in the cult of polysemy, dispersion, and ambiguity. Its coyness lies in its self-conscious sophistication.

As he states in a recent interview with Javier Escudero: "busco la ambigüedad completa del poder del contagio ... una obra que tenga todas las lecturas posibles. No se puede leer el libro con una lectura reductiva, no puedes juzgar una obra por una lectura unívoca. Lo profundo es la polisemia total" [I seek the complete ambiguity of the power of contagion ... a work which permits all possible readings. The book cannot be read reductively; you cannot judge a work on the basis of a univocal reading. What is profound is total polysemy] (Escudero 133). Goytisolo is here referring to the novel that follows *Paisajes, Las virtudes del pájaro solitario*, and specifically to Escudero's queries about the role of AIDS in that novel. AIDS, Goytisolo acknowledges, plays an important role in *Las virtudes*, but ultimately as only one of any number of other terrible events.[23] Ambiguity and metaphorical contagion are, he asserts, the true measure of creativity and freedom by which apparatuses of domination, exploitation, and control falter and fall. Given that identification, reduction, and focalization have been, and continue to be, tactics used by an oppressive status quo, Goytisolo's point is well taken: but only if it is not taken unambiguously, only if it is not taken as meaning that ambiguity is always positive and identity always negative.

For the fact is that ambiguity, while positive for the text, can be, in Goytisolo's view, far too positive for the body. Metaphorical contagion may be the wondrous stuff of literature, but when it is itself literalized, it becomes something else entirely. In the very same interview in which Goytisolo says that he seeks "the complete ambiguity of the power of contagion," he also says the following: "De la gente que yo sabía que eran homosexuales que conocía en Nueva York creo que han muerto todos. Ha sido una hecatombe. Por fortuna he sido siempre muy selecto. Nunca he tenido ambigüedad con europeos. Sólo me ha interesado lo que yo llamo la zona sotádica y nunca me he acostado con homosexuales sino con heterosexu-

ales que ocasionalmente pueden ser bisexuales. Entonces, esto yo creo que
en cierto modo me ha salvado de la hecatombe. . . . Me costó mucho hacer
la primera prueba. Realmente no sabía si había cometido algún error" [I
think that the people whom I knew to be homosexual in New York have all
died. It has been a hecatomb. Fortunately, I have always been very se-
lect(ive). I have never had ambiguity with Europeans. I have only been
interested in what I call the Sotadic Zone and I have never gone to bed
with homosexuals, but only heterosexuals who can occasionally be bisexual. Thus, I believe that that saved me in a way from the hecatomb. . . . It
was very hard for me to get tested. I really didn't know if I had made some
mistake] (Escudero 132).[24] This is an extraordinary confession, not because it comes amid repeated refusals to discuss his "personal convictions"
(Escudero 124, 127, 128), nor because Goytisolo is "selecto" rather than
"selectivo," select or selected rather than selective, but because he presents
ambiguity as signifying gay sex, and gay sex, in turn, as European. Afraid
of having contracted AIDS through some sort of error or ambiguous slip,
he later recognizes that his fears were unfounded: fortunately for him, he
has never had "ambiguity" with Europeans. The ambiguity that he has
had—outside the grotesquely open book, of course—is not exactly ambiguity either: he has never gone to bed with homosexuals, and certainly not
gay men, but has satisfied himself instead with heterosexuals who can
occasionally be bisexual, with men, that is, whose ambiguity is only occasional and always partial. These "occasional bisexuals," like the protagonist
of *Paisajes*, like Goytisolo himself, maybe even like André Gide, are perhaps married to women, as so many heterosexual, and apparently more
than a few homosexual, men are. If this may sound as if it leads to ambiguity, apparently it does not. For it is his astonishingly unambiguous ability
to identify an HIV-positive person on the basis of where he comes from
and what he calls himself, not on what he does or does not do, that saves
Goytisolo from the slaughter, from the hecatomb.

The word Goytisolo twice uses to refer to AIDS allows for an interesting trace from the quasi-confessional arena of the interview to that of
Paisajes.[25] A hecatomb is a large-scale sacrifice or slaughter (originally, of a
hundred oxen) and resonates, in the modern ear, with a classical strangeness, possibly even with an echo of the tomb (in Spanish, *-tombe, tumba*).
It is also, as I briefly mentioned, the word that opens and closes *Paisajes*,
where it signifies the catastrophe of signification. That catastrophe is there

not the effect of AIDS but the effect of immigration, multicultural clash, racism, and terrorism. It is not an unambiguous catastrophe, for in it, through it, the fragmentation of identity that the protagonist, narrator, or author celebrates is attained.[26] Thus, for their part, the Red Fags are, after a fashion, the bearers of what is most desired. Desire can be terrifying, of course, and what is perhaps most terrifying is, as Goytisolo knows, that sexuality, however private and personal, is also always political and collective. Or rather, what is most terrifying is that sexuality can be politicized and collectivized in a way that excludes, censors, or otherwise controls private and personal fantasy, play and creativity: what is most terrifying is that the Red Fags command a confession devoid of falsity, fiction, and imagination.[27]

On this score, once again, Goytisolo's fiction intersects with his words to Escudero: "A mí nunca me ha interesado, y algunos me lo reprochan dentro del movimiento gay, el que no haya transformado mi homosexualidad en un instrumento político de combate. . . . No me ha interesado nunca este tipo de militancia, fuera de la despenalización y de lo que puede ser la discriminación. En los países islámicos es algo totalmente inconcebible, les parece el colmo del absurdo" [I have never been interested—and some people within the gay movement reproach me for it—in transforming my homosexuality into an instrument of political combat. . . . This type of militancy, outside of decriminalization and what might be discrimination, has never interested me. In the Islamic countries it is something totally inconceivable; to them it seems the height of absurdity] (Escudero 141). Never mind that the height of absurdity may well be that Goytisolo continues to pit an idealized and totalized Islam (based more on Morocco and Turkey than on Iran and Yemen) against a degraded and totalized West;[28] never mind that sodomy is a capital offense in more than one Islamic nation, or that it is illegal in many others,[29] or that the much-touted tolerance of *male* homosexuality (lesbianism is another story altogether) in still others may be repressive too (to turn a title of one of *Paisajes*' chapters on Goytisolo himself: interpret Marcuse correctly!);[30] never mind that silence and invisibility and the concept of the absurd may harbor violence themselves; never mind that problems of (de)criminalization and sexual discrimination exist in *both* Islamic and the Western nations, and that Goytisolo is, for all his plays with fragmentation, parody, and dispersion, too unambiguously binary in his oppositions; never mind any of this, Goytisolo's stance, in the West, seems clear: gay and lesbian activism, militantly combative, repeats the doctrinaire excesses of communism. Using virtually the same language he uses in *Paisajes* to criticize social realism, Goytisolo presents his resistance to the gay and lesbian movement as a defense of artistic creativity, openness, polysemy, and heterogeneity. As Goytisolo styles it, gay activism is tendentiously fixated on reference and responsibility; it reifies identity, essentializes sexuality, reduces meaning, and, worst of all, instrumentalizes pleasure, including the pleasure of the text.

Against such single-mindedness, Goytisolo advances, in both *Paisajes* and his interview, the Sufi ideal of degradation and detachment, of fragmentation, dispersion, and loss. This is certainly a compelling ideal, one that Leo Bersani has suggested as a response to the fragmentation and loss occasioned by AIDS.[31] But Goytisolo, before AIDS and after *Paisajes después de la batalla*, is on the whole strangely unambiguous about his views on the gay movement. Goytisolo parodies communism and gay and lesbian activism in the name of freedom. In *Paisajes*, these parodies are often funny, more often bitingly sarcastic, and even more often both. And yet what is not so funny, it seems, is speaking, or writing, in the name of freedom (*Libertad, libertad, libertad*, as he titles a book of essays). Within as well as without the text, Goytisolo speaks and writes in the name of freedom, particularly when it comes to Islam and literature, with considerable seriousness. He does so by fragmenting language and dispersing, ostensibly, the subject. And yet, through it all, he remains bound to a curious integrity. He remains unambiguous in his celebration of ambiguity and all but univocal in his praise of polyvocality. He is, in this, closer to a significant fragment of the gay movement than he may acknowledge, and yet he is still so far away.[32]

But he is also closer to another movement, another effect, of power. I am thinking of what Pierre Bourdieu calls "the oracle effect," the ability to assume an ever greater authority by abolishing the self and speaking in the name of others or in the name of an ideal. In the words of Bourdieu, "[i]t is when I become Nothing . . . that I become Everything. . . . The oracle effect is a veritable *splitting of personality:* the individual personality, the ego, abolishes itself in favour of a transcendent moral person" (211). The symbolic power of Goytisolo's moral person has been noted by a number of writers and critics from Guillermo Cabrera Infante to Susan Sontag.

Goytisolo himself, in his recent writings from Bosnia, appears reluctant to relinquish that power, to abandon some form of the Sartrean concept of writing as engagement that was crucial to the social realism that he subsequently, and ambiguously, abandoned.[33] He appears reluctant, in the end, to write the author, the person, out of morality: even, if not especially, in *Paisajes'* "fábula sin ninguna moralidad" [fable without a moral].[34] I, for my part, am not concerned so much with refuting or reducing that moral person, with setting it straight, as with considering what is at stake in its self-declared narrative fragmentation, what privilege it obscurely secures in letting privilege go, what moral authority it holds in disauthorizing morality and killing off the author, even the effect of the author. Of course, another aspect of the oracle effect, of speaking in the name of a group, is not just the demand, but the reprimand, the reproach. According to Bourdieu, "[t]he right of reprimanding other people and making them feel guilty is one of the advantages enjoyed by the militant" (211). I must here, in reprimanding Goytisolo, reprimand myself. It is, after all, my advantage, the sign of something queerly militant, to reprimand him, and myself, for *not* being sufficiently militant, for not enjoying the militant's advantages, for also being guilty of speaking, at times too shrilly, in the name of others. To that, I confess. In ambiguity. It is not, again, of my imagination alone. The Red Fags, *los Maricas Rojos,* are at the door.

Notes

This essay appeared in a slightly different form in *Significant Violence: Oppression and Resistance in the Narratives of Juan Goytisolo, 1970–1990,* by Brad Epps (New York: Oxford University Press, 1996).

1   I use the word *dilemma* in its dictionary sense as "a form of argument involving an opponent in choice between two (or more) alternatives, both equally unfavorable" and as "a position of doubt or perplexity; a difficult situation." Given the context of my argument, the celebration of fragmentation and difference *tout court,* the declaration that one is, *once and for all,* favorable, is to *identify* difference, to *unify* fragmentation, as *always* politically, ethically, or even aesthetically superior.

2   An apparent contradiction in terms, hermetic openness is the measure of a certain Barthesian writerliness, a quality that cannot be *read* according to a predetermined political or ethical system of value: the radically writerly in-

cludes the possibility of rewriting Barthes's suggestion that the writerly is "progressive" and the "readerly" conservative. Barbara Johnson acknowledges that "writerliness is . . . something that can take on diametrically opposed political values, but it is something about which it is somehow not irrelevant—indeed, it seems urgent—to *raise* political questions" (27).

3   At times the narrator, or protagonist, appears affiliated with both the Martel and Oteka groups, although at one point he declares that his work on behalf of the Martel group (the extreme right) is a deceptive, somewhat cynical, tactic to keep the situation tense and combative (211). It is as if Goytisolo, whether as author or textual effect ("goytisolo"), could not bear that his work might actually be read as being beyond *a certain* morality.

4   Goytisolo links himself to Dodgson in *Coto vedado,* translated by Peter Bush as *Forbidden Territory: The Memoirs of Juan Goytisolo, 1931–1956.* Referring to his fear of persecution in Spain, Goytisolo says that "the sequence with the Reverend Charles Lutwidge Dodgson at the Police Headquarters in . . . *Paisajes después de la batalla* is the faithful transcription of one of its versions in which sex and politics, exhibitionism and revolutionary militancy are subject to sarcastic attack by a chorus of inspectors" (254 original; 215 translation). These inspectors are the ones who reveal "the perverse eventuality of my *defects* and *weaknesses*" (254; 215, italics in the original). These "defects and weaknesses" relate to his "nocturnal habits and sexual inclinations," mentioned shortly before. A number of things are of interest here: Goytisolo makes explicit the ties between one autobiography (*Coto vedado*) and another (the "grotesque" autobiography of *Paisajes*); the defects and weaknesses in question are associated with homosexuality; a faithful transcription of something "real" into the fiction of *Paisajes* is accompanied, in the realm of fiction itself, by a resistance to faithful transcription (the narrator, protagonist, or implied author resists a fully straight account of his life, however queerly demanded); and, perhaps most interestingly, the police inspectors who are described in *Coto vedado* as "mocking" and "attacking" revolutionary militancy are accompanied, indeed overshadowed and outmaneuvered, in *Paisajes* by revolutionary militants themselves. In *Coto vedado,* however, it is the revolutionary militants who are overshadowed: Goytisolo's nightmares of persecution, feeding on and into the reality of Francoist Spain, are transcribed in the "real" autobiography of *Coto vedado* without the "grotesque" company of the Maricas Rojos.

5   The author is elsewhere reluctant to concede so much authority to Lewis Carroll. In *El bosque de las letras,* Goytisolo declares that the author, creator, or maker drawn in *Paisajes* is based on Jean Genet (96). Genet is the author

whom Goytisolo describes in *En los reinos de taifa*, translated by Peter Bush as *Realms of Strife: The Memoirs of Juan Goytisolo, 1957–1982*, as his "only adult influence on the strictly moral plane" (153 original; 128 translation). In *Disidencias*, Goytisolo presents Genet as "perhaps the only serious moralist of our time" (301; translation mine). Morality, once again, colors the "amoral" or "extramoral" landscape of *Paisajes*.

6 Luce López-Baralt 3–4; Guillermo Cabrera Infante, "Paisajes con Goytisolo al frente" 56–59; and Julián Ríos underscore the comic tone of *Paisajes*. They are certainly right to do so, but only because laughter, as even Bakhtin knew, can be derisive, mocking, cutting, and vicious.

7 The "creative author" is also a scribe or copier (of Sufi poetry, among other things). Separated from his wife, estranged from friends and colleagues, hounded by intense sexual and political obsessions, "he does not pick up the phone, he does not answer messages or letters, he has disconnected the doorbell and, when some obstinate visitor knocks on the door, he holds his breath, [and] plays dead" (97 original; 46 translation). So portrayed, the author, whoever he is, is less dead than playing dead, an actor alienated from the human community. And although Goytisolo indicates that the author in question is Lewis Carroll or Jean Genet, his signs of identity indicate that he is closer to Goytisolo himself. Like the author of the text, the author *in* the text has a somewhat unconventional marriage and an apartment in the Sentier. This coincidence needs to be noted without being overestimated (i.e., the author of the text is exactly the same as the author in the text) or discounted (i.e., the author of the text is entirely different from the author in the text). The author is *a subject in question*, which is not to say that we know nothing at all about him.

8 Among the "grotesque" signs of the narrator's, protagonist's, or author's "grotesque autobiography" is "his grotesque swooning in the presence of well-built, dark-skinned young men laboring in the mysterious public-works trenches repeatedly being redug" (217–18 original; 145 translation). The descriptions of awe before the "dark bodies" of Turkish and North African laborers are scattered throughout a number of Goytisolo's texts, including *Reivindicación del Conde don Julián, Juan sin tierra, Makbara*, and *Las virtudes del pájaro solitario*. Their parodic potential is undercut by the interplay of Goytisolian texts, including interviews and critical essays. In other words, if Goytisolo reiterates some of the most problematic stereotypes of the (homo)sexual imperialist, of the westerner who finds (homo)sexual adventure and release in a realm beyond Europe and European values, his revelations, confessions, and discussions of his own (homo)sexual practice render

the very notion of parodic distance dubious. And here, amid doubt, one may doubt that this "awe" is all that different from the awe of other Europeans in face of a non-European Other: the awful awe of erotic fetishization.

9 I wish to thank my friend and colleague Doris Sommer for her suggestions here. See also Alter, "Sodom as Nexus," in which he examines among other things the "scandal" of Lot's offering his daughters to protect his guests from "being known" (i.e., being possessed) by the Sodomites.

10 For more on parody in *Paisajes,* see Genaro J. Pérez.

11 See Bhabha, *The Location of Culture.*

12 The accepted word in Spanish for the Marxian concept of estrangement, or alienation (*alienación*), is *enajenación,* meaning to make distant, detached, alien, or foreign (*ajeno*). *Extrañamiento* is more properly associated with banishment and, more commonly, bewilderment or surprise. But both *ajeno* and *extraño* are signifiers of the strange, the foreign, the odd, and the different, of something other, outside, and away. The María Moliner dictionary makes the connection explicit: *ajeno* is defined as *extraño, extraño* as *ajeno,* and one of the first uses given is the following: "ajeno/extraño a la familia" [strange to the family].

13 This particular parody, by which communists heighten rather than eliminate estrangement, is not exactly new or unfamiliar: it may be found in any number of anticommunist works before, but especially after, World War II.

14 I am using "ideology" in the more ample and "neutral" sense used by Lenin and Gramsci. For Marx, "ideology" is of course profoundly negative.

15 It is not necessary to rehearse the communist critique of anarchism to see that, however subtly, homophobia inflects it as well (or, inversely, that the fear of anarchy inflects the communist view of homosexuality).

16 Social or socialist realism was adopted as doctrine by the first Soviet Writer's Congress in the fall of 1934. It is related but not equivalent to the proletarian literature that preceded it and that stipulated that the writer come for the proletariat. Furthermore, unlike nineteenth-century realism, socialist realism was less concerned with "mirroring" society than with portraying its heroic overcoming. Others have pointed out the differences between Soviet-inspired socialist realism and the social realism practiced in Spain. See, for example, Blanco et al.

17 The narrator, protagonist, or author of *Paisajes* is thus not only Juan Goytisolo, Lewis Carroll, and Jean Genet, but also Heberto Padilla. There are, of course, other "contributors"—not all of them nameable—to the text. For a selection of documents related to the Padilla case, see Casal. Goytisolo gives his own version of the case in *En los reinos de taifa.*

18 This quote is italicized in its entirety in the text.

19 One thing is "homosexualism" or "homosexuality," and another thing is organized gay activism, in which Goytisolo has not been engaged.

20 For a strikingly similar, though decidedly nonparodic, listing of sexual identities, see Gayle Rubin, "Thinking Sex." Although championing what she describes as a radical position, Rubin herself is uneasy with the "label" of "libertarianism" (29–30, note).

21 Foucault, in a series of late interviews, speaks at length about the details of sexual practice, the limit experiences of S-M, the lessons of the bathhouses, and the possibilities for "reinventing" gay friendship. He is often cautious about the gay movement, but Foucault, unlike Goytisolo, is increasingly engaged with the gay movement. See, for example, "Sexual Choice, Sexual Act," in *Foucault Live*, in which Foucault, wary of speaking for "gay people," states: "I am of course regularly involved in exchanges with other members of the gay community. We talk, we try to find ways of opening ourselves to one another" (229).

22 "Coyness," we should remember, means "shy and retiring; artfully or affectedly demure; annoyingly unwilling to make a commitment."

23 Judith Butler's reading of Slavoj Žižek's work is apposite to Goytisolo's work as well. Goytisolo, like Žižek, elaborates a series, or chain, of catastrophic events that include the Holocaust, the Gulag, and, for Goytisolo, the Inquisition, Chernobyl, and AIDS. This "chain" is what Goytisolo describes in terms of contagion, with one element contaminating another. As Butler points out in *Bodies That Matter: On the Discursive Limits of "Sex,"* such a chain is itself an ideological construct, one in which the individual links "instantiate the same trauma" (202). Goytisolo's attention to AIDS is similarly constructed, serving as an instance, *as yet another instance,* of a trauma whose liberal humanist version is "man's inhumanity to man." Goytisolo's attention to AIDS is overlain with inattention, the specificity of the instance shot through with a lack of specificity. If Goytisolo inscribes "estrangement" in his text, it is not of a Brechtian sort.

24 What Goytisolo calls the Sotadic Zone is derived from the work of Sir Richard Burton. Goytisolo develops this in an essay on Burton titled "Sir Richard Burton, peregrino y sexólogo," in *Crónicas sarracinas*, translated by Helen R. Lane as "Sir Richard Burton, Pilgrim and Sexologist." Simply put, the Sotadic Zone (from Sotades, "a Greek poet of the Third Century B.C. noted for his licentious writings") is an area that encompasses the Mediterranean coast, North Africa, the Middle East, Persia, Afghanistan, and the Indian subcontinent. In it, homosexuality is "popular and endemic, and regarded even in the very worst of cases as a mere peccadillo" (170 original; 32 translation). Al-

though Goytisolo describes Burton's theories as "discutibles y peregrinas" [debatable, and indeed downright odd] (170; 32), he revives and extends them. However "peregrina," however odd, strange, or queer, such a theory of sexuality may be, it certainly seems to travel well with Goytisolo.

25 Referring to the less than favorable reception of the text when it first appeared, Goytisolo tells Escudero that "*Paisajes* is now finding its audience for the simple reason that it is a book which is, in some way, quite prophetic about what is happening throughout the cities of the world" (137).

26 The reader is repeatedly reminded of the importance of fragmentation: "A rereading of the 170 pages [248 in the original Spanish] of his manuscript reveals the existence of a fragmented being" (*Paisajes* 221; *Landscapes* 148).

27 "Your future, your life thus lay in your own hands: they depended solely on the sincerity of your confession" (216; 144).

28 Goytisolo's claims to present a *parodic* vision of Western fears of Islam are inconsistent and insufficient; they do not, in other words, authoritatively "resolve" the problems of his fiction (see, for example, the essay titled "De Don Julián a Makbara" in *Crónicas sarracinas*). As Paul Julian Smith observes, the "abstraction and aestheticization of the Arab body (which always remains the same, which cannot be distinguished from the desert it inhabits) makes it impossible for Goytisolo to offer a historical account of Arab or Moslem cultures comparable to the one he makes for Spain. . . . One would hardly suspect from the novels that many of the countries he describes remain subject to dictatorships as bloody and repressive as the regimes of Franco and Castro so mercilessly parodied in the trilogy [*Señas de identidad, Reivindicación del Conde don Julián,* and *Juan sin tierra*]; or that in at least one of them homosexuality is punishable by death" (*Laws of Desire* 87–88). Indeed, Goytisolo often speaks of Islam as if it were devoid of inner tensions or differences (Sunni, Shi'ite, Kharijite) and as if Sufism and Moroccan social polity provided the full measure of "los países islámicos" [the Islamic countries]. The challenge, as I see it, is to interrogate sexual ideology not only *between* but also *within* national spheres, questioning the Western vision of Islam (including Goytisolo's) *and* the Islamic vision of the West.

29 Although the status of "homosexuals" and homosexuality in many Islamic countries remains obscure, a number of things are quite clear. Amnesty International has paid special attention to Iran, where sodomy is punishable by death. The organization states, in *Breaking the Silence: Human Rights Violations Based on Sexual Orientation,* that "what is clear is that homosexuality is a capital crime in Iran" (33). Frequently the "crime" of homosexuality is linked to, or hidden beneath, the crimes of spying and sedition (once again, the idea of the homosexual as traitor). Other countries where homo-

sexuality is a *hadd* offense—an offense against the divine will under *Shari'a*—
Islamic law or code of ethics—include Mauritania and the Arab Republic
of Yemen. According to the same Amnesty International report: "In other
countries where Shari'a is the basis for penal codes, lesbians and gay men
[*sic*] may be vulnerable to human rights abuses. Although sodomy and
homosexuality may not be mentioned, many of these penal codes criminalize
a wide range of sexual behavior outside marriage. Countries which have such
laws include Saudi Arabia, Pakistan, the Sudan, and Oman" (34). I should
point out that the very formulation "lesbians and gay men" is of dubious
applicability to many, if not most, Islamic countries, inasmuch as it designates sociopolitical identities constructed, or identified, in the West. "Homosexuals" and "homosexuality" are arguably less problematic, but "sodomy"
and "sodomites" seem the least problematic terms available in translation.
"Sodomy" designates an "act" whereas "homosexuality" designates, or can
designate, an identity. Nevertheless, "sodomy" does function metonymically
to figure a "homosexual actant" (a sodomite) who can be held, in a curious
looping, "responsible" for, or "guilty" of, the act of sodomy. The "act" thus
functions as an "identity-effect," saturating the subject as moral-legal subject
(i.e., subject *to* the law). When the law defines death as that which is due the
act, when it *enacts* death as that which follows from the act, the act is hardly as
discrete as it may seem (I am thinking of the Foucauldian distinction between
act and identity). In such circumstances, before such a law, the act is presented as something ontological, and our fretting over the appropriateness or
propriety of one term as opposed to another—"gay," "homosexual," "sodomite"—seems of *nominal* significance.

30 On the issue of repressive tolerance, see Marcuse. He posits tolerance as an
objective (an ideal) rather than an existing condition (a fact): "The realization of tolerance would call for intolerance toward prevailing policies, attitudes, opinions and the extension of tolerance to policies, attitudes, and
opinions which are outlawed or suppressed. . . . what is proclaimed and
practiced as tolerance today, is in many of its most effective manifestations
serving the cause of oppression" (81). That tolerance may be repressive and
oppressive, that it may mask something intolerable, is a proposition whose
validity, or invalidity, is played out globally. In this sense, the "tolerance" of
homosexuals, in Sweden or in Morocco, is a proposition that is not beyond
question and critique. Goytisolo suggests the contrary, declaring that beyond
issues of "despenalización" and a vague "discriminación," such critique is
absurd. Goytisolo also suggests that critique is motivated by guilt, something
that he has lost "totally and absolutely." He goes on to tell Escudero that "[i]n

the Islamic world there is not guilt [over homosexuality] even though there are 'aleyas' in the Koran that condemn sodomites. Male homosexuality is totally integrated into society; it is not conflictive as long as it is not mentioned. As long as it remains implicit it is not a problem for anybody" (131, translation mine). This is yet another astonishingly secure, and hopelessly contradictory, declaration: total integration involves communal (self)censorship and silencing; guilt is divorced from law; and no one has a problem at all, provided they are less explicit about certain things than Goytisolo. Goytisolo's ability to penetrate the silence and to articulate the individual realities behind it—"it is not a problem for anyone"—speaks for itself. Rex Wockner quotes several Islamic men who cast a rather different light on Goytisolo's validation of what sounds strangely like a "don't ask, don't tell" position. According to one, many of the men who "engage" in homosexual acts "are very comfortable. They think it's the best of all possible worlds. Since nobody recognizes homosexuality as even existing, they can get away with things we cannot get away with here. But if you start actually talking about homosexuality, they get very uncomfortable" (106). Here too, Foucault's understanding of a "repressive hypothesis" and an "incitement to discourse," both developed in *The History of Sexuality*, vol. 1, may reveal their geopolitical and historical limits. Wockner describes lesbianism as "all but invisible" in Islamic countries, a "perception"—or "misperception"—related to the "perception" of female sexuality in Islam in general. For a more nuanced perspective on women in Islam, see Mernissi, especially 153–71. For information concerning lesbianism and Islam, see Tohidi, who includes a selection of articles from the Bill of Retribution [*Qisas*] that pertain to women. As Tohidi indicates, the *hadd* for lesbianism [*mosaheqah*] in Iran is 100 lashes; the fourth offense is punishable by death (264).

31 See Bersani. There is of course also the following in *Paisajes:* "His virtues are kept modestly hidden, and to further conceal them he delights in practices that are contemptuous and base: he therefore not only brings upon himself the reprobation of his fellows, but provokes them into ostracizing and condemning him. Beneath his masks and veils the aim of writing is disdain: the proud rejection of the sympathy or admiration of others as the indispensable requisite for the attainment of that inner alchemy practiced beneath the disguise of mocking and sarcastic chronicle, of incidents and adventures in a deliberately grotesque autobiography . . . the map of universal stupidity" (224). The latter is a reference, used by Goytisolo in *En los reinos de taifa*, to Flaubert's *Bouvard et Pécuchet*, a work cited as an epigraph to *Paisajes*. Besides providing for a wonderful intertextual play, it also serves as a brilliantly

defensive *authorial* move, preempting criticism by claiming to seek it. Antic-ipating rejection, rejection is apparently rendered inoperative; debunking the integrity of the author, the author is left alone.

32 "The privileging of ambiguity," writes Barbara Johnson, "would always ap-pear to be an avoidance of action" (30). On a certain level, that is true. And yet, what a significant *fragment* of the gay *movement* has shown is that ambi-guity can be the call to action, and that it can be performed, and not just championed, as collective, imaginative, and political. Goytisolo is not oblivi-ous to such a performative ambiguity (after all, the Red Fags are extrava-gantly attired and adept at mimicry and manipulation), but he presents it as if it were a ruse, as if ambiguity were here the mask of a deeper, more disturbing, dogmatism.

33 See Goytisolo's *Cuaderno de Sarajevo: Anotaciones de un viaje a la barbarie* and *El sitio de los sitios*.

34 When the story seems to be summed up as a "fable without a moral"; when the protagonist, or implied author, is identified as "our misanthrope"; when López Baralt approvingly affirms that the text "neutralizes the seriousness of political ideals and of literature itself" (4); when Sánchez Robayna in his introduction to *Paisajes* declares that it "erases every moralizing impulse to retain only the signs of free and liberating laughter" (26); and Annie Perrin—in "Un casse texte explosif"—asserts that the particular significance of con-flicting ideologies "matters little" (219); when so much points to the irrele-vance of thought and action alike, ethics and politics are indeed hard-pressed. Francisco Javier Blasco is one of the few critics to resist the risible neutraliza-tion of ethical categories in *Paisajes* (they are funny, they are defused, but only in part and at times) and holds that ethics converges and conflicts with aesthetics in a kind of insoluble cultural palimpsest (18, 11). But Blasco is not alone. Given the importance of Lewis Carroll in *Paisajes,* we may do well to recall, as Julián Ríos does, the words of the Duchess in *Alice's Adventures in Wonderland:* "Tut, tut, child! . . . Everything's got a moral, if only you can find it" (Carroll 70). What is erased and matters little may just be what Goytisolo, whatever his intentions, writes as mattering most.

Abjection and Ambiguity: Lesbian Desire in

Bemberg's *Yo, la peor de todas*

⟡

Emilie Bergmann

The poems are really all we have. . . . I have wanted not to produce another romance about this woman who lived long ago.—Page duBois, *Sappho Is Burning*

In a slow-paced scene of domination and seduction in María Luisa Bemberg's film about Sor Juana Inés de la Cruz, the poet's patroness, the vicereine of Nueva España, declares her desire for intimate knowledge of her brilliant protégée: "Jamás he conocido a una mujer como tú: más poeta que monja, más monja que mujer. Hace años que me pregunto: ¿Cómo es Juana cuando está sola, cuando nadie la mira?" [Never have I known a woman like you: more poet than nun, more nun than woman. For years I have asked myself: what is Juana like when she's alone, when no one is looking at her?]. After commanding the nun to remove her veil, performing an awkward striptease from the neck up, the condesa kisses her, claiming "Esta Juana es mía. Solamente mía" [This Juana is mine. Only mine]. Staging the attempt to fix an identity for this elusive figure as object of desire, Bemberg's imperious vicereine repeats a gesture enacted by generations of readers, critics, novelists, and dramatists in search of a Sor Juana of their own.

Yo, la peor de todas is shaped by a narrative of female abjection, the defeat of a risk-taking, exceptionally gifted, and accomplished woman crushed by the patriarchal social order. The film draws heavily on the textual source cited in the opening credits, Octavio Paz's *Las trampas de la fe* (*The traps of faith*). Bemberg, however, goes farther than Paz to posit a causal relationship between this defeat and the homoeroticism that can be read in some of Sor Juana's poems to her patronesses. Thus, Bemberg's project is implicated in Paz's homophobic readings of Sor Juana's expressions of passionate friendship toward the vicereine, despite her earlier creation of what was probably the first significant and sympathetic role for a homosexual character in Argentine cinema, in *Señora de nadie* (1982).[1]

Bemberg's condesa problematizes Sor Juana's gender in the scene described: as nun, her sexuality is neutralized; as poet, she engages in a masculine activity, and the condesa wishes to uncover the woman behind these social roles. But the shorn head of the unveiled Sor Juana reveals submissiveness rather than a desiring female body. This scene and the selection of poems in *Yo, la peor de todas* exemplify the problem of representing lesbian desire:

> The difficulty in defining an autonomous form of female sexuality and desire in the wake of a cultural tradition still Platonic, still grounded in sexual (in)difference, still caught in the tropism of hommo-sexuality, is not to be overlooked or willfully bypassed. It is perhaps even greater than the difficulty in devising strategies of representation which will, in turn, alter the standard of vision, the frame of reference of visibility, of *what can be seen.* (de Lauretis, "Sexual Indifference" 152)

Bemberg's film creates the fleeting image of two women looking at each other with a desire that is historically situated and not "hommo-sexual" but homoerotic. Her choice of poetic texts recited by the actors and her statements about the film obscure the lesbian reading of that image.

Because public recognition and scholarly work were generally limited to men in the early modern period, Sor Juana's erudite poetry, publication, and fame within her lifetime created gender troubles that haunt her earliest biographies, including her own self-representations. Central to Bemberg's representation is the attribution of sexual desire, both heterosexual and homosexual, to the Condesa de Paredes[2] while characterizing the homoeroticism of Sor Juana's poetry as sublimated, distanced, and "Platonic." Bemberg stages a causal connection between Sor Juana's passionate poems to the condesa and her persecution by ecclesiastical authorities, which requires that Sor Juana's devotion to the condesa be perceived as threatening to the social order. The film's characterization of the condesa as bisexual reflects fairly accurately an early modern context in which, as Valerie Traub suggests, "desire may have been allowed to flow more freely if less sensationally between homoerotic and heterosexual modes," as long as homoeroticism was not "perceived as a threat to the reproductive designs of heterosexual marriage" (78–79).[3] The cinematic interpretation of the relationship between patroness and poet ensures that this threat is only a delusion of leering, misogynistic clerics and does not implicate Sor Juana as desiring subject.

Scholars and biographers from Calleja in the eighteenth century to Paz in the twentieth have struggled with the problem of identifying Sor Juana's powerful intellect as "masculine," together with the troubling perception of homoerotic desire as masculine-identified sexuality toward the women to whom she dedicated love poetry and verbal portraits. Questions of gender and sexuality had already been addressed in Sor Juana's poetry and the autobiographical account in her Respuesta a sor Filotea [Response to Sor Filotea]. Her verses to a Peruvian correspondent "diciendo que se volviese hombre" [saying that she should become a man] (*Obras Completas* 1: 136–39) exploit her knowledge of Latin, the language reserved for men in power, to wittily challenge gender categories. In her *Respuesta a sor Filotea,* Sor Juana recalls that she wished to cross-dress in order to study Latin at the University in Mexico City (*The Answer* 48–49). From that anecdote, Bemberg elaborates a flashback that suggests a view of gender as performance. At the deathbed of the poet's mother, the girl Juana is dressed as a boy and reveals, while winking directly into the camera, that she became a nun because she wasn't allowed to dress in male clothing.

Despite the struggle with the "masculinity" of intellectual achievement, Paz and other scholars have found in Sor Juana's prose, poetry, and theater a feminine subjectivity that explicitly challenges this categorization and celebrates the learning of female saints and pre-Christian deities (Bénassy-Berling 275–78; Sabat-Rivers 305–26; Martínez-San Miguel), as well as the everyday world of domesticity, affection, and maternity (Scott, "Ser mujer"). Three scenes in the film focus on the vicereine's pregnancy and on celebration at the convent over the birth of her son, probably as a result of Bemberg's consultation with Scott.

Paz's struggle with seventeenth-century categories of "masculinity" and twentieth-century concepts of "Sapphism" leads to an analysis in terms of gender binaries and finally to a definition of Sor Juana's sexuality as "erotic ambiguity, which is not the same as bisexuality."[4] He devotes more than one chapter to discussing "the poems of loving friendship [amistad amorosa] for María Luisa Manrique de Lara. But even those inflamed poems cannot be described as Sapphic, except in the sublimated sense of the Renaissance Platonic tradition" (*Traps* 506).[5] Paz's conclusion, however, does not succeed in closing off discussion and speculation.[6] As Frederick Luciani has shown, numerous recent fictionalizations of Sor Juana's life center on her sexuality. As one of Mexican culture's three foundational icons, Sor Juana is as subject to nationalist distortion and exploitation of her sexuality as Malintzín/La Malinche and the Virgin of Guadalupe. Although Paz insists that she could not possibly have had homoerotic desires (*Traps* 111; see also 196–230), her lesbianism is taken for granted by Latino/a and Spanish American lesbian and gay poets who have adopted her as their patron saint. Mexican poet Juan Carlos Bautista imagines her smiling on the development of gay and lesbian activism (16). Alicia Gaspar de Alba weaves together the erotic and intellectual life of Sor Juana in an imaginary "Sapphic Diary."[7] Sor Juana's poetry, however, challenges her readers' search for narratives to represent the poet and explain her life: "No soy yo la que pensáis . . . y diversa de mí misma / entre vuestras plumas ando" [I am not at all what you think. . . . Borne on your feather-pens' plumes / my flight is no longer mine] (*Obras Completas* 1: 159, no. 51. ll. 13, 17–18; trans. Trueblood, 103).

In discussing the undeniable emotional intensity of the poems dedicated to the Condesa de Paredes, Paz struggles with the sexuality of his most distinguished literary predecessor, declaring that "[t]o think that she felt a clear aversion to men and an equally clear attraction to women is absurd [descabellado]." He continues in a xenophobic vein: "Only by attributing to her an intellectual and sexual license more appropriate to a Diderot heroine than to a girl of Juana Inés's age and social class in New Spain could she cold-bloodedly have chosen as refuge an institution inhabited exclusively by persons of the sex that supposedly attracted her. . . . it is futile to try to learn what her true sexual feelings were. She herself did not know" (*Traps* 111). Holstun's and Traub's scholarship in early modern cultural studies supports Eileen Myles's witty response to Paz, "Where else would one go in 17th Century Mexico? The bars?" Traub's point of departure for the study of female homoeroticism is the "absence" and "silence" late-twentieth-century scholarship finds in searching for evidence of recognizable early modern versions of "lesbian" desire and subcultures. She suggests that it is precisely in relationships among apparently heterosexual or celibate women that the homoerotic was articulated.

Bemberg's project of making a film about Sor Juana is a feminist trope: bringing to life the exemplary woman of three centuries ago, representing her internal contradictions and interpersonal conflicts. The film rehearses interpretations of Sor Juana's writing: almost every scene in the first two-thirds of the film is based on a literary text or (auto)biographical document. The title, *Yo, la peor de todas,* a telling misquotation, inscribes the film in a narrative of public defeat.[8] The title alludes to Sor Juana's general confession in 1693 and her abjuration of her past intellectual life, signed in her own blood in 1694 (*Obras Completas* 4: 518, no. 409).[9] This is the scene of renunciation that closes Bemberg's film. The title's constellation of references address the relative power of religious and secular institutions, the reasons for Sor Juana's renunciation of her studies, intellectual questions of the inscription of the female body with a woman poet's blood, and questions of feminine desire in her poetry and in her cultural context. In the process of making the textual visible, the film places writing and the cinematic image in collusion and contradiction.

Scholarship on Sor Juana's remarkable intellectual and artistic production and her renunciation of this activity have centered around the enigma of capitulation and apparent self-accusation by a woman who is seen as both strong and independent. Her early death is implicitly linked to this renunciation, and the figures of Phaëton and the phoenix in her poetry have been taken as evidence that she saw the problem of her gender in terms of self-destruction, glorious aspiration and ultimate defeat. Despite Paz's general adherence to this narrative scheme in *The Traps of Faith,* he makes a convincing argument against it based on legal documents (*Traps* 464). His suspicions that Sor Juana never completely renounced her intellectual pursuits have been confirmed by Teresa Castello's recent discovery of the inventory of Sor Juana's cell after her death and Elías Trabulse's examination of the convent's account books, which clarify the pressures under which Sor Juana handed over her library and reveal her use of her financial skills to recover a portion of her formerly vast library.[10] These discoveries offer an alternative to the highly seductive image of crushing defeat as punishment for excessive feminine ambition, and posthumous fame as the only possible reward, the paradigm that shapes Bemberg's Sor Juana.

Although the opening credits of the film cite Paz's *Las trampas de la fe* as textual source, Bemberg's depiction of the events leading up to Sor Juana's capitulation to ecclesiastical authority deviates from Paz's version. Enrico Mario Santí exposes the political motivation of Paz's "poetics of restitution," which positions the seventeenth-century poet as colluding with powerful bureaucracies, and being betrayed not so much by them as by her own misguided intervention in their conflicts (Santí, "Sor Juana" 115–17).[11] Bemberg shows Sor Juana as a victim caught between rivals within the church hierarchy, the bishop of Puebla, Manuel Fernández de Santa Cruz, and the notoriously misogynistic archbishop of Mexico, Francisco de Aguiar y Seijas. In addition, Bemberg's *Yo, la peor de todas*, like her 1984 film *Camila*, is a historical film in which feminine desire upstages political conflicts, and the physical desire that Paz denies is made visible and necessary to the plot. As Nina Scott has pointed out, Bemberg "underscores erotic elements in the relationship between Sor Juana and María Luisa. . . . Whereas Paz maintained that the passion of Sor Juana's verses to María Luisa was strictly poetic convention, Bemberg's film portrays a definite physical attraction" (Scott, "Sor Juana" 153).

As Paz uses critical interpretation to close off the transgressive gesture of Sor Juana's intellectual work and the homoeroticism of her poetry, so Bemberg uses poetic citations and statements in interviews at the time of the film's release to deny the homoerotic desire that Nina Scott perceived in *Yo, la peor de todas*. None of the controversial poems dedicated to "Filis," the Condesa de Paredes, or to her predecessor "Laura," Leonor Carreto, Marquesa de Mancera, are cited in the film. The plot structure clearly points to the religious hierarchy's perception of Sor Juana's legible passion for the vicereine as the deciding factor in their condemnation of her "worldly" pursuits that led to her retreat from writing and study. However, Bemberg insists on the inaccuracy of an interviewer's perception of "un rapporto lesbico" [a lesbian relationship] (Vernaglione 481). In addition, Bemberg's account of the relationship inverts the economy of desire as it is depicted in the film: "È vero che c'è un legame d'amore e credo che ci sia stata una passione da parte di Juana ma credo sublimata" [It is true that there was a bond of love and I believe that there was passion on that part of Juana but I believe it was sublimated] (Vernaglione 481). In summarizing the plot of *Yo, la peor de todas* in an interview, however, Bemberg mentions only Paz's political interpretation: "The script is based on a biography by Octavio Paz and he shows—it's all documented—how her harassment by the Church finally broke her in the same way that dissidents in certain countries are being induced to recant" (Whitaker 120). Bemberg's statement about her reversal of roles in her earlier historical film *Camila* suggests a political reason for her image of the sexually "pure," passive nun in *Yo, la peor de todas:* "I think it was a good idea to have the priest seduced by the woman, to have a role reversal, because all the stories tell of the beautiful, innocent Camila who was seduced by the nasty priest. It helped me with the Church since he was the 'pure' one" (Whitaker 118).

In the opening scene of the film, the Marqués de la Laguna, newly arrived viceroy of Nueva España, establishes the secular power that will later protect Sor Juana against the church hierarchy until he is recalled to Spain. The marqués is shown at a table opposite the archbishop of Mexico, Francisco Aguiar y Seijas, in an austerely symmetrical arrangement that alludes visually to the techniques of Baroque composition. The binary opposition of the opening scene carries over into a self-consciously Baroque framing scene that inscribes Sor Juana in a seventeenth-century cultural context. The Marqués de la Laguna and his wife, the Condesa de Paredes, are contrasting figures framing the brightly illuminated figure of Sor Juana as she emerges from the wings in triumph after the opening performance of her play, *Los empeños de una casa* [The trials of a household]. The first of a series of excerpts from Sor Juana's poems is introduced by the viceroy, who recites the familiar opening lines of her satirical ballad "Hombres necios" [Foolish men]. Shifting to Sor Juana's perspective, the camera angle changes to reveal the *dramatis personae* of a different scene: her ally Fernández de Santa Cruz, the bishop of Puebla, is seated directly behind the couple, who praise her beauty, passion, and wit while the spitefully misogynistic archbishop of Mexico, Aguiar y Seijas, growls truculently from the shadows. The camera briefly positions the playwright as audience of a drama, just beginning, into which she is about to be drawn.

Bemberg's selection of poetic texts and the voices in which they are read contribute an illusion of historical veracity to her cinematic version of the poet's sexuality. Significantly, they do not include the poems that haunt Sor Juana's readers with the welcome or feared phantom of homoeroticism. Among the poems that have attracted critical speculation is her description of the physical attributes of the condesa in the *romance* "Lo atrevido de un pincel" [Phyllis, a brush's boldness] (*Obras Completas* 1: 54–59). The poem's title may have been added by an editor, as if to fend off speculation about the poet's sexuality: "Puro amor, que ausente y sin deseo de indecencias, puede sentir lo que el más profano" [A pure love, however distant, eschewing all unseemliness, may feel whatever the most profane might feel]. Key to debates about eroticism in her poetry have been such lines as "Ser mujer ni estar ausente, / no es de amarte impedi-mento / pues sabes tú que las almas / distancia ignoran y sexo" [That you're a woman far away / is no hindrance to my love: / for the soul, as you well know, / distance and sex don't count] (*Obras Completas* 1: 57, ll.109–10; trans. Trueblood 39). The imagery of the poem, both Neoplatonic and passionate, referring to the risks and dangers in the female speaker's de-sire, and to the "lazos estrechos" [closely knit embrace] in which elements of the natural world are drawn together by love, constitutes a significant challenge to the film's representation of the condesa's articulation of desire and Sor Juana's reticence. Another important example is the physical description of the condesa's beauty in the *romance decasílabo* [ten-syllable ballad] "Lámina sirva el cielo al retrato" [May Heaven serve as plate for the engraving] (*Obras Completas* 1: 171–73). None of these poems, nor any of the love sonnets in which a possibly feminine lyric voice is directed toward a female object, is cited in the film.

One conventional answer to generations of readers' questions about the nature of the eroticism in Sor Juana's poems dedicated to the marquesa is that, whatever one or both might have felt, they were separated by the convent walls and the bars of the *locutorio,* the visitors' room that served as Sor Juana's salon. Novelists and playwrights have contrived various means to penetrate that barrier or to allow their Sor Juana a physical or imagi-nary escape.[12] Early in the film, Bemberg introduces the framing device of the gleaming iron bars of the *locutorio,* the grillwork that divides visitors from the cloistered women in the convent. In her first visit to the convent, as the vicereine notes the similarities in their restricted lives, the grillwork dominates the scene, and other iron bars are visible behind the vicereine. A few scenes later, Sor Juana and her confessor Antonio Núñez de Mi-randa are in sharp chiaroscuro, with the camera as well as the light on Sor Juana's side of the bars while from the darkness Núñez (called "Miranda" in the film) warns her about her secular poems to the viceroy and his wife. Bemberg explains in an interview that this scene symbolizes the entire story of the film, placing Sor Juana in the context of medieval women persecuted as witches and accomplices of the devil. The filmmaker concludes: "È l'oscurantismo che vince" [It is the darkness that wins] (Vernaglione 480).[13]

The ominous confrontation between the poet and her religious adviser is immediately followed by a scene in which the condesa appears within Sor Juana's light-filled study, without revealing the opening through which she, in her voluminous brocaded gown, managed to penetrate the division of secular world from cloister. With her strong Habsburg chin and a history of films in which she plays coldly beautiful women who make dangerous object choices (*The Garden of the Finzi-Continis, The Conformist*), Dominique Sanda is cast as the sexually aggressive bisexual vicereine. The poet, played by Assumpta Serna, seems much younger than the vicereine, although historically both women were in their early thirties when they met. Bemberg's Sor Juana is a fresh-faced ingenue, with hardly a trace of the femme fatale—quite literally—that Serna played in Pedro Almodóvar's *Matador*. This Sor Juana has apparently plucked the heavy dark Frida Kahlo eyebrows she has in all her portraits. Her powerful intellectual presence wanes, and she appears increasingly subjugated as the plot unfolds.

Exerting the greater power of the secular state established in the first scene, and unsatisfied with small talk in the convent locutorio, the condesa occupies the exclusively feminine space of Sor Juana's study in the cloister, initiates physical contact, and speaks explicitly about desire. As Sor Juana passes through a gauzy curtain to join her, the condesa explains, "No soporto los barrotes de tu locutorio" [I can't stand the iron bars of your locutory]. The scene in Sor Juana's study is structured around the intellectual danger of books, the sexuality of the pregnant vicereine, and the play of religious and secular authority. Like Núñez in the previous scene, the vicereine cautions Sor Juana, observing dangerous books on her study table: Descartes, Gassendi, Kircher.[14] Her vivid memory of an *auto-da-fé* causes the pregnant vicereine to become faint, and she asks Juana to loosen her bodice. This scene foregrounds the inequalities and differences in temperament and experience between the two women. The dialogue casts Sor Juana as a scholar so absorbed in intellectual passion and ignorant of feminine sexuality that she is shocked by the vicereine's pregnancy. The figure of the vicereine brings together two aspects of feminine sexuality, lesbian desire and maternity, traditionally perceived as mutually exclusive. In addition to positioning the vicereine as desiring subject, this sequence balances her unusual sympathy toward the victims of the In-quisition with her status as noblewoman born and raised to command her social inferiors, and unable to release herself without help from the con-strictions of seventeenth-century dress. The dialogue clearly supports a homoerotic interpretation. In response to Sor Juana's need for silence and solitude, the vicereine invokes Nature and God in favor of the "deseo de amar" [desire to love]. As Sor Juana conducts a guided tour of her collec-tion of scientific and musical instruments, the condesa comments, "¡Qué bella eres cuando te apasionas!" [How beautiful you are when you're excited!].

Bemberg does not cite the transgressive poetic portraits of her pa-tronesses that might have accompanied a later scene in which the vicereine sits for a painter. Instead, she invents an exchange in which Sor Juana is the passive recipient of a miniature portrait of the vicereine, which the nun secretly wears around her neck where she would ordinarily wear a scapu-lar. Sitting in a sunny patio outside the palace while the painter works, the vicereine reads Juana's lyrical expressions of the agony and melancholy of love, in her *redondillas*, "En que describe racionalmente los efectos irra-cionales del amor" [In which she describes rationally the irrational effects of love] (*Obras Completas* 1: 213–16, no. 84; trans. Trueblood 79), a poem probably written at an earlier time.

In this witty appropriation of tropes traditionally used by male poets to complain about their beloveds' "ingratitude," Sor Juana weaves concep-tual oppositions of love as suffering, with verbal intricacies of "passion" and "reason," "blame" and "justice." Bemberg reads Sor Juana's poetry in light of Paz's discussion of "Platonic" love and "amorous ambiguity": "Per lei l'amore è una idea e che si tratta di un amore impossibile, ed è l'amore migliore, quello che non tiene ai premi, alle ricompense, agli asservi-menti" [for her, love was an idea and she wrote about an impossible love, which is the best, that love whose devotion is not rewarded] (Vernaglione 481). These observations explain why Bemberg chose courtly conceptual wordplay and the absence of graphically physical desire in the verses re-cited in this scene. Their tone matches the spiritual devotion suggested in Sor Juana's faithful wearing of the miniature, rather than the erotic energy and playfulness of some of the poems explicitly dedicated to the condesa, such as "Lámina sirva el cielo al retrato," and "Lo atrevido de un pincel."

The closing quatrain of these redondillas assumes common ground with the male speakers in other Petrarchist poems: anyone who has loved will understand and forgive the speaker's irritability and shifting moods. This is a poem closer to imitation, however problematic, of the masculine poetic tradition than to the confrontation and resistance that characterizes much of Sor Juana's work.

One of the most effective scenes in the film shows Sor Juana's salon in the convent locutory at the height of her poetic powers and social prestige. Her vanity and self-assurance are dramatized as she prepares to meet her visitors, putting cologne on her hands, and a jet bracelet on her wrist, historically accurate details of the relaxed discipline in the Hieronymite convent (Scott, "Sor Juana" 153). She stands on a small platform while her servant brushes her habit. She sits regally in a chair while the camera focuses on her face and then on the faces of her *tertulia* [salon] of male intellectuals. The camera always includes some part of the iron grillwork, no matter what the angle, a semiotically necessary element, however architecturally impossible. Sigüenza y Góngora argues that Phaëton signifies "imprudence," whereas Sor Juana interprets the mythological figure as a symbol of intellectual aspiration and knowledge without limits. Her confessor asks if Phaëton perhaps symbolizes the attraction of the abyss, implying a warning, and Sor Juana replies, "El conocimiento es siempre una transgresión. Y más para una mujer." She pauses a moment, sips hieratically from her elegant porcelain cup, and adds, "Y si no, preguntadselo al arzobispo" [Knowledge is always a transgression. And more so for a woman. And if you don't believe it, ask the archbishop]. At the insistence of her admirers, she recites her sonnet on the risk of undertaking a lifelong commitment to the convent or marriage (*Obras Completas* 1: no. 149), only to be interrupted by the entrance of the condesa, bearing an enormous headdress of quetzal feathers. Fernández de Santa Cruz and Sigüenza y Góngora remark on the appropriateness of the quetzal, which they term "our sacred bird," "the Mexican bird." Sor Juana accepts the gift and steps back from the bars, so that the camera frames her through them. She puts on the headdress, bows, and remarks wittily, "Moctezuma se cae postrado a los pies del conquistador" [Moctezuma falls prostrate at the feet of the conquistador].

The gift of the headdress of quetzal feathers serves multiple purposes: it inscribes this discourse in a Mexican context, it re-creates a gift Sor Juana commemorated in a poem, it pictures Sor Juana as an ingenious rara avis in her cage, and it creates a self-conscious scene of colonial dominance and submission. This episode communicates power and the erotic through the rapt expressions on the nun's and the vicereine's faces, and the harpsichord music that announces the vicereine's entrance on the soundtrack. But the episode also corroborates Jean Franco's reading of the passionate friendship between Sor Juana and her patroness as clearly mediated by their hierarchical power relationship in its colonial context: "It is impossible to separate personal love from love of the body politic, and love of the body politic included the recognition of authority" (50).

Although the passionate poems to the vicereine are textually absent, interpretations of them as "Platonic," as courtly performance and as homoerotic, are brought together with the noblewoman's maternity in a scene in the viceregal palace in which a voice-over of Sor Juana recites amorous verses while the vicereine caresses her son's head. The poet's voice and her immediate audience, the condesa, embody and weave together the feminine in the forms of virgin, mother, and wise woman that Sor Juana celebrated in her long philosophical poem *Primero sueño* [First dream]. The setting each one occupies, however, is a scene of patriarchal power that will separate them. The correspondence of sound to image, voice with body, are shattered as the voice changes to the viceroy's and the camera shifts from the vicereine to her husband, reading the same poem aloud.

These shifts in voice and image signal a change in Sor Juana's fortunes. Her poetry is no longer a private form of communication between two women. The viceroy comments urbanely, "¡Qué pasión! Sigues haciendo estragos, María Luisa" [What passion! You keep on breaking hearts, María Luisa]. The lines are the tercets of a sonnet: "Baste ya de rigores, mi bien, baste; . . . pues ya en líquido humor viste y tocaste / mi corazón deshecho entre tus manos" [So, beloved, put an end to harshness now . . . since, in that flood of tears, you saw and touched / my broken heart within your very hands] (*Obras Completas* 1: 287, no. 164, ll.9–14; Trueblood 81). The mental confusion of the lines cited earlier in the portrait scene gives way to suggestively physical imagery in these lines.

The use of voice-overs continues in the transition to the next scene, accompanied by the ethereal sound of the nuns' singing. While Sor Juana sings innocently in choir, her enemies enter her study and copy out her poems to the vicereine. With an implication of causality leading up to Sor Juana's persecution and final renunciation, the poems are examined by a group of clerics convened by the archbishop. Once again, the sonnet chosen for discussion in this scene was not written for the Condesa de Paredes. Its lyric speaker, of indeterminate gender, advises a jealous man, "Alcino," in love with "Celia," and enumerates the stages of love: "Amor empieza por desasosiego, / solicitud, ardores y desvelos; / crece con riesgos, lances y recelos, / susténtase de llantos y de ruego" [Love begins with restlessness, / solicitousness, ardor and wakefulness; / it grows with risks, daring, and misgivings, / and feeds on tears and prayers] *Obras Completas* 1: 297–98, no. 184).

The clerics' scrutiny of Sor Juana's poetry initiates a series of scenes that become increasingly speculative. Núñez, Juana's confessor, affirms the autonomy of poetry. He claims that it is not subject to religious judgments and insists that he finds no perverse intention. He rehearses Paz's argument that these tropes of praise and adoration are still used by poets all over Europe. But two unidentified clerics leer over the poems, one referring to Sor Juana's "enfermiza sexualidad" [diseased sexuality], a term worthy of Pfandl. The archbishop finds her poetry "profoundly disturbing." In the following scene, the door to Juana's study is barred and sealed. Núñez, despite his defense of her writing among his peers, appears to recognize the homoeroticism in her poems. He warns her, "En el convento esos desordenes amorosos no pueden llevarte más que al castigo. Tampoco en el mundo hay esperanza para ellos" [In the convent those amorous disorders can lead only to punishment. Nor is there any hope for them in the secular world]. Bemberg's sequence departs from Paz's political arguments by implying that Juana's troubles begin with these expressions of love by one woman to another, and that Sor Juana's contemporaries did not need to read Diderot to find the lesbian in them.

In the transition to the next scene, a voice-over of the condesa assures Sor Juana, "Mientras estemos en Mexico nadie te puede tocar" [As long as we are in Mexico nobody can touch you]. Her disembodied voice is prophetic of the disasters to follow, because the viceregal couple is about to return to Spain, leaving Sor Juana without their powerful patronage and protection. The long, slow-paced scene of seductive domination that follows the debate about the eroticism of the nun's poems to the condesa is an ambiguous response to the question of Sor Juana's sexuality that displaces sexual desire and agency from the *criolla* poet to the powerful condesa.

The camera cuts to the condesa in Sor Juana's study, wondering who this woman is, more nun than woman, more poet than nun, then cuts again to the vicereine standing behind Sor Juana with a gaze of power and possession: "Quítate el velo. Es una orden" [Take off your veil. That's an order]. Sor Juana looks submissively over her shoulder and obeys hesitantly, taking off only the outermost layer of her habit. The condesa commands her to remove everything, then turns her around to face her with her shorn hair, completely dominated by her patroness. "Esta Juana es mía. Solamente mía" [This Juana is mine. Only mine], she says before kissing her on the mouth. What the condesa says after the kiss, "Para recordar" [To remember], echoes an earlier flashback of Juana's years at the palace, in which a young man kisses Juana, and she reciprocates with surprising fervor. "Para recordar," she tells him. Thus, the chastity of the Hispanic "Décima Musa" is protected, and she is depicted as acting only on exclusively heterosexual desire: when the Condesa de Paredes kisses Juana, she does not return the physical gesture.

Reiterating her claim to believe that the relationship was "platonic," Bemberg explains why she decided not to film a scene of passion between the two women: "Perché sentivo che sarebbe stata una scelta opportunista." [Vernaglione:] "Nella scena dell'incontro tra Juana e Maria Luisa tutto è esplicito. Si pensa che ci sia un rapporto tra le due donne." [Bemberg:] "Credo che tutte le suore, tutte le donne che portano un abito religioso siano misteriose. Dunque quello che vuole la viceregina è conoscere. Perché conoscere è possedere" [Because I thought it would have been an opportunistic decision. [Vernaglione:] In the encounter between Juana and Maria Luisa everything is explicit. One would think that there was a relationship between the two women. [Bemberg:] I think that all nuns, all women who wear a religious habit are mysterious. Therefore what the Vicereine wants is knowledge. Because knowledge is possession] (Vernaglione 481). Bemberg's response is evasive, in light of the overt homoeroticism in the scene, although lesbian subjectivity is exclusively attributed to the vicereine. The omission throughout the film of the poems Sor Juana dedicated to this powerful noblewoman obscures her role as desiring subject and simplifies the relationship along binaries of political power.

In her interview with Vernaglione, Bemberg defends her avoidance of an explicitly lesbian scene whose physicality could be perceived as "opportunistic." It can be argued that there is historical veracity in the voluminous clothing that surrounds female bodies in almost every scene. The exceptions are not scenes of sensual pleasure, but rather scenes of suffering from an epidemic, accompanied by moaning and vomiting, followed by shots of the nuns' bare backs, bloodied from flagellation, and the humble, barefoot bodies of plague victims. Nakedness in this seventeenth-century context connotes degradation and suffering rather than sexual release. The film problematizes twentieth-century encodings of sensuality: once freed of its veil, Sor Juana's dull, unevenly chopped hair presents her vulnerability. The condesa, who earlier expressed identification with her, now expresses a desire to possess the nun's unknowable complexity and commands her to reveal what she is without the trappings of her social status. The only scene in which physical contact is associated with pleasure is the one in the viceregal palace in which the condesa reads Sor Juana's lines, "Baste ya de rigores, mi bien, baste," while stroking her son's hair.

The denouement of the film refers to documented events, adding fictional confrontations to dramatize the filmmaker's interpretation of events. Sor Juana's theological critique of a sermon by the Brazilian theologian Vieyra, who was much admired by the archbishop of Mexico, was probably published as the *Carta Atenagórica* [Athenagoric letter][15] by his rival the bishop of Puebla, who then donned the pseudonymous drag of "Sor Filotea" to reprimand the nun for transgressing the exclusively masculine boundaries of theological discourse. Bemberg includes passages from Sor Juana's strong feminist response to "Sor Filotea" but fabricates an implausibly violent confrontation between Sor Juana and her ecclesiastical superiors. The camera captures Sor Juana from the visitors' side of the iron grillwork. She appears, and behaves, like an animal in a cage, in sharp contrast to the witty urbanity of her salon in better days. Soon after this scene, Núñez resigns as her confessor, and Mexico is devastated by famine, plague, and hunger riots, which contribute to the pressures on Sor Juana that culminate in renunciation and handing over her library to be sold by her ecclesiastical superiors.

In a capsule biography of Sor Juana in her interview with Whitaker, Bemberg does not mention the condesa: "[Sor Juana] ended up looking after the nuns in the convent, which is what the Church wants women to do: to scrub, to sew, to wash, but never to think, to be creative and audacious" (120). Scrubbing is precisely what Sor Juana is doing at the end of the film, but contrary to her summary, Bemberg's version of Sor Juana's abjection focuses on the gesture of renouncing her love for the condesa. The camera angle exaggerates the humiliation of her position at the feet of her confessor, who says that he has waited twenty years for this Juana, "abnegada, entregada al servicio de Dios" [self-abnegating, surrendering to the service of God]. In a melodramatic moment, Núñez de Miranda blames her intellectual pursuits and her love of the condesa for the recent floods and plague: "Amaste demasiado a esa mujer" [You loved that woman too much]. Juana's reply is a succinct Neoplatonic theory of love: "Más la amaba, más me sentía cerca de Dios" [The more I loved her, the closer I felt to God]. After agreeing to give up all her worldly belongings, Sor Juana finally tears off the concealed miniature of the condesa she has been wearing around her neck.

The voice-body split in the voice-overs within the film replicates the other contradictions between Bemberg's verbal summaries of the biographical plot of the film and the representation of desire in the film, as well as among the poetic texts included, the circumstances that produced them, the possible interpretations, and the images they accompany in the film. There is, in addition, a curious mismatch between the sound track and the dissonant movements of Dominique Sanda's mouth throughout the film. The final credits resolve that mystery: Cecilia Roth provided her voice, suggesting another, ironic reading to Paz's insistence that only a French woman could have felt the lesbian desire attributed to Sor Juana. After the camera work ends, the epilogue appears on a black screen: Sor Juana died shortly after her profession of faith signed in her own blood, and she was considered "Uno de los más grandes poetas del siglo de oro español" [One of the greatest poets of the Spanish Golden Age]. With the problematic "uno" of this epilogue, both unmarked and marked as masculine, and the assimilation into the peninsular Spanish poetic pantheon, Sor Juana's writing continues to be framed and constricted by gender and by political categories. And she continues to defy them.

Notes

I thank Kathleen Newman and David Eng for sharing their expertise in film theory, and Frederick Luciani and Nina Scott for their helpful discussions of representations of Sor Juana during the preparation of this essay.

1 Production of "Señora de nadie" was postponed because the military regime considered the protagonist's separation from her husband and her friendship with a homosexual to be subversive: "They told me that it was a very bad example for Argentine mothers and that we couldn't put a maricón (which is a terrible word for a homosexual) in the film. The colonel said that he would rather have a son who had cancer than one who was homosexual, so I couldn't do it" (Whitaker, 115).

2 María Luisa Manrique de Lara y Gonzaga, Marquesa de la Laguna by marriage and Condesa de Paredes through her mother's lineage, was the wife of Tomás Antonio de la Cerda, Viceroy of Nueva España from 1680 to 1688.

3 Traub chooses the term *homoeroticism* to avoid the historical specificity of terms like *homosexual* and *lesbian* and to include possibilities still relatively unexplored in the early modern period. Although her study of feminine homoeroticism is limited to early modern England and France, Traub's argument is useful in studying the instability of gender within categories of sexuality and articulating a "discourse of desires and acts" (64) in this period in Spain and Colonial Spanish America.

4 Ludwig Pfandl's term *intersexual,* as it is cited by Paz in the Spanish original, was used by early-twentieth-century "sexologists" to refer to sexual deviation toward masculine appearance and behavior among independent women (Jeffreys 175; see also Smith-Rosenberg 268, on the related term "intermediate sex"). Paz, however, elides the embedded meanings in Pfandl's text by interpreting "intersexual" as meaning "bisexual" in the late-twentieth-century sense of sexual attraction toward both sexes: "Claro está que sor Juana era intersexual pero ¿qué se quiere decir con esto? Sólo una minoría del género humano no es intersexual" [Of course Sor Juana was bisexual, but what does that say? All but a handful of humanity is bisexual] (*Trampas* 604; *Traps* 506).

5 Because Paz made some significant changes in the text as it appears in the 1988 English version, and Margaret Sayers Peden's translation is very reliable, my citations are from *The Traps of Faith.*

6 Further evidence of Paz's uneasiness with Sor Juana's sexuality is his marginalization of the discussion of Pfandl's outrageous psychoanalytic theories of the 1940s concerning Sor Juana's "intersexuality," "father fixation," and "difficult menopause." In the 1982 Spanish original, *Las trampas de la fe,* Paz

addresses them in the first biographical chapter and the penultimate chapter (92–95 and 603–6), but they are isolated in the final "Notes on Sources" in the 1988 English translation, *The Traps of Faith.*

7 Arenal and Powell (Juana Inés de la Cruz, *The Answer* 8–12) and Scott ("Ser mujer" 160–61) give succinct accounts of the scholarly debate about eroticism in Sor Juana's poetry. Scott cites serious scholarly errors in Victoria Urbano's biography, casting doubt on her strong claims about Sor Juana's erotic relationships with her patronesses (Scott, "Sor Juana and Her World" 150–51).

8 In a brief document intended to be inscribed with the date of Sor Juana's death, she referred to herself as "Yo, la peor del mundo" [I, the worst woman in the world] and as "La peor que ha habido" [the worst woman who ever existed] (*Obras Completas* 4: 523, no. 413).

9 As Paz points out, only the title, superimposed by an editor, and not the text of the document written by Sor Juana and signed on 5 March 1694, refers to a renunciation of secular studies: "Protesta que, rubricada con su sangre, hizo de su fe y amor a Dios la Madre Juana Inés de la Cruz, al tiempo de abandonar los estudios humanos para proseguir, desembarazada de este afecto, en el camino de la perfección" [Confession that, signed with her blood, Mother Juana Inés de la Cruz made of her faith and love of God, at the moment of abandoning human studies to continue, freed from this burden, on the road to spiritual perfection]. "There is not a word about humane studies [in the text]. Moreover, no one has seen the original document. . . . There is, therefore, *not a single declaration in which Sor Juana formally and expressly renounces letters.* I have no doubt that she defended herself to the last and refused to sign an abdication and nullification of her entire life" (*Traps* 463; emphasis in Paz's text).

10 Among her other duties, Sor Juana also kept the convent's financial records. Trabulse's paper, "Los años finales de Sor Juana: una interpretación" and Castello's paper (title unannounced in the program) were read at a conference held 13–17 November 1995, "Sor Juana y su mundo a 300 años de su muerte . . . una mirada actual," sponsored by the Universidad del Claustro de Sor Juana, and are forthcoming in the *Actas* of the conference. In 1982 Paz drew on the research published by Dorothy Schons in "Nuevos datos" (1929) on the financial transactions between Sor Juana and the church hierarchy in the last years of her life, and on a lawsuit filed in 1698 against the archbishop's heirs, "with the aim of recovering some portion of the loans and requisitions he had coerced from different persons and institutions," including jewels and money from Sor Juana's cell in the convent of San Jerónimo (*Traps* 468).

11 Santí traces Paz's metaphor of "the traps of faith" to his attacks on Stalinism, which coincided with the first stages of his work on Sor Juana in the 1950s.

Thus, his explanation of the biographical enigma of Sor Juana's renunciation in *Las trampas de la fe* is modeled on the ideological "trap" in which Soviet intellectuals found themselves in the 1950s (102–3; 115–17).

12 The scenes in two plays based on Sor Juana's life, Rosario Castellanos's *El eterno femenino* (1975) and Coral Aguirre's *La cruz en el espejo* (1988), for example, involve dream and memory to transcend the limitations of physical space and verisimilitude. Alicia Gaspar de Alba's "Sapphic Diary" uses letters and memory to cross those boundaries.

13 How great a threat the Inquisition posed to Sor Juana's intellectual activity is debatable: it was not the Holy Office itself that placed pressure on her.

14 Paz discusses the possibility, still open to debate, that Sor Juana might have read or heard summaries and discussions of prohibited works by these authors (*Traps* 258–59). The film depicts a fallible process of censorship in which Sigüenza y Góngora attempts to slip a few banned books into a stack of approved ones.

15 The popular but inaccurate translation "Letter Worthy of Athena" has no conceptual or grammatical basis; the allusion is to the second-century Christian apologist Athenagoras.

Cuban Homosexualities: On the Beach with

Néstor Almendros and Reinaldo Arenas

~

Paul Julian Smith

Exile, homosexuality, a courageous response to the prospect of early death: it is not these similarities between Néstor Almendros and Reinaldo Arenas that are initially apparent, but rather the differences between them. Barcelona-born cinematographer and critic Almendros left his adopted homeland of Cuba in 1962, just three years after Castro entered Havana; the autobiography Almendros first published in French in 1980 is rigorously restricted to his professional life, the very model of discretion. Novelist and poet Arenas, on the other hand, left his native Cuba only in 1980 with the Mariel exodus, after suffering many years of harsh repression; his autobiography of 1992 is scandalously indiscreet, extravagantly confessional. The respective titles of the autobiographies are symptomatic: Almendros's *Días de una cámara* (literally "Days of a camera," translated as *A Man with a Camera*) characteristically effaces the writer's subjectivity, fuses him with his professional instrument; Arenas's *Antes que anochezca* [Before night falls], on the other hand, invites the reader to share the urgency of the scenes of its writing: first in Havana's Lenin Park, where the author, a fugitive from the Castroist security forces, could write only by daylight before night fell, and later in New York exile, where he struggled to rewrite the manuscript when facing the definitive darkness of death. A photograph reproduced in *Antes que anochezca* might also be read as emblematic: seated on a sofa with mutual friends at a private house in Spain, Arenas gestures vividly to unseen spectators outside the frame; Almendros looks down, apparently immersed in reading an exotic newspaper. Extravagance and reticence, these are the overt messages of both text and picture.

Both Almendros and Arenas left complimentary references to each other's work in their respective works. But where they most clearly coincided was in Arenas's participation in the feature Almendros codirected with fellow exile Orlando Jiménez Leal, the documentary *Mauvaise conduite* [*Improper Conduct*, 1984]. Ten years have now passed since the film's then unprecedented indictment of revolutionary Cuba's homophobia. And it is possible to look back, more dispassionately perhaps, at the polemic the film provoked and to reread that polemic in the context of the two autobiographies.

The questions raised by *Improper Conduct* are more fundamental than they at first appeared, and they are posed all the more urgently now that the eclipse of Marxism as a political and theoretical force has rendered the articulation of new forms of resistance a priority. Those questions are drawn from the three broad areas of representation, nationality, and identity. First, *Improper Conduct* offers itself, like Arenas's subsequent autobiography, as pure transparency, with film simply a vehicle for the imaging of truth. Almendros spoke at the time of the film's release of his wish to include all the testimony spoken by the witnesses without editing of any kind; the two-hour final cut was edited down from an eight-hour version that Almendros considered to be the "true" film. Shot full face, often in tight close-up, and illuminated for the most part by available light sources, the film's twenty-eight witnesses speak as if directly to the spectator, without interference from the cinematic mechanism. But, of course, film is not, or not only, ontology, the representation of subjects and objects that precede it; it is also language, a complex means of representation serving actively to construct those subjects and objects. As we shall see, *Improper Conduct* was criticized on its release for precisely this theoretical naïveté, for its apparent faith in the unmediated presence of truth in art. The problem remains: how can we reconcile this skepticism toward artistic truth, so commonplace in cultural studies since the seventies, with the respect due to the testimony of the survivors of totalitarianism? Or to put it more bluntly, why did the critique of representation become an apology for dictatorship?

This leads on to the second question, that of nationality. There seems little doubt that the Castro regime's treatment of homosexuals has proved to be a unique point of contention both on the island and amongst supporters and detractors abroad. Given the prevalence of homophobia throughout Latin America and elsewhere, it is by no means inevitable that this should have been the case. Why is it that homosexuality has been such a sensitive issue in and for Cuba? And how did foreign responses vary according to the nationality of the spectator? As we shall see, Anglo-American readings of the film differed sharply from those of French critics, who were perhaps more sympathetic to Latin American homosexualities than were English speakers, whether gay or straight; and it seems likely that any answer will have both a historical and a psychic dimension.

Here we come to the third question, that of identity. Neither in *Improper Conduct* nor in the two autobiographies do we find gay identities of a kind familiar to U.S. or U.K. spectators. One British lesbian critic complained that only two of the film's speaking heads identified as gay on screen, and they were readily identifiable queens, whose "improper conduct" was already flagrantly visible. But to criticize the reticence of Almendros's autobiography and his witnesses on film may be simply to impose foreign norms on differing forms of subjectivity. What are those forms, and how are they rendered visible to us?

One much-reproduced still from *Improper Conduct* is of Arenas calmly seated on a chair, illuminated by a window to the right. A French film magazine ran this picture with the caption "La lumière naturelle" ("Les Films du mois" 26). The caption might seem to reconfirm that "natural" simplicity shared by both Almendros and Arenas in their faith in personal testimony. However Almendros's career as a cinematographer in Europe and the United States reveals that "natural light" is not as simple to achieve as it might at first appear. I shall argue that far from being naive, as has often been supposed, both Almendros and Arenas share in their artistic practice a healthy awareness of the limits of representation and of identity, of the necessary collusion between fiction and the real. If truth, light, and life are inextricable in what Derrida once called the "white mythology," then Cuba stands as a twilight zone in which contraries merge and fuse or, in Freud's resonant phrase, are "reversed into their opposites." In contrast to this crazy "up and down dream" of the Castristas is Almendros's and Arenas's vision of the beach: the erotic location par excellence in which anonymous bodies are set in motion, silhouetted against the water, against the light.

Let us look more closely at *Improper Conduct* itself and its detractors' objections to it before moving on to the autobiographies. As Almendros himself explained after a screening of his film at New York University in 1984 ("Almendros and Documentary" 50–54), the two hours of screen time are structured according to a three-part movement: the first part has "innocent testimonies" offered by nonintellectual witnesses such as Caracol, a gloriously extravagant Afro-Cuban queen; the second part has intellectuals (Guillermo Cabrera Infante, Juan Goytisolo, Susan Sontag) reflecting on that testimony; the third part has the testimony of those who had "the most terrible experiences," such as René Ariza (condemned to eight years in prison because his writings were judged to attack Castro and "lack literary value"), with whom the film ends. This structural movement (from testimony to reflection and back to testimony) is complemented by a chronological narrative: the first part treats the notorious UMAP camps of the 1960s (their motto: "Work Will Make You Men"), in which gays were condemned to forced labor; the second, the impact of new laws on "extravagance" and "dangerousness" in the 1970s; the third, the Mariel exodus and its consequences in the 1980s. Almendros notes that the editing is as "unadorned" as possible, leaving jump cuts where material has been omitted; that the mise-en-scène is equally minimalist ("the less . . . the better"); and that, most unusually for a film by a cinematographer, sound takes precedence over image, the spoken word over visuals. There is no background music to detract from the testimony, and the only distractions from Arenas's and Jiménez Leal's original footage (shot of necessity outside Cuba) are archive shots of the revolutionaries' entry into Havana, of Cuban crowds dutifully demonstrating against the "vermin" of the Mariel, and of Castro himself vigorously denying the existence of repression in Cuba.

Almendros laments that he was unable for financial reasons to shoot in thirty-five millimeter because it "is closer to reality than [the] 16 mm" he was obliged to use in *Improper Conduct,* and he claims that "faces [are] shown frontally, because in profile one sees only half of the truth of the face." With witnesses' eyelines adjusted as far as possible to the lens, "the audience . . . feel[s] that the people being interviewed were almost talking to them." Such statements are clearly a gift to critics who believe that on the contrary, film is by no means innocent and "reality" is called into being by those media that claim, simply, to reflect it. Ironically, however, the same critics who marshaled the skeptical arsenal of critical theory against Almendros's modest documentary give evidence elsewhere of a credulity toward Castroism that can only be called theological. Typical here is Sean Cubitt's review in the then left-leaning London listings magazine *City Limits,* which both encourages its readers to "get out their critical scalpels" for a film that "promises to tell the whole Truth" and suggests that to criticize Cuba at all is to play into the hands of the U.S. imperialist enemy (23).

Let us look at two influential critics in the United States and the United Kingdom. B. Ruby Rich's piece in *American Film,* run under the unfortunate title "Bay of Pix," attacks *Improper Conduct*'s use of talking heads, claiming that by editing out the historical and social context of such testimonies, the film becomes "fiction, not documentary":

> The film is so determined to ignore the advances in standard of living, education, health, and access to culture that it is crucial to remember what is omitted. In place of history, the film offers myth. In place of data or documented sources, there is only first-person testimony. In place of understanding, only shock. *Improper Conduct* cynically uses homosexuality as a wedge to splinter what little sympathy for Cuba remains among American intellectuals. (59)

We are far here from Almendros's faith in the revelation of truth, caught full face in natural light. And Rich's skeptical attention to the power of montage (its capacity to create meaning through omission as well as selection or combination) would have to be taken seriously if the film had indeed failed to address the historical context she erroneously claims it neglects.[1] Elsewhere, however, Rich promises *American Film*'s readers the "true story of homosexuality in Cuba" and the "real story behind the film's making." Skeptical epistemology would thus seem to have its limits. And there is throughout the piece an appeal to a rhetoric of reversal that is curiously emphatic: thus "the stories ring true in inverse proportion to the viewer's familiarity with Cuba" (58), or again "only ignorance regarding the anti-Castro *émigré* network could cause audiences to accept this film as a defense of homosexuality, when the issue is simply being used as a sort of intellectuals' MX missile, aimed not at Christopher Street, but at Havana" (59). In the twilight zone of Cuban polemic, geographic and epistemological positions are reversed, with New York changing places with Cuba, and the revelations offered by the film condemned as the obscurity of propaganda.

Another critic who makes quite explicit his identification with the "socialist ideals" of Cuba is Briton Michael Chanan, author of an exhaustively documented history of Cuban cinema. Chanan's *The Cuban Image* opens with an attack on *Improper Conduct*, then recently released (he was also prominent in attacking Almendros when he presented his film at the London Film Festival). In Chanan, as in Rich, but more explicitly, the critique of representation fuses with an overt political commitment that leads its author into sophistries based once more on a rhetoric of reversal. Thus Chanan's introduction claims that "film is an incomparable means, in the right hands, with which to show the way things are (whatever the theoretical status you ascribe to the image in its quality as a sign)" (2). Struggling to reconcile film as ontology ("to show the way things are") with film as language ("the theoretical status of the sign"), Chanan is forced to appeal to the external legitimation of political control ("in the right hands"). There is no doubt for Chanan that those hands are not Almendros's. Dismissing *Improper Conduct* as "tactical propaganda" ("a theory and a concept which go back to the Nazis") (5), Chanan attacks the film for its "relentless disregard for dialectical argument, [lack of] exploration of the contradictions [the interviews] posed, or respect for the viewer's powers of discrimination" (5). "In the end," he writes, "one has to doubt whether all of these stories can be true." On the one hand, then, Chanan claims that in his own case, no "apologia is required for showing commitment," "no apology" is needed for writing a "partisan history" (4, 6); on the other hand, he attacks Almendros for failing to observe those theoretical fetishes (dialectic, contradiction) beloved by Marxist cultural critics, and for making his own political commitment embarrassingly clear.

Most grotesquely, in a curious variation of the "things are getting better" argument offered by many apologists for Castro, Chanan blames revolutionary homophobia on the supposed success of Cuban feminism:

[The repression of gays] seems to me . . . the result of the advancement of women within the Revolution. . . . Especially in a society as intensely machista as Cuba, the advancement of women represents a threat to men, or to a certain kind of man, and men whose own sexuality is thus threatened are all too liable to start taking it out on other men. (6)

For Chanan, the focus of identification thus shifts from gay men, the victims of surveillance, imprisonment, and exile, to their heterosexual tormenters, stricken by an identity crisis whose blame can safely be assigned to overassertive women.

Hence in this rhetoric of reversal marshaled by apologists for dictatorship, bottom becomes top, knowledge ignorance, and light dark. Oppressed and powerless lesbians and gays are dismissed as the unwitting (or sometimes witting) instruments of an omnipotent oppressor, the United States. The knowledge of oppression exiles bring with them is branded as ignorance of the revolution's true motives and effects, which, in the final instance, must be in the interests of all Cuba's unwilling citizens. Finally, the enlightenment of witnesses' testimony (to themselves, to others) is transformed into a cloud of false consciousness, the obscurity of a subjectivism wholly untheorized and nondialectical. At best, such witnesses are stigmatized as ingenuous fools who know not what they say; at worst, they are culpable criminals, aiming cinematic missiles at the ever vulnerable revolutionary citadel.

Chanan's account of the Cuban film industry in the early years of Castroism coincides in outline with Almendros's, in the brief version in his autobiography; but Chanan also offers further evidence of the uneasy coalition between leftist politics and critical theory in the 1980s. The emergence of an independent Cuban film sector after the revolution was preceded by the *aficionado* movement of the 1940s and 1950s, which itself focused on the first *cine-club* in the country, set up by Almendros and Guillermo Cabrera Infante, among others.[2] With the arrival of the long-haired revolutionaries (much admired by Arenas) in 1959 and the setting up of ICAIC, the national film institute, the stage was set for the production of documentary and subsequently full-length features in a national and more latterly socialist vein. Directors such as Tomás Gutiérrez Alea were to win Cuba much-coveted film prizes from abroad.[3] Dissension was immediate, however. Almendros's own short documentary on beach life

Gente en la playa [People on the Beach], filmed informally and mainly with a hidden camera, was confiscated and had to be edited clandestinely. The autobiography reproduces a tantalizing still: bodies silhouetted against a burned-out background, the blinding light of the tropical sun reflected on the ocean. A more celebrated short called *P.M.*, directed by Saba Cabrera Infante and *Improper Conduct*'s Orlando Jiménez Leal, was also banned. Now dismissed from ICAIC, Almendros gave *P.M.* a favorable review in his role as critic for the magazine *Bohemia.*[4] The ensuing conflict culminated in Castro's much debated 1961 speech "Words to the Intellectuals" and in the closing down of *Lunes de Revolución,* the cultural supplement edited by Guillermo Cabrera Infante. In Chanan's version of this polemic, the banning of *P.M.* can no longer be called "the Revolution's first act of censorship." Rather, he argues, "it is more enlightening to see [the controversy] as the denouement of the incipient conflict between different political trends which lay beneath the surface during the period of the *aficionado* movement in the 50s" (105). Just as previously the manifest injustice of the regime's treatment of homosexuals was deflected onto the supposed latent identity crisis of its heterosexual men, so here a conspicuous act of repression is transmuted into the imperceptible stirrings of hidden cultural conflict.

But what interests me here is not Chanan's servility (he faithfully transcribes each interruption for "applause" in Castro's speech), nor his sophistry (he cites official sources claiming that the closing of *Lunes* "established better conditions for different artistic tendencies to engage with each other on more equal terms"); it is rather his appeal to film theory to justify state censorship. Thus *P.M.*'s depiction in free cinema style of the mainly black, working-class bars of the waterfront was intolerable not because of its lack of uplifting revolutionary moral but because its "irresponsibility" was aesthetic as well as political:

They had begun to sense at ICAIC that the camera was not the unproblematic kind of instrument the apologists for *P.M.* supposed. It does not—to paraphrase the French film theorist Serge Daney—involve a single straight line from the real to the visible and thence to its reproduction on film, in which a simple truth is faithfully reflected. . . . Daney says "in a world where 'I see' is automatically said for 'I understand' such a fantasy has probably not come about by chance. The dominant ideology which equates the real with the visible has every interest in encouraging it." At ICAIC they were beginning to perceive that revolutionary change required a rupture with this equation, which meant among other things being constantly on guard against received aesthetic formulae. (103)

It is an unfortunate irony, unmentioned by Chanan, that one reason for Almendros's flight from Cuba was his realization that he was unable to make those revolutionary changes in lighting that were to win him such fame as a cinematographer abroad. Cuban cinema still clung to received aesthetic formulae even as it proclaimed its definitive rupture with the political past. But of course the point Chanan borrows from Daney is not technical, but theoretical: it is only by challenging the white mythology that collapses light, visibility, and truth that the cinematic apparatus can be denaturalized and the actual relations between spectator, cinema, and society can be rendered intelligible. But if the equation between sight and understanding is a fantasy promoted by the dominant (capitalist) ideology, then visibility is itself placed under suspicion. It must be interrogated for its unspoken compliance with a spectatorial regime as pervasive as it is insidious.

Here then is the theoretical justification for dismissing the testimony provided by *Improper Conduct*'s witnesses: it is their very visibility (full-face close-ups, flooded with natural light) that is unforgivable, that renders them complicit with the regime of political and aesthetic norms fostered by international capitalism. But this theoretical question is also national. For in Cuba, also and much more immediately, the trial of visibility was enforced as a criterion for measuring the degree of "social pathology" exhibited by gay men. Thus the Declaration of the First National Congress on Education and Culture of 1971 stressed the need to "differentiate between cases" and establish their relative "degree of degradation" (reproduced in Almendros and Jiménez Leal, *Conducta impropia* 177). Proposing preventative measures such as the "extension of the coeducational system" and the prohibition of "known homosexuals" influencing "the development of our young people," the declaration also dealt with "fashions, customs, and extravagant behavior," asserting "the necessity of maintaining the monolithic and ideological unity of our people . . . [through] direct confrontation in order to bring about the elimination of extravagant aberrations" (180). Ironically, then, the Cuban witnesses whose testimonies were discounted by foreign intellectuals from the safety of New York or London ("finally we must ask if all these stories can be true") had already suffered a more rigorous trial of visibility in which their appearance had been scrutinized for its divergence from preset ideological norms.

All too visible for Anglo-American critics, the very transparency of their testimony rendering them suspect to theoretical eyes and ears, still Almendros's speakers were not yet visible enough. Why, foreigners asked, did so few of them (Arenas included) identify themselves as lesbian or gay? Jane Root wrote in the London *Monthly Film Bulletin* that *Improper Conduct* was "both an attack on and a betrayal of the relaxed, self-affirming warmth generated by gay films in the *Word Is Out/Harvey Milk* tradition" (220–21). More sympathetic critics might consider that those who had been persecuted for their excessive visibility had some reason to be circumspect even in exile, and that Cuban refugees should not be expected to pay obeisance to North American documentary styles. Indeed, Arenas's autobiography is, as we shall see, scathing in its dismissal of a U.S. gay lifestyle it sees as anything but "relaxed" and "warm." Moreover, if we look at French responses to the film, which were much more favorable than those in the United States and the United Kingdom,[5] we find possible answers to both the question of nationality (why is homosexuality so important for Cuba?) and that of identity (why do Cuban lesbians and gays appear so reluctant to "affirm" themselves?).

Michel Celemenski, in *Cinématographe*, claims that "the uprooting [*extirpation*] of homosexuality has a vital role in the erection of socialism" (27). Most telling for him is not the brutality with which laws of "extravagant behavior" and "improper conduct" are enforced, but rather the ideological implications of "reeducation." Whereas the Nazi appeal to work (*Arbeit macht frei*) was merely cynical, one of the lies intended to ensure the docility of death camp victims, the communist belief in the salutary value of labor (Work Will Make You Men) is naively proclaimed as a scientific truth. This "supernatural" status of work, at the heart of Marxist "folklore," makes it available to the authorities as a form of shock treatment, to be administered with "Ubu-esque" zeal. Communist puritanism and terror are thus derived from a tenacious attachment to metascience:

Communism is a form of morality, and its structuration depends on the rigorous integration of all human functions and, a fortiori, the function of love. Life is production, love reproduction. . . . The relegation by Marxism of secondary elements of alienation (such as the *condition* of women, the *question* of the Jews, the *problem* of nationality) is no mere tactical sideline of the Communist project. The teleological hypothesis of Marxism . . . bears witness to a universal mission seeking not to ensure the development of a future liberated . . . society, but rather to forge a uniform identity in the image of the industrial ideals from which [Communism] itself emerged and on whose behalf it acts in the Third World countries it has colonized. (Celemenski 27)

The language would be familiar to those who framed the Cuban decree on "extravagance," bent as they were on preserving the "monolithic . . . unity of the people." But if the homophobia of Cuba is deeply embedded in its Marxist ideology, then that same homophobia manifests itself in the most transparent ways: an attachment to appearance, whereby a readily visible homosexuality is thought to be more "serious" a crime than the invisible, closeted variety; and a totalitarian system of surveillance that "possesses the unique ability of rendering any gesture suspicious" (Celemenski 28).

For French critics, then, better versed in theory than their English-speaking opposite numbers, the oppression of gays in Cuba is by no means accidental but is rather structurally determined by the centrality of the labor theory of value to Marxist doctrine. Writing in *Cahiers du Cinéma,* Charles Tesson further suggests that the power of *Improper Conduct* lies in Cuba's particular vulnerability to attack by cinematic means: unable or unwilling to lay bare the contradictions of its own history on film, Cuba lays itself open to cinematic critique (47–48). Like Celemenski, Tesson also stresses the way repression operates in the field of the visible: the body is interrogated for supposed external signs of inner vice, such as clothing, hairstyle, gesture, and posture. This he calls a "physical violation" that takes place "in the intimacy of bodies and their representation" (48). It is perhaps significant that Tesson begins his piece by referring to Almendros's early documentary *Gente de la playa* and claims that the love of natural light has been Cuba's continuing contribution to Almendros's distinguished career in Europe and the United States.[6]

But if French critics prove more sensitive than English speakers to both theoretical nuance and physical sensation (paying particular attention to the quality of light and sound in the film), what is clearly lacking from their accounts is the sense of responsibility toward a lesbian and gay audience we find in British and North American reviewers. This absence is even more extreme in Spanish responses: trade journal *Cineinforme*, reporting that the film had won a major award, manages to avoid informing its readers of the nature of the oppression the film documents; even Almendros speaks laconically in his autobiography of "repression in Cuba." However, what seems like closetry to English speakers may have a different meaning in Latin cultures. And Anglo-American binaries would prove quite incapable of coping with the actual range of sexual preferences revealed outside the film by *Improper Conduct*'s talking heads: from Arenas's scorn of U.S. gay male separatism to Goytisolo's limitation of his male sexual partners to Arabs who consider themselves heterosexual.

Unwilling as they are simply to assume the existence of a clearly delimited lesbian and gay community, Cubans, French, and Spaniards are obliged to examine homophobia in the context of other forms of oppression and are unable to draw a neat dividing line between them. There is thus a final irony in the film's reception: although critics such as Chanan claimed that *Improper Conduct* allowed no space for the audience to exercise its own judgment, they also attacked the film at precisely that point where it chose not to specify and refused to direct its spectators. Deprived of explicit guidance as to the sexual identity of the participants, we are left suspended before faces bathed in light, tempted to retrace once more that trial of visibility to which some were subjected with such terrible consequences in Cuba.

François Truffaut's introduction to *A Man with a Camera* notes that one aim of the cinematographer is "to interpret the desire of a director who knows exactly what he does not want but can't explain what he does want" (viii). This modestly self-effacing role (of interpretation without direction) is confirmed by Almendros himself in his opening section, "Some Thoughts on My Profession": "The director of photography . . . does everything and nothing. . . . [He must] immerse himself in the director's manner. It is not 'our' film, but 'his' film" (3, 4). Tracing the history of movie lighting from the mannered direct lighting of the 1940s to the more subtle reflected lighting of the New Wave and after, Almendros reclaims a narrative invisible to most cinemagoers, and one that aspires to ever-increasing transparency and "naturalness." Thus Almendros scorns from the very beginning artificial filters, gauzes, and diffusers (10) and is impatient with the clinched backlighting he was taught when studying in Rome, supposed capital of neorealism (31). Experimenting with "available light" (that is, without artificial supplements), his first short was *58–59*, a record of New Year's celebrations in Times Square in which people are shown "in silhouette against a luminous background" of neon billboards and shopwindows (32). This clearly anticipated the Cuban-made *Gente de la playa*, in which Almendros was confirmed in his belief that "natural light [was] more beautiful than artificial" (36).

Exiled by Castro (as he had been by Franco and Batista), Almendros lends his skills to the deceptively simple projects of New Wave directors in the 1960s. Thus his innovative use of reflected light for interiors complements Eric Rohmer's severely "functional" image and direct sound (Almendros, *Man with a Camera* 61); his "justification" of light sources on period sets (candles, lamps, and bonfires) aids Truffaut's meticulously "calligraphic" reconstructions (104); and his discreet camera work echoes Maurice Pialat's "respect for reality" (119). But if Almendros's great innovation was the use of documentary lighting for feature films, that naturalness was often the result of meticulous and ingenious experiment. For example, in Truffaut's *Adele H.* (1974), the "justified" lighting that appears to come from period oil lamps was in fact derived from household electric bulbs whose cords ran to batteries hidden under the actors' clothes (104). And Almendros approaches the reconstruction of a period not through direct documentary evidence but rather with reference to a contemporary school of painting (102). Moreover, if Almendros loves to "light by eye" and "look through the viewfinder [him]self," he is constantly aware of the technical limits to filmic representation: "I need the frame with . . . its limits. . . . There is no artistic transposition without limits. . . . What counts in two dimensional art is not only what is seen but what is not seen, what does not let itself be seen" (12). In his professional practice, Almendros thus knows full well that omission is as significant as inclusion, and that it is the invisible that enables the visible to be seen.

Famous in France, Almendros was invited to work more frequently in the United States in the 1970s. Most important here was his contribution to Terence Malick's *Days of Heaven* (1976), for which Almendros won an

Academy Award. Once more, Almendros attempted an absolute simplicity: "Subtract[ing] technical aids . . . to leave the image bare" (*A Man with a Camera* 171); using hand-operated heads for pan shots (instead of mechanical gears) so that "the operator becomes all of a piece with the camera" (175); and shooting "characters silhouetted against the flames" of buring wheat fields in a tour de force of natural lighting (181). However, *Days of Heaven* also led Almendros to heights of ingenuity: in outdoor scenes involving crosscut dialogue, both actors were shot in the same spot with their backs to the sun. Cinematic continuity (the need for a background with the same luminous value) here led to what Almendros calls a "flagrant contradiction in realist ethics" (181). The reliance on natural light in extreme conditions forces Almendros to hold the lens stop wide open, leading to a minimal depth of field (184). The preference for working "in the camera," thus avoiding optical effects in the laboratory, led him to run film backward so that locusts dropped from planes would appear to be rising out of the fields (185). And Almendros's later work in the 1980s makes explicit this collusion between nature and artifice. "Stylization" is, he notes, essential to convince the viewer of "historical realism" (220); the use of directional lighting in Truffaut's Occupation drama *Le Dernier Métro* (1980) is "ironic" (251); in the final analysis, there can be no simple dividing line between naturalism, stylization, and verisimilitude (269).

What is striking, then, about Almendros's meticulous professional autobiography is that it shows how just as he brought documentary lighting to features, so he brought feature techniques to documentary: the "transparent" devices of *Improper Conduct,* most particularly the quest for a natural light justified within the frame itself, were ones Almendros had spent more than twenty years perfecting. Significant here is the reference to Vermeer as an artistic precedent for light slanting through the window: Almendros uses it to describe both *Improper Conduct* and *Days of Heaven.* However, to claim that Almendros was indeed, contrary to his critics, skeptically aware of the limits of representation and the language of film is not to invalidate the artistic and political project of *Improper Conduct.* Rather it is to endow that project with greater dignity and seriousness. For just as the limits of the frame throw the objects within it into luminous relief, so the limits of human mortality lend that professional and personal life a resonant pathos.

Almendros tells us that much of *Days of Heaven* was shot, at the director's insistence, at the brief "magical hour" between sunset and nightfall:

All day we would work to get the actors and the camera ready; as soon as the sun had set we had to shoot quickly, not losing a moment. For these few minutes the light is truly magical, because no one knows where it is coming from. The sun is not to be seen, but the sky can be bright, and the blue of the atmosphere undergoes strange mutations. . . . Each day, like Joshua in the Bible, Malick wanted to stop the sun in its imperturbable course so as to go on shooting. (182)

That moment of radiance, all the more precious because of its brevity, is not only the truncated career of Almendros, professional of light; it is also Reinaldo Arenas's experience of desire and of writing, enjoyed all the more intensely because of the awareness that it takes place in the shadow of dictatorship and mortality.

Reinaldo Arenas's persona, extravagant, humorous, spiteful, could hardly be further from Almendros's studied seriousness. Yet Arenas also appeals to a criterion of naturalness or authenticity that will have cultural critics reaching for their theoretical scalpels. Just as Almendros sought to draw a straight line from the real to the visible by flooding faces with natural light, so Arenas attempts (with scant regard for "the theoretical status of the sign") to shed light on the darkness of Cuban dictatorship and speak the truth of his experience as a gay man, dissident writer, and political prisoner. However, as in the case of Almendros once more, truth and nature will prove to be stubbornly indefinable, their stability undermined by the very homosexuality that Arenas insists on rendering gloriously, extravagantly visible. Moreover, Arenas's erotic and literary adventures are framed by the brief narrative of his AIDS-related illness with which he begins his autobiography and the unforgiving suicide note with which he ends it. Like Almendros's "magical" twilight hour, the truncated time span of *Antes que anochezca* is rendered all the more intense, all the more radiant, by its pathetic brevity.

Composed in extremis (dictated into a tape recorder and subsequently revised), *Antes que anochezca* aspires to the condition of a speaking voice: loquacious, undisciplined, shamelessly egocentric. This oral register is confirmed by Arenas's narration of his childhood, characterized by an unmediated closeness to nature: his first memory is of the excretion of a monstrous centipede, the product of his infantile habit of eating earth (17). The trees of his provincial home hold a secret life to be "deciphered" by the child who climbs them (22); its flooded rivers offer the prospect of merger and annihilation (36). Little Reinaldo is the fortunate possessor of a boundless, nonspecific eroticism, roused by animals and plants, by the bouncing of his buttocks on his uncle's swollen penis as they trek to town on horseback (40). And as he grows to adulthood, by way of a desultory participation in the campaigns against Batista and a move to the longed-for capital, his innumerable erotic encounters come to stand as a "territory of beauty" that challenges the "anti-aesthetic" tedium of dictatorship (113). It is an erotic rebellion typified by his frantic coupling with a naked recruit by the side of a highway, their bodies lit by the headlights of speeding vehicles.

But the natural element of love is water. For the child, the sight of men bathing in the river, their genitals shining in the sun, had been a "revelation" (26); for the adult, the beach is the erotic location par excellence: in the huts of La Concha, respectable married men give themselves up to fevered gay desires (126), and Arenas's invaluable flippers even give him access to underwater intimacies (127). The flashing of sun on sea, the brief mystery of the tropical sunset glimpsed while swimming (136), these are not merely sensual but fully sexual pleasures.

A shamelessly explicit narrative of sex, *Antes que anochezca* is also simultaneously a chronicle of writing that is equally obsessive and repetitive: Arenas will be condemned constantly to rewrite lost or confiscated manuscripts. Having procured a nominal post in the National Library, Arenas is free to pursue his literary education, aided by friendship with distinguished gay writers such as Virgilio Piñera. The bodily rhythm of writing is parallel to that of cruising the parks and beaches, and the regime's repressive vigilance makes unauthorized composition and conjugation equally taboo, equally hidden from sight. However, if sex and writing are authentic activities that tolerate no prohibition, they are also insidiously affected by the state censorship that would keep them under wraps. On Castro's entry into Havana in 1959, it is the splendid hair and beards of the revolutionaries that attract Arenas's amorous attention (68), and the youth and labor camps of state socialism are ideal breeding grounds for

264 ~ PAUL JULIAN SMITH

same-sex desire. On the paradise of the Isla de los Pinos, the "erotic fury" of five thousand military recruits is in direct proportion to their revolution-inspired repression (119). And more than once, Arenas hints that the transcendent importance of literature in Cuba derives in part from the regime's implacable policing of those who seek to practice it. If, as Almendros claims, there can be no artistic transposition without limits, then those limits are in Cuba fragrantly, brutally clear.

What Arenas prizes above all in sex is spontaneity and freedom from convention. This is why he suspends all sexual activity when incarcerated in Havana's notorious Morro prison on a trumped-up charge of corruption of minors. But on closer examination, the "naturalness" of his homosexuality is shot through by cultural convention and role play. Thus Arenas gives a tragicomic categorization of "four kinds of queens" in Cuba (103–4) and defines himself as a *loca* who seeks his opposite: a "real man" (132). Lamenting from exile the tedious reciprocity of gay sex in the United States, he eulogizes the objects of his love in Cuba: men who have wives or girlfriends but enjoy penetrating other men. Just as such men cannot be defined by conventional binaries, so Cuban beaches or clubs are undivided along sexual lines (133). Civil rights may be all very well for First World gays, but the U.S. lifestyle Arenas encounters in exile is "desolate."

Ironically, it was this imprecision of definition that facilitated Arenas's inclusion in the Mariel exodus of 1980. Having been imprisoned for "public scandal," Arenas presented himself to the authorities not as a dissident writer but as a passive queer (the active variety was not considered to be homosexual and was therefore denied permission to leave) (301). Asked to walk in front of a panel of psychologists, he had no trouble in persuading them which category he belonged to, in spite of the fact that the autobiography tells us with some relish of the times he enjoyed "playing the man" in bed. Having passed this final trial of visibility, Arenas was to submit himself to what he would call the third tyranny he was to suffer: after Batista and Castro came the equally unforgiving U.S. dollar.

One response to *Antes que anochezca* from inside Cuba expresses affectionate incredulity toward Arenas's gleefully hostile treatment of former friends;[7] we may indeed come to doubt whether all of Arenas's stories can be true. To dismiss the book as tactical propaganda against Castro would, however, be a mistake. Relentlessly obsessive in his concern for the body, Arenas barely attempts to take up that abstracted position from which

Truth is handed down to the believers. If this is a partisan history, it quite rightly makes no apology for its commitment. After dragging himself, mortally sick, to Miami Beach to await the end in his preferred location, Arenas is disappointed once more: like bureaucracy, death is always subject to delay (9). It is in such moments of mordant humor that *Antes que anochezca* transcends the skepticism that its details may provoke and inspires the respect due the memoirs of a distinguished survivor.

In chapter 6 of *The Interpretation of Dreams*, Freud gives two examples of "reversal into opposite" characteristic of the dreamwork. The first is the "Up and Down Dream" (288). A man notices that as he carries a woman up a staircase, she becomes lighter, not heavier, the further they go; it is as if the positions of up above and down below have been reversed. In the second, "Goethe's Attack on Herr M.," the dreamer believes that the celebrated author had denigrated his unknown friend, whereas in fact it had been the other way round. As Freud puts it in Strachey's translation: " '[J]ust the reverse' has to be put straight," by drawing out the "contemptuous indications of the phrase 'turning one's back on something' " (the German *kehrseite* meaning literally "backside"). "It is remarkable to observe," notes Freud dryly, "how frequently reversal is employed in dreams arising from repressed homosexual impulses" (327).

This last phrase is taken from the section of the chapter on "the means of representation" under (psychic) censorship. I have argued that a similar rhetoric of reversal occurs in U.S. and British responses to homosexuality in Cuba. Turning their backs on victims of oppression, refusing to see what a recent critic has called "the palpable dignity of abused survivors,"[8] film scholars have claimed up is down, and light dark. Ironically, it is also a technique consciously employed by Almendros and Arenas: in *Improper Conduct* Castro's inspection of a labor camp is compared to that of the grand lady visiting her serfs; in the first story of Arenas's novel *Viaje a la Habana* (written as the laws on extravagance and improper conduct came into force), a bizarre couple are terrified by the notion that someone in Cuba may not be watching them as they parade through the streets in impossibly extravagant costumes.[9] Repeating and reversing the trial of visibility to which so many were to be subjected, shadowing the trek over the island that Arenas himself undertook in his quest for the freedom to love and to write, the novel reveals that "in the right hands," reversal is an

incomparable technique for showing "the way things are" in a dictatorship. There is thus a certain collusion between fiction and the real, with
the oblique allegory of the novel pointing perhaps more clearly than the all
too explicit autobiography to what is not seen, to what does not let itself be
seen, to the space, at once necessary and impossible, that lies beyond the
frame.[10]

The critique of representation derived from theorists such as the early
Barthes and Althusser was originally devised to combat those ideological
state apparatuses that served to exile dissident viewpoints outside of a self-
mythologizing bourgeois culture. As long as "I see" meant "I understand,"
received aesthetic and political criteria were mutually supporting and impossible to challenge. We have shown that Anglo-American critics re-
trained that powerful critique on the victims of totalitarianism, whose
access to any form of representation was meager indeed: Almendros struggled to fund and distribute his documentaries, especially in the United
States; Arenas's literary production, undertaken under such tragically reduced circumstances, received only the slightest of financial rewards. Both
were branded as agents of the CIA or worse. Ten years after the release of
Improper Conduct, it is clear that a certain idea of "Cuba" served as a
projection or (in Chanan's word) an "identification" for leftists in the
United States and United Kingdom who suffered in the 1980s under tri-
umphalist governments of the Right. For France and Spain, on the other
hand, who spent most of the decade under self-styled socialist administra-
tions, Cuba had long ceased to be the fetish it had been in the 1960s, when
the exiled Almendros had been subject to barracking from leftist intellectuals on his arrival in Barcelona.[11] Much better versed in Marxism than
their North American counterparts, French intellectuals were also more
active in articulating alternative forms of resistance associated with a certain postmodernism: from the Levinas-derived "respect for the other" of
Finkielkraut to the celebration of the "little narratives" of the Gulag by
Lyotard.

I have suggested, however, that such national differences are psychic as
well as historical. Reversing testimony into its opposite, Anglo-American
critics, troubled perhaps by homosexual impulses that had been "repressed" in both senses of the word, refused the process of identification
that Almendros offered them all too nakedly in *Improper Conduct.*[12] However, if homosexual relations and identities vary from one culture to an-

other, that is no excuse for failing to respond to the truth of the face. What is required is a critical identification that is (as Freud suggests once more) no mere hysterical imitation of the symptom, but rather a quest for the historical causes of repression. The challenge and the danger of the other's body is that in Arenas's words, "being oneself it can give us the pleasure of being another" (*Viaje* 148). On the beach, that most unproductive of locations, bathing in light, that most neglected of resources, we may come to share with Almendros and Arenas the pleasures and perils of visibility, the vulnerability of the artist who seeks, naively, obstinately, passionately to tell the truth.

Notes

This essay originally appeared in *Vision Machines: Cinema, Literature, and Sexuality in Spain and Cuba, 1983–93*, by Paul Julian Smith (London: Verso, 1996).

1 For Almendros's and Jiménez Leal's response to Rich, see "Improper Conduct."

2 For Cabrera Infante's account of ICAIC, *P.M.*, and *Improper Conduct*, see "Cuba's Shadow."

3 In 1993 Alea shot *Fresa y chocolate*, based on a short story by Senel Paz in which a gay man and a heterosexual revolutionary confront each other.

4 The review has recently been republished in *Cinemanía*, the collection of writings that Almendros edited just before his death.

5 One exception is the review by "Hitch," in the U.S. trade journal *Variety*, which calls *Improper Conduct* "an important film of lasting value" that "clearly can find its place before sophisticated audiences in congenial art theaters."

6 See also the favorable review by "M.C." in *Positif.*

7 See Tomás Robaina's text, which was handed to Catherine Davies in Havana by the author and is introduced by Verity Smith. Robaina writes that one copy of Arenas's book has been circulated amongst members of the official Cuban writers' union (UNEAC) by José Rodríguez Feo.

8 Here, Ana M. López is discussing Almendros's later documentary *Nadie escuchaba* [Nobody listened, 1988]. Her account of *Improper Conduct* is heavily dependent on Chanan and Rich.

9 This first story ("Que trine Eva") is dated 1971. For this unrepentant exhibitionism, compare his volume of poetry, *Voluntad de vivir manifestándose.*

10 For Arenas's fusion of history and fiction, see his historical reworkings *El*

mundo alucinante and *La loma del ángel.* For Hispanic autobiography as "mask" and "impossibility," see Sylvia Molloy (*At Face Value* 1).

11 See Terenci Moix's memoir, "Mi Néstor Almendros." Moix suggests that in spite of his misfortunes, Almendros was more camp and humorous in private than he chose to reveal in his published writings.

12 As he notes in the March 1984 issue of *Cinématographe* (26).

Virgilio Piñera:

On the Weight of the Insular Flesh

~

José Quiroga

Because the past is written in code, in a language always permanently about to be lost, the gay critic is like a scholar of ancient Ugaritic—the one who recuperates a trembling historical bloodline, writing an imminent *parole* before the codes to the *langue* are ossified or about to disappear. We assume, nevertheless, that no language can ever remain undeciphered, no code can hold its flesh so close to its bone. So we revisit works and uncover the weight that made them possible, even if in the process we risk losing what initially beckoned us to their site. There is always a loss, and also a gain—there is imminent danger in going back to works circumscribed by sexual marginality. For the negotiations as to silence and voice that made possible that primary text in the first place, that account for its subtlety, for its deliberate *pentimento* of sex into style, may disappear completely when critics bring to light the invisibilities that seduce in the text.

Gay readings of gay books ultimately trace their own bloodlines on themselves; they reveal what the primary text can only visibly encode. But because this primary text, in turn, encodes by means of metaphors, these metaphors insinuate themselves into the bloodline where another gay reader comes forth. Critics go back, we return, to a particular site where codes, figuration, but above all metaphors themselves seem to be the very blood of the poet, a blood that allows a particular kind of body (of text) to exist. But gay criticism, in its search for visibilities, tends to forget that metaphor in gay texts, that linkage between A and B, is always *more* than just a linkage; it is something that produces a surplus that in turn the gay critic decodes. The filial circuit passes through the blood that is distilled by gay texts, and this blood also flows into gay readings of gay texts as a return. Because coding, as Thomas Yingling said, is already embedded in the way homosexuality works in society, we are particularly sensitive to the taste of that blood (34–35). These negotiations, as I hope to show in this essay, belong to a story that gets assembled by means of circuitous blood-lines, which are all written in blood, and on whose surface considerable blood has been shed.

This essay reflects on the work of the Cuban writer Virgilio Piñera (1912–1979), and on its reception as "gay" discourse. Blood is particularly apt as a metaphor in this case, because revolution, as a historical event, is circum-scribed by a filial sense of rupture that traces its bloodline on itself. The son of a working-class family, Piñera lived most of his life in Cuba, with brief sojourns in Buenos Aires (1946–1947, 1950–1954, 1955–1958), where he met Borges and his circle, and the motley crew assembled around Polish expatriate writer Witold Gombrowicz, whose *Ferdydurke* Piñera, among others, translated into Spanish. He was an important, if somewhat marginalized, writer in Cuba, because he openly dissented with the im-mensely influential *Orígenes* group, led by José Lezama Lima—a poet who became, in a sense, Piñera's antithetical double.[1] Although Piñera died in 1979, most of his work was published before the revolution of 1959. Prac-tically an unknown figure *outside* Cuba, within, Piñera was venerated by a small circle of disciples even as he was ostracized by the revolutionary state. Because a dead revolutionary is more seductive than a real-life one, Piñera's status in the Cuban pantheon of literary heroes has only increased over time, especially since the late 1980s, when the collapse of the Soviet Union was accompanied in Cuba by an acute sense of social and economic impasse. Thus, Piñera's "rehabilitation" in Cuba falls into two broad cate-gories: on the one hand, Piñera has been rescued as a social satirist and absurdist writer; on the other, he has become a saint and martyr to those marginalized by revolutionary homophobia. Although both are related, I will concern myself principally with the latter, because it is accompanied by the appearance, since the late 1980s, of at least one other important work that features homosexuality and its relationship to the revolution. I am referring, of course, to Senel Paz's *El lobo, el bosque y el hombre nuevo* from 1991, which won the prestigious Juan Rulfo Prize and was in turn filmed by Tomás Gutiérrez Alea as *Fresa y chocolate* (1993).[2]

One should clarify the ambivalent representation of homosexuality, its still-contested terrain, for in the constant ideological battle over anything Cuban, the fact that the openly homosexual Piñera remained in Cuba after the revolution takes different meanings according to the angle critics take in the convoluted histories of the Cuban family romance. For some, like Guillermo Cabrera Infante and Reinaldo Arenas, Piñera is the example of the moral dissident, alienated by the republic and then by the revolution of 1959. For others, that he was published during the sixties and remained in Cuba throughout the seventies until his death proves that the revolution in its more Stalinist phase (what Cubans term "el quinquenio gris," 1971–1976) exercised a repressive, but not a silencing, function (Arguelles and Rich). To both camps, however, Piñera is a slippery signifier, one who assumed a moral pose: the homosexual who, after the revolution, never again openly proclaimed his homosexuality in printed, published works, but one that, on the contrary, registered his approval or discontent in silence.

The whole issue of outing a text in Cuba, then, is fraught with political dispute. Not only is the competition for Piñera's body part of a general "coming to terms" with the history of homosexuality and the revolution, but it also forces us to ponder the limits (the gains and the losses) of visibility as it colludes with the designs of the state. It is because of my skepticism as to the consequences of such visibility that I purposely choose to render the whole issue of *outing* a text as densely as possible, not in an openly political manner as this is generally understood in the fractious Cuban context (it is not my intention to revisit the polemical relationship of revolution to sexuality) but in an indirect, albeit not wholly apolitical, sense. If to celebrate the existence of a precursor entails coming to terms with his or her particular legacy, then how do we negotiate this visibility when the legacy also speaks of silence and inner exile? Perhaps a digression is in order here, for I would rather work my way around the issue of Piñera's visibility, of revolution, in a roundabout way and stack code on code to the topic at hand.

To a certain extent, the issues of bloodlines, of visibilities in relation to Piñera's "gay" texts can be seen clearly in the dispute that originated when David Leavitt set out to write *While England Sleeps*, a historical novel with an openly gay plot, based on an episode out of Stephen Spender's memoirs—a book that does not necessarily belong to the category of "gay literature." It is well known that Spender was not precisely taken in with the use of his affair with a working-class lad and sued Leavitt. Spender's side of the story was that in essence Leavitt had first of all plagiarized not a life but actually a finished work—one that was also an autobiography. Furthermore, Spender argued that Leavitt used that work to create a story line that had a series of gratuitous "pornographic" scenes. For Spender, a life may not have the same status as a finished work, but the finished work has a *particular* status if it also happens to be an autobiography, one whose coded sexual messages have to be inscribed as part of a wider antifascist struggle against oppression and censorship in the 1930s. For Spender, outing is not the issue; sexuality—understood in terms of describing sexual acts—is. Spender explained that the sex in *While England Sleeps* added nothing to character development and, as a matter of fact, circumscribed those characters, flattened them out, trivialized them. Spender defended a work (his own) that refused to be marginalized as a "gay book" contra Leavitt's "gay book," one that is presented as an act of purely imaginative freedom. The case was settled out of court, but not before Spender demanded withdrawing the current edition of *While England Sleeps,* forcing Leavitt to issue a revised edition, which he prefaced with a self-defense: "Stephen Spender published *World within World* when he was 41. I am 32 and I have never written an autobiography; but if I ever do, and if something in its pages grabs some young novelist's attention, I hope he'll feel free to take whatever he wants from the story. Indeed, I can't think what greater homage could be paid a writer than to see his own life serve as the occasion for fiction" (Leavitt 37). "Imagine freely," says Leavitt, concluding his defense, to his future reader, to whom so much of his novel is seemingly addressed. Imagination, in the sense of writing what was not written in the text (namely sex, as Spender sees it), is the central tenet of Leavitt's revision on Spender, an imagination that Spender sees, rather, as stripping all complexity from the work.

That the attendant codes embedded within Spender's work were trivialized by Leavitt's showing and telling should already warn us about the economies of gain and loss involved in the reductionism that outing entails. But the more urgent question provoked by the debate between Spender and Leavitt, a debate that I am recalling here to read a Cuban gay writer, bears on them both: for why collaborate with imagination if imagination itself collaborates with the closet? This gay family romance, taking place in this day and age, would be better served by arguing for freedom *from* imagination, in order to liberate imagination to think of something other than the coded panic of this and other gay family romances. Spender's self-defensive view, in spite of his pleas for the reader to understand the context of obscenity laws in the thirties, is still a response from within the closet by a writer who nevertheless refuses to be pegged onto the gay niche where Leavitt, even in spite of himself, seems to reside. To imagine and reinvent, to narrate sex where sex was merely implied, forms part and parcel of the epistemology of the closet, where—we should say—both Leavitt and Spender dwell in different ways. Sex defines the boundaries of the permissible; it relegates and apportions the private and the public spaces where imagination and utterance keep each other in perpetual silence. Leavitt, like all gay readers of gay texts, needs to break a silence, and *out* the historical text while also tracing, in *it* and in *him*, the bloodlines of his own gay family romance. Like all unhappy families, the son or daughter prolongs dysfunctionality by adding complication on complication on the tale, by inscribing it as an imminent story that negotiates distance by reinforcing the perverse bloodline of the marginal. By outing the text, Leavitt, as writer and critic, wants to be the child who is the parent of the closeted self, who is then beckoned *out* but also *into* a world of renegotiated power, where the child will be the father to the man. Spender's warning, on the other hand, entails the revenge of the repressed, for Leavitt has turned a political tale into a tale of sexual mores. Even though Spender might not understand sex in Leavitt's political sense, Leavitt's self-indulgent search has produced a gain and a loss that Spender was probably at pains to avoid.

One of the many questions that is pertinent not only for Spender but also for Piñera can be summed up as follows: does outing in this context (of canonized literary precursors) allow us merely to *gain* a certain kind of body—a collection of weightless lives on paper—and *lose* another kind of flesh? And even if outing is beside the question, what kind of attention must be placed on writers' homosexuality, especially if those writers, in contexts different from our own, cannot—but, more important, do not want to—identify as "gay"? Does not excessive attention run the risk of collaborating with a homophobic cultural imaginary, one that consigns these authors to a specific *place* where they might be controlled and normatized and returned as stereotypes, emptied of their flesh and blood?

The bloody consequences that may follow precisely from our outing are ones that some immediate precursors never allow us not to keep in mind—just as Spender *openly* reminds Leavitt of a particular context and, *implicitly,* distances himself from the category of "gay writer" as defined by Leavitt and by his context. Because these writers' choices were then, as now, choices between silencing their homosexuality and stereotyping it, between repression and the dead weight of a weightless body, I think Piñera, among others, understood that the future reader would return to extract the blood of the confession. Piñera, in turn, negotiated precisely his own life and works with the thickest blood that he was able to fling unto the text to come.

Virgilio Piñera's homosexuality has never been disputed. But one could see his outness, as a matter of fact, as a misleading pose: that of the self-conscious "faggot" or "queen." Piñera, however, was no amateur when it came to homosexual politics. Since the 1950s, in the Cuban magazine *Ciclón,* Virgilio (as he is generally called in Cuba) demanded that Cubans appreciate the complex and sometimes baroque codes that authors use to talk about their lives and, particularly, their homosexuality. In "Ballagas en persona," an already classic essay published in 1955, Virgilio tackled the work of Emilio Ballagas, one of Cuba's foremost modernist poets. Introducing the essay with a quote from Roland Barthes, Piñera decries the whitewashing that has soiled accounts of Ballagas's life. After his recent death, Virgilio says, all traces of Ballagas's complex and tormented homosexuality have been cast aside by his friends. Attacking Cintio Vitier's somewhat ecumenical reading of Ballagas—one that merely alludes to, but does not face up to, what Virgilio seems to term Ballagas's very human imperfections—Piñera explains:

> Si los franceses escriben sobre Gide tomando como punto de partida el homosexualismo de este escritor; si los ingleses hacen lo mismo con Wilde, yo no veo por qué los cubanos no podamos hablar de Ballagas en tanto que homosexual. ¿Es que los franceses y los ingleses tienen la exclusiva de tal tema? No por cierto, no hay temas exclusivos ni ellos lo pretenderían, sino que franceses e ingleses nunca estarán dispuestos a hacer de sus escritores ese lechero de la Inmortalidad que tanto seduce a nuestros críticos. (42)

[If the French write about Gide taking as a point of departure this writer's homosexuality; if the English do the same with Wilde, I don't see why we Cubans cannot speak of Ballagas as homosexual. Is it that the French and the English have the exclusive rights to that theme? Of course not, there are no exclusive themes nor would they pretend that there are, it's just that the French and the British would never be prone to turn their writers into that source of Immortality that so seduces our critics.][3]

To appreciate the revolutionary character of this essay, one should recall, as Piñera does, that Ballagas was deeply religious, and that he married and fathered a child while still writing some of the more erotically charged Cuban poetry of all time. In spite of and because of this, Piñera clarifies that Ballagas's poetry has to be read taking into account the poet's struggle with homosexuality: "Todos sus actos, comprendiendo en esos actos su obra entera, es [sic] el reflejo de esa lucha a brazo partido con el pecado. ¿Qué es esta obra, en definitiva, sino un largo y reiterado De Profundis del cual quizá Ballagas habría salido victorioso de no haber muerto tan joven?" [All of his acts, including in these acts his work as a whole, are the reflection of a fight against sin. What is this work but a long and reiterated De profundis from which Ballagas perhaps would have emerged victorious had he not died so young?] (42). For Piñera, Ballagas's tortured homosexuality structures the entire work; it endows what is said and what is not said with a particular weight; it soils the page with its notion of homosexuality as pleasure and as sin.

Piñera is at all times conscious of the risks entailed in making an initial claim for Ballagas as part of a homosexual tradition—hence his deliberate outing of the writer himself as tormented being. Still, this outing is deliberately political, because it was written for Ciclón, a journal financed by the wealthy gay patron José Rodríguez Feo after his rift with José Lezama Lima (whose journal Orígenes Rodríguez Feo also financed). Ciclón valued scandal and openness, particularly as a follow-up to the more sedate Orígenes: in the late fifties, Ciclón published excerpts from Sade's 120 Days of Sodom as well as essays on Oscar Wilde, on Freud, on Gide, and on pornography. As a self-conscious cultural elite (I underscore cultural because its members by no means came from the wealthy class), the writers of Ciclón saw their mission as that of opening up Cuban discourse in the waning days of Batista's dictatorship. For a time after the revolution, most of its members, including Guillermo Cabrera Infante, Antón Arrufat, Pablo Armando Fernández, and the recently deceased Severo Sarduy, went on to write for the even more anarchic *Lunes de revolución*, with Virgilio Piñera as their guiding mentor, until *Lunes* itself was closed down by the revolutionary government, and most of its members chose either exile (as did Cabrera Infante) or tempered their irreverence in view of the more complex cultural politics that followed.

In many ways, Piñera's future history within the revolution is inversely proportional to Ballagas's previous history: Piñera decided to live his *life* openly as a homosexual while his *texts* only marginally dealt with homosexuality. His life and texts, in spite of their apparent simplicity, are densely textured within the inversely proportional relationship that they sustain with each other: open, crystalline life, that of the "faggot"; a writer of "simple" tales in a colloquial, even impersonal language that actually represses more than what it says. Inversion, in any case, was one of Piñera's favorite narrative tropes. Most of his work deals with a world upside down, askew, out of joint, antithetical but also parallel to ordinary existence.

For a writer known as a "flaming queen" before and after the revolution, one who defended Ballagas against his own acolytes, the repression of homosexuality in Piñera's texts has to be profoundly disturbing. Given that Piñera, before 1959, was openly and publicly arguing against a simplified vision of the relationship between writers and their works, and that after 1959 this kind of reading is found nowhere else in his work except, perhaps, in allegorical terms, outing Piñera really depends on who does the outing, in what context it is made, and to what political or social ends. The gay critic is in many ways deeply implied in all this, for Piñera flings his own sexuality to the critic-to-come in statements such as the following, taken from several published fragments of his autobiography, *La vida tal cual:* "Claro que no podía saber a tan corta edad que el saldo arrojado por esas tres gorgonas: miseria, homosexualismo y arte, era la pavorosa nada" [Of course I could not know at such an early age that the price to pay for these three gorgons: misery, homosexuality and art, was a terrible void]. Briefly put, the critic who outs Piñera will find himself or herself squarely in the realm of a homosexuality written in terms of agony and sin. What do we learn from such a precursor? And what kind of morally superior register does outing imply over this sense of damnation? Piñera's reading of Ballagas is a challenge whose only response could be Piñera's later silence. Paraphrasing Piñera's own words on Ballagas, what was Piñera's whole life but a struggle with and against sin?

In spite of what in all accounts has been underscored as Piñera's very "open" or "uncloseted" homosexuality, the undercurrent of damnation from which Piñera always speaks of it in writing is part and parcel of his circumstance. This circumstance is encoded throughout his work and is one of the most important points of origin for his critique on Cuban literature. But what happens when the poet disrobes, when everything is apparently offered to the reader as a surface that can be *openly* read? The initial response to that question forces us to see how disrobing is, in fact, the prelude to further coding of information. The stereotypical queen that appears in other writers' memoirs on Piñera is precisely that, a foil that allows the reader only partial access to the very real sense of damnation that Piñera keeps barely under the surface, and that has to be taken into account in the process of claiming Piñera as part of a homosexual writing continuum. Let us see, for example, the first line of one of Piñera's more tormented works, *La isla en peso* (1943), a long, rambling poem that resembles Aimé Césaire's *Cahier du retour au pays natal*.[4] The poem begins with an implicit question that affirms an enigma:

La maldita circunstancia del agua en todas partes me obliga
a sentarme en la mesa de café.
Si yo no pensara que el agua me rodea como un cáncer, habría
podido dormir a pierna suelta

[The damned circumstance of water on all sides forces me to sit on the coffee table. / If I did not think that water surrounds me like cancer, I could have slept like a log]

What is the circumstance? A first approach to this question is, of course, insularity (or insularism), a signifier that has slipped in and out of Cuban discourse since José Lezama Lima's famous "Coloquio con Juan Ramón Jiménez," where Lezama argued for the essential exceptionality of insular lives. The coffee table Piñera is literally thrown onto (but also off of), is an island unto itself, circular, spherical, surrounded on all sides by water but also reproducing itself in the circular black hole of a cup of coffee as a black sun. The concentric circles repeat themselves as surface upon surface is indelibly surrounded by a water that always condemns everything within its borders to live in a kind of amniotic sac, where Piñera anticipates a resolution to Fernando Ortíz's impasse of tobacco and sugar in *Contrapunteo cubano del tabaco y el azúcar* by means of a third drug: the black bilious sun of caffeine. Water occupies the same place in *La isla en peso* as flesh does in Piñera's later work—particularly in his best novel, *René's Flesh*. In both cases, its weight needs to be apprehended as the weight of the void that is within, as a profound materiality that dissolves as soon as it is touched:

> Esta noche he llorado al conocer a una anciana que ha vivido
> ciento ocho años rodeada de agua por todas partes.
> Hay que morder, hay que gritar, hay que arañar.
> He dado las últimas instrucciones
> El perfume de la piña puede detener a un pájaro
> Los once mulatos se disputaban el fruto
> Los once mulatos fálicos murieron frente a la orilla de la playa
> He dado las últimas instrucciones
> Todos nos hemos desnudado.

[Tonight I cried when I met an old woman who has lived for one hundred and eight years surrounded by water on all sides. / One has to bite, one has to shout, one has to scratch. / I have given the final instructions / The pineapple's perfume can stop a bird / The eleven mulattoes fought for the fruit / The eleven phallic mulattoes died on the seashore / I've given the final instructions / We have all undressed.]

There is no oblivion, but there is nakedness, and as any reader of *René's Flesh* will appreciate, both are not the same thing. In *La isla en peso*, the tropical Saint Sebastian is about to be penetrated by naked bodies on the literal and metaphorical border of the text (on the beach). Because weight itself is both inside and outside the subject and the text, Piñera demands that we read *La isla en peso* with the degree of immanence that this very weight endows to all things: "[S]iempre más abajo hasta saber el peso de su isla / el peso de una isla en el amor de un pueblo" [always below until one knows the weight of one's island / the weight of an island in the affections of a people]. Because the water in this text is not so much an event as it is a circumstance, it is not only water and flesh but also blood. Damnation is the mode taken by a poet who damns everything to such an extent that its weight turns the poem upside down, into a kind of inverted and perverse celebration. The white ocean that surrounds the text is punctured by an epigraph. It is a dialogue where two voices named only as "Uno" [One] and "Otro" [Other] call and respond to each other. Uno says, "¿alaba o maldice?" [Does he praise or damn?], to which Otro responds, "Eso no importa" [It doesn't matter].

How are we to read the damned circumstance of which Piñera speaks? Are we to read it as homosexuality and put Piñera's "gorgon" center stage, as he did with Ballagas? Piñera's insistence on the lack of importance of being damned or celebrated seems to point toward an essential ambivalence of the code, to a kind of bisexuality of emotive affection. But what does matter here is that what the text says is damned—*maldita*, but also *mal dicha*, because Piñera is aware that his poem is an imperfect child of an already dense and damned space. The poem lives in a no-man's-land between the space of two possibilities. It exposes a bloody past of conquest and a cursed future that will arise from the present circumstance, but it also reacts to the moral and social decay of the Cuban Republic by coding a response to what had been presented, at that time, as one of the possible avenues of salvation for the republic: the formal perfection of the weighted cultural body delineated by another Cuban poet who may (or should) be called gay, José Lezama Lima, in his poem "Muerte de Narciso" (1937)—perhaps one of the most formally complex, one of the "heaviest" poems, in all of Latin American literature. "Muerte de Narciso" is profoundly marked by culture—it is a text that, given the time and place where it was written, argued for the kind of timelessness of culture as the only salvation for "the Cuban condition." As hermetic allusion is webbed to hermetic allusion in a dense intertextual code, Lezama aims toward perfection by means of a dense incorporative frenzy: everything belongs, and is brought into, the space of the island; nothing is emptied from within.

For Piñera, Lezama's voracious cultural incorporation was, in this context, tantamount to avoidance and repression. Culture, literally, was a *detour*. To *devour* culture was to forget the enemy within, to avoid the encounter with one's own malaise. As Piñera said, *La isla en peso* was "el antilezamismo en persona" [antilezamism in person], a poem where the poet "paga sus culpas y pecados con el lezamismo" [pays up his guilt and his sins with lezamism]. *Culpas y pecados* is an interesting turn of phrase— guilt and sin—an astoundingly religious language used by a man who in 1940 had complained that the journal that he and Lezama (who was then his friend) belonged to, *Espuela de plata,* had turned into a Catholic journal because, as Lezama had stated, all of its members were practicing Catholics: "Tuve que soportar que ese maniqueísmo, con un impudor e insinceridad que eran de esperarse por su propia condición maniqueísta, me comunicase, como un gran descubrimiento, que *Espuela de plata* era una revista católica" [I had to withstand the fact that that Manichaeanism, with a lack of modesty and sincerity that were to be expected because of its own Manichaean condition, would communicate to me, as if it were a great discovery, that *Espuela de plata* was a Catholic journal]. It was this same Manichaeanism that further provoked Piñera to write an essay in the same *Espuela de plata* in 1941 on Emilio Ballagas and Lezama titled "Dos poetas, dos poemas, dos modos de poesía" [Two poets, two poems, two modes of poetry] in which he read Lezama's as the work of a painfully narcissistic poet whose byzantine mosaic demanded a reader initiated into an apparent verbal chaos that was Lezama's "atmósfera gongorina; doloroso rigor, siempre solicitando la perfección que muere de rodillas" [Gongorine atmosphere; dolorous rigor, always beckoning a perfection that dies on its knees]. It was against this perfection that Piñera wrote *La isla en peso,* telling Lezama, in coded language, that the density and weight of the Neo-Baroque was not the way to redeem the island from its damned condition, and that the formal complications of language had the effect of hiding a circumstance that the poet and his language needed to undress.

"La isla en peso," then, deploys a series of codes that are (pardon the redundancy) encoded within each other. But the paradox is that Piñera demands that we read the poem as a text *against* encoding (or against interpretation), *for* nakedness and against allusion. It seems that even when he tries to disrobe, Piñera ends up further trying to say what he means only by means of allusion. But this indirection is at all points deliberate. It allows *La isla en peso* to be read, within the Cuban milieu, as a poem about culture, and not as a text on homosexuality. But culture becomes, in this work, a coded word that means homosexual, and homosexuality is what structures the question as to the cultural damnation or redemption of the republic. Indeed, within this context and in terms of Virgilio Piñera and José Lezama Lima, every time we use the word "culture" and aggregates such as "Cuban condition" or the "malaise" of the republic, we should actually read "homosexuality." To argue for culture (as Lezama does) means to argue against outing. To take the opposite side of the debate, to argue, as Piñera does, against culture, means arguing for unveiling, for a "damned" form of outing. But *La isla en peso* represents, nevertheless, an unfulfilled disrobing, for the text also encodes and sublimates what it really means to say. "El ligerísimo Virgilio" [the weightless Virgilio] (Rodríguez Feo 75), as Lezama called him in a letter to José Rodríguez Feo, demanded the outed expression of a damned circumstance, but his "once mulatos fálicos" [eleven phallic mulattoes] have collapsed on the beach while the writer and his public take off their clothes and wait for the hand of a redeemer.

There are at least two questions that have been encoded in the relationship between critic and poet (subject and object) in this essay and that must now be given some tentative state of closure. What is to be done if rescuing the bloodline that passes through the bodies of gay texts and gay readers at different points in time merely allows us to uncover a trembling code addressed to some future deliverance from the repressive state of marginality? The second question follows from the first: why should we deliver those texts only to consign them to a more insidious and weightless marginal existence as "gay" texts? I intend to make my way through the labyrinth of these bloodlines and of my deep allegiance to them by quoting the account of one of Piñera's and Lezama's fights, as narrated by Guillermo Cabrera Infante in 1980. My reason for quoting Cabrera, of course, is because his open treatment of Virgilio and Lezama—indeed, his very deliberate outing of these two writers, framed and described according to their sexual "weaknesses" by a "heterosexual" narrator—allows us to see what happens to a homosexual polemic within a "heterosexual" context when sexuality is brought out into the open and fetishized. We must note that at the crucial moment in Cabrera's essay that I will quote, all allusion to culture or to literature has been excised for the sake of levity. Lest one be accused of not having a sense of humor, let us follow Cabrera as he sets the scene, when Lezama and Piñera meet in Havana at some point in the early forties, at the Lyceum and Lawn Tennis Club (English in the original):

I never found out if Virgilio and Lezama met in the library or in the exhibition hall—it happened in the afternoon. What I do know is that they both went out to the street to settle their fight in the macho Cuban way ("Come outside and we'll settle this"—I simply can't see either Virgilio, so pugnacious, or Lezama, so stable, voicing such a challenge) or the way of the laconic cowboys from old Westerns. But ritually or silently they went out to the street and no sooner had they uttered two words or a sudden silence, then Virgilio jumped over the short hedge to enter the gardens. He didn't pay any attention to the sign ("Don't walk on the grass") and poking around the giant flamboyant tree he looked for something. A buried treasure? A murder weapon? Lezama didn't hit upon guessing what Virgilio's quest was (the philosopher's stone, perhaps) until he saw that it wasn't a stone but pebbles. When Virgilio figured he had enough garden pebbles he started to throw them at Lezama, aiming at the powerful legs, at the flat feet of his once literary friend now mortal enemy. Every time Lezama saw a small stone coming he took a leap, (Or rather a little hop: what his girth would allow him). Virgilio was laughing diabolically or amused. As a response Lezama was aiming verbal threats at Virgilio, a Havana still in his mouth, fuming, warning: "Virgilio, I'm going to chastise you." But this smoking Goliath wasn't doing anything to reach his opponent, stone-throwing David.

Soon there was a mob of street urchins who were gleefully witnessing the skirmish—the strife of stones against speech. At the end the urchins included themselves in the combat as a chorus: "Make the fat man jump! Make the fat man jump!" Which didn't get any points with Lezama who never tolerated being called fat—not even affectionately. Finally the stoning stopped because Virgilio ran out of ammunition and the boys began to vituperate Virgilio. With the irregular duel over, each opponent went back to his literary corner—but they didn't speak to each other again for thirty years. (Cabrera Infante 338)

Cabrera weds his erotic and literary links into lives that are read with the sense of flatness possessed by opera buffa. Imagination (and here we should perversely recall David Leavitt) centralizes sex, glosses over the real and the coded debates of the time, and leaves us two bodies emptied of flesh, mannequins that battle for some elusive goal. Why did the fight take place? Some say it was because of La isla en peso; others prefer to think that it was because Piñera had critiqued Lezama and had favored Ballagas in *Espuela de plata*. But the point is, only the fight between two faggots can be negotiated as a love affair inscribed in their very marginal choice of love objects. The irony is, of course, that no other Cuban writer has dared to out Piñera and Lezama like Cabrera has in his essayistic memoirs, and from what I have been able to read in Cabrera's correspondence with Virgilio, the two were tied by the singular affection of a friendship that spoke openly and frankly about sex. I mention this to underscore that we may call Cabrera sexist, but there is no doubt in my mind that he is a sympathetic observer, one who is not condemning at all the homosexuality of the principal characters of the tale but rather voyeuristically enjoying it. On the contrary, their homosexuality is rendered as central to the tale of Cuban culture precisely because of its "exceptional" nature.

The sense of homosexual damnation and sin that we see in some of Piñera's work, as well as in the stoic and dignified silence of his later years, does not arise solely as reaction to a hostile setting. Piñera's insular weight precludes the simple acceptance of doom as a response. Indeed, as he at times seems to imply, in a perverse twist on Lezama's insular essence, the very nature of insularity is directly related to the sense of damnation that the insular inhabitant feels. This is why Piñera's disrobing, his arguing for nakedness, cannot be anything but a profoundly ambivalent act—as ambivalent as outing him is. For what he means by nakedness, which in this context I am using as a synonym for outing, as saying everything without the code, without the allusion, runs counter to the very act that Piñera always forced himself to play: that of the buffoon, the "loca," the vapid sprite of *levitas*. Piñera's postrevolutionary silence in terms of his homosexuality—precisely after he had found a way of outing himself via Ballagas—has to be seen in terms of the repressive nature of the Cuban state. But it also has to be seen in the more tragic sense as a failure of, and a fear of, voice. The "queen" could never again publish, but she opted not to risk banishment or imprisonment. Neither a sinner nor a saint, but a subject who seems to prefer a slow disappearance. As the picaresque tales of his life after the revolution multiply, and as the editions of his unpublished work find more and more of a space in Cuba after his death, we are forced to try to understand those years of silence. It is the silence of a certain kind of fear, but also the result of the deep sense of fatality and damnation that the homosexual poet flings out to his heirs. It is as ambivalent a cipher as any homosexual writer could fling to his heirs: an act of absolute passivity *and* power.

Lest we adopt a high moral tone in respect to this silence, let us remember that to invoke, as Cabrera Infante does, the weightless body of the stereotype does not do justice to the flesh that Piñera wanted us to pierce. To honor the blood of the ancestor also entails the risk of passing on, of transmitting, his sense of sin. To say that who does the telling is important, that it is all a question of who does the outing, seems to me an ancillary point—in essence, all citizens of the republic should do the telling, but only in the present or at some future point, because there should be, in theory, no telling to do. The narrative, nevertheless, as Piñera understood it, is going to be comic and tragic, for the Manichaean sensibility of homophobia demands the tragic buffoon that can only be given a borrowed space—one that can easily be withheld. The whole bloody text that is written by Virgilio Piñera and by other gay men in Latin American literature seems to want and demand, at this point, for the future reader to disrobe. But we can only hope to give voice to a different set of choices, one in which subjects retain the sense of agency that is their right—not as impertinent sons that continue a dysfunctional bloodline, but by noticing again and again how the water that surrounds these texts is a flesh that is thicker than blood.

Notes

I want to thank my late and deeply missed colleague Roberto Valero for many talks on Piñera and for his recollections of the members of Piñera's circle. I also want to thank Enrico Mario Santí for providing a copy of the first edition of *La isla en peso*, Elissa Marder for reading an early draft of this essay, Princeton University Libraries, and particularly Peter Johnson, for their invaluable help during the summer of 1994.

1 Piñera felt that Borges and the *Sur* group replicated Lezama and his *Orígenes*, hence his never feeling comfortable with either, and his deliberate self-marginalizing from perhaps the two most important Latin American literary circles, both in Argentina and in Cuba.

2 The revaluation of the whole library circle around *Ciclón* and *Lunes de Revolución* (about which more later) also involves, to an extent, the issue of sexuality and, more specifically, of homosexuality, as can be seen in Roberto Pérez León's *Tiempo de Ciclón*, published in part in Havana, although I have

only been able to consult a more complete manuscript still unpublished outside of Cuba.

3   Unless otherwise noted, all translations are mine.

4   All quotes from *La isla en peso* are taken from the first edition (Havana: Espuela de Plata, 1942). The first publication of Césaire's *Cahier* was in the Paris periodical *Volontés*, no. 20 (August 1939), but its first French edition, as well as publication in book form, are from 1947. I have no documentation as to whether Piñera did or did not read Césaire's poem.

Works Cited

Aguirre, Coral. *La cruz en el espejo (pieza dramática en dos actos)*. Buenos Aires: Torres Agüero Editor, 1988.

Alderson, Michael. "Introduction: About the Author." *The War of the Fatties and Other Stories from Aztec History*. Trans. Michael Alderson. Austin: University of Texas Press, 1994. ix–lviii.

Alfonso X. *Las siete partidas del sabio rey Don Alfonso X / nuevamente glosadas por el Licenciado Gregorio López, del Consejo Real de Indias de su Magestad* [Facsimile edition of the 1555 text]. Madrid: Boletín Oficial del Estado, 1974.

Almendros, Néstor. "Almendros and Documentary." *Sight and Sound* 55.1 (winter 1985–1986): 50–54.

——. *Cinemanía*. Barcelona: Seix Barral, 1992.

——. *A Man with a Camera*. London: Faber, 1984.

Almendros, Néstor, and Orlando Jiménez Leal. *Conducta impropia*. Madrid: Playor, 1984.

——. "Improper Conduct." *American Film* 9.10 (Sept. 1984): 18, 70–71.

Alter, Robert. "Sodom as Nexus: The Web of Design in Biblical Narrative." *Reclaiming Sodom*. Ed. Jonathan Goldberg. New York: Routledge, 1994.

Alvarez-Curbelo, Silvia, and María Elena Rodríguez-Castro, eds. *Del nacionalismo al populismo: Cultura y política en Puerto Rico*. Río Piedras: Ediciones Huracán, 1993.

Amnesty International. *Breaking the Silence: Human Rights Violations Based on Sexual Orientation*. New York: Amnesty International Publications, 1994.

Anzaldúa, Gloria. *Borderlands/La frontera: The New Mestiza*. San Francisco: Aunt Lute, 1987.

Arenal, Electa, and Stacey Schlau. *Untold Sisters: Hispanic Nuns in Their Own Words*. Albuquerque: University of New Mexico Press, 1989.

Arenas, Reinaldo. *Antes que anochezca.* Barcelona: Tusquets, 1992.

——. *The Assault.* New York: Viking, 1994.

——. *Before Night Falls.* Trans. Dolores Koch. New York: Penguin, 1993.

——. *The Ill-Fated Peregrinations of Fray Servando.* Trans. Andrew Hurley. New York: Penguin, 1987.

——. "La isla en peso con todas sus cucarachas." *Necesidad de libertad. Mariel: testimonios de un intelectual disidente.* Mexico City: Kosmos-Editorial, 1986. 115–31.

——. *La loma del ángel.* Barcelona: Dador, 1989.

——. *El mundo alucinante.* Mexico City: Diógenes, 1978.

——. *Viaje a la Habana.* Miami: Universal, 1990.

——. *Voluntad de vivir manifestándose.* Madrid: Betania, 1989.

Arguelles, Lourdes, and B. Ruby Rich. "Homosexuality, Homophobia, and Revolution: Notes toward an Understanding of the Cuban Lesbian and Gay Male Experience." *Signs: Journal of Women on Culture and Society* (summer 1984): 683–99; (autumn 1985): 120–36.

Azize, Yamila. *La mujer en la lucha.* Río Piedras: Editorial Cultural, 1985.

——, ed. *La mujer en Puerto Rico.* Río Piedras: Ediciones Huracán, 1987.

Barbazza, Marie-Catherine. "Un caso de subversión social: el proceso de Elena de Céspedes (1587–1589)." *Criticón* 26 (1984): 17–40.

Barradas, Efraín. *Apalabramiento. Diez cuentistas puertorriqueños de hoy.* Hanover, N.H.: Ediciones del Norte, 1983.

——. "El machismo existencial de René Marqués." *Sin nombre* 8.3 (1977): 69–81.

Barrientos, Juan José. "Reynaldo Arenas, Alejo Carpentier y la nueva novela histórica hispanoamericana." *Revista de la Universidad de México* 40.416 (Sept. 1985): 16–24.

Barthes, Roland. *Roland Barthes.* Trans. Richard Howard. Berkeley: University of California Press, 1994.

Bataille, Georges. *La part maudite. Précéde de La notion de dépense.* Paris: Minuit, 1967.

Bataillon, Marcel. Introduction. *La vie de Lazarillo de Tormes.* Trans. A. Morel Fatio. Paris, Aubier: Éditions Montaigne, 1958.

Baudelaire, Charles. "Le peintre de la vie moderne." *Oeuvres complètes.* Paris: Gallimard, "Pléiade," 1954.

Bautista, Juan Carlos (Colectivo Masiosare). "La sonrisa de sor Juana." *fem* 14.95 (Nov. 1990): 13–16.

Beaver, Harold. "Homosexual Signs (In Memory of Roland Barthes)." *Critical Inquiry* 8 (fall 1981): 99–119.

Bejel, Emilio. "Senel Paz: homosexualidad, nacionalismo y utopía." *Plural: Revista Cultural de "Excelsior"* 269 (Feb. 1994): 58–65.

Benassar, Bartolomé. "El modelo sexual: la Inquisición de Aragón y la represión de los pecados 'abominables.'" *Inquisición española: poder político y control social*. Ed. Bartolomé Benassar. Barcelona: Editorial Crítica, 1981.

Bénassy-Berling, Marie-Cécile. *Humanismo y religión en Sor Juana Inés de la Cruz*. Trans. Laura López de Belair. Mexico City: Universidad Nacional Autónoma de México, 1983.

Benjamin, Walter. "The Work of Art in the Age of Mechanical Reproduction." *Illuminations*. Trans. Harry Zohn. New York: Schocken Books, 1969.

Bergmann, E. L., and Paul Julian Smith, eds. *¿Entiendes? Queer Readings, Hispanic Writings*. Durham: Duke University Press, 1995.

Bersani, Leo. "Is the Rectum a Grave?" *October* 43 (1987): 197–222.

Bhabha, Homi. *The Location of Culture*. New York: Routledge, 1994.

Blanco, José Joaquín. *Crónica de la poesía mexicana*. Mexico City: Editorial Katún, 1983.

Blanco, Aguinaga Carlos, Julio Rodríguez, and Iris M. Zavala, eds. *Historia social de la literatura española (en lengua castellana)* 3. Madrid: Castalia, 1983.

Blasco, Francisco Javier. "El palimpsesto urbano de *Paisajes después de la batalla*." *Anales de la Literatura Española Contemporánea* 10.1–3 (1985): 11–29.

Borges, Jorge Luis. *Discusión*. 1936. Buenos Aires: Emecé, 1964.

Boswell, John. *Christianity, Social Tolerance, and Homosexuality: Gay People in Western Europe from the Beginning of the Christian Era to the Fourteenth Century*. Chicago: University of Chicago Press, 1980.

Bourdieu, Pierre. *Language and Symbolic Power*. Ed. John B. Thompson. Trans. Gino Raymond and Matthew Adamson. Cambridge: Harvard University Press, 1991.

Braun, Lucille V. "Inside and Outside: Topology and Intertextuality in Juan Goytisolo's *Paisajes después de la batalla*." *Revista Canadiense de Estudios Hispánicos* 14.1 (1989): 15–34.

Bullough, Vern L., and Bonnie Bullough. *Cross Dressing, Sex, and Gender*. Philadelphia: University of Pennsylvania Press, 1993.

Burshatin, Israel. "Elena alias Eleno: Genders, Sexualities, and 'Race' in the Mirror of Natural History in Sixteenth-Century Spain." *Gender Reversals*. Ed. Sabrina Petra Ramet. New York: Routledge (in press). 105–22.

Butler, Judith. *Bodies That Matter: On the Discursive Limits of "Sex."* New York: Routledge, 1993.

——. *Gender Trouble: Feminism and the Subversion of Gender*. New York: Routledge, 1990.

Cabrera Infante, Guillermo. "Cuba's Shadow." *Film Comment* 24.3 (May–June 1985): 43–45.

——. *Mea Cuba*. Trans. Kenneth Hall and Guillermo Cabrera Infante. New York: Farrar Straus Giroux, 1994.

——. "Paisajes con Goytisolo al frente." *Quimera* 27 (1983): 56–59.

Cadden, Joan. *Meanings of Sex Difference in the Middle Ages: Medicine, Science, and Culture*. Cambridge: Cambridge University Press, 1993.

Calinescu, Matei. *Faces of Modernity: Avant-Garde, Decadence, Kitsch*. Bloomington: Indiana University Press, 1977.

Capistrán, Miguel. *Los Contemporáneos por sí mismos*. Mexico City: Consejo Nacional para la Cultura y las Artes, 1994.

Carrasco, Rafael. *Inquisición y represión sexual en Valencia. Historia de los sodomitas (1565–1785)*. Barcelona: Laertes, 1985.

Carrier, Joseph. *De los otros: Intimacy and Homosexuality among Mexican Men*. New York: Columbia University Press, 1995.

Carroll, Lewis. *Alice's Adventures in Wonderland*. Ed. Donald J. Gray. New York: W. W. Norton, 1992.

Casal, Julián del. *Obra poética*. Havana: Editorial de Letras Cubanas, 1982.

Casal, Lourdes. *El caso Padilla: Literatura y revolución en Cuba: Documentos*. Miami: Ediciones Universal, 1972.

Case, Sue-Ellen. "Toward a Butch-Femme Aesthetic." *Making a Spectacle*. Ed. Lynda Hart. Ann Arbor: University of Michigan Press, 1989.

Castellanos, Rosario. *El eterno femenino*. Mexico City: Fondo de Cultura Económica, 1975.

Castle, Terry. *The Apparitional Lesbian: Female Homosexuality and Modern Culture*. New York: Columbia University Press, 1993.

Castrejón, Eduardo. *Los 41: Novela crítico-social*. Mexico City: Tipografía Nacional, 1906.

Celemenski, Michel. Review of *Improper Conduct. Cinématographe* 98 (March 1984): 27–28.

Césaire, Aimé. *The Collected Poetry*. Trans. Clayton Eshleman and Annette Smith. Berkeley: University of California Press, 1983.

Céspedes, Elena de. *Legajo 234, Expediente 24, Sección Inquisición*. Archivo Histórico Nacional, Madrid.

Chanan, Michael. *The Cuban Image*. London: BFI, 1985.

Chodorow, Nancy. *The Reproduction of Mothering: Psychoanalysis and the Sociology of Gender*. Berkeley: University of California Press, 1979.

Cohen, Ed. "Who Are 'We'? Gay 'Identity' as Political (E)motion (A Theoretical Rumination)." *Inside/Out: Lesbian Theories, Gay Theories*. Ed. Diana Fuss. New York: Routledge, 1991. 71–92.

Copjec, Joan. "The Sartorial Superego." *October* 50 (fall 1989): 57–95.

Covarrubias Orozco, Sebastián de. *Tesoro de la lengua castellana o española, según la impresión de 1611, con las adiciones de Benito Remigio Noydens publicadas en la de 1674.* Ed. Martín de Riquer. Barcelona: S. A. Horta, 1943.

———. *Tesoro de la lengua castellana o española* [1610]. Madrid: Turner, 1970.

Cruz-Malavé, Arnaldo. *El primitivo implorante. El "sistema poético del mundo de José Lezama Lima.* Amsterdam: Rodopi, 1994.

———. "Toward an Art of Transvestism: Colonialism and Homosexuality in Puerto Rican Literature." *¿Entiendes? Queer Readings, Hispanic Writings.* Ed. Emilie Bergmann and Paul Julian Smith. Durham: Duke University Press, 1995: 137–67.

Cubitt, Sean. "Cube libre?" *City Limits* 171 (1 Nov. 1985): 14.

———. Review of *Improper Conduct. City Limits* 171 (1 Nov. 1985): 23.

Cuesta, Jorge. *Poesía y crítica.* Mexico City: Consejo Nacional para la Cultura y las Artes, 1991.

———. *Sonetos.* Intro. C. Múgica. Astrological Chart, V. del Valle, C. Múgica. Mexico: UNAM, 1987.

———, ed. *Antología de la poesía mexicana moderna.* 1st contemporary edition. Intro. G. Sheridan. Mexico City: Fondo de Cultura Económica, 1985.

Darío, Rubén. *Obras completas.* 5 vols. Madrid: Afrodisio Aguado, 1955.

Daston, Lorraine, and Katharine Park. "Hermaphrodites in Renaissance France." *Critical Matrix: Princeton Working Papers in Women's Studies* 1.5 (1985): 1–19.

Dauster, Frank. *Xavier Villaurrutia.* New York: Twayne Publishers, 1971.

Davis, Lisa. "Oscar Wilde in Spain." *Comparative Literature* 25 (1973): 136–52.

———. "La traducción de *Salomé* de Guerra Mondragón." *Sin Nombre* (Puerto Rico) 10.4 (1981): 26–39.

Debroise, Olivier. *Figuras en el trópico: Plástica mexicana 1920–1970.* Mexico City: Océano, 1984.

Delany, Samuel R. *The Motion of Light in Water.* New York: Arbor House, 1988.

de Lauretis, Teresa. "The Lure of the Mannish Lesbian: The Fantasy of Castration and the Signification of Desire." *The Practice of Love: Lesbian Sexuality and Perverse Desire.* Bloomington: Indiana University Press, 1994. 203–53.

———. "Sexual Indifference and Lesbian Representation." *Theatre Journal* 40.2 (May 1988): 155–77. Reprinted in *The Lesbian and Gay Studies Reader.* Ed. Henry Abelove, Michèle Aina Barale, and David Halperin. New York: Routledge, 1993. 141–58.

Deleuze, Gilles. *The Logic of Sense.* Trans. Mark Lester. New York: Columbia University Press, 1990.

Deleuze, Gilles, and Félix Guattarí. *Anti-Oedipus: Capitalism and Schizophrenia.* Trans. R. Hurley, M. Seem, and H. R. Lane. Minneapolis: University of Minnesota Press, 1992.

de Man, Paul. "Autobiography as De-facement." *The Rhetoric of Romanticism.* New York: Columbia University Press, 1984, 67–80.

D'Emilio, John. "Capitalism and Gay Identity." Ed. Ann Snitow, et al. *Powers of Desire: The Politics of Sexuality.* New York: Monthly Review Press, 1983. 100–113.

———. *Sexual Politics, Sexual Communities: The Making of a Homosexual Minority in the United States, 1940–1970.* Chicago: University of Chicago Press, 1983.

Derrida, Jacques. *De la grammatologie.* Paris: Minuit, 1967.

———. "La parole soufflée." *Writing and Difference.* Trans. Alan Bass. Chicago: University of Chicago Press, 1978. 169–95.

Díaz Alfaro, Abelardo. *Terrazo.* San Juan: Editorial Yaurel, 1948.

Díaz Arciniega, Víctor. *Querella por la cultura "revolucionaria" (1925).* Mexico: Fondo de Cultura Económica, 1989.

Díaz Quiñones, Arcadio. *Conversación con José Luis González.* Río Piedras: Ediciones Huracán, 1976.

———. "Los desastres de la guerra: para leer a René Marqués." *El almuerzo en la hierba (Lloréns Torres, Palés Matos, René Marqués).* Río Piedras: Ediciones Huracán, 1982. 133–68.

Díaz Valcárcel, Emilio. "El asedio" [1958]. *Panorama: Narraciones 1955–1967.* Río Piedras: Editorial Cultural, 1971. 11–18.

Didi-Hubermon, Georges. *Invention de l'hysterie: Charcot et l'iconographie photographique de la Salpêtrière.* Paris: Macula, 1982.

Donoghue, Emma. "Imagined More than Women: Lesbians as Hermaphrodites, 1671–1766." *Women's History Review* 2 (1993): 199–216.

Dowling, Linda. *Language and Decadence in the Victorian Fin de Siècle.* Princeton: Princeton University Press, 1986.

du Bois, Page. *Sappho Is Burning.* Chicago: University of Chicago Press, 1995.

Dunn, Peter. *The Spanish Picaresque Fiction: A New Literary History.* Ithaca: Cornell University Press, 1993.

Edelman, Lee. *Homographesis: Essays in Gay Literary and Cultural Theory.* New York: Routledge, 1994.

El Saffar, Ruth. "Ana/Lysis/Zayas: Reflections on Courtship and Literary Women in María de Zayas's *Disenchantments of Love.*" *Indiana Journal of Hispanic Literatures* 2.1 (1993): 9–28.

Epps, Bradley. "Proper Conduct: Reinaldo Arenas, Fidel Castro, and the Politics of Homosexuality." *Journal of the History of Sexuality* 6.2 (1995): 231–83.

Epstein, Julia. "Either/Or—Neither/Both: Sexual Ambiguity and the Ideology of Gender." *Genders* 7 (1990): 99–142.

Escamilla, Michèle. "A propos d'un dossier inquisitorial des environs de 1590: les étranges amours d'un hermaphrodite." *Amours légitimes amours illégitimes en Espagne (XVIe–XVIIe siècles)*. Ed. Augustin Redondo. Paris: Publications de la Sorbonne, 1985. 167–82.

Escudero, Javier. "Muerte, erotismo y espiritualidad: Entrevista con Juan Goytisolo." *Revista de Estudios Hispánicos* 27 (1993): 123–39.

Ette, Ottmar, ed. *La escritura de la memoria*. Frankfurt am Main: Vervuert Verlag, 1992.

Fanon, Frantz. *Black Skin, White Masks*. New York: Grove Press, 1967.

Ferré, Rosario. *Maldito amor*. Río Piedras: Ediciones Huracán, 1988.

——. *Papeles de Pandora*. Mexico City: Joaquín Mortiz, 1976.

"Les Films du mois: Néstor Almendros et Orlando Jiménez Leal." *Cinématographe* 98 (March 1984): 23–26.

Flores, Juan. *Divided Borders: Essays on Puerto Rican Identity*. Houston, Tex.: Arte Público Press, 1993.

Folch Jou, Guillermo, and María del Sagrario Muñoz. "Un pretendido caso de hermafroditismo en el siglo XVI." *Boletín de la sociedad española de historia de la farmacia* 93 (1973): 20–33.

Fontanella, Francesc. *Vexamen*. "Context i text del *Vexamen* d'academia de Francesc Fontanella." Kenneth Brown. *Lengua i Literatura* 2 (1987): 173–252.

Forster, Merlin H. *Los contemporáneos 1920–1932: Perfil de un experimento vanguardista mexicano*. Mexico City: Ediciones de Andrea, 1964.

——. *Fire and Ice: The Poetry of Xavier Villaurrutia*. North Carolina Studies in the Romance Languages and Literatures, Essays 11. Chapel Hill: Department of Romance Languages, University of North Carolina, 1976.

Foster, David William. *Gay and Lesbian Themes in Latin American Writing*. Austin: University of Texas Press, 1991.

Foucault, Michel. "The Ethic of the Care of the Self as a Practice of Freedom." *The Final Foucault*. Ed. James Bernauer and David Rasmussen. Trans. J. D. Gauthier. Cambridge: MIT Press, 1988.

——. *Foucault Live (Interviews, 1966–1984)*. Ed. Sylvère Lotringer. Trans. John Johnston. New York: Semiotext(e), 1989.

——. *The History of Sexuality*. 3 Vols. Trans. Robert Hurley. New York: Vintage, 1978, 1985, 1986.

——. *Madness and Civilization*. Trans. Richard Howard. New York: Random House, 1965.

——. *Mental Illness and Psychology*. Trans. Alan Sheridan. Berkeley: University of California Press, 1987.

Fowler, Victor. "Arenas: Homoerotismo y crítica de la cultura." *Apuntes Postmodernos/Postmodern Notes* 6.1 (fall 1995): 20–35.

Franco, Jean. *Plotting Women: Gender and Representation in Mexico.* New York: Columbia University Press, 1989.

Fraser, Nancy. "Rethinking the Public Sphere." *The Phantom of the Public Sphere.* Ed. Bruce Robbins. Minneapolis: University of Minnesota, 1993.

Freud, Sigmund. " 'A Child Is Being Beaten': A Contribution to the Study of the Origin of Sexual Perversions" [1919]. *The Standard Edition of the Complete Psychological Works of Sigmund Freud.* Ed. James Strachey. London: Hogarth Press and the Institute of Psycho-Analysis, 1957–1973. SEXVII: 175–204.

———. *Inhibitions, Symptoms, and Anxiety.* Trans. A. Strachey. New York: W. W. Norton, 1959.

———. *The Interpretation of Dreams.* New York: Basic, 1960.

———. "Psychoanalytic Notes upon an Autobiographical Account of a Case of Paranoia (Dementia Paranoides)" [1911]. *Three Case Histories.* New York: Collier, 1993. 83–160.

———. "Three Essays on the Theory of Sexuality" [1905/1924]. *The Freud Reader.* Ed. Peter Gay. New York: W. W. Norton, 1989. 239–92.

Fuss, Diana. "Inside/Out." *Inside/Out: Lesbian Theories, Gay Theories.* Ed. Diana Fuss. New York: Routledge, 1991. 1–10.

———. *Inside/Out: Lesbian Theories, Gay Theories.* New York: Routledge, 1991.

———. "Pink Freud." *GLQ: A Journal of Lesbian and Gay Studies* 2.1–2 (1995): 1–10.

Garber, Marjorie. *Vested Interests: Cross-Dressing and Cultural Anxiety.* New York: Routledge, 1992.

García, Mario. "Identity and Gender in the Mexican-American *Testimonio:* The Life and Narrative of Frances Esquivel Tywoniak." *Identity and Migration.* Ed. Rina Benmayor and Andor Skotnes. New York: Oxford University Press, 1994. 151–66.

García Ramis, Magaly. *La familia de todos nosotros.* San Juan: Instituto de Cultura Puertorriqueña, 1976.

———. *Felices días, tío Sergio.* Río Piedras: Editorial Antillana, 1986.

Gaspar de Alba, Alicia. "Excerpts from the Sapphic Diary of Sor Juana Inés de la Cruz." *Frontiers* 12.3 (1992): 171–79.

Gates, Henry Louis, Jr. *The Signifying Monkey: A Theory of African-American Literary Criticism.* New York: Oxford University Press, 1988.

Gelpí, Juan. "Desorden frente a purismo: La nueva narrativa frente a René Marqués." *Literatures in Transition: The Many Voices of the Caribbean Area.* Ed. Rose Minc. Gaithersburg, Md.: Montclair State College/Ediciones Hispamérica, 1982.

———. "La escritura transeúnte de Manuel Ramos Otero." *Literature y paternalismo en Puerto Rico.* Río Piedras: Editorial de la Universidad de Puerto Rico, 1993. 137–54.

———. *Literatura y paternalismo en Puerto Rico.* Río Piedras: Editorial de la Universidad de Puerto Rico, 1993.

Gilroy, Paul. *The Black Atlantic: Modernity and Double Consciousness.* Cambridge, Mass.: Harvard University Press, 1993.

Glaessner, Verina. "'*Yo, la peor de todas*' [I, the Worst of All]." *Sight and Sound* (November 1991): 56–57.

Gómez Carrillo, Enrique. *Almas y cerebros.* Paris: Garnier, n.d.

———. *En plena bohemia.* Madrid: Mundo Latino, n.d.

González, José Luis. *El país de cuatro pisos y otros ensayos.* Río Piedras: Ediciones Huracán, 1980.

González Echevarría, Roberto. *Celestina's Brood: Continuities of the Baroque in Spanish and Latin American Literature.* Durham: Duke University Press, 1994.

———. *Myth and Archive: Towards a Theory of Latin American Narrative.* Cambridge: Cambridge University Press, 1990.

———. *La ruta de Severo Sarduy.* Hanover, N.H.: Ediciones del Norte, 1987.

Goytisolo, Juan. *El bosque de las letras.* Madrid: Alfaguara, 1995.

———. *Coto vedado.* Barcelona: Seix Barral, 1985.

———. *Crónicas sarracinas.* Barcelona: Seix Barral, 1989.

———. *Cuaderno de Sarajevo: Anotaciones de un viaje a la barbarie.* Madrid: El País/Aguilar, 1993.

———. *Disidencias.* Barcelona: Seix Barral, 1977.

———. *En los reinos de taifa.* Barcelona: Seix Barral, 1986.

———. *Forbidden Territory: The Memoirs of Juan Goytisolo, 1931–1956.* Trans. Peter Bush. San Francisco: North Point Press, 1989.

———. *Landscapes after the Battle.* Trans. Helen Lane. New York: Seaver Books, 1987.

———. "El mundo erótico de María de Zayas." *Disidencias.* Barcelona: Seix Barral, 1977. 63–115.

———. *Paisajes después de la batalla.* Ed. Andrés Sánchez Robayna. Madrid: Espasa-Calpe, 1990.

———. *Realms of Strife: The Memoirs of Juan Goytisolo, 1957–1982.* London: Quartet Books, 1990.

———. *El sitio de los sitios.* Madrid: Alfaguara, 1995.

———. *Reivindicación del conde don Julián.* Barcelona: Seix Barral, 1982.

———. *Space in Motion.* Trans. Helen R. Lane. New York: Lumen, 1987.

Gutmann, Matthew C. *The Meanings of Macho: Being a Man in Mexico City.* Berkeley: University of California Press, 1996.

Hall, Radclyffe. *The Well of Loneliness* [1928]. New York: Anchor Books, 1990.

Hansen, Miriam. Foreword. *Public Sphere and Experience: Toward and Analysis of the Bourgeois and Proletarian Public Sphere.* By Oskar Negt and Alexander Kluge. Minneapolis: University of Minnesota Press, 1993.

Hayles, N. Katherine. *Chaos Bound: Orderly Disorder in Contemporary Literature and Science*. Ithaca, N.Y.: Cornell University Press, 1990.

Henríquez Ureña, Max. *Breve historia del modernismo*. Mexico City: Fondo de Cultura Económica, 1962.

Herdt, Gilbert, ed. *Third Sex, Third Gender: Beyond Sexual Dimorphism in Culture and Society*. New York: Zone Books, 1994.

Herrero, Javier. "The Ending of Lazarillo: The Wine against the Water." *Modern Language Notes* 93.2 (1978): 313–19.

——. "The Great Icons of the Lazarillo: The Bull, the Wine, the Sausage, and the Turnip." *Ideologies and Literature* 1.5 (1978): 3–18.

Hitch. Review of *Improper Conduct*. *Variety* 25 Apr. 1984.

Hocquenghem, Guy. *Homosexual Desire*. Trans. D. Dangoor. Durham: Duke University Press, 1993.

Holmes, M. Morgan. "Queer Cut Bodies: Homophobia in Medical Treatment of Intersexuality." Unpublished conference paper, 1995.

Holstun, James. "Will You Rent Our Ancient Love Asunder? Lesbian Elegy in Donne, Marvell, and Milton." *ELH* 45 (1987): 835–67.

Hyde, H. Montgomery. *The Trials of Oscar Wilde*. New York: Dover, 1962.

Ingenieros, José. "Nuevos estudios sobre la psicología de los simuladores." *Archivos de Psiquiatría, Criminología y Ciencias Afines* 3 (1904): 647–709.

——. "Psicología de los simuladores." *Archivos de Psiquiatría, Criminología y Ciencias Afines* 2 (1903): 449–87.

——. *Simulación de la locura. Obras completas*, II. Buenos Aires: Ediciones L. J. Rosso, 1933.

——. *La simulación en la lucha por la vida. Obras completas*, I. Buenos Aires: Ediciones L. J. Russo, 1933.

Irigaray, Luce. *This Sex Which Is Not One*. Trans. Catherine Porter. Ithaca, N.Y.: Cornell University Press, 1985.

Jameson, Fredric. "On Negt and Kluge." *The Phantom Public*. Ed. Bruce Robbins. Minneapolis: University of Minnesota Press, 1994.

Jay, Karla, and Joanne Glasgow. *Lesbian Texts and Contexts: Radical Revisions*. New York: New York University Press, 1990.

Jeffreys, Sheila. *The Spinster and Her Enemies: Feminism and Sexuality, 1880–1930*. London: Pandora/Routledge, 1985.

Johnson, Barbara. *A World of Difference*. Baltimore: Johns Hopkins University Press, 1987.

Johnson, Hillary, and Nancy Rommelmann. *The Real Real World*. New York: MTV Books/Pocket Books/Melcher Media, 1995.

Jones, Ann Rosalind, and Peter Stallybrass. "Fetishizing Gender: Constructing the Hermaphrodite in Renaissance Europe." *Body Guards: The Cultural Politics of*

Gender Ambiguity. Ed. Julia Epstein and Kristina Straub. New York: Routledge, 1991. 80–111.

Juana Inés de la Cruz, Sor. *The Answer/La respuesta: Including a Selection of Poems.* Ed. and Trans. Electa Arenal and Amanda Powell. New York: Feminist Press, 1994.

———. *Obras completas.* Ed. Alfonso Méndez Plancarte and Alberto G. Salceda. Mexico City: Fondo de Cultura Económica, 1951–1954.

———. *A Sor Juana Anthology.* Intro. and Trans. Alan S. Trueblood. Cambridge: Harvard University Press, 1988.

Katz, Alejandro. *Jorge Cuesta, o la alegría del guerrero.* Mexico City: Fondo de Cultura Económica, 1989.

Koestenbaum, Wayne. *Double Talk: The Erotics of Male Literary Collaboration.* New York: Routledge, 1989.

Krafft-Ebing, Richard von. *Psychopathia Sexualis: A Medico-Forensic Study.* New York: G. P. Putnam's, 1965.

Lacan, Jacques. "El estadio espejo como formador de la función del yo [je] tal como se nos revela en la experiencia psicoanalítica." *Escritos 1.* Trans. Tomás Segovia. Mexico City: Siglo XXI, 1984. 86–93.

———. *Psychoses.* Trans. R. Grigg. New York: W. W. Norton, 1993.

———. *The Seminar of Jacques Lacan II. The Ego in Freud's Theory and in the Technique of Psychoanalysis 1954–1955* [1988]. Trans. Sylvana Tomaselli. New York: W. W. Norton, 1990.

———. "La significación del falo." *Escritos 2.* Trans. Tomás Segovia. Mexico City: Siglo XXI, 1984. 665–75.

Lagos, María Inés. "Confessing to the Father: Marks of Gender and Class in Ursula Suárez's 'Relación.'" *MLN* 110 (March 1995): 353–84.

Laqueur, Thomas. *Making Sex: Body and Gender from the Greeks to Freud.* Cambridge: Harvard University Press, 1990.

Lazarillo de Tormes [1554]. Ed. Francisco Rico. Madrid: Ediciones Cátedra, 1987.

Lea, Henry Charles. *A History of the Inquisition of Spain* IV. New York: Macmillan, 1907.

Leavitt, David. "Did I Plagiarize His Life?" *New York Times Magazine* 3 Apr. 1994: 36–37.

Leiris, Michel. "The Autobiographer as Torero" [1963]. *Manhood.* Trans. Richard Howard. Chicago: University of Chicago Press, 1992.

León Caicedo, Adolfo. *Soliloquio de la inteligencia: La poética de Jorge Cuesta.* Mexico City: Instituto Nacional de Bellas Artes/Leega, 1988.

Leyland, Winston, ed. *Now the Volcano: An Anthology of Latin American Gay Literature.* San Francisco: Gay Sunshine Press, 1979.

Lezama Lima, José. *Coloquio con Juan Ramón Jiménez*. Havana: Dirección de Cultura, 1937.

Li, Victor. "Towards Articulation: Postcolonial Theory and Demotic Resistance." *Ariel* 26 (Jan. 1995): 167–89.

Limentani, Adam. *Between Freud and Klein: The Psychoanalytic Quest for Knowledge and Truth*. London: Free Association, 1989.

López, Ana M. "Cuban Cinema in Exile: The 'Other' Island." *Jump Cut* 38 (1993): 51–59.

López Baralt, Luce. "Juan Goytisolo aprende a reir: Los contextos caribeños de *Makbara* y *Paisajes después de la batalla*." *Insula* 468 (1985): 3–4.

Luciani, Frederick. "Recreaciones de sor Juana en la narrativa y teatro hispano/norteamericanos, 1952–1988." *Y diversa de mí misma entre vuestras plumas ando: Homenaje internacional a Sor Juana Inés de la Cruz*. Ed. Sara Poot-Herrera and Elena Urrutia. Mexico City: Colegio de México, 1993. 395–408.

Ludmer, Josefina. "Tretas del débil." *La sárten por el mango*. Ed. Patricia González and Eliana Ortega. Río Piedras: Huracán, 1984. 47–69.

Lugo-Ortiz, Agnes. "Community at Its Limits: Orality, Law, Silence, and the Homosexual Body in Luis Rafael Sánchez's '¡Jum!' " *¿Entiendes? Queer Readings, Hispanic Writings*. Ed. Emilie Bergmann and Paul Julian Smith. Durham: Duke University Press, 1995. 115–36.

Luna, Juan de. *Segunda parte del Lazarillo* [1620]. Ed. Pedro Piquero Ramírez. Madrid: Cátedra, 1988.

Lyotard, Jean-François. *The Inhuman*. Stanford, Calif.: Stanford University Press, 1991.

——. *The Postmodern Explained*. Trans. D. Barry, B. Maher, J. Pefanis, V. Spate, and M. Thomas. Minneapolis: University of Minnesota Press, 1993.

M.C. Review of *Improper Conduct*. *Positif* 279 (May 1984): 72–73.

Maldonado Vázquez, Salvador. *Ensayo sobre orientación sexual para México y Latinoamérica*. Mexico City: Diana, 1976.

Marañón, Gregorio. *La evolución de la sexualidad y los estados intersexuales* [1930]. 2d ed. Santiago de Chile: Nueva Época, 1933.

Marcuse, Herbert. "Repressive Tolerance." *A Critique of Pure Tolerance*. Ed. Robert Paul Wolff, Barrington Moore Jr., and Herbert Marcuse. Boston: Beacon Press, 1965. 81–117.

Marín, Guadalupe. *La única*. Mexico City: Jalisco, 1938.

Marqués, René. *Otro día nuestro*. San Juan, 1955.

——. "El puertorriqueño dócil." *Ensayos (1953–1971)*. Río Piedras: Editorial Antillana, 1972. 153–215.

——, ed. *Cuentos puertorriqueños de hoy* [1959]. 8th ed. Río Piedras: Editorial Cultural, 1985.

Márquez Villanueva, Francisco. *Espiritualidad y literatura en el siglo XVI.* Madrid: Alfaguara, 1968.

Martí, José. *Epistolario: Antología.* Madrid: Editorial Gredos, 1973.

——. *Obras completas.* Havana: Editorial de Ciencias Sociales, 1975.

——. *Poesía mayor.* Havana: Editoria Arte y Literatura, 1977.

Martín Morán, José Manuel. "*Paisajes después de la batalla:* La verdad, la ficción y el vacío." *Escritos sobre Juan Goytisolo: Coloquio en torno a la obra de Juan Goytisolo, Almería 1987.* Almería: Instituto de Estudios Almerienses, 1988. 147–67.

Martínez, Jan. "Manuel Ramos Otero o los espejuelos de Mahoma." *El mundo* 10 Nov. 1985: 52–53.

Martínez, José Luis. *La expresión nacional.* Mexico City: Oasis, 1984.

Martínez–San Miguel, Yolanda. "Engendrando el sujeto femenino del saber o las estrategias para la construcción de una conciencia epistemológica colonial en sor Juana." *Revista de Crítica Literaria Latinoamericana* 20.40 (July–Dec. 1994): 259–80.

Matos, Nemir. *Las mujeres no hablan así.* Río Piedras: Editorial Atabex, 1981.

Meléndez, Concha. *Antología de autores puertorriqueños: El cuento.* San Juan: Ediciones del Gobierno del Estado Libre Asociado de Puerto Rico, 1957.

Méndez, José Luis. "Sartre y la literatura puertorriqueña." *Para una sociología de la literatura puertorriqueña.* Río Piedras: Editorial Edil, 1983. 27–44.

Mernissi, Fatima. *Islam and Democracy: Fear of the Modern World.* Trans. Mary Jo Lakeland. Reading, Mass: Addison-Wesley, 1992.

Meyer, Moe, ed. *The Politics and Poetics of Camp.* New York: Routledge, 1994.

Mitchell, Juliet. "From King Lear to Anna O and Beyond: Some Speculative Theses on Hysteria and the Traditionless Subject." *Yale Journal of Criticism* 5.2 (1992): 91–107.

——. "Whatever Happened to Don Juan? Don Juan and Male Hysteria." *Mitos* (Biblioteca peruana de psicoanálisis) 2–3.5 (1990): 77–84.

Moix, Terenci. "Mi Néstor Almendros." *El País* [Madrid] 7 Mar. 1992: 11.

Molho, Maurice, ed. Introduction. *Romans picaresques espagnols.* Paris: Gallimard, 1968.

Molloy, Sylvia. *At Face Value: Autobiographical Writing in Spanish America.* Cambridge: Cambridge University Press, 1991.

——. "Decadentismo e Ideologia: Economias de Desejo na América Hispánica Finissecular." *Literatura e História na América Latina.* Ed. Ligia Chiappini and Flávio Wolf de Aguiar. São Paulo: Editora da Universidade de São Paulo, 1993. 13–26.

——. "Diagnósticos de fin de siglo." *Cultura y tercer mundo 2: Cambios de identidades y ciudadanías.* Ed. Beatriz González Stephan. Caracas: Ediciones Nueva Sociedad, 1996, 171–200.

——. "Disappearing Acts: Reading Lesbian in Teresa de la Parra." *¿Entiendes? Queer Readings, Hispanic Writings.* Ed. E. L. Bergmann and Paul Julian Smith. Durham: Duke University Press, 1995. 230–56.

——. "Too Wilde for Comfort: Desire and Ideology in Fin-de-Siècle Spanish America." *Social Text* vol. 10, nos. 2–3 (1992): 187–201.

Monsiváis, Carlos. "Ortodoxia y heterodoxia en las alcobas." *Debate feminista* 6.11 (Apr. 1995): 183–212.

——. "Salvador Novo: Los que tenemos unas manos que no nos pertenecen." *Amor perdido.* Mexico City: Biblioteca Era, 1977. 265–96.

Monter, William. *Frontiers of Heresy: The Spanish Inquisition from the Basque Lands to Sicily.* Cambridge: Cambridge University Press, 1990.

Montero, Mayra. *La última noche que pasé contigo.* Barcelona: Tusquets/La Sonrisa Vertical, 1991.

Montesquieu, Charles de Secondat, baron de. *Lettres Persanes.* Ed. Paul Vernière. Paris: Garnier Frères, 1975.

Moretta, Eugene L. *La poesía de Xavier Villaurrutia.* Mexico City: Fondo de Cultura Económica, 1976.

Muñoz, José E. "*Choteo*/Camp Style Politics: Carmelita Tropicana's Performance of Self-Enactment." *Women and Performance: A Journal of Feminist Theory* 7.2–8.1: 14–15, 39–52.

——. *Disidentifications.* Minneapolis: University of Minnesota Press, forthcoming.

——. "Flaming Latinas: Ela Troyano's *Carmelita Tropicana: Your Kunst Is Your Waffen* (1993)." *The Ethnic Eye: Latino Media Arts.* Ed. Chon A. Noriega and Ana M. López. Minneapolis: University of Minnesota Press, 1995.

Murray, Steven O., ed. *Latin American Homosexualities.* Albuquerque: University of New Mexico Press, 1995.

Negrón-Muntaner, Frances. "Echoing Stonewall and Other Dilemmas: The Organizational Beginnings of a Gay and Lesbian Agenda in Puerto Rico, 1972–1977." *Centro* 4.1–2 (1992): 77–115.

Negt, Oskar, and Alexander Kluge. *Public Sphere and Experience: Toward and Analysis of the Bourgeois and Proletarian Public Sphere.* Trans. Peter Labanyi, Jamie Owen Daniel, and Assenka Oksiloff. Minneapolis: University of Minnesota Press, 1993.

"Néstor Almendros gana el premio del Festival de Cine de Derechos Humanos de Estrasburgo." *Cineinforme* 130 (May 1984): 9.

Newton, Esther. "The Mythic Mannish Lesbian: Radclyffe Hall and the New Woman." *Hidden from History; Reclaiming the Gay and Lesbian Past.* Ed. Martin Duberman et al. New York: Meridian, 1990. 281–93.

Novo, Salvador. *XVIII sonetos.* Mexico City: Punto por Punto Editores, 1986.

——. *Las locas, el sexo, los burdeles.* Mexico City: Editorial Novaro, 1972.

———. "Memorias." *Política sexual: Cuadernos del Frente Homosexual de Acción Revolucionaria* 1 (n.d. [1979?]): 4–10.

———. "Memoirs." *Now the Volcano: An Anthology of Latin American Gay Literature.* Ed. W. Leyland. San Francisco: Gay Sunshine Press, 1979. 11–47.

———. *Poesía.* Mexico City: Fondo de Cultura Económica, 1961.

———. *Toda la prosa.* Mexico City: Empresas Editoriales, 1964.

Nugent, Georgia. "This Sex Which Is Not One: Deconstructing Ovid's Hermaphrodite." *differences: A Journal of Feminist Cultural Studies* 2 (1990): 160–85.

Oboler, Suzanne. *Ethnic Labels, Latino Lives: Identity and the Politics of (Re)Presentation in the United States.* Minneapolis: University of Minnesota Press, 1995.

Olea Franco, Rafael, and Anthony Stanton, eds. *Los Contemporáneos en el laberinto de la crítica.* Mexico City: Colegio de México, 1994.

Olivier, Guilhem. "Conquérants et missionnaires face au 'péché abominable,' essai sur l'homosexualité en Mésoamérique au moment de la conquête espagnole." *Caravelle* 55 (1990): 19–51.

Ortiz, Fernando. *Contrapunteo cubano del tabaco y el azúcar* [1940]. Caracas: Ayacucho, 1978.

Palmer, Neyssa. *Las mujeres en los cuentos de René Marqués.* Río Piedras: Editorial de la Universidad de Puerto Rico, 1988.

Panabière, Louis. *Itinerario de una disidencia: Jorge Cuesta (1903–1942).* Trans. A. Castañón. Mexico City: Fondo de Cultura Económica, 1983.

Park, Katharine, and Robert A. Nye. "Destiny Is Anatomy." Review of *Making Sex: Body and Gender from the Greeks to Freud,* by Thomas Laqueur. *New Republic* 18 Feb. 1991: 53–57.

Parker, Andrew, Mary Russo, Doris Sommer, and Patricia Yaeger, eds. *Nationalisms and Sexualities.* New York: Routledge, 1992.

Paz, Octavio. "Hieroglyphs of Desire." Xavier Villaurrutia and Octavio Paz. *Nostalgia for Death and Hieroglyphs of Desire.* Trans. E. Allen. Port Townsend, Wash.: Copper Canyon Press, 1993. 93–148.

———. "Homenaje a Sor Juana Inés de la Cruz en su tercer centenario." *Sur* 197 (1951): 48–76.

———. *El laberinto de la soledad* [1950/72]. 3d ed. Mexico City: Fondo de Cultura Económica, 1989.

———. *Sor Juana Inés de la Cruz, o las trampas de la fe.* Mexico City: Fondo de Cultura Económica, 1983.

———. *Sor Juana Inés de la Cruz, or the Traps of Faith.* Trans. Margaret Sayers Peden. Cambridge, Mass.: Harvard University Press, 1988.

———. *Xavier Villaurrutia en persona y en obra.* Mexico City: Fondo de Cultura Económica, 1978.

Pellón, Gustavo, and Julio Rodríguez-Luis. *Upstarts, Wanderers, or Swindlers:*

Anatomy of the Picaro. A Critical Anthology. Amsterdam: Editions Rodopi B.V., 1986.

Pérez, Genaro J. "Desconstrucción paródica en *Paisajes después de la batalla* de Juan Goytisolo." *Hispania* 71.2 (1988): 242–48.

Pérez de Ayala, Ramón. *Las máscaras* II. Madrid: Renacimiento, 1924.

Peri Rossi, Cristina. *Lingüística general.* Valencia: Prometeo, 1979.

Perrin, Annie. "El laberinto homotextual." *Escritos sobre Juan Goytisolo: Coloquio en torno a la obra de Juan Goytisolo, Almería 1987.* Almería: Instituto de Estudios Almerienses, 1988: 75–81.

——. "Un casse texte explosif ou les aventures d'un personnage auteur et de son petit rat blanc dans *Paisajes después de la Batalla* de Juan Goytisolo." *Le personnage en question.* Toulouse: Université de Toulouse-Le Mirail, 1984. 217–25.

Perry, Mary Elizabeth. *Crime and Society in Early Modern Seville.* Hanover, N.H.: University Press of New England, 1980.

——. *Gender and Disorder in Early Modern Seville.* Princeton, N.J.: Princeton University Press, 1990.

——. "The Nefarious Sin in Early Modern Seville." *The Pursuit of Sodomy: Male Homosexuality in Renaissance and Enlightenment Europe.* Ed. Kent Gerard and Gert Hekma. New York: Harrington Park Press, 1989. 67–89.

Piedra, José. "Nationalizing Sissies." *¿Entiendes? Queer Readings, Hispanic Writings.* Ed. Emilie L. Bergmann and Paul Julian Smith. Durham: Duke University Press, 1995.

Piñera, Virgilio. "Autobiografía." *El espectador* 491 (20 Sept. 1992): 7.

——. "Dos poemas, dos poetas, dos modos de poesía." *Espuela de plata* (Aug. 1941): 16–19.

——. "Emilio Ballagas en persona" *Ciclón* 5 Sept. 1955: 41–50.

——. *La isla en peso.* Havana: Espuela de Plata, 1942.

Ponce, Aníbal. "Prólogo." *La simulación en la lucha por la vida.* By José Ingenieros. *Obras completas* I. Buenos Aires: Ediciones L. J. Rosso, 1933.

Quintero Rivera, Angel. *Conflictos de clase y política en Puerto Rico.* Río Piedras: Ediciones Huracán, 1976.

Ramos Collado, Lilliana. *Reróticas.* San Juan: Editorial Nómada, 1995.

Ramos Mejía, José María. *Los simuladores de talento* [1904]. new ed. Buenos Aires: Editorial Tor, 1955.

Ramos Otero, Manuel. *Cuentos de buena tinta.* San Juan: Instituto de Cultura Puertorriqueña, 1992.

——. *Invitación al polvo.* Río Piedras: Plaza Mayor, 1987.

——. *El libro de la muerte.* Maplewood, N.J. and Río Piedras: Waterfront Press/Editorial Cultural, 1985.

———. *Página en blanco y staccato.* Madrid: Playor, 1987.

Rich, B. Ruby. "Bay of Pix." *American Film* 9.9 (Aug. 1984): 57–59.

Ríos, Julián. "Paisaje después de la batalla." *Vuelta* 80 (1983): 35–39.

Robaina, Tomás. "Carga acerca de *Antes que anochezca,* autobiografía de Reinaldo Arenas." *Journal of Hispanic Research* 1 (1992): 152–56.

Rodó, José Enrique. *Ariel.* Ed. Gordon Brotherston. Cambridge: Cambridge University Press, 1967.

———. *Ariel.* Trans. Margaret Sayers Peden. Austin: University of Texas Press, 1988.

———. "Rubén Darío. Su personalidad literaria. Su última obra," en *Obras completas.* Madrid: Aguilar, 1967.

Rodríguez Castro, María Elena. "Las casas y el porvenir: nación y narración en el ensayo puertorriqueño." *Revista Iberoamericana* 162–63 (Jan.–June 1993): 44–53.

Rodríguez Feo, José. *Mi correspondencia con Lezama Lima.* Havana: Ediciones Unión, 1989.

Rodríguez Monegal, Emir. "Encuentros con Rubén Darío." *Mundo nuevo* 7 (1967): 5–21.

Root, Jane. Review of *Improper Conduct. Monthly Film Bulletin* 52.618 (1984): 220–21.

Rubenstein, Hal. "Pedro Leaves Us Breathless." *Poz* 1.3 (Aug.–Sept. 1994): 38–41, 79–81.

Rubin, Gayle. "Thinking Sex: Notes for a Radical Theory of the Politics of Sexuality." *The Lesbian and Gay Studies Reader.* Ed. Henry Abelove, Michèle Aina Barale, and David M. Halperin. New York: Routledge, 1993. 3–44.

———. "The Traffic in Women: Notes on the Political Economy of Sex." Ed. Rayna Reiter. *Toward an Anthropology of Women.* New York: Monthly Review Press, 1975. 157–210.

Sabat-Rivers, Georgina. *Estudios de literatura hispanoamericana. Sor Juana Inés de la Cruz y otros poetas barrocos de la colonia.* Barcelona: Promociones y Publicaciones Universitarias, 1992.

Said, Edward. *Representations of the Intellectual.* New York: Vintage, 1996.

Salessi, Jorge. *Médicos, maleantes y maricas.* Rosario, Argentina: Beatriz Viterbo, 1995.

Sánchez, Luis Rafael. "¡Jum!" *En cuerpo de camisa* [1966]. 5th ed. Río Piedras: Editorial Cultural, 1990.

———. "Las divinas palabras de René Marqués." *Sin nombre* 10.3 (1979): 11–14.

Santí, Enrico Mario. "Sor Juana, Octavio Paz, and the Poetics of Restitution." *Indiana Journal of Hispanic Literature* 1.2 (Apr. 1993): 101–39.

———. "Textual Politics: Severo Sarduy." *Latin American Literary Review* 8.16 (1980): 152–60.

Sarduy, Severo. *De donde son los cantantes* [1967]. Barcelona: Barral, 1980.

———. *De donde son los cantantes.* [1967] Edición de Roberto González Echevarría. Madrid: Cátedra, 1993.

———. *La simulación.* Caracas: Monte Avila, 1982.

Schneider, Luis Mario, ed. *El estridentismo México 1921–1927.* Mexico City: Universidad Nacional Autónoma de México, 1985.

———. Introducción. *Homenaje Nacional a los Contemporáneos: Antología poética.* Mexico City: Instituto Nacional de Bellas Artes, 1982. 5–6.

———. *Ruptura y continuidad: La literatura mexicana en polémica.* Mexico City: Fondo de Cultura Económica, 1975.

Schons, Dorothy. "Nuevos datos para la biografía de sor Juana." *Contemporáneos* 9 (1929).

Schwartz, Kessel. "Themes, *Écriture,* and Authorship in *Paisajes después de la batalla.*" *Hispanic Review* 52.4 (1984): 477–90.

Scott, Nina M. " 'Ser mujer ni estar ausente, / no es de amarte impedimento': los poemas de Sor Juana a la condesa de Paredes." *Y diversa de mí misma entre vuestras plumas ando: Homenaje internacional a Sor Juana Inés de la Cruz.* Ed. Sara Poot-Herrera and Elena Urrutia. Mexico City: Colegio de México, 1993. 159–70.

———. "Sor Juana and Her World." *Latin American Research Review* 29.1 (1994): 143–54.

Sedgwick, Eve Kosofsky. *Between Men: English Literature and Male Homosocial Desire.* New York: Columbia University Press, 1985.

———. *Epistemology of the Closet.* Berkeley: University of California Press, 1990.

Sheridan, Guillermo. *Los contemporáneos ayer.* Mexico City: Fondo de Cultura Económica, 1985.

———. "Introducción: Los poetas en sus relatos." *Homenaje Nacional a los Contemporáneos: Monólogos en espiral: antología de narrativa.* Mexico City: Instituto Nacional de Bellas Artes, 1982. 5–11.

Shipley, George A. "The Critic as Witness for the Prosecution: Making the Case against Lázaro de Tormes." *PMLA* 97 (1982): 179–94.

———. "Lazarillo de Tormes Was Not a Hardworking, Clean-Living Water Carrier." *Hispanic Studies in Honor of Alan D. Deyermond.* Ed. John S. Miletich. Madison, Wis.: Hispanic Seminary of Medieval Studies, 1986. 247–55.

Sicroff, Albert A. "Sobre el estilo del Lazarillo de Tormes." *Nueva Revista de Filología Hispánica* 11.2 (1957): 157–70.

Sieber, Harry. *Language and Society in "La vida de Lazarillo de Tormes."* Baltimore: Johns Hopkins University Press, 1978.

Sifuentes Jáuregui, Benigno. "Scars of Decisions: Transvestism and Other Versions of Masculinity in Contemporary Spanish American Literature." Ph.D. diss. Department of Spanish and Portuguese, Yale University, 1994.

Silberman, Lauren. "Mythographic Transformations of Ovid's Hermaphrodite." *Sixteenth Century Journal* 19.4 (1988): 643–52.

Silverman, Kaja. *The Acoustic Mirror: The Female Voice in Psychoanalysis and Cinema.* Bloomington: Indiana University Press, 1988.

Simmons, Jon. *Foucault and the Political.* New York: Routledge, 1995.

Sinfield, Alan. *Cultural Politics—Queer Readings.* Philadelphia: University of Pennsylvania Press, 1994.

———. *The Wilde Century: Effeminacy, Oscar Wilde, and the Queer Moment.* New York: Columbia University Press, 1994.

Sin nombre [special issue on René Marqués], 10.3 (1979).

Smith, Paul Julian. *Laws of Desire: Questions of Homosexuality in Spanish Writing and Film, 1960–1990.* Oxford: Clarendon Press, 1992.

———. *Representing the Other: "Race," Text, and Gender in Spanish and Spanish American Narrative.* Oxford: Clarendon Press, 1992.

Smith-Rosenberg, Carroll. "Discourses of Sexuality and Subjectivity: The New Woman, 1870–1936." *Hidden from History: Reclaiming the Gay and Lesbian Past.* Ed. Martin Duberman et al. New York: Meridian, 1990. 264–80.

Solá, María. "René Marqués ¿Escritor misógino?" *Sin nombre* 10.3 (1979): 83–97.

Solomon, Alisa. "Not Just a Passing Fancy: Notes on Butch." *Theater* 24.2 (summer 1993): 35–46.

Spender, Stephen. "My Life Is Mine; Not David Leavitt's." *New York Times Magazine* 4 Sept. 1994: 10–12.

Surtz, Ronald E. *The Guitar of God: Gender, Power, and Authority in the Visionary World of Mother Juana de la Cruz (1481–1534).* Philadelphia: University of Pennsylvania Press, 1990.

Suslow-Ortiz, Tamra. "Outsiders at the Center: The *Contemporáneos* and the Construction of Culture in Post-Revolutionary Mexico." Unpublished paper.

Tesson, Charles. "Docteur Fidel et Mister Raul." *Cahiers du Cinéma* 358 (Apr. 1984): 47–48.

Thompson, B. Bussell, and J. K. Walsh. "The Mercedarian's Shoes (Perambulations on the Fourth *Tratado* of *Lazarillo de Tormes*)." *Modern Language Notes* 103.2 (1988): 440–49.

Tohidi, Nayereh. "Gender and Islamic Fundamentalism: Feminist Politics in Iran." *Third World Women and the Politics of Feminism.* Ed. Chandra Talpade Mohanty, Ann Russo, and Lourdes Torres. Bloomington: Indiana University Press, 1991. 251–67.

Tomás y Valiente, Francisco. "El crimen y pecado contra natura." *Sexo barroco y otras transgresiones premodernas.* Madrid: Alianza Editorial, 1990. 33–55.

Traub, Valerie. "The (In)significance of 'Lesbian' Desire in Early Modern England." *Queering the Renaissance.* Ed. Jonathan Goldberg. Durham: Duke University Press, 1993. 62–83.

Ulner, Arnold L. *Enrique Gómez Carrillo en el modernismo, 1889–1896.* Ph.D. diss. University of Missouri, 1972.

Urbano, Victoria. *Sor Juana Inés de la Cruz: Amor, poesía, soledumbre.* Potomac, Md.: Scripta Humanistica, 1990.

Vega, Ana Lydia. *Esperando a Loló y otros delirios generacionales.* Río Piedras: Editorial de la Universidad de Puerto Rico, 1994.

Vera León, Antonio. "A Garden of Forking Tongues: Bicultural Subjects and an Ethics of Circulating In and Out of Ethnicities." *Postmodern Notes/Apuntes Postmodernos* 3.2 (1993): 10–19.

Vernaglione, Paolo. "Conversazione con Maria Luisa Bemberg." *Filmcritica* 41.408 (Sept.–Oct. 1990): 480–81.

Villaurrutia, Xavier. *Nocturno de los ángeles.* Facsimile edition of 1936 edition and manuscript. Mexico City: Ediciones del Equilibrista, 1987.

——. *Obras.* 2d ed. Mexico City: Fondo de Cultura Económica, 1991.

Villena, Luis Antonio de. "Salvador Novo: Ultima poesía erótica." *Los Contemporáneos en el laberinto de la crítica.* Ed. Rafael Olea Franco and Anthony Stanton. Mexico City: Colegio de México, 1994. 207–12.

Villiers de l'Isle Adam, Auguste. *L'Eve future. Oeuvres complètes* I. Genève: Slatkine Reprints, 1970.

Warner, Michael. "Introduction: Fear of a Queer Planet." *Social Text* 9.4 (1991): 3–17.

Weber, Alison. *Teresa of Avila and the Rhetoric of Femininity.* Princeton: Princeton University Press, 1990.

Weeks, Jeffrey. *Coming Out: Homosexual Politics in Britain from the Nineteenth Century to the Present.* London: Quartet, 1977.

Whitaker, Sheila. "Pride and Prejudice: María Luisa Bemberg." *Monthly Film Bulletin* (Oct. 1987): 292–94. Reprinted in *The Garden of Forking Paths: Argentine Cinema.* Ed. John King and Nissa Torrents. London: British Film Institute, 1988. 115–21.

White, Edmund. "The Wanderer: Juan Goytisolo's Border Crossings." *Village Voice Literary Supplement* June 1991: 18–21.

Wilde, Oscar. *The Complete Works of Oscar Wilde.* New York: Harper Row, 1989.

Wockner, Rex. "Homosexuality in the Arab and Moslem World." *Coming Out: An Anthology of International Gay and Lesbian Writing.* Ed. Stephan Likosky. New York: Pantheon, 1992. 103–16.

Xirau, Ramón. "Presencia de una ausencia." *Tres poetas de la soledad.* Mexico City: Antigua Librería Robredo, 1955. 21–35.

Yingling, Thomas E. *Hart Crane and the Homosexual Text: New Thresholds, New Anatomies.* Chicago: University of Chicago Press, 1990.

"*Yo, la peor de todas.*" Film directed by María Luisa Bemberg. Argentina: GEA Cinematográfica, 1990. Distributed by First Run/Icarus Films.

Zayas, Manuel Ramón de. "Sangre y Arenas: Machismo, homosexualidad y subversión." *Apuntes Postmodernos/Postmodern Notes* 6.1 (fall 1995): 3–19.

Zayas y Sotomayor, María de. *Parte segunda del Sarao y entretenimiento honesto [Desengaños amorosos].* Ed. Alicia Yllera. Madrid: Cátedra, 1983.

Ziolkowski, Jan. *Alan of Lille's Grammar of Sex: The Meaning of Grammar to a Twelfth-Century Intellectual.* Cambridge, Mass.: Medieval Academy of America, 1985.

Contributors

DANIEL BALDERSTON is Professor of Spanish and Portuguese at Tulane University. His most recent books are *Out of Context: Historical Reference and the Representation of Reality in Borges* and a translation of Ricardo Piglia's *Artificial Respiration* (both from Duke University Press) and (coedited with Donna J. Guy) *Sex and Sexuality in Latin America.*

EMILIE BERGMANN is Professor of Spanish at the University of California, Berkeley, specializing in gender studies in early modern Spain and Spanish America. She is coauthor of *Women, Culture, and Politics in Latin America* (1990) and coeditor, with Paul Julian Smith, of *¿Entiendes? Queer Readings, Hispanic Writings* (Duke University Press, 1995).

ISRAEL BURSHATIN is William R. Kenan Jr. Professor of Spanish at Haverford College. He has published numerous studies on the cultural role of Moriscos and Moors in medieval and Golden Age writing, including "The Moor in the Text: Metaphor, Emblem, and Silence," in Henry Louis Gates Jr., ed., *Race, Writing, and Difference* (1986), and, most recently, "Playing the Moor: Parody and Performance in Lope de Vega's *El primer Fajardo,*" in *PMLA* (May 1992). He is currently working on a book-length study of the trial of Eleno de Céspedes.

BRAD EPPS is Professor of Romance Languages and Literatures at Harvard University. He has written and published on Spanish, Latin American, French, and Catalan literature, film, and art from the nineteenth and twentieth centuries. His publications include *Significant Violence: Oppression and Resistance in the Narratives of Juan Goytisolo* (1996). He is currently working on two books: one on modern Spanish culture, and another on gay and lesbian writing in Spain, Latin American, and U.S. Latino cultures.

JOSÉ ESTEBAN MUÑOZ teaches in the Performance Studies Program, Tisch School of the Arts, New York University. He is the author of *Disidentifications* (forthcoming) and coeditor of *Pop Out: Queer Warhol* (Duke University Press, 1996), *Everynightlife: Culture and Dance in Latin/o America* (Duke University Press, 1997) and a special issue of the journal *Women and Performance* titled "Queer Acts." His articles have appeared in *TDR, Screen, GLQ,* and *Social Text,* as well as in several anthologies of critical theory.

MARY S. GOSSY is Associate Professor of Spanish, Women's Studies, and Comparative Literature and director of the Graduate Program in Women's Studies at Rutgers University. She is the author of *The Untold Story: Women and Theory in Golden Age Texts* (1989), *Freudian Slips: Women, Writing, the Foreign Tongue* (1995), and articles on narrative from feminist and psychoanalytic perspectives. New and continuing work includes essays on Spain's meaning for Freud, and a study of pleasure called "Magic Wand."

ROBERT MCKEE IRWIN is a Ph.D. candidate and MacCracken Fellow at New York University. He has published articles on the rhetoric of masculinity in twentieth-century Mexican literature in *La otredad,* in *La seducción de la literatura,* and in the forthcoming *En el ambiente.*

AGNES I. LUGO-ORTIZ is Assistant Professor of Women's Studies and Latin American Literature at Dartmouth College. Her publications include essays on Julián del Casal, Victoria Ocampo, José Martí, and twentieth-century Caribbean literatures. Her book *Identidades imaginadas: Biografía y nacionalidad en el horizonte de la guerra (Cuba 1860–1898)* is forthcoming from the University of Puerto Rico Press.

SYLVIA MOLLOY is Albert C. Schweitzer Professor of Humanities at New York University. Her most recent book is *At Face Value: Autobiographical Writing in Spanish America* (1991). She is currently working on a book on decadence, national health, and the construction of sexualities in turn-of-the-century Latin America.

OSCAR MONTERO is Professor of Spanish American Literature at Lehman College and the Graduate Center of the City University of New York. He is the author of *The Name Game: Writing/Fading Writer in "De donde son los cantantes"* (1988) and *Erotismo y representación en Julián del Casal* (1993). He is a member of the Board of the Center for Lesbian and Gay Studies of the City University of New York.

JOSÉ QUIROGA is an Associate Professor at the Department of Romance Languages and the Latin American Studies Program at George Washington University. He has published essays on twentieth-century Latin American poetry, and his book on Octavio Paz is forthcoming from the University of South Carolina Press. The essay in this volume will form part of a book tentatively titled *Queer Tropics in Revolution,* which he has recently completed.

RUBÉN RÍOS AVILA is Professor of Comparative Literature at the University of Puerto Rico. He is a member of the editorial board of *Postdata* and the literary critic of *El mundo.* He edited the gay issue of *Piso Trece* and writes on contemporary Spanish-American and Puerto Rican literatures.

B. SIFUENTES JÁUREGUI teaches Latin American literature at Rutgers. He has published articles on Latin American and gender studies. Presently, he is completing a project entitled *Facing Masculinity: Transvestism and Spanish American Literature.*

PAUL JULIAN SMITH is Professor of Spanish at the University of Cambridge. His eight authored books include *Laws of Desire: Questions of Homosexuality in Spanish Writing and Film 1960–1990* (1992); and his three coedited books include *¿Entiendes? Queer Readings, Hispanic Writings* (Duke University Press, 1995). Forthcoming from Cambridge University Press is *The Theatre of García Lorca: Text, Performance, Psychoanalysis.*

Index

~

Library of Congress Cataloging-in-Publication Data
Hispanisms and homosexualities / Sylvia Molloy and Robert
McKee Irwin, editors.
p.   cm.
Includes bibliographical references and index.
ISBN 0-8223-2181-5 (cloth : alk. paper). —ISBN 0-8223-2198-X
(paperback : alk. paper)
1. Spanish American literature—History and criticism.
2. Spanish literature—History and criticism.   3. Homosexuality
and literature.   I. Molloy, Sylvia.   II. Irwin, Robert McKee.
PQ7081.A1H5735   1998
860.9'353—dc21   98-3312
                                                CIP